W. SHELBY COATE
(June 17, 2013)

Descent to Suez

Descent to Suez

Diaries 1951–56

Evelyn Shuckburgh

Selected for Publication by
John Charmley

W·W·NORTON **& C**OMPANY
New York   London

Library of Congress Cataloging in Publication Data

Shuckburgh, Evelyn, 1909-
Descent to Suez.

Includes index.
1. Eden, Anthony, Earl of Avon, 1897-
2. Great Britain—Foreign relations—1945-
3. Near East—Foreign relations—Great Britain.
4. Great Britain—Foreign relations—Near East.
5. Egypt—History—Intervention, 1956. 6. Shuckburgh,
Evelyn, 1909-   —Diaries. 7. Diplomats—Great Britain
—Diaries. I. Charmley, John. II. Title.
DA566.9.E28S58   1987   962′.053   86–18167

ISBN 0-393-02414-8

W. W. Norton & Company, Inc., 500 Fifth Avenue, New York, N.Y. 10110
W. W. Norton & Company Ltd., 37 Great Russell Street, London WC1B 3NU
1 2 3 4 5 6 7 8 9 0

'Put that down on your tablets, Evelyn'

ANTHONY EDEN TO EVELYN SHUCKBURGH

CONTENTS

ILLUSTRATIONS

Eden and I enter the United Nations Assembly in Paris, November
  1951
On the job at the United Nations
In the library at the British Embassy in Paris
Eden, Robert Schuman and Dean Acheson, June 1952 (*BBC Hulton
  Picture Library*)
King Hussein of Jordan, 1953 (*BBC Hulton Picture Library*)
Eden with Eisenhower, Washington, March 1953 (*Popperfoto*)
Return from convalescence, 23 July 1953 (*Popperfoto*)
Photographs of Nancy and me at High Wood by Francis Russell
The corner cupboard (*Graham Stone*)
Francis Russell of the US State Department (*US State Department*)
Eden with John Foster Dulles, October 1953 (*Popperfoto*)
Downing Street (*Associated Newspapers*)
The Prime Minister with his Foreign Secretary (*both photos BBC Hulton
  Picture Library*)
Being met at Tehran airport, 1954
The Conference of Middle East Ambassadors, Beirut, 1954
Anthony Nutting and Colonel Nasser sign the Anglo-Egyptian Agreement,
  October 1954 (*Popperfoto*)
Music-making at home
Brief amity: Eden and Nasser in Cairo, 21 February 1955 (*Popperfoto*)
Harold Macmillan at his desk at the Foreign Office, April 1955 (*Crown
  copyright, Macmillan Family Archives*)
With the last British and the first Sudanese Sudan Agent in London, 1955
Eden with John Foster Dulles at No. 10 during the Suez crisis, August
  1956 (*BBC Hulton Picture Library*)
Dulles, Selwyn Lloyd and Winthrop Aldrich walking from the Foreign
  Office to lunch with Eden, September 1956 (*BBC Hulton Picture
  Library*)

EDITORIAL NOTE

The full text of the diaries, bound in five volumes, comes to about 400,000 words; this book contains about half that text.

The delicate task of cutting them down to a manageable size has been performed for me by Dr John Charmley, distinguished historian and author at the University of East Anglia. The main sections omitted are the passages covering the Berlin Conference of 1953 and the tour of Middle East countries which I made with my wife in 1954. Other cuts are spread throughout the diary. Dr Charmley's objective has been to allow the main features of the diary to emerge unscathed; the routine of the Foreign Office and its atmosphere, the portraits of Churchill and Eden, the foreign policy problems and difficulties of a Great Power in decline and, finally, the character of the diarist. I am deeply appreciative of the skill and sensitivity with which he has performed this task.

Because of the extensive nature of the cuts, they have not been indicated by the use of ellipses; a rash of dots on every page would be unsightly and distracting. Footnotes are confined for the most part to the identification of persons named in the text. A list of members of my family (with the abbreviations used in the diary) and of the main protagonists will be found in an appendix.

My special thanks are due to Dr Roger Bullen and Mrs Heather Yasamee of the Historical Branch, Foreign and Commonwealth Office, and to Miss Linda Osband of Weidenfeld's for invaluable professional advice and assistance throughout the preparation of this volume. I must also mention the encouragement and support which I have received from the Librarian of the Foreign and Commonwealth Office, Miss P. M. Barnes, and her staff.

Part One

Private Secretary
1951-54

The diaries which form the substance of this book cover the period from the autumn of 1951, when I was appointed Principal Private Secretary to the Secretary of State for Foreign Affairs, to December 1956, the morrow of the Suez debacle. For the first three years – to May 1954 – I was Anthony Eden's closest diplomatic assistant and for two years after that Under-Secretary in charge of Middle East Affairs at the Foreign Office. I was released from the Foreign Office on 20 June 1956, to become Senior Civilian Instructor at the Imperial Defence College. By that time, as the reader will not fail to notice, I was badly in need of a rest.

The diaries fall naturally into these two parts, though certain themes run through them both: the relationship with Eden, for example, and his relations with Churchill, the defence of Britain's interests in the Middle East and the search for a Palestine settlement. Taken together, they offer a sidelight on the events which led to the Suez tragedy of 1956 and this justifies the title which I have given them here – Descent to Suez. They were not intended to be a continuous account of events. I had no clear idea why I was keeping a diary at all, unless it was to interest my wife (for many of the entries took the form of letters home) or just to let off steam. I do know that, in the later stages especially, the thought of being able to write about it all in private before I went to bed was a consolation for the daily stresses of the job.

There was at one time an attempt by the Cabinet Office to forbid the keeping of diaries by top civil servants. But Ministers were writing diaries themselves and they knew that some of us did so too. Eden was fully aware, of course, that I kept a diary and used often to ask me to record something or other about himself in my 'tablets' as he called them. I did not intend to publish them, but regarded them rather as source material for future historians. I only do so now because thirty years have elapsed since the events they describe and the official documents of the period are becoming open to public scrutiny.

My three years with Eden were not the first experience I had had of being a Private Secretary. In 1937 I had been posted as a Third Secretary to the Embassy in Cairo, to be Private Secretary to the Ambassador, Sir Miles Lampson. Although the conditions and duties of this estate are very different abroad from what they are in London, there are similarities and I find that, reading through my 1951–54 diaries, I am reminded of my 1937–39 experiences in many ways. I daresay the earlier experience hardened me somewhat for the later.

Sir Miles Lampson maintained, for an Ambassador, an exceptionally grandiose establishment. Quite apart from his large Chancery, which contained such distinguished orientalists as Walter Smart and John Hamilton, he had, working in his Residence, a diplomatic Private Secretary (myself), a Comptroller, two ADCs, an accountant and two male clerks, one of whom was exclusively occupied with keeping his diary and his game book. The Comptroller and the ADCs shared a large room adjacent to HE's study and this was known to be the jolliest corner in the establishment. My small room led off it, and I was constantly distracted from my desk work by the gay social life next door.

The Ambassador's house guests, ranging in infinite variety from his delightful daughter Mary to such figures as the great Lord Lloyd, Noël Coward and Sir Ronald Storrs, were constantly drifting in to this ADCs' room for relaxation and gossip.

I had some Chancery work of my own, mainly to do with cultural relations (I was secretary to the Ambassador's Education Committee, chaired by Sir Robert Greg[1]). But my main duties were social rather than diplomatic. I wrote no diary at that time, but my father kept the letters I wrote home and they give some of the colour of my functions. On 27 November 1937 I wrote to him at the Colonial Office (where he was in charge of Palestine problems), as follows:

No, I'm afraid you do not see my hand in any of the Cairo telegrams. After 'thinking myself so grand' in the Spanish crisis,[2] I now spend my time writing drafts about the purchase of a Union Jack for the local club; whether Mohammed Abdin Nokrashi Hassanein Bey is a suitable person to be admitted to Balliol College, Oxford; the great regret with which His Excellency declines an invitation to the YWCA Ball; the unfortunate incident at dinner with the PM when the Minister's wife was placed below the wife of the President of the Chamber of Commerce etc. On all these subjects I am by way of becoming an acknowledged expert,

1 Sir Robert Greg was at that time the leading Englishman in the cultural and educational world in Egypt. He was amongst other things Chairman of the Quarantine Board and British Commissioner on the Caisse de la Dette. He had a beautiful house and garden on the Nile.
2 I had been Secretary to the Non-Intervention Committee during the Spanish Civil War.

expertise

though my expertism [*sic*], like all official expertisms, is an entirely *ex officio* acquisition.... I think it was in my third day here that a senior member of the staff, resident in Egypt for fourteen years, asked me with sincere deference whether I thought it advisable that HE should attend a public function at which there was some risk of student riots. 'Ask the Private Secretary: he ought to know' – how well I know it.

I was, of course, expected to know the leading Egyptians by sight and by name, and to make sense in conversation with them before and after the Ambassador received them. Guests arriving for dinner at the Embassy were not received by the Lampsons in the usual way; they were assembled by the ADCs and myself in the large drawing-room, and when they were all present doors were thrown open and Their Excellencies entered. I took the Ambassador round the lined-up guests, naming each one to him, and I soon acquired the knack of holding in my memory, for a few moments at least, the various extensive combinations of Abdullah, Mohammed, Ibrahim, etc., of which their names consisted, together with their titles and denominations.

After dinner the two ADCs and I, having accomplished what was known as the 'second *placement*' (i.e. putting each important person on a chair or sofa next to someone he or she had not been next to at dinner), were expected to stand for the rest of the evening in the doorways of the drawing-room, ready to retrieve any mistake we might have made in the second *placement* and in particular to catch the desperate signals which the Ambassadress emitted as soon as she had had enough of the person beside her. It was not exactly what I had been trained for in the Foreign Service, but it was Experience.

In this field of endeavour, as in any other, terrible mistakes can be made. Early in my period of office, the Ambassador gave a dinner party to which the principal diplomats in Cairo were invited. Consulting the local diplomatic list I noted that the Minister of (Republican) Spain was the senior diplomat invited, so I put him on Lady Lampson's right. I noted also, beneath his name on the list, a Senora with the same name, so I put her on Sir Miles's right. When they arrived it was observed that she was young and attractive and HE sat down to dinner well pleased. But before long doubts arose, glances were exchanged and there was discomfort. The Private Secretary was asked, when we rose from table, what kind of a solecism he had committed this time and further research revealed that the lady was not the Minister's wife but his daughter-in-law, acting as his hostess for the season. She should, of course, have been sitting next to me at the far end of the table. I was instructed the following day to put on a morning coat and call on all the offended Ministers to apologize. Most of them kindly said that they had seen nothing amiss, but one said, '*Oui, en effet, ma femme a remarqué ça.*'

The Ambassador was so grand that he never carried money on his person. Nor did he take personal responsibility for his glasses, his cigarette case, his fly whisk or any other appurtenance required when he went out of the grounds, even for a picnic in the desert. I sat behind him in church on Sunday and supplied at the appropriate moment the half crown he contributed to the collection. He had, by courtesy of the Egyptian Government, the best duck shoot in the Nile Delta, and I was responsible for drawing up the list, each week in the season, of sportsmen who might be expected to do credit to his game book. He demurred once when I included his young son Graham, on holiday from school, because, he said, he would spoil the averages of the bag. The ADCs and I used to make fun of this obsession with records of the chase and one of our favourite quotations from the Ambassador's lips was, 'I like coot; they kill so well.' Everybody in Egypt shot duck on a Friday, so that the migrating birds had no safe place to settle. Every stretch of water great or small had its quota of armed men concealed in hides from earliest dawn, with decoys floating on the surface. Naturally there was a buyer's market for duck on Saturday, but the Ambassador found means of holding back large numbers until Monday, despite the heat of the season, and got a better price.

It seems in retrospect to have been a strange thing that after the Anglo–Egyptian treaty of 1936, when we gave independence to Egypt, we should have kept on as Ambassador the same man who had been High Commissioner (i.e. Governor) under the previous dispensation. There he still was, behaving in much the same way as before the Treaty, with his special train and all, flying his flag in the same conspicuous Residence, associated in every Egyptian mind with British rule since Cromer. There were British troops in Cairo as well as on the canal, and Russell Pasha commanded the police. I remember seeing him, a splendid figure on a white horse, in the centre of the Kasr El Nil Bridge, heading off a minor riot.

Sir Miles Lampson drove through the streets of Cairo with two motor-cyclists blowing whistles before him. His attitude towards the various Prime Ministers who rose and fell in his time was avuncular and overbearing. Only the British were allowed to have an Embassy in Cairo; the rest had to be content with Legations. All this seemed to be more or less accepted as natural and right at the time; Egypt, though independent, was still regarded as outlying territory of the Raj. But fifteen years later, when I was dealing with our Middle East affairs and we were trying to get on terms with people like Colonel Nasser and his contemporaries, I could not help wondering whether seeds of resentment had been sown at that time which need not have been sown. Against this, however, it must be said, as Frank Roberts my predecessor in Cairo has written, that 'Lampson's prestige, partly linked to all this outward show, served us well during the war, in dealings with our own side, soldiers, Ministers, etc. as well as with the Egyptians.'

As for Nancy and me, we were newly married, starting a family and remarkably carefree and happy despite the looming threat of war. My letters home were all about amateur dramatics, tennis at the Gezireh Sporting Club (to which Egyptians were not admitted), expeditions into the desert, riding the polo ponies of officers who had been sent off to Palestine or the Western Desert, and dancing in the night-clubs of Alexandria. I described shooting Sudan doves with HE (Lampson 93, Shuckburgh 17), going with him to the races in Heliopolis, accompanying him aboard the flagship in exercises of the Mediterranean fleet. The only political topic which seems to have worried me seriously (and I kept writing about it to my father) was Palestine. I will recall some of this in Part II of this book, since it relates to my subsequent involvement in the Middle East.

When a young diplomat is given a Private Secretarial post at an Embassy abroad he has to realize (at least it was so forty years ago) that he is entering a magnetic field where the master–servant relationship operates, and he may not like its application to himself. The chief is an important and busy person leading a public life, who does not necessarily make nice distinctions between the various subordinates who assist him or between his public and his private requirements. There were times in Cairo when this seems to have irked me. I wrote to my father:

I am not feeling altogether pleased with life at present. Apart from having a large amount of paper work which I never get five minutes peace to do in, I have to arrange the lives of both HE and Lady Lampson and to be treated more or less as a hired footman by both. Lampson is ... very charming when he wants to be, but entirely oblivious of the lives or interests of his subordinates and expecting everything from them. Nobody who works for him enjoys his *complicity*, if you see what I mean. Even if you are going out shooting with him, you remain a member of his personal staff whom he is at liberty to curse and order about.... He refuses to employ a private secretary for Lady Lampson and the result is an insidious pressure on the ADCs and myself of work which is entirely private in nature.

These are, I imagine, the occupational complaints of Private Secretaries the world over. In return, they are given responsibilities well beyond their years and enjoy the acquaintance of interesting people in every walk of life long before they could otherwise expect it.

When I was appointed Private Secretary in 1951, Harold Nicolson told my father that it was in his opinion the most interesting and, I think he said, the most important job in the Office. But I entered upon the duties with fairly modest expectations. The first thing you are conscious of is your sudden exposure to new aspects of public life. You are a youngish man in your early forties and you have hitherto managed a busy department in the Foreign Office, supported by clever young Foreign Service officers, archivists and secretaries and covered against too much personal responsibility by the Under-Secretary and the Permanent Under-Secretary above you, both older and wiser than you. Your duties have been carried out for the most part at your own desk and in working hours (though you frequently took work home), and the only regular social element in your official life has consisted of receptions and dinners at the Embassies of the countries you were dealing with and occasional Government Hospitality meals for those same people. Suddenly, you are enlarged.

The Private Office is a most exciting place; it buzzes like the centre of the hive. It has been excellently described by Nico Henderson,[1] who occupied my desk there some twelve years later. But it is not the Private Secretary's only place of work. Several other localities claim his constant presence. First, there is the Secretary of State's place of residence – No. 1 Carlton Gardens in the case of Eden – where the Private Secretary becomes a familiar figure, bringing in boxes of official papers and taking them out again, occupying the telephone, perching on chairs to write minutes and telegrams and generally keeping the Secretary of State 'happy' during hours when normal people are resting from their labours. Eden had acquired from Churchill (who presumably acquired it during the war from his contemplation of Alexander the Great or Louis XIV) the habit of doing business from his bed, so that part of the Private Secretary's duty was to conduct moderately important persons such as junior members of the Government, Assistant Under-Secretaries and frightened heads of Foreign Office departments upstairs to his bedroom, standing by them there and seeing them off again. There were also innumerable lunches and informal meetings over drinks, most agreeable and interesting, at which the Private Secretary played a sort of ADC role and learned to know his chief in a wider context than that of the Office. Here I met Eden's private friends, including his future wife, and his political circle, and here I was first made aware of the difference between serving the Minister in his office, which was so to speak a limited liability, consisting of ensuring that the right papers and the right people were brought before him at the right time, and

1 Nicholas Henderson, *The Private Office* (Weidenfeld & Nicolson, London, 1984).

spending hours alone with him at home trying to make an adequate response to his high-powered curiosity about every aspect of foreign affairs and public life. I soon discovered that Eden did not have many close friends, or seem to want them. Jim Thomas[1] is the only one I can remember coming to see him voluntarily, as it were, and without a business reason; and even in his case I was sometimes asked to interrupt with 'work' if he should stay too long. With other visitors – women as well as men – this was almost routine practice.

Secondly, there was the Secretary of State's room in the House of Commons, a place of horror for the Private Secretaries, charged with an electric atmosphere wholly outside one's bureaucratic experience. When Parliament was sitting the Secretary of State might spend as much time there as in the Foreign Office, but it was impossible to know in advance on which of his perches he would be resting at any given moment. You did not know from hour to hour whether you would have to send the French Ambassador round to the House for his appointment or keep him in the Ambassador's Waiting Room until your chief's return. If you started work on tomorrow's speech at your own desk in the Office you were likely to be in trouble for not being in the House listening to today's speech from the officials' box. I think that I got more out of breath and risked my life more often running between Downing Street and the House of Commons in those years than at any other period of my life. When there was a Foreign Affairs debate, life in the Secretary of State's room in the House of Commons could be so terrible as to become quite thrilling. Ministers, Chief Whips, Lobby correspondents, distracted experts from the Office, sometimes even Prime Ministers, poured in and out through the small cubby-hole which served as the Private Secretary's room in which you were trying to find suitable words for the Secretary of State to use in winding up after the Opposition's attacks. This was where, in the heat of battle, we (and I mean I myself and the assistant Private Secretaries) forged invaluable understandings and alliances with the Foreign Secretary's political colleagues, the Ministers of State, the Parliamentary Under-Secretaries and the Parliamentary Private Secretaries. Tony Nutting[2] and Robert Carr,[3] for example, rapidly became close friends and allies and made it all possible to bear and enjoy.

In that small and chaotic place of work one saw aspects of Foreign Affairs which seldom obtruded themselves within the Foreign Office itself;

1 J. P. L. Thomas, First Lord of the Admiralty 1951–53; later Lord Cilcennin.
2 Anthony Nutting, Under-Secretary of State at the Foreign Office 1951–54; Minister of State at the Foreign Office 1954–56, when he resigned over Suez.
3 Robert Carr, Parliamentary Private Secretary to Eden 1951–55; Home Secretary 1972–74; now Lord Carr of Hadley.

the political background, the party pressures, the personal ambitions of Ministers, the strains of hostile debate. The Private Secretary became better able than his colleagues to understand why the Minister often cannot follow up policies which, intellectually and in the seclusion of the Office, he might have agreed were right. One came also to see what an enormous proportion of the Foreign Secretary's emotional and mental energy is burned up by parliamentary anxieties and by the strains of the House of Commons, so that the immense task of coping with the conduct of Britain's foreign relations is only a part – and perhaps the lesser part – of his burden. This is, of course, why the Office often feels happier under a Foreign Secretary in the Lords, despite the disadvantages which that entails; it then has a chief who can give more undivided attention to its affairs. Having spent these two years operating at the point of contact between the political and the professional forces which contribute to the formulation of policy, I think I can see why politicians are different from the rest of us. Perhaps the main reason is that we hardly ever get shouted at in public.

Finally, one's 'enlargement' extended in the time scale; office hours were nothing. Although he was always considerate to his staff Eden required attention at many unconventional times and the job itself forced one to regard oneself as available. I had devoted assistants in Freddie Leishman, John Priestman and others. We divided the duties as best we could, but it undoubtedly imposed great sacrifice on our wives and families. When Eden was ill, for example, I frequently had to spend the whole weekend at Binderton, his house in Sussex, in order to provide a link with the Office, and I travelled all round the world with him.

It was Herbert Morrison, not Anthony Eden, to whom I was appointed Principal Private Secretary in August 1951. I had for the two previous years been Head of the 'Western Organizations Department' of the Foreign Office, a new department specially established to handle the institutional aspects of post-war European reconstruction and the early beginnings of the Atlantic Alliance. I suppose that I was more or less wished upon Herbert Morrison, who had hardly met me before my name was put to him. But he was given a chance to say no; I was included in his delegation to the Council of Europe in Strasbourg and spent several days there with him, knowing that I was 'on appro' and knowing that he knew I knew it. I got on well with him and I liked him. He had little experience of foreigners and was inclined to think that continental socialists wore cloth caps, which was not the case, but he was confident that he would be able to handle them all, given time, as he had handled the London County Council and the Festival of Britain. He was courageous and quick in the uptake. He did not have the deep human resources which had enabled Bevin, his predecessor, to thrive instantly in an unfamiliar international scene. He had no languages. This had not incommoded Bevin and might not have been a great disadvantage to Morrison, had it not been that by the early 1950s we were moving into the era of multilateral diplomacy (with the Brussels treaty, Council of Europe, NATO, etc.) in which Foreign Ministers were increasingly called upon to meet one another in groups, rather than *tête-à-tête*, and were trying to develop a 'community' attitude amongst themselves. At their official meetings there was, of course, interpretation, but at working lunches and informal gatherings when several languages were being spoken it was becoming a definite handicap to know none but one's own. Morrison also suffered from having to fill the space previously occupied by Bevin; it would have taken a man of considerable stature not to appear a bit disappointing after that portentous European figure. Those were colourful and emotional days in Europe, with heavy wartime personalities still moving around on the stage, and a lot was still expected of the British. Labour Ministers were in a particularly awkward position over their European relationships, because of the great play which the Conservatives were making with the ideals of the European Movement. Twice I remember sitting in a hotel room on the main square in Strasbourg, helping first Bevin and then Morrison to determine coolly how much British sovereignty they would be justified in giving away, while outside on the square the great Winston Churchill and the popular but less great Duncan Sandys[1] were promising Union Now to applauding multitudes. When, in October 1951, Herbert Morrison went out of office, I was really sorry to be parted from him, as I think my diary shows.

The return of Anthony Eden to the Foreign Office has been described by many contemporaries and I will not repeat the descriptions. I was relatively junior and young and I probably did not cotton on so quickly as my seniors to the fact that we now had a professional diplomat as Secretary of State. Not many days passed before I put my foot in it. The American Ambassador came to pay his first call. I showed him into the Secretary of State's room in the usual way and, when they were both seated, took a third chair myself with my notebook at the ready. Eden looked astonished and said, 'I think we can manage on our own, dear,' and I slunk from the room. I soon learned to judge the varying degrees of privacy to be accorded to the Foreign Secretary in his contacts with others. In any complicated or technical or potentially embarrassing encounter the appropriate 'expert' (usually the Head of the Department concerned) or one of the Private Secretaries would be present to take a note. But with old friends like the American Ambassador or for calls which were delicate politically Eden preferred to be on his own. In that event it was my duty to ensure that

1 Duncan Sandys, Conservative MP and Churchill's son-in-law.

one of the Secretary of State's ladies went to his room after the visitor had left, to take down a record from dictation.

British Foreign Secretaries, so far as I know, always accepted – in principle at any rate – that they must make a record for the Office of their talks with foreign representatives. But when, years later, I was Political Adviser to M. Spaak, Secretary-General of NATO, I could not persuade him to keep me informed of his interviews. In the first place it had not been his habit to make such records as a Minister in the Belgian Government and secondly, of course, I was not of his nationality. He could not wholly accept that I might have a loyalty to him, as an international officer, which would stand its ground with my loyalty to the British Government. Up to a point he was right; if he had asked me to keep something secret from the British delegation which they really ought to have known, then he would have been foolish. But the same would be true on the national level. If your own Minister asked you to do something against your family loyalties or your personal standards, that too would be unwise. But neither of these things need happen. I used to think that the little difficulty between M. Spaak and myself about his confidence in me and my loyalty to him illustrated rather well one of the hurdles which international institutions have to surmount if they are to become effective. The spectacle of international officials running straight round to their respective Embassies to report whenever they pick up anything of interest is a very discouraging one. I suppose it is a commonplace in the UN and I have seen it in the International Red Cross (the League, of course, not the International Committee of the Red Cross). I wonder how far they have got in the last thirty years towards acceptance in European institutions of a 'European loyalty' not overriding but co-existing with national loyalties.

Eden knew all about the Office and he seemed to me to know all about international affairs. On his arrival my role as Private Secretary suddenly took on a different aspect; instead of being concerned to explain and justify the Foreign Secretary to the Office I found myself justifying the Office to the Secretary of State and defending startled officials from his all too experienced and well-documented strictures. Morrison, I vividly remembered, had called the Under-Secretaries and top advisers into the Ambassador's Waiting Room within the first few days of his reign and had addressed them as if they were a meeting of shop stewards. Formidable persons like Ivone Kirkpatrick,[1] Gladwyn Jebb[2] and Roger Makins[3] had been told in front of their subordinates that they must not be afraid to give

1 Sir Ivone Kirkpatrick, Permanent Under-Secretary at the Foreign Office 1953–57.
2 Sir Gladwyn Jebb, British Representative at the United Nations 1950–54; later Ambassador to France, now Lord Gladwyn.
3 Roger Makins, Deputy Under-Secretary of State 1948–52; later Ambassador to the US 1953–56 and Joint Permanent Secretary at the Treasury 1956–59; now Lord Sherfield.

him their honest opinion on matters of foreign policy though it was he, Morrison, who would take the decisions 'at the end of the day'. Eden had no need to hold such rallies; he knew the ropes, he was at home.

It was the same thing abroad. His return to office seemed to be everywhere greeted with delight and relief, as if a popular cricket captain had returned to the field. I shall never forget walking with him into the Assembly on his first appearance at the United Nations in Paris in November 1951: Foreign Ministers and diplomats crowding up to welcome him on every side and everyone – including Eden himself – feeling that a new era had begun for Europe and for the cause of peace.

From that time on, until I handed over the Private Secretaryship to Tony Rumbold in Geneva in June 1954, I was Eden's man; or to be more accurate I was the Office's man at Eden's side. I think that my diary throws some light on the complexities and difficulties as well as the rewards of that relationship. The main point to realize – and it explains the great difference between the diary I wrote in those years and the fuller, less subjective entries of 1954 to 1956 – is that the Private Secretary is not an official adviser to the Secretary of State, nor is he the 'expert' on any foreign policy matter. He is a relatively junior officer whose duty is to provide the link between the Secretary of State and his advisers. He does his best – at least I did my best – not to let his own opinions intrude unduly. This is not always easy especially when one is abroad with the Secretary of State, when the proper advisers may not be available. I read with some embarrassment my diary entry for mid-February 1952 where I seem to have expressed astonishingly self-confident views to Eden in Lisbon about sterling and the gold standard, about which I knew nothing. That is a natural hazard of the job: you are so continuously closeted with the Secretary of State that you are compelled to take a share in all his preoccupations. It is not possible to keep saying, 'I am sorry, Sir, but I cannot express an opinion on that; you must wait until I can get hold of Sir Bloggins', especially if you know that Sir Bloggins is far away and that the Secretary of State does not think much of him anyway. I am afraid that the diaries show me to have been opinionated and sometimes presumptuous. They also show, as you would expect, that as the Private Secretary becomes more familiar with the issues and enters more fully into the thinking of his chief and of the Office, he becomes more and more confident in expressing opinions. His private diary naturally highlights these. It is necessary to remember that at international meetings, such as the Berlin and Geneva conferences covered by these diaries, the Secretary of State was receiving continuous advice, written and oral, from his official delegation and was not, as some of the entries would seem to suggest, entirely beholden to his Private Secretary for enlightened guidance.

In the first months of my time with Eden we made many journeys abroad, mainly to Paris and Washington but also to Strasbourg, Bonn, Rome and so on, as my diary shows. The dominant preoccupation for me during these tours was the Secretary of State's ill health. He was constantly having trouble with his insides. We used to carry round with us a black tin box containing various forms of analgesic supplied by his doctor, ranging from simple aspirins to morphia injections, and we dealt them out to him according to the degree of his suffering. It was understood that if an injection was required the detective was sent for to perform it; this task at least the Private Secretary was spared. The truth is that Eden's complaint had not been properly diagnosed and when I expressed concern to his doctor about all these pain-killers, he replied that he was responsible for a very important national figure and conceived it to be his duty 'to keep him on the road'. When Eden acquired a loving wife, Sir Harold Evans was called in and a proper diagnosis was made. But it was very late in the day.

These pains nagged at him throughout all the important negotiations which he conducted at home and abroad up to the time of his three operations and they undoubtedly coloured his judgement. For one thing, they deprived him of sleep. One of the many things which I remember of him with affection was his belief that the sun's rays could bring him relief; he would take off his shirt in any garden and behind the window of any New York hotel to let the winter sun play upon his chest. I also sympathized with his love of flowers, which was more than purely visual pleasure. 'Dear dahlias,' he once said as we walked down the herbaceous border at Binderton, 'you're thirsty. Dear Evelyn, do get some water for the dahlias.'

My second preoccupation was his constant anxiety about the premiership: impatience with the Prime Minister for staying on and fear lest some other aspirant might overtake him in the race for the succession. So much has been written about this that I will leave without further comment the various passages in the diary which relate to it. Of course it affected his relations with his colleagues and presented the private offices at No. 10 and at the Foreign Office with some difficult problems. David Pitblado, Jock Colville[1] and I agreed early on that it was our duty to smooth down these difficulties, whatever we might individually feel in loyalty to our respective masters, and I think we were fairly successful. Relations between No. 10 and the Foreign Office were not bad in our time; they have certainly been much worse on occasions both before and since. A facet of Eden's worry about the succession was his intense preoccupation with what was said about him – or not said about him – in the press. The post of Head of News Department, occupied for most of my time by William Ridsdale, was for this reason often a painful one. Neither of the Edens could wholly rid themselves of the idea that Foreign Office influence with the press,

---

1 Joint Principal Private Secretaries to Churchill.

such as it was, should be used to support the Secretary of State's personal ambitions in the Government.

The disaster of Suez in 1956 has established a sort of road block, or curtain, which prevents us seeing clearly Eden's achievements as Foreign Secretary in the Churchill Government of 1951 to 1955. He is judged to an unfair degree by what happened *after* he had achieved his ambition to become Prime Minister and after his intestines had ceased to serve him properly. Prior to that he had been one of the great operators on the post-war international scene, an acutely sensitive and skilful player of the diplomatic game. I am not saying that he had original policies (there is probably no such thing) or any particular philosophical approach to foreign affairs; his approach was pragmatic. He was interested in settling problems, in bringing people together and working out agreements. And he was good at it. His first reaction, when he heard the speeches which the Americans and Russians were making to one another in the United Nations in 1951, was that he must somehow reduce the shouting and persuade people to talk to and not at one another. His own first speech was composed with that end in view. 'Working for Peace', which was a phrase he insisted on my inserting in one form or another in every speech I drafted for him, meant for him just that: getting people negotiating. (The word 'peace' had not yet been devalued by Soviet misuse nor the words 'working for' by London metropolitan misuse.)

His great speciality was to remember always the third parties and the fourth parties in the international confrontations with which he was involved. At the Geneva Conference on Indo-China in 1954, for example, I remember being astonished by his indefatigable determination to keep in touch, not only with Canada, Australia and New Zealand but also with the Prime Ministers of India, Pakistan, Ceylon and many others not represented at the conference. This, of course, had the effect of enlarging his own influence and facilitating his task as co-chairman (with Molotov) of the conference. The complexities and the excitements of that conference gave, I should think, as much real joy to Eden as anything in his life. It was an atmosphere which he really loved and in which he moved with professional assurance. He was, in my opinion, a great Foreign Secretary, and this judgement is not invalidated by the evidence so frequently displayed in these diaries that he had weaknesses and was difficult to work with.

All outstanding British Foreign Secretaries since the war, from Bevin to Carrington and beyond, have had roughly the same policy, for the simple reason that they have represented the same country and faced roughly the same circumstances. Eden wrote of Bevin in *Full Circle* (page 5) that 'though my handling of some events would have been different from his, I was in agreement with the aims of his foreign policy and with most that he did'. There was much in common in their outlook. They both saw 'a broader picture'. In the very scrappy diary which I kept in the year 1948, when I was Head of South American Department, I find the following entry which, if the reader will forgive the brashness of the author's commentary, contains an interesting version of Bevin's vision:

> 5 November. Dr Bramuglia, the Argentine MFA [Minister of Foreign Affairs], arrived from Paris at 9.10 Victoria, with his wife, simpering daughter and young son, Under-Secretary Vignes with an artificial blonde wife plastered in diamonds, three Heads of Section with their wives and a fairly respectable interpreter called del Campo. Met by Mayhew,[1] Marcus Cheke,[2] self, Argentine Ambassador (Labougle) and a crowd of Argentines. In the afternoon Bramuglia, Vignes and Labougle called upon Mr Bevin and had an hour's talk. I was present, with an interpreter whom I had briefed.

> Bevin gave a survey of his policy 'for stopping the submergence of Europe by the Slavs'. He compared the Berlin issue with the turning-back of the Turks at the gates of Vienna. He said that Stalin had said to him at Yalta that France was 'finished for fifty years'. He was going to prove this a miscalculation. With our help, and the help of ERP [European Recovery Project], France would revive in ten years. Also it was his aim to 'bring Germany west and reconcile her for ever with France'. In the great vision of a revived western Europe, 'one economy up to the Oder', it was essential to consider South America, no less than USA and Canada, as forces behind, backing the project. Thus he showed Bramuglia Argentina's proper part in the world struggle. In thanking Bramuglia for his support at Paris about the Italian colonies, Bevin also drew a picture of the Middle East as a key to the strategic defence of the whole Western world. 'Without the Middle East we could not prevent them overrunning Africa, threatening your coasts and laying the whole Atlantic open.'

> This seemed to make an impression on the insignificant and feather-headed Bramuglia, in so far as it is possible to speak of making an impression on so light a mind.[3]

Eden would not have dissented from any of this. He would particularly have approved of the appeal to Argentina's own interest in the broader

---

1 Christopher Mayhew, Labour MP and Under-Secretary at the Foreign Office.
2 Marcus Cheke, Vice-Marshal of the Diplomatic Corps 1946–57.
3 An explanation of this impertinent and certainly unjust judgement of the Argentine Foreign Minister is perhaps to be found in the following excerpt from what I wrote the next day:

> 6 November. After taking the Argentine party to the Opera we had supper at their Embassy where Bramuglia solemnly assured us that Peron has found a new way of telling whether he has the support of the people. He gets a crowd of half a million and calls out to them 'Are you in favour of my Government or not?' Bramuglia says that if Peron thought there was a lack of enthusiasm in the response he would resign!!

struggle ('threatening *your* coasts'), which was the equivalent of his own line with Nehru and Krishna Menon in 1954, when he impressed upon them that India also 'had a concern in limiting the onward rush of communist forces' (*Full Circle*, page 124). He always managed to make the representatives of smaller powers feel they were being let into his confidence and that the intricacies of Great Power politics had relevance for them. But he did not often talk in such general terms. His aim, he used to say, was 'to grasp definite and limited problems' and try to settle them bit by bit, one by one. There were plenty of these when he came to office; troubles in Egypt, the Persian oil fields lost, disagreement in Europe over the future of Germany, confusion over the European Army, etc. He used to make a tally of these problems from time to time, as if he were a juggler handling numerous dumb-bells, and would ask me what I thought his chances were of 'settling' one or two of them in the near future. He was conscious, as Bevin had been, that we were 'over-stretched' world-wide despite the winding up of the Indian Empire, and he was concerned to reduce our commitments to what our capacity would bear. But in his effort to achieve this he was less fortunate than Bevin, for he had behind him an influential body of opinion in his own party (and indeed a Prime Minister) to whom the idea of withdrawal by agreement from any exposed position was tantamount to treason and derided as a policy of 'scuttle'. This nefarious word, first used against the Labour Government when they refrained from sending a battleship to Abadan against Mossadeq,[1] was then applied to Eden's efforts to reach agreement with Egypt over the Canal Zone base. It was used against him also over Cyprus, over Iraq and over the Sudan, and it ended by having a serious effect on his morale. Of the many strands of personal and political pressure which led to the humiliation of Suez I think that one of the most powerful was Eden's indignation at being called a 'scuttler' by his own party and his determination to show himself responsible and strong.

It was, in a way, the same story with regard to his European policy. Eden's doubts and hesitations about committing Britain too deeply into a European set-up were no different essentially from those which leaders of all parties have felt, and still feel, when in office. Eden's trouble was that his Prime Minister and many influential figures in his party had committed themselves, when not in office, to very much more glamorous and idealistic attitudes and he felt upstaged on this matter. Some actors do not mind unduly being upstaged, but Eden was not one of these. He did not take the naïve view that the Anglo-American 'special relationship' or the new Commonwealth provided alternative roles for Britain which would enable

1 Prime Minister of Iran April 1951–August 1953.

us to dispense with a close European association. But he did believe that we had responsibilities, experiences and qualities of thought of a world-wide nature which we ought not to jeopardize. Some of it sounds a little over-optimistic today, but it was not ridiculous: the idea that the British had an unusual understanding of what are now called 'North–South relationships' and an unusual instrument, the Commonwealth, for handling them; the idea that our language and our history gave us a special role in relation to the United States; the fact that our popular traditions and connections were so widely spread around the world. He was, of course, himself a cultured and convinced European, speaking European languages, knowing European literature, thinking as a European. But he used to say to me that if you were to open the personal mail arriving from overseas in any post office in England you would find that 90 per cent of it came from beyond Europe, from Australia, Canada, India, Africa, anywhere, indeed, where British soldiers and administrators had served or British families settled. How could we ignore all that? That was what he meant by 'feeling it in his bones'. Eden's thought, if I can epitomize it correctly after all these years, was that we must be free to make the most of our own influence in the world, particularly our influence for peace. We must see ourselves as an active and enlightened European nation with a world role and not as a limb of Europe.

The accusation that he personally stifled the pro-European inclinations of the Churchill administration of 1951 rankled with him to the end of his life. In April/May 1969 he wrote me three letters on the subject and sent me a copy of a five-page memorandum which he had prepared refuting suggestions to this effect by Mr Macmillan, Lord Boothby[1] and others. The very last time I saw him before his death he asked me whether I could not find, amongst my papers or my memories, material for proving the contrary.

People who had committed themselves to federalism and European union and found that their own Conservative Government was no more prepared to support such things than the Labour Government had been, naturally liked to attribute this to the short-sightedness or folly of individual colleagues rather than to the mood of the country. My reply to Eden's question in 1969 was that I did not think he should worry so much about his record on this point; he had, in my opinion, been correct in his judgement as to how far the British could be persuaded to go towards integration in Europe. In my last letter to him, of 12 May 1969, I said, 'It still seems to me quite clear that the British were not ready to put their forces into anything like the EDC[2] in 1951.'

---

1 Robert Boothby, Conservative MP.
2 European Defence Community, see footnote on page 82.

I think subsequent experience has endorsed this. The agreements of 1954, which brought the Federal Republic of Germany into NATO and into the Western European Union, and which included undertakings by the United States and the United Kingdom to keep forces on the Continent, were more realistic and have been the main foundation of European security for the last thirty years. They were to a great extent Eden's creation and they should be sufficient to protect his memory against the vain imaginings of Lord Boothby.

Another achievement for which I think we should be grateful to Eden is the smooth conduct of our first post-war contacts with the Russians and then with the Chinese. He had a large share of responsibility for preventing our becoming involved in war in the Far East in the 1950s. On these achievements my diaries throw some light. But they also show one respect in which perhaps he failed to come to terms with reality. Considering his heady experiences as a young dictator-slayer before the war and as a much-admired Foreign Secretary in the days of our triumph, he had his feet pretty firmly on the ground. He recognized the decline in the power and influence of Britain, but he could never quite reconcile himself to its inevitable consequence – growing American dominance and self-assurance in international affairs, epitomized for him in the attitudes first of Mr Acheson[1] and then of Mr Dulles.[2]

The Foreign Office in those days had, and I am sure still has, an elaborate and efficient system for ensuring that telegrams received from Embassies abroad were seen by the right people and dealt with by the right person. The 'action copy' went to the department concerned in a jacket providing space for comment, having been 'entered', i.e. recorded, by the registrars. But dozens of other copies were made. The daily distribution of Foreign Office telegrams was an immensely complicated business. Inside the Office it was based more or less on a 'need to know' basis, but Foreign Office Ministers received everything of importance and there was a distribution outside to the Prime Minister and others. The Foreign Secretary, and occasionally other Ministers, might be minded to make comments and propose action on the basis of their own, non-action copies, especially when there was some international crisis on foot which interested them. It was one of the Private Secretary's duties to ensure that these ministerial observations and instructions were correlated with the advice being sent up to the Foreign Secretary through the official hierarchy on the cover of the 'entered' copy. Every morning, before the Secretary of State's arrival at the office, a box would come over from Carlton Gardens containing the

1 Dean Acheson, US Secretary of State 1949–53.
2 John Foster Dulles, US Secretary of State 1953–59.

work he had done at home the night before, and this would almost always include copies of telegrams on which he had scribbled his comments. These I would send down at once to the appropriate department; it was a quick way of letting them know how the Secretary of State's mind was working and it often helped to ensure that the submission which they subsequently sent up, and the draft reply which they perhaps suggested, would be more or less acceptable to him. It was rare for the Minister himself to draft an instruction to an Ambassador abroad; he almost always waited until a draft was submitted through the Permanent Under-Secretary, on the basis of the 'entered' copy of the message under reply. If he did not like the draft he would either amend it or, more probably, call his advisers in to discuss it. This system enabled a certain consistency to be maintained in the expression of Britain's foreign policy; it made a synthesis between the personal or political instincts of the Minister and the professional opinions, practices and style of the permanent officials.

But it did not always work out like that. On page 119 of his memoirs, *Full Circle*, Eden quotes in full a somewhat petulant telegram which he sent to Roger Makins in Washington in April 1954, which anyone can see was not drafted in the Foreign Office. The style and personal colour of the message would be convincing evidence enough that this was Eden's own draft but, as it happens, my diary entry for the period 16–19 April confirms it. Our system evidently broke down on this occasion. It was the Easter weekend and the Secretary of State was down at Binderton. He received in his telegram distribution a message from Washington relating to Dulles and the Far East which irritated him, and wished to send a sharp rejoinder. Being unable to contact his Private Secretary (me) or the Under-Secretary concerned (Denis Allen)[1] or the Permanent Under-Secretary (Kirkpatrick), he wrote his own reply round the edges of the incoming telegram. I imagine that this text was telephoned to the Resident Clerk in London, who despatched it on his instructions, and the original will have been collected by me on one of the days following. Apart from its interest as a case where our normal system did not operate, this telegram illustrates very well the personal irritation which Eden was beginning to feel with Dulles, and his growing sense of indignation over the lack of deference which, he felt, the Americans were showing towards their British ally. In contrast to this example of Eden's marginalia, I find also amongst my papers a copy of a telegram from Cairo, describing the cool Egyptian reactions to the abdication of King Farouk, on which the Prime Minister had written indignantly in red ink, 'They have lost their King!' Churchill's comments were usually couched in this succinct, dramatic style and were highly prized in

1 Denis Allen, Under-Secretary in charge of Far Eastern Affairs; later Ambassador to Turkey.

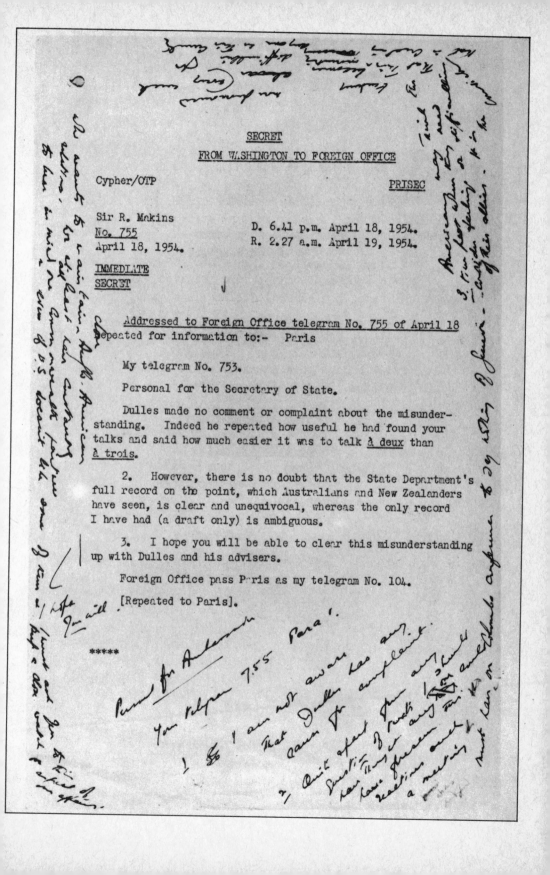

SECRET

FROM WASHINGTON TO FOREIGN OFFICE

Cypher/OTP   PRISEC

Sir R. Makins   D. 6.41 p.m. April 18, 1954.
No. 755   R. 2.27 a.m. April 19, 1954.
April 18, 1954.

IMMEDIATE
SECRET

Addressed to Foreign Office telegram No. 755 of April 18
Repeated for information to:-   Paris

My telegram No. 753.

Personal for the Secretary of State.

Dulles made no comment or complaint about the misunderstanding.   Indeed he repeated how useful he had found your
talks and said how much easier it was to talk à deux than
à trois.

2.   However, there is no doubt that the State Department's
full record on the point, which Australians and New Zealanders
have seen, is clear and unequivocal, whereas the only record
I have had (a draft only) is ambiguous.

3.   I hope you will be able to clear this misunderstanding
up with Dulles and his advisers.

Foreign Office pass Paris as my telegram No. 104.

[Repeated to Paris].

*****

PRIORITY
SECRET

27 July 1952

Addressed to Foreign Office telegram No. 201 of 27th July,

Repeated for information to Alexandria
                          Washington.

Farouk's abdication has been received without excitement here, but general feeling is of satisfaction.

No news of any reaction throughout the country, and I see no reason why we should have any trouble.

Foreign Office pass Alexandria and Washington as my telegrams Nos. 104 and 71 respectively.

[Repeated to Alexandria and Washington].

ADVANCE COPIES:
Head of African Department
Head of News Department
Resident Clerk

44444

20
They have lost their King !

28.vii

the office when they did not outrage our established ideas.

The Eden–Dulles relationship, already a subject of concern to us during my Private Secretary days, emerges more prominently as a disturbing historical factor in the second part of these diaries when I am concerned primarily with Middle East problems. By that time I had in a sense a more impartial stance on the subject, partly because I no longer had the Private Secretarial relationship with Eden, and partly because, having been deputed (with Francis Russell of the State Department) by both Eden *and* Dulles to search for Palestine solutions, I had a sort of allegiance to Dulles as well. I saw a great deal of him, as the diaries show, and I had considerable respect for him. The trouble, so far as his relations with Eden were concerned, was that the tempo of his mind was entirely out of harmony with Eden's. They were like two lute strings whose vibrations never coincide. On 4 May 1954 I wrote from Geneva to Freddie Leishman, 'A lot of the trouble I think has been due to the fact that Master and Foster do not really understand one another. Foster talks so slowly that Master does not wait to hear what he has to say, while our man talks in so roundabout and elusive a style that the other, being a lawyer, goes away having failed to make the right guesses.' On numerous occasions I was aware of this and could see misunderstandings and suspicions arising. Sometimes it was possible on the 'Private Secretary net' to nip these in the bud, and naturally I have often wondered whether, had I still been in that position in 1956, I could have prevented the total breakdown of confidence between these two which finally took place. Probably not.

At the end of this Part I still have a close relationship with Eden and despite some of the things which I wrote in my diary at the time it was a relationship of respect and affection on my side. It is sad to note that this did not long survive the quite different circumstances of the next period.

Chapter One

Eden at the Foreign Office, 1951–52

The diary opens on the day after the general election of 1951, at which Attlee's Labour Government was defeated and Churchill, now aged seventy-four, formed his first peacetime administration. Anthony Eden became Foreign Secretary for the third time in his career.

Having been appointed Principal Private Secretary three months previously by Herbert Morrison, I now found myself serving Eden.

26 October

By 3 o'clock in the afternoon it was clear that the Conservatives would probably have a majority, though it would be a very small one, and we all assumed that the weekend might be spent in discussion as to whether Mr Churchill would form a Government at once or whether there might be some delay. The Secretary of State (Morrison) came back from his constituency to No. 11 at about 5 but showed no inclination to come to the Foreign Office. I went over to get a decision from him about expelling some Italian Communists from Libya but he (rightly) would not take responsibility for this in view of his knowledge that the Government were almost certainly defeated. He said that if there were any delay in the appointment of a new Foreign Secretary, he would take the decision on Monday.

Half an hour later we were informed by No. 10 that Mr Attlee had resigned and Mr Churchill had been invited to form a Government; also that the King would hold a Council the following morning at 10.30 to swear in new Ministers. It was therefore clear to me that there was a risk that a new Foreign Secretary might walk into the Foreign Office during the course of the next morning. Meanwhile Mr Morrison had gone to Miss Donald's flat announcing that he would go straight home to bed and did not wish to be woken before lunchtime on Saturday.

Obviously, therefore, I had to get him back and had a painful half-hour at No. 11 in which I stripped him of his Foreign Office key, box, and pass and obtained authority to send over the seals to Buckingham Palace. He was plainly feeling very deflated and very tired. He asked whether it was constitutionally right of me to take away his keys, etc., before the new Foreign Secretary had been announced. I said, 'no'; he remained Foreign Secretary until his seals had been handed over the following morning. But, as he wished to sleep the following morning, I had to perform the operation tonight. He accepted this and was very friendly about me. He is clearly disappointed at leaving the Foreign Office just when the job is beginning to intrigue him. I accompanied him downstairs and through the communicating door into No. 10 and out through the front door into his car. Just as I was shaking hands with him, he was recognized by the crowd, who booed him the whole way down Downing Street; they had come, of course, to see the new men, not the old. I felt very sorry about this but assumed politicians are used to this kind of thing. I, on the contrary, was disconsolate on the pavement.

27 October

We learned from No. 10 this morning that Mr Eden was the Prime Minister's appointment for Foreign Secretary and, although the King's approval had not yet been obtained, I got in touch with his secretary, Mrs Maltby, at 4 Chesterfield Street and offered my services. He at once invited me to join Sir William Strang and Jim Bowker[1] at lunch with him. He also said that he would like to come into the Foreign Office after the Council (postponed till 3 p.m.) and hoped Mr Morrison would agree to this. We did not wake the latter up until 12.15 but he of course agreed, and it was arranged that he would come and see the new Secretary of State on Monday.

When Strang, Bowker and I arrived at 4 Chesterfield Street, we found Eden having a heated telephone conversation about whether or not he was to be described as Deputy Prime Minister in the forthcoming announcement of the new Government. We thought he was talking to Winston. He was protesting strongly that he had been promised this title, that Attlee had had it during the war and Morrison in the recent Government and he did not see why he should not have it, and that it would give him the authority he needed over his colleagues. He did not seem to be getting very far and eventually said he was thoroughly unsatisfied with the situation. There was a pause and Winston came to the 'phone. At once he agreed and there was a great deal of 'thank you, dear'. Eden then told us that it had been Norman Brook (Secretary to the Cabinet) and the King's Private

1 Strang was the Head of the Foreign Office 1949–53 and Bowker an Assistant Under-Secretary 1950–53, later Ambassador to Turkey and Austria.

Secretary (Lascelles) who had been arguing against the appointment. They had alleged that it was an infringement of the King's prerogative that a man should be named Deputy Prime Minister; the King was free to choose whoever he liked to succeed a PM. William Strang told Eden he thought he was perfectly justified in insisting.

4 November

We flew to Paris in the morning for the United Nations Assembly and stayed a week. This was the first of a whole series of trips abroad, which, combined with my own newness to the job of Private Secretary, prevented my keeping a diary at all for the next five months. What follows until April is done from memory (with the assistance of odd notes).

Main impressions of the Assembly. First the Commonwealth dinner on 5 November at the Embassy when we had the Foreign Ministers of all the Commonwealth countries alone. Although Zafrullah [Pakistani Foreign Minister] and the Indian [Pandit Nehru, the Prime Minister] have very different ideas from the rest of us about how to deal with the Russians, there they were, talking very frankly, like the members of a family. Second, the really terrifying violence of Vishinsky's[1] speech on 6 November and the almost equal violence of Acheson's reply three days later. Vishinsky and A.E. had quite a friendly-looking encounter in front of hundreds of photographers at the General Assembly, but there was of course no private exchange between them.

I was rather horrified by the way speeches at the Assembly are not addressed to anybody present but solely to each man's public opinion at home and to the world propaganda platform. It was at once clear that A.E. had a great opportunity to plead for more moderate talk. I worked a lot at his speech; spent one night till about 2 in the morning in Selwyn Lloyd's[2] suite at the Bristol Hotel going through a draft and drinking neat whisky. Ended up still lucid and enjoying the exercise though flat on the floor. As the day approached (12 November) A.E. got pretty nervous and in the middle of Sunday night Freddie Leishman and I had to get a doctor to give him injections for 'spasms' in the stomach which, of course, he and we thought were a return of his duodenal ulcer. A great deal of secrecy over this. I was instructed to tell Acheson's private secretary in the utmost confidence and only the Prime Minister and William Strang at home were told. Fortunately it turned out to be a false alarm. The last evening on the speech was the most exciting and I contributed a chunk at the end about

---

1 Andrei Vishinsky, Soviet Foreign Minister 1949–55.
2 Selwyn Lloyd, Minister of State at the Foreign Office 1951–54; later Minister of Supply 1955, Minister of Defence 1955 and Foreign Secretary 1955–60.

the Commonwealth. I also succeeded in inserting an idea from a letter from Gerald Bailley of the Quakers about improving the tone of discussions between peoples and nations. The speech itself had a really remarkable reception.

We had a disagreeable couple of meetings with Acheson about Persia. He seemed to be quite out of sympathy with our position there. He was insisting that we should make concessions to the Persians all along the line for fear that they would go Communist if Mossadeq were to fall. He seemed irritated by our experts – Donald Fergusson[1], Leslie Rowan[2] and Flett[3] of the Treasury – when they explained the damage which might be done to our interests all over the world if we gave the Persians a premium for having seized our installations. A.E. was extremely calm and moderate but it certainly went very badly. Taking Acheson down the stairs afterwards, I said that we felt very depressed, especially over the effect of all this on our economic position. He said, 'You must learn to live in the world as it is,' which I thought a very offensive remark, as it no doubt was meant to be. This was a bad day.

21 November

Off again to Paris for Three-Power talks on Germany, followed by talks with Adenauer.[4] Thence by train to Rome, arriving on the Sunday. When A.E. was in bed, I managed to get out to the Appian Way with Lady Mallet[5] and a friend for a short walk in the rain. Picked up some pieces of marble and Roman tile for Julian.[6] Also had an hour of tennis with Michael Wilford[7] on the Embassy court. But altogether there was too little sleep, too much food and far too much nervousness during this visit. At least I have started off my time with A.E. in the most intimate way, having my bedroom next to his and hearing every groan. It is discouraging that his health should be so bad.

30 November

Took the 4.10 from Paddington at the last moment with A.E. for Warwick in order to help him with his speech to the Young Conservatives Club at Leamington. Arrived to find myself a guest at Warwick Castle, sleeping in Cardinal Wolsey's bed: a most glorious affair of ivory and ebony. A.E. went off to his meeting and I was left with a pleasant evening of wine and

1 Sir Donald Fergusson, Permanent Under-Secretary at the Ministry of Fuel and Power.
2 Sir Leslie Rowan, Second Secretary at the Treasury.
3 Martin Flett, Under-Secretary at the Treasury.
4 Konrad Adenauer, Federal Chancellor 1949–63.
5 Wife of the Ambassador, Sir Victor Mallet.
6 Our son, then aged eleven.
7 Michael Wilford, Assistant Private Secretary to Eden; later Ambassador to Japan.

looking at pictures with Fulke [the Earl of] Warwick and his nice secretary, Miss Cavendish. We sat in a room entirely furnished with Canalettos, most of them of Warwick Castle itself.

There was a small snuff box on the dinner table wonderfully worked in metal and wood in the seventeenth century, which I admired very much, particularly because the artist had done the under side as well as the others. When I confessed that my veneered cigarette box had got green baize (albeit pre-war) at the bottom, they were all very contemptuous.

In the morning, I awoke to find myself looking far out across Warwickshire from a high mullioned window with a river tumbling below. Very conscious of the fact that my ancestors come from these parts and must often have come in and out of Warwick Castle.[1] Tonight for the first time I had a *faint* sensation that I enjoyed this job. Spent Saturday morning on a little balcony in the sun going through papers with A.E., and then back home for the weekend. On Leamington station I bought a copy of *Picture Post* with a rather good picture of Anthony and me in the Paris Embassy.

16 December

The third visit to Paris, this time with the Prime Minister. We left Victoria at 9 in the evening. Winston got on at Sevenoaks, having had the train stopped for him. There was a crowd on the platform there to see him off, and it was a question whether A.E. would get any of their attention.

The object of this visit was to show the French that we were taking their opinion before the PM's visit to Washington. Tremendous reception at the Gare du Nord, slightly marred by roving journalists and cameramen (though nothing like so badly as the later arrival in New York). This was not an easy visit for A.E. as he had all the time to play second string. The Embassy full of the PM's personal staff, but I was glad of this because it enabled me to get to know David Pitblado and Jock Colville. We are agreed about the need to smooth from time to time the relations between our two masters. One tremendous evening spent in the small study with the PM, A.E., Bob Dixon,[2] Oliver Harvey[3] and Freddie Leishman polishing the draft communiqué about the visit. The PM kept sending it back to be

---

1 The Shuckburgh family had lived on Shuckburgh Hill, between Southam and Daventry, since before the Norman Conquest and still do so. I am descended from a younger brother of Richard Shuckburgh who fought with Charles I at Edgehill and received a baronetcy at the Restoration. The two branches of the family have remained fitfully in touch. I used often to stay at Shuckburgh as a boy when Sir Gerald, father of the present baronet, taught me the country pursuits.
2 Sir Pierson Dixon, Deputy Under-Secretary of State 1950–54; Representative to the UN during the Suez crisis.
3 Sir Oliver Harvey, Ambassador in Paris 1947–53.

retyped and having new thoughts, cutting out words, striding about the room and consuming whisky while everyone else got sleepier and sleepier. He made a tremendous attack on the Egyptians late at night when A.E. was talking about the troubles with them. Rising from his chair, the old man advanced on Anthony with clenched fists, saying with the inimitable Churchill growl, 'Tell them that if we have any more of their cheek we will set the Jews on them and drive them into the gutter, from which they should never have emerged.' He then sank back, exhausted, into his chair. None of this seemed very helpful, but it was most amusing. He talked at great length about the war and about his trips to the Middle East at that time – fascinating reminiscences which obviously interest him much more than today's problems.

We visited the SHAPE [Supreme Headquarters Allied Powers in Europe] headquarters at Fontainebleau. PM and A.E. had lunch with Ike[1] and Winston stayed on to talk to the officers of SHAPE. The PM always seems to recognize me whenever he sees me, but unfortunately calls me Makins.

The following passage relates to a speech by Mr Churchill on 30 January.

One lunchtime I was summoned over to his bedroom at No. 10, in connection with a passage in a speech he was to make that afternoon in the House of Commons. It dealt with the problem of Egypt and the Middle East Command, and in his draft he was proposing to repeat the rather unfortunate suggestion for 'token American forces' to be stationed in Egypt, which he had made in speaking to Congress in January. I found him sitting up in bed in white silk pyjamas looking very red in the face and smoking a large cigar, dictating and issuing orders to his private secretaries, of whom there were three in the room. After reading the passage about Egypt, I made a few amendments in pencil, most of which he accepted. But when he came to the point where I had put a bracket round the phrase 'token American forces' he shouted, 'No, you silly owl – I beg your pardon. That is the whole point. I must say that.' But he eventually agreed that I should re-write the passage and clear it with A.E. by telephone. I hope this has not done too much damage to Roger Makins's reputation!

Had four days clear for Christmas at home. Fairly mild weather and so able to do a lot to tidy up the garden. Very pleased with my cuttings this year. It has been mild since autumn and I have about fifty oddments

1 General Dwight D. Eisenhower, Supreme Commander NATO forces in Europe 1950–52; later President of the United States 1953–61.

stripped from various shrubs in the Eshers'[1] former garden near Bath all doing well. I finished off the veneered cigarette box with engraved glass panel by Laurence Whistler[2] and presented it to Nancy for Christmas. A great success. But the French polishing is not satisfactory. I have not yet discovered the trick of French polishing very small surfaces. Started on a project for making a corner cupboard with six vertical panels on which I may get John Piper to draw some design. He has just started an intensive study of drawing human figures, hitherto noticeably absent from his paintings. He has bought and redecorated the Kenton Theatre in Henley and is planning a series of repertory shows there. I fear it is over-ambitious as there is not a large enough audience in Henley to support such an undertaking without a great deal of assistance from London.

29 December

Off to America. I arrived at Waterloo with A.E. rather late (the detectives having sworn that the Prime Minister would be even later) to find a lot of floodlights and cameramen and Winston sitting in the special coach with Mrs Churchill, Lord Ismay, Lord Cherwell and Lord Moran. I could not see any of my official colleagues and got stuck in this coach for about ten minutes, being called Makins from time to time. After that the coach suddenly moved off and the cameramen waiting outside never got a picture. Winston leapt up and stuck his head out of the window in protest but to no effect. We were then hitched on to the main train and Mrs Churchill was able to get out. I eventually found the rest of the party in the next coach, as follows: Norman Brook, Leslie Rowan, Sir Kenneth Maclean,[4] Jock Colville, David Pitblado. Freddie Leishman was at Southampton to meet us and Roger Makins joined us next morning on the *Queen Mary*.

I found myself in a most luxurious cabin shared by Freddie. A.E. had a suite about ten yards along the passage and the Prime Minister another beyond that. Having arrived very late at night, we went straight to bed and did not look around us till the morning. We were due to sail at noon and I was with A.E. and a few others in the PM's bedroom (the old man looking cherubic in bed) when the Captain and local representatives of the Cunard Company came in, looking very shamefaced and evidently expecting an explosion, to say that the anchor was stuck and we could not sail for twenty-

1 See list of family members.
2 Laurence Whistler, engraver on glass, poet and author.
3 Lord Ismay, Secretary of State for Commonwealth Relations 1951–52; General Secretary NATO 1952–57; old wartime friend of Churchill's. Lord Cherwell, Paymaster-General; scientific adviser to Churchill. Lord Moran, Churchill's doctor.
4 Sir Kenneth Maclean, professional soldier; Chief Staff Officer at the Ministry of Defence.

four hours. Winston was in a great hurry to get to America and this was bad news. But he saw it immediately in terms of the telegram he would send to Truman:[1] 'The anchor is fouled. We cannot proceed.' He at once thought what fun it would be to sail to the Isle of Wight, but the afternoon was too choppy and he stayed in bed instead. We were quite glad of the respite to read briefs, to hold meetings, etc., in preparation for the talks, as we knew there were bad storms in the Atlantic and thought we should probably feel less like work once we sailed. This proved all too true.

Not a very pleasant voyage, except for the last two days, when we got out of the storms. I was only saved by hyacin tablets. The most amusing thing was to see Winston in a very short silk dressing-gown with white knobbly legs sticking out below, and large beetroot head above, toddling down the passage to A.E.'s stateroom for a morning talk. He invited us all to see the New Year in with him and gave us champagne. After hearing Big Ben strike and the BBC announcer wish us all a happy New Year, we turned the machine off and looked to Winston, who had risen, with his champagne glass in his hand and was swaying gently with the swell. Everyone thought he was going to make a speech, but he simply said, 'God save the King,' and we all drank his health. He refused to go up to the main lounge where the other passengers were longing to see him. In fact he never moved at all from his suite during the whole voyage. This and A.E.'s similar inaccessibility caused great disappointment to the five British journalists who had come aboard especially to 'cover' the trip. They got no news at all except what they could extract from reluctant officials.

I started the first draft for A.E.'s main public speech in America while still on board and made quite a bit of progress dictating to my secretary, Daphne Lumsden. I did not show it to A.E. until we got to America. The delegation was very well organized under Norman Brook. I had little other work to do apart from talking to A.E. and ministering to his health.

5 *January* 1952

Arrival in New York. We got off the *Queen Mary* on to a cutter and bounced across rather choppy water in the rain, feeling as if we were about to be thrown to the lions. A tremendous reception on shore with bands and flags and troops, marred by the wholly undisciplined behaviour of hundreds of cameramen who swarmed all over and all around the scene. While Winston and A.E. were standing to attention for the National Anthems, there were cameramen shouting 'Look this way, Mr Churchill,' '*Please*, Mr Eden,' and so on. My old friend Jack Simmonds is the head of Protocol and responsible for looking after us.

1 Harry S. Truman, President of the United States 1945–53.

As we drove from the docks to the airport, the roads were lined with Irish placards saying: 'Go home Churchill,' etc. A very comfortable flight to Washington in the President's aircraft and a really well-organized reception there. My hairdresser in London afterwards said he saw me on television descending from the aircraft. Shook Truman's hand and drove off with Acheson and A.E. to Blair House (where the President is living – the White House being under repair) for the President's lunch. I was left outside and found I had no car to get me to the Embassy. After some telephoning, the State Department provided one. A negro driver very interested in that curious anomaly England.

I attended most of the meetings with Truman in the White House Annexe. Thought him a very cheerful and nice man, though performing an act of continuous hearty efficiency, romping through the agenda with a loud, gay voice. He was quite abrupt on one or two occasions with poor old Winston and had a tendency, after one of the old man's powerful and emotional declarations of faith in Anglo-American co-operation, to cut it off with a 'Thank you, Mr Prime Minister. We might pass that to be worked out by our advisers.' A little wounding. It was impossible not to be conscious that we are playing second fiddle. Our own side (including A.E., Lord Cherwell and Lord Ismay) were a good deal concerned by the PM's readiness to give away our case, both in regard to the Far East and on raw materials. On the latter subject, when we were trying to get steel in return for tin and some other metals, but were known to be unable to meet the Americans over copper, Winston electrified us by himself raising the question of copper, just at the point when agreement was about to be reached without it. He gave quite a little lecture on the need to develop copper production in the British African colonies, and appeared to be under the impression that he was addressing the British Cabinet. The American officials bravely and loyally extracted us from this difficulty.

The President's offices are decorated in the worst possible taste. The walls are covered with the most frightful cartoons of Mr Truman and relics of his past political campaigns, and the main feature of his study – apart from the Stars and Stripes – is an enormous television set which I was offered the privilege of seeing in action by one of the negro guards.

My work on A.E.'s Columbia speech became more and more hectic and I was at it practically all night for the last three nights, greatly helped by Paul Gore-Booth.[1] I got A.E. through various readings of it in his bedroom and by skilful manœuvring prevented Roger Makins from scuppering the whole text, which I felt in my bones he desired to do. Fortunately, on the

---

1 Paul Gore-Booth (later Lord Gore-Booth), Director of British Information Services in the US. Later Head of the Office.

last night, when he was brought in, A.E. had become attached to my favourite passages and refused to see them cut out.

Spent several pleasant evenings with the Burrows[1] during one of which I was made to do square-dancing in their cellar, with about ten others. Great fun. Bernard absolutely in his element, calling the figures through a megaphone. Inez offered to go and buy me a nylon nightdress for Nancy and got one starting scarlet at the bottom fading to white at the top. My bedroom was next to Norman Brook's and I saw a lot of him. I like him, but ... he is not always too helpful in the differences of mood between A.E. and Winston. Jock Colville and David Pitblado do their best, but do not seem to be allowed very much influence with their master. He seems to keep them mainly for company late at night playing cards and reminiscing, but does not pay much attention to what they say.

One day I was walking along the passage with some papers in my hand, when Winston popped out of his bedroom looking as if he had been deserted, saw me and shouted, 'Have you got something there you wish to show me?' I said, 'No, sir.' 'Have you got something there you do *not* wish to show me?' he then asked, so I showed him my copy of the *New York Herald Tribune*. He asked whether I was the son of my father, with whom he said he had done important work in the old days over Middle East questions – 'At least we thought it was important at the time.' This was at least an improvement on what he had said to Norman Brook when shown my name on the list of those going to Washington. On that occasion he had said, 'Ah, Shuckburgh. Yes, I know him. I used to work with him,' being evidently under the impression my poor father, at this late date, was A.E.'s Private Secretary.

After the Washington talks we went to New York by train for the Columbia speech.

The speech went down very well. After it was over A.E. and I were driven out to Ophir Farm by Whitelaw Reid to spend two nights and Saturday in the country. A most welcome break and at last two good nights' sleep. The second evening they had a dinner party for us to which they asked a number of interesting pro-Eisenhower Republicans, including Mrs Ogden Reid (Whitelaw's mother and owner of the *Herald Tribune*), Mr Cowles and his politically and socially active wife Virginia, the former editor of a fashion magazine called *Look* and author of a scandalous book about Mrs Perón of the Argentine (comparing her and her husband with the dictator Rosas and his mistress), and Nancy's cousin, Augie Heckscher, and his nice French wife Claude. A most interesting evening on the

1 Bernard and Inez Burrows. He was Counsellor at the Embassy in Washington; later Ambassador in Ankara.
2 Home of Mr Whitelaw Reid of the *New York Herald Tribune*, a personal friend of Eden.

prospects for this year's presidential elections. This is the subject all Americans have uppermost in their minds, and our problems in Europe are really quite secondary.

The visit to Washington was followed by trips to Canada and then Paris. The entries for these trips are omitted.

6 February

A telephone call from Anthony early in the morning that the King has died in his sleep. This was still unknown to the public and we had to pretend for two hours in the Office that nothing was amiss, until the announcement was made from No. 10. I broke the news to William Strang and Roddie Barclay,[1] who has to make all the arrangements. Poor Princess Elizabeth, who is in Rhodesia on her way to Australia, is flying straight back. (A few days later there was a touching picture of her in *The Times* walking down the steps from the aircraft with the Privy Council lined up to greet her. One could see just the backs of their poor old heads: Winston, Attlee, A.E., Woolton and so on. The twentieth-century version of Melbourne galloping to Kensington Palace, falling on his knees before Victoria in her nightdress. The mystery is, where did she get her black clothes from? I have since heard that Queen Mary has laid it down as a principle of life never to go anywhere without a black dress – 'in case something should happen.' It is said that the young Duke of Kent wrote to his mother: 'Hard cheese about Uncle Bertie. But we couldn't have played footer anyway that day as it was freezing.')

15 February

I saw the funeral procession from the window of 6 St James's Street. Joanna and George[2] came too. After it was over I walked round to No. 1 Carlton Gardens, to see what A.E. was up to. Found a party of people there who had been watching the procession from the terrace. Amongst them Clarissa Churchill,[3] whom I later discovered to play a large part in A.E.'s life. I am hoping that he can be induced to marry her. Nobody needs a wife more than he.

Mid-February

A series of meetings leading up to the North Atlantic Council in Lisbon. First Acheson, Schuman[4] and Adenauer came to London and good progress

---

1 Roderick Barclay, Assistant Under-Secretary of State, superintending Protocol Department; later Ambassador to Denmark and Belgium.
2 See list of family members.
3 Clarissa Churchill, niece of Winston Churchill; married Eden, August 1952.
4 Robert Schuman, French Foreign Minister 1948–53.

was made over the German contract at meetings in the Secretary of State's room. I decided not to sit in throughout the meetings, but went in and out a good deal. Then we flew off to Lisbon.

    A very alarming departure from London airport. First one of the engines of our aircraft was losing power when they tested it out on the tarmac, and after two hours repairing it (during which we drank a great many cocktails at the expense of the Company) we set out again, starting our run across the airfield, only to hear the engine pack in again and have a dreadful fear for one moment that we had gone too far to stop. Back again to the V I Ps' room for dinner with champagne, all on the house, and eventually departed in another aeroplane rapidly taken off the Far East run. A.E. had become somewhat nervous by the end of all this and we had a little trouble. His reaction at the delay so scared the officer in charge of the airport that he told us we could go aboard the new aeroplane before it was really ready, this causing another outburst when the crew explained that they had not yet got their radio set to the new wavelengths. I am beginning to learn how to be a lightning conductor on these occasions, to save innocent bystanders from scenes which appear far more serious to them than I now know them to be.

    We arrived in Lisbon at about two in the morning, very tired. I had already had some rather chilly correspondence with Nigel Ronald[1] about accommodation in the Embassy, and the moment we arrived I realized that he was going to be unhelpful. He had refused to allow desks and chairs to be put into the study which Michael Wilford and I were given to work in, so we had to work on tiny marqueterie desks and wicker chairs, with no room to put anything. Nigel Ronald is a fussy valetudinarian and irritated us all considerably. He showed no interest in any of our work and gave no help over it, nor did his staff. All he seemed to be interested in was offering extra vests and doses of quinine to A.E., who caught a cold the second day.

    The Conference went well and agreement was reached over the German contribution to Western defence and the relationship of the E D C with N A T O. But the effect of all this on the public was spoilt by the insistence of the Americans on issuing an over-optimistic communiqué which spoke of the West having fifty divisions by next year – which is manifestly impossible. One of the meetings with Acheson and Schuman took place in the beautiful French Embassy, which I was shown over afterwards by the Ambassador and his wife. It overlooks the river and was built for one of the Governors of Lisbon in the sixteenth century who watched from his windows the galleons coming in from the New World up the Tagus. This romantic and beautiful house somewhat comforted me for easily the worst

1 Sir Nigel Ronald, Ambassador in Lisbon.

scene I have so far had with A.E. The chauffeur and detective, thinking they knew better than our instructions, had taken us off to the American Embassy at the far end of the town and we were half-way there before we realized what had happened. Being already late for the meeting (I had persuaded A.E. to take a rest in the garden after visiting the British Council offices) this extra delay seemed intolerable, and the annoyance was for some minutes uncontrolled. It developed into a physical struggle between me trying to shut the window between us and the driver, so that the lower classes might be insulated from these troubles, and A.E. leaning forward to wind it down so that he might call them bloody fools! All ended amicably as usual.

We paid a call on Salazar,[1] and I wrote a long letter to Nancy, sitting in the ante-chamber. We also visited de Gasperi[2] at the Italian Embassy. But I never got a record out of A.E. This was unfortunate as de Gasperi later greatly exaggerated the importance of the conversation and mis-understanding arose.

At the height of this visit to Lisbon there came out from London Eric Berthoud[3] with very grim news about the UK balance of payments and a really alarming plan worked out by the Bank of England and accepted by the Chancellor[4] for dealing with the situation. In brief the plan, so far as A.E. and I could understand it, was to block the Commonwealth and other sterling balances (except for limited amounts which would be released) and to make sterling convertible. The effect and object of this would be to throw the burden of the adverse trade balance off the reserves (which were rapidly running right out) and on to the home economy and the standard of living. It would have meant abandoning the policy of full employment and a controlled economy to which both parties had been pledged at the election.

Berthoud's instructions were to consult A.E. and Plowden[5] only, but I was present throughout.

Berthoud made it clear to us that the plan was strongly favoured by the Prime Minister and the Chancellor and also by a great section of the economic planners and senior officials in the Treasury. Lord Cherwell and Lord Swinton[6] were said to be very doubtful about it. So was Robert Hall [Cabinet Office] and Lionel Robbins [London University], who had been

1 Antonio de Oliveira Salazar, dictator of Portugal 1932–70.
2 Alcide de Gasperi, Italian Prime Minister 1945–53.
3 Eric Berthoud, Assistant Under-Secretary of State superintending the economic departments; later Ambassador to Denmark and Poland.
4 R. A. Butler, Chancellor of the Exchequer 1951–55.
5 Sir Edwin Plowden, Chief Planning Officer at the Treasury; later Lord Plowden.
6 Lord Swinton, Chancellor of the Duchy of Lancaster 1951–52, Secretary of State for Commonwealth Relations 1952–55.

consulted privately. It was clear that it was a bankers' plan: logically unassailable, perhaps, but open to the very gravest political objections. We could not help being at first attracted by the argument that it would force this country automatically to live within its means and thereby give us a rock-bottom start from which we could climb out of the series of crises which have marked the last few years. At this stage I suggested to A.E. that the only possible way of putting it across would be for the Government to announce the plan and go to the country on it. They could not possibly put it through with their small majority, in defiance of their election policy. A.E. agreed with this and for a time was quite keen on the idea of an appeal to the country. He had little doubt the Government would lose the election, but at least then they would have told the people the truth and prescribed the honest remedy.

The more we thought about it, however, the more A.E. became doubtful about the premises on which it was based. Plowden's reaction was to doubt whether the situation really warranted such drastic measures and he thought it looked as if the Chancellor had allowed himself to be rattled by the Bank of England. Plowden and Berthoud flew straight back to London with a cautious manuscript letter from A.E. to the Prime Minister suggesting that a good deal more careful thought should be given to it. I was then left the only person in Lisbon with whom A.E. could share this disquieting burden. The more we thought about it the more it seemed to us that the plan was premature. A.E.'s inclination was to distrust the automatic character of the plan and to think that the proper course would be to cut back the rearmament programme very substantially, reduce imports further on a selective basis and see whether this could not suffice to restore confidence in sterling without sacrificing the controlled economy and the policy of full employment.

I have recorded this at some length because, when we got back to London it became clear that there was a strong body of opinion which felt this way. The Treasury was sharply divided. Plowden had by this time produced an alternative and much less drastic scheme. The position in the Cabinet, we were told, turned entirely on what A.E. would do, and he went into the fray to kill the plan. The Budget had been postponed by a week, but there was very little time. After a series of evidently very stormy meetings, the Cabinet rejected the plan. It was impossible not to be sorry for Rab Butler, but Whitehall as a whole was profoundly relieved. In the event, the Budget was remarkably well received in the country and abroad, and the position of sterling dramatically strengthened. Even A.E. was, I think, a little surprised at this since in the event it had not been found possible (for international reasons) to make much of the cut in rearmament. (The opponents of the plan had been insisting that the one way to restore confidence abroad in our economy was to declare openly that our rearmament burden was too great and would be cut.) However, during the next three months the sterling drain was very greatly reduced and it does seem possible that we may get by.

A.E. rightly takes credit for these developments. It has, however, left a scar on his relations with the Chancellor, who was for a time very disgruntled at his plan having been rejected, and there was a marked tendency in the Treasury to cry 'stinking fish' about the prospects of sterling for quite a time afterwards. But the fact is that the economists and the planners are greatly divided and uncertain what we should do in our grave economic plight.

Eric Berthoud came out of all this extremely well, I thought. He was convinced throughout that Roger Makins, his chief, would think as he did, and this proved to be very much the case. When Roger got back from his tour in the Persian Gulf he became the leader of the anti-Plan group in Whitehall. The Chancellor has great confidence in him.

By a curious twist, Rab's successful Budget started off a series of suggestions in the press that he had taken the lead over A.E. in the Cabinet and was a serious rival for the succession to Winston. This is still believed by quite a lot of people, but I regard it as completely unreal. I do not think Rab has much political sense, and he certainly has no political following in the country. I am sure he would not want to go in above Anthony.

12 March

Another short visit to Paris: for the Committee of Ministers of the Council of Europe. On this occasion, A.E. launched a new British plan for giving the Council serious work to do. The idea is that it should provide the political institutions for the E D C and the Schuman Plan. It was extremely well received, and for the first time at a meeting of the Council in my experience the United Kingdom was not 'dragging its feet'. The credit for the plan goes to Ken Gallagher,[1] who worked it out.

Eisenhower came to breakfast one morning, and I had a few moments' conversation with this great man. He gives an impression of sense and solidity.[2]

15 March

Arrived back by air just in time to motor down to Cothill for Julian's school concert. He sang 'I know that my Redeemer liveth' quite beautifully, and played a Mozart minuet on the piano.

---

[1] F.G.K. Gallagher, Assistant in Western Organizations Department; later Ambassador to OECD.

[2] In 1969 I added a footnote here: 'But I recall that he said to A.E. that he would only consent to become President of the U S if there was a "unanimous call" from the nation; and that he was determined "not to become involved in politics" – surely a most naïve attitude.'

3 April

Lunch with the Foreign Press Association at the Dorchester. Another big speech by A.E., written almost entirely by me. Rather boring. I sat next to Mrs Matthews, wife of a member of the News Department, whose first remark to me was, 'Who wrote Mr Eden's speeches when he was out of office? I thought they were so much better than those he makes now.'

[17] April

Walter Gifford, the American Ambassador, came round with a letter from Dean Acheson to A.E. about an unpleasant article in *Newsweek* describing the alleged incompatibility of character between the two Secretaries of State. I helped A.E. with his reply.

There is a great deal of concern in the Conservative Party about the lack of leadership in home affairs. The P M has made a mess of the question of railway and bus fares and what with the disaster of the municipal elections ten days ago the Government is in a very bad way. There is no doubt that the old man ought to retire, but it is said that he is determined to stay until the coronation. A.E. tells me that in a month or two he will be under the strongest pressure to give up the Foreign Office and resume leadership of the House so that he can co-ordinate home policy.[1] He will be very reluctant to do this unless in the meantime he can have got a settlement in Egypt and perhaps with Persia, and seen the E D C and German contract safely established. Even then there will be the problem of Russia, and it will be a very difficult decision. It is a great pity that he and Rab do not combine more easily.

A.E. has been X-rayed and they have found the cause of his pains and sleepless nights. It is *not* an ulcer but has a long name which sounds like a flower or an exotic shrub [diverticulitis]. He will have to diet, but not too severely.

Negotiations were in progress for an agreement to replace the Anglo-Egyptian treaty of 1936, which had been abrogated by Egypt in October 1951. This treaty, due to expire in any case at the end of 1956, provided for the stationing of British troops in Egypt. Also under discussion was the future of the Sudan, then an Anglo-Egyptian condominium.

15 April

Returned from Easter holiday to find that we were still not agreed with the Egyptians on a formula for the 'basis of negotiations'. The latest

---

1 Eden had been appointed Leader of the House when the Government was formed but had been relieved of the office, at his own request, shortly afterwards in favour of Captain Crookshank.

Egyptian proposal is a new version of the formula of evacuation of the Canal Zone and defence, which might be agreed right away subject to later agreement on the Sudan clause. Although rather unhappily worded from our point of view, this formula seemed to William Strang and Roger Allen[1] adequate for our purpose. It did not exclude our discussing Egyptian participation in Middle Eastern defence or anything else we might think necessary as a result of the withdrawal of our forces from the Canal Zone. But when I read it over the telephone to A.E. (who was still at Binderton) he was indignant against it and said that he could not possibly get it through Cabinet and would not try. Later in the day we went through it with him and suggested some amendments. Particular difficulty now is to avoid saying that we will take the R A F out of the Zone.

21 April

A.E. had a meeting this afternoon with Ralph Stevenson[2] from Cairo and the Governor-General of the Sudan, Bob Howe,[3] to see whether any possible formula could be found which would meet the Egyptians' demand for our recognition of the King's title to the Sudan without breaking our pledges to the Sudanese. The result was in effect a complete deadlock. A.E. started by suggesting that we might let the Egyptians say that in their view Farouk is King of the Sudan while we, for our part, would say that we regarded the Condominium as still subsisting, and 'all rights deriving from it'. Perhaps we could call the Governor-General a Viceroy and find other means of making the arrangements more palatable to the Egyptians, while satisfying the Sudanese that their progress towards independence would not be halted. He put the matter in the broad setting of our economic weakness and the burden of keeping large numbers of troops in the Canal Zone, which would be greatly reduced if we could reach an agreement with the Egyptians.

This argument went on for ten days, with meetings almost every day, during which a formula was eventually worked out which Ralph does not think the Egyptians will accept, except possibly if the King is told in the firmest terms by the Americans that they will get nothing better out of us. The unreal part of all this is that the formula is not even intended as an agreement, but merely as a basis for negotiations. It becomes more and more clear that the effort (insisted upon by the Egyptians) of laying down the principles on which you will negotiate before you have negotiated is quite hopeless. It is one thing to defend in the House a formula which has

1 Roger Allen, Head of African Department; later Assistant Under-Secretary of State at the Foreign Office 1953–54, and Ambassador to Greece, Iraq and Turkey.
2 Sir Ralph Stevenson, Ambassador in Cairo 1950–53.
3 Sir Robert Howe, Governor-General of the Sudan 1947–55.

been the subject of an agreement and is therefore to that extent satisfactory as having achieved something, but quite another to defend a formula before its implications have been worked out between the parties. Recognizing this, A.E. has bit by bit made the formula less acceptable to the Egyptians in order to make sure that he cannot be accused of going behind or weakening our pledges to the Sudanese.

Every kind of bright idea has been thought of, from making HM the Queen joint sovereign with Farouk over the Sudan (this clearly had to be ruled out on psychological grounds) to calling Farouk 'King of the Nile Waters' and other subterfuges.

We have not yet (30 April) heard whether the Americans will support our formula. Nuri Pasha, the Prime Minister of Iraq, who had lunch with the Secretary of State today, thinks we should be able to divide the Sudan question from the Canal Zone problem. This would suit us well, and he is trying to be helpful, but it appears that the Egyptians are in too exalted a frame of mind over the Sudan to allow this. One cannot see what will happen. Perhaps the hot weather in Egypt will come in time to enable Hilaly[1] to get through the summer without any agreement at all with us.

27 April

Drove up from home in the Sunbeam in the morning and worked with A.E. at his flat. A.E. tells me that the Party are more and more concerned about the conduct of the Government, especially Winston's lack of grip and the fumblings of the Leader of the House. All reports show that the Government has lost a great deal of support. The trouble is lack of co-ordination on the home front and for this Lord Woolton is to blame. Jock Colville says he is becoming slower and more ineffective every day. Jock said, incidentally, that he had been astonished to find, when discussing the question of a CH for E. M. Forster, that Winston had never heard of him and had not read *A Passage to India*. Some concern about the PM's health. It is announced that he has a bad cold.

After finishing our work we waited half an hour in the street for Robert Carr and his wife who were to drive A.E. down to Binderton. Great patience was displayed.

High Wood[2] was looking beyond words beautiful this weekend. The beeches coming out, bluebells in the woods, all our new trees and shrubs bursting forth and tulips and blossom everywhere.

---

1 Egyptian Prime Minister.
2 Our home on the Chiltern escarpment near Christmas Common, Watlington. Designed by my brother-in-law, Lionel, for his parents in 1937 and given to my wife by them after the war.

30 April

The draft reply to the Soviet note,[1] resulting from discussion between the officials of the US, UK and France, turned out a terribly turgid affair which A.E. rejected as too long and badly written. William Strang asked me in great secrecy to have a shot at improving it, which I did. But I don't know whether this version will come to light, as it is said the Americans want a complete re-draft.

A.E. tells me that there is more concern over the PM's health than had been apparent. The Palace, Lord Salisbury and Lord Moran – his doctor – have been holding something back. The old man himself admits to being extremely tired and told A.E. the night before last that it would not be very long now before he gave up. But he mentioned no dates! A.E. said today that there had been some talk of trying to get him to accept a peerage. There has been a lot of vacillation as to whether the PM or A.E. should make the Party Broadcast on Saturday night, 'The First Six Months of the Government', but the PM finally decided to do it, greatly to our relief.

General Templer has been giving pep talks to the British community in Malaya, telling them that they should play less golf and attend fewer cocktail parties while the struggle against Communist guerrillas is on, and that they should be less stand-offish in their relations with the Malays. When I suggested to Anthony that he might make some approving reference to this in a speech, he did not like it at all. He said, 'Is not it all rather Montyish?' He is remarkably unsympathetic to the ordinary masculine simplifications of the English mind. He dislikes bishops, boy scouts and almost all soldiers except Eisenhower. Yet he also dislikes playboys and smarties, including the Mountbattens. His only real friend in the Cabinet (apart from Winston, who obviously has a lasting fascination for him) is Jim Thomas, though he admires the Lord Chancellor [Lord Simonds]. Apart from these, Tony Nutting and Robert Carr seem to be his only intimates, now that the Douglases[2] have gone away.

14 May

Anthony had to make two speeches today, first opening the Foreign Affairs debate and again in the evening at the United Nations Association dinner. This was a great strain – not only on him! Nancy was in the Strangers' Gallery. Before the debate I was buttonholed by Jim Thomas, First Lord, and told all about his troubles with A.E. He thinks that the attitude of the

---

1 This note of 10 March proposed immediate four-power discussions on the conclusion of a peace treaty for Germany and formation of an all-German Government.
2 Lew Douglas, US Ambassador in London 1947–50. He and his wife were personal friends of Eden.

Daily Telegraph, which has been regularly hostile to A.E., may be partly due to Michael and Pamela Berry[1] being offended at A.E.'s neglect of her 'salon'. Also they were upset by some occasion when Antony Head[2] was ticked off.

All this came on top of great agitation about last-minute arrangements for the reply to the Soviet note.

Eden went to Paris on 21 May for talks with Robert Schuman before going on to Strasbourg for the Committee of Ministers of the Council of Europe. He then went to Bonn for the signature of the Contractual Agreements and back to Paris for signature of the European Defence Community treaty.

23 May

Flew from Strasbourg after lunch and were in the Schloss Röttgen[3] by 6.30.

24 May

Spent the whole day in the Bonn Parliament for the talks on the Contract. The French in a terrible state of indecision. I have never seen Schuman so obstinate and unreasonable, putting himself into the worst light before Adenauer. They cannot make up their minds in Paris to have the slightest confidence in the Germans, to whom at the same time they are offering this long-term unity and merging of sovereignty. Schuman even refused to agree to the abandonment of the principle of taking reparations out of current production until eventually he was able to state that France did so under pressure from the US and UK.

In the evening there was a party given by the High Commissioners at which I sat next to General Heusinger and his wife and an American of German origin called Bohlen.[4] The dinner broke up early and the argument resumed in private session in McCloy's[5] office till after midnight. This was a very entertaining session, at which Jessup[6] and I had the most enjoyable sport of producing drafts and formulae to meet the Ministers' difficulties. Bathurst, Legal Adviser to the United Kingdom High Commissioner, was

1 Later Lord and Lady Hartwell. He was then editor-in-chief of the *Daily Telegraph*.
2 Antony Head (later first Viscount Head), Secretary of State for War 1951–56.
3 The official residence of the UK High Commissioner in Germany, a country house some fifteen miles outside Bonn.
4 Charles (Chip) Bohlen, American diplomat; later Ambassador in Moscow and Paris.
5 John J. McCloy, US Ambassador-at-large.
6 Walter Jessup, US Ambassador-at-large.

very helpful, and M. Sauvagnargues, Schuman's second adviser, very unhelpful.

The Secretary of State and Kirkpatrick escaped me to their car and I was left standing at the door. Fortunately the police car also failed to catch them. I loaded into that and had a hair-raising drive for twenty miles at highest speed with five policemen, four of them German. Frank [Roberts][1] arrived shortly afterwards and I felt in honour bound to wait up (in my dressing-gown) while he read out telegrams recording the day's events. Bed at about 3.00 a.m., full of whisky and very weary.

25 May

Further meeting in the morning at which finally all the outstanding points were settled. I did not attend most of these but dictated replies to various Foreign Office telegrams.

Dinner with the Chancellor. When I broke it to the Secretary of State just before dinner that we should have to start from home at 9.15 the next morning, he was very irritated at the long drive home to Schloss Röttgen. We therefore decided to spend the night in Bonn in the Villa Spiritus, and the admirable A D C arranged everything in a flash, fetching down all our clothes from Röttgen twenty miles away and rearranging all the security, etc. Enjoyed the dinner very much. Sat next to the Minister of Refugees, Herr Lukachek, and one Frau Kleiber. After dinner a massed male choir from Bonn and Cologne sang Mozart and German folk songs outside in the dark.

After I had got off to sleep, Con O'Neill[2] came on Frank's instructions, to tell me about last-minute French hesitations. But I did not awake the Secretary of State.

26 May

Up early in the Villa Spiritus on the Rhine. The signature of the German Contract took place at 10.00 organized by the Germans. Freddie was shocked to see two German soldiers in uniform standing at the door of the Chancellor's house. After the signature there was a buffet lunch with the Chancellor, during which Adenauer came round and talked to Frank and

---

1 Frank Roberts, Assistant Under-Secretary. He had been my predecessor both in Cairo before the war and in the Private Office, and was subsequently my predecessor on the North Atlantic Council. He was later Ambassador to the U S S R and to the German Federal Republic.

2 Con O'Neill, at that time on the Control Commission for Germany; later Head of FO News Department and Ambassador to the European Communities in Brussels. Led the official team negotiating British entry into the EEC 1969–72.

Wife of the Ambassador, Sir Oliver Harvey.

me about the difficulties of dealing with Berlin as well as diplomatic problems. Talking of the number of questions asked in Parliament, he said that he was comforted by the saying 'one fool can answer a lot more questions than ten wise men'.

We took off from the military airport after lunch for Paris and arrived in time for a dinner at the Embassy to which Acheson, Perkins, Jimmy Dunn, Walter Gifford and Jessup and a Middle East expert called Stabler came. Acheson in tremendous form, told several improper stories during dinner, one of great length about a New Zealand judge who had to settle a case in which some ewes, sold as having been 'joined' by the rams, had turned out not to be in lamb. The case, he said, turned on the meaning of the word 'joined'. If, for example, I say I joined my wife at the railway station, I do not mean what you sheep farmers think I mean.

The discussions went on till 1 o'clock and I was dead tired by the time I got to bed. It was very stuffy and oppressive.

27 May

I was still having my breakfast in bed when Freddie came in to say that the Secretary of State thinks he should perhaps abandon his visit to Hanover in order to be able to have further talks with Schuman and Acheson. Bob Dixon was in favour of this because Acheson has some new ideas about Indo-China which he feels we should be in on. After some argument it was agreed that we should stay. I 'phoned Kirkpatrick who took it very well, and the Americans and French seemed delighted.

I spent most of the morning dictating records of last night's talks with Acheson. The Secretary of State and the Ambassador went to lunch with Schuman and we had a very pleasant lunch on the terrace with Maudie Harvey,[1] discussing the weaknesses of the French.

The E D C was signed in the afternoon – a great scrimmage with cameras and newspapermen breathing down our necks and burning us with arc lamps. Adenauer gave me his autograph for Julian.

The ceremony appeared to attract no interest whatever from the Paris population. There was not a soul at the gates. Even in Bonn yesterday in the rain there were quite reasonable little crowds for the German Contract. However, A.E. got a telegram from Winston congratulating him in the name of the Cabinet and is purring.

1 Wife of the Ambassador, Sir Oliver Harvey.

Chapter Two

Eden at the United Nations, 1952

In September I accompanied the Secretary of State on visits to Yugoslavia and Austria, but the diary written on these visits is omitted here. On 7 November, after a brief visit to Paris for a meeting of the Organization for European Economic Co-operation (OEEC), we went to New York for the seventh session of the United Nations General Assembly, where Eden played a lively part in the efforts to break the deadlock in the negotiations for an armistice in the Korean war. He was in the unusual position of having to deal with both an outgoing and an incoming United States administration, for on 5 November the Republican candidate, General Dwight D. Eisenhower, had been elected President of the United States. Acheson's days at the State Department were numbered. John Foster Dulles came on stage.

In the meantime, in August, Eden had married Churchill's niece, Clarissa Churchill. His loneliness, which had been so painful to witness, was at an end.

3 November

I have kept no diary between the Yugoslav trip and today (3 November).

We went to Paris for the OEEC meeting where A.E. had a personal success in persuading the Europeans of United Kingdom interest on the economic side. Admittedly, the Americans have been busy with their election. There is no doubt that we have greatly enhanced our influence in Europe by these visits.

At Paris we all but succeeded in bringing the French and Germans together in a solution of the Saar problem. It was therefore very galling to A.E. when he returned to London and reported to the Prime Minister that all Winston had to say was 'What have you done about getting the Duke of Windsor invited to the Embassy in Paris?' This sort of comment, which is constant, and the irrational interference in all sorts of small matters, combined with a persistent attack upon him by the Beaverbrook press, is making A.E.'s position most difficult and irritating for him. There is a suspicion in the party that the PM's intimates, e.g. Randolph Churchill,

Duncan Sandys, Soames,[1] etc., and even possibly the PM himself, are behind these press attacks. Certainly the P M has done nothing to disown them. The calculation may be that by blackening the one possible successor they may keep the old man longer in office. Or they may be genuinely thinking they can groom Rab Butler for the succession.

Rab himself makes every now and then mild gestures of loyalty to A.E. through William Strang and through me, but never does anything direct. There is a deadlock between him and the Chiefs of Staff about the defence budget. A.E. will have to resolve this. It is a matter of about 75 millions.

4 November

Talk with the Lord Chancellor in A.E.'s room at the House of Commons about Maclean and Burgess question and Kenneth de Courcy's allegations [in the *Sunday Times*]. Lord Chancellor strongly opposed to libel action. A.E.: 'I am longing for an opportunity to get at this man!' Lord Simonds: 'You are the kind of man lawyers dream of.'

5 November

News of Eisenhower's victory. General disappointment here. Roger Makins thinks that from the long-term point of view it is good because:

 (i) it saves the two-party system in the United States;
(ii) it breaks down the split between the North and the South, but it will make great difficulties for us in the immediate future, especially if Dulles becomes Secretary of State.

High Wycombe by-election announced at lunch. Government have increased their majority. This is a personal triumph for A.E. Before he visited the constituency on Saturday the Gallup Poll put the Tories four points down. By Monday they were two points up. Numerous letters from constituents protesting against the Beaverbrook campaign to put Rab Butler in the lead for the succession.

Prime Minister was very cross because we were hesitant about his sending a telegram of congratulation to Eisenhower and wanted to consult Oliver Franks[2] first. He did not wait for the reply.

7 November

Drove into Reading to meet Catherine[3] (half-term holiday) and after an hour there left for London and America.

1 Randolph Churchill, Churchill's son; Christopher Soames, PPS and son-in-law to Churchill.
2 Sir Oliver Franks, British Ambassador in Washington 1948–52.
3 Our daughter, then aged thirteen.

Suggestions in the paper that Eden might go to Korea with Eisenhower. He passed a note to the PM in Cabinet: 'Do you want me to go?'

Went over at 7 p.m. to Carlton Gardens and sat with Anthony and Clarissa waiting for the aeroplane. Over an hour late, held up four hours in Shannon in the middle of the night. A.E. heavily drugged, stayed in the aircraft but had a bad recurrence of his pain and got practically no sleep. Austin[1] gave him an injection.

8 November

Arrived very bedraggled at Idlewild. Selwyn Lloyd, Oliver Franks and Gladwyn Jebb met us but were not allowed onto the aeroplane. Long drive to Gladwyn's house for lunch. Discussion at lunch whether A.E. should see Eisenhower. Oliver thinks very unlikely Ike will want to see him. He is busy trying to fill up his Government. The party having been twenty years out of office, it is difficult to find experienced Ministers. Oliver said, 'Don't press, ask Acheson.'

The Whitelaw Reids came to dinner to meet Anthony, but he was in bed. Whitey asked at dinner what Europe would say if the Americans used atomic weapons tactically in Korea to get a decision. When I said they would not like it at all, he replied, 'But you would expect us to use them if Europe were attacked?' Gladwyn answered, 'But that would threaten the life of the United States as well as the United Kingdom, whereas an attack in Korea is not vital to either.' I said also, 'You should not use your atomic weapon until you absolutely must. Its deterrent power is far greater before it has been used.' But it is very clear the Americans are becoming impatient of the Korean conflict and some want to get out.

9 November

Worked all morning on speech with Selwyn and Charles Johnston[2] at Gladwyn's house, where we are staying (Wave Hill, along the riverside drive with a fine view of the Hudson River).

Acheson, Jessup, Gross,[3] Schuman, Hoppenot and Lacoste came to lunch. Discussion first on Tunis and Morocco. A. E. dissuaded Schuman from announcing in the Assembly that he will walk out of the Committee if they discuss Tunis and Morocco.

On Korea, Acheson seemed agreeable to our working on the Indian kind of formula, but he seemed very scared of the Pentagon, because anything the

1 Eden's detective.
2 Charles Johnston, Head of China and Korean Department at the Foreign Office; later Governor of Aden and High Commissioner in Australia; author and poet.
3 Ernest Gross, US Representative at the UN.

State Department does, even with Truman's support, which the Pentagon doesn't like, Eisenhower will denounce. 'Whereas, if we carry the Pentagon, they will carry Ike along.'

A social dinner party at which I sat next to Mrs Ronald Tree and a Mrs Ryan, who seemed to know London society very thoroughly and talked of everyone by their Christian names.

This session of the General Assembly was dominated by the question of the Korean war. The Indian Representative at the UN, Krishna Menon, put himself forward as a mediator between East and West.

10 November

Gladwyn says the Secretary of State spoke to him about his going to Paris next year. He is delighted, but suggests he could double the role of Ambassador and NATO Representative. He is an expert on NATO and wants hard work, and there should not be 'two Kings in Brentford'. I mentioned this to A.E., who was not keen.

Moved into the Waldorf-Astoria, twenty-third floor. Romantic view over the East River.

First Committee of the Assembly. Greatly impressed by the new United Nations building, especially the outside and the corridored Committee Rooms. I don't like the main Assembly Hall, which looks like a super cinema, with a vast nightmarish organ half-way round it.

Vishinsky's speech. Very disagreeable. Interruption through some hammering in the cellars below.

Worked all day on the speech. Mrs Pandit [Nehru's sister] and Krishna Menon are sponsoring a resolution on Korea which we might accept. A.E. is setting out in his speech the principles which he thinks must be preserved and thus will give an opening to the Indians to table a resolution. He thinks it might be useful for the United Kingdom and India to share the honours, if any.

Resignation of Trygve Lie[1] announced unexpectedly today. A.E. knew this (Lie told some weeks ago in great confidence). But the secret was well kept. . . .

Remark of the day: A.E.: 'Can one get any ice in this hotel?'

11 November

A.E.'s speech in the Assembly. Main points: an attack on the Communist hate campaign; defence of British colonial policy; warning to the United Nations not to stretch the Charter by interference in internal affairs of

---

1   Norwegian Secretary-General of the United Nations.

member states; and the formula for Korea.

Very well received by the Americans. The French delighted with support on Tunis and Morocco. The Indians also pleased, though Krishna Menon said the passage about the hate campaign was 'un-British'. He said the Russians 'go away and lick their wounds' after attacks of that kind.

Sobolev, the second Russian delegate, came up to A.E. in the afternoon. A.E.: 'Do you think my speech has opened the door even an inch?' Sobolev: 'Perhaps two inches.' A.E. encouraged by this reply and reported it home. Doubt whether it means anything much.

Walked round outside the new buildings with A.E. Cameras, women admirers, police. Thought what one atomic bomb could do here!

Selwyn Lloyd gave lunch to A.E., Kraft (the Danish Foreign Minister) and me in the UN restaurant. Very crowded, bad service, filthy food. Kraft spoke of the NATO meeting in December. He is Chairman. He wants it held though the Annual Review is not ready. He said John Foster Dulles had asked to see him and that he might consult him. We advised him against this. J.F.D. also asked to see Anthony but A. thinks he is trying to make himself Secretary of State and is stalling.

Dined at a nice club with Augie and Claude. Augie very disappointed with Eisenhower. At the Convention, where the battle was against Taft and the Old Guard, the young Republicans were to the fore and the Party seemed vigorous and enlightened. Later the old gang got back. Augie spoke with tremendous admiration of [Adlai] Stevenson. His 'pure spirit and intellectual clarity'. A really great man. He would never say the obvious thing. He would never say, 'Korea shall have top priority with me,' though that would have been an election move, because it was obvious. He did not cash in on his settlement of the Illinois gaol riot. Augie thinks Stevenson's future of tremendous importance for America. He may never put up again, on the other hand he may succeed in drawing together and symbolizing all the most enlightened hopes of America. Various stories showing what an impression Stevenson's speeches made on intellectuals of all classes (known by the Republicans as 'egg heads'). Augie thinks Ike's visit to Korea should have a good effect because of his military reputation. 'He will say, we have got to carry the war, and the people will believe him.'

12 November

Krishna Menon came round early to advocate his resolution, first to Acheson on the twenty-eighth floor and then to A.E.[1]

---

1 Menon proposed handing over prisoners of war in Korea to a Repatriation Committee of neutral powers as a means of breaking the deadlock on the question which was preventing the negotiation of an armistice.

Thinks the Americans want to keep as many Chinese prisoners of war as possible. A.E. not sympathetic to his draft. Wonders whether he is really a Communist. Could be – but I think not. He seems to be guided mainly by the love of playing an important part.

Meeting with Acheson. Perkins and Jessup there. A.E. put me off by telling me not to take notes. Later Acheson put me at ease by asking if his man should stop taking notes too. By that time we were both doing it surreptitiously. Discussion on state of France, chances of EDC ratification. 'Europe hangs by the thin threads of the lives of Adenauer and Schuman.'

Acheson produced a new plan for Trieste which he explained on a map. It would give Italy Capodistria and compensate Yugoslavia in the hinterland of Zone A. Obviously inspired by concern over the Italian elections. Tone very anti-Yug. De Gasperi to be given a chance to say whether he 'can live with it'. If so, Tito to be told he must. We pointed out some difficulties, but did not make substantial comment. Later, the Americans alleged that A.E. had said there 'might be something in the plan'.

A.E. told Acheson about progress of talks with Neguib.[1] He hoped Americans could persuade Neguib that, if he kept quiet and refrained from anti-British speeches, we might be able to find a way of getting our troops out. Much would turn on the review we are making of our strategic needs in the Middle East. But Winston would probably make one last attempt, with Eisenhower, to get United States troops into Egypt.

Lunch in drugstore with Freddie. Hamburgers. Went shopping at Altmanns: nylon shirt, nightdress, stockings for Nancy.

Nicholas Eden arrived. Mike Pearson,[2] Selwyn and Charles Johnston all very active with Krishna Menon's plan. S.L. says we 'are nearing a major confrontation. Is it worth making concessions to get an Indian resolution which the Communists will almost certainly not accept? We see the great propaganda advantages of thus demonstrating the unity of view between Asiatic nations and the Western powers. But Acheson dare not, being afraid that anything he does will be attacked by the Republicans.'

13 November

Meeting with Acheson, Schuman, Webb (New Zealand), Pearson (Canada) and Spender (Australia) to discuss what to do about Krishna's resolution. Acheson very hostile to it. Made three good points:

(1) Principle of no forcible repatriation not sufficiently clearly stated;

---

1 General Neguib led a successful army coup against King Farouk in July 1952, together with Colonel Nasser. Two years later he was himself deposed by Nasser.
2 Rt Hon. Lester Pearson, Canadian Secretary of State for External Affairs 1948–57; later Prime Minister 1963–68.

(2) Plan gives every opportunity for blackmail of prisoners of war in the transit camps;

(3) There is no indication what would happen to POWs who still refused to go back.

But I think his hostility deeper than that. Spender strongly supported him. This annoyed A.E. very much as Casey[1] had only the day before taken the contrary view. Pearson rather vague and woolly.

Dewey[2] called in the afternoon. Asked me to spell my name.

A.E.'s talk to Foreign Relations Committee. Afterwards an interview with John Foster Dulles, who gave A.E. all sorts of assurances that policy won't be changed. Like Dewey, he was most friendly and apparently anxious to dispel British fears of Republican policy. I sat in adjacent room alone. Did not smoke today.

14 November

More Krishna Menon. He is hoping to be able to accept substantially the amendments to his resolution.

NATO meeting in Acheson's suite called by Kraft. All Ministers there very sleepy and with difficulty decided to hold the December meeting of NATO. Then followed quite a row between Pearson and Acheson about Menon's activities. A. tried to warn Pearson off, but got no change.

Cocktail party at Gladwyn's house. Vishinsky and Gromyko[3] surrounded by thugs. Zorin[4] and his wife arrived late and at once recognized me. I swallowed my disgust at his role in Czechoslovakia and introduced him to A.E. A Mrs Hamilton Galt came up and told me she was a Miss Shuckburgh, but I had no time to enquire further.

Dined with Mr and Mrs Ronnie Tree. Large house, full of wonderful furniture, pictures. Great luxury. Ed Murrow[4] held forth about the influence of television on political opinion. He takes the line that the *metteur-en-scène* can entirely control the effect which any public speaker on TV has upon his audience. He guaranteed he could make Mr [Aneurin] Bevan appear as honest and impressive as Mr Eden himself. This did not go down well. Others present were Mike Pearson and his wife, Charmian Douglas[6] who offered to do all my shopping for me, and a banker from Philadelphia

1 R. G. Casey, Australian Foreign Minister.
2 Thomas Dewey, Republican Governor of New York 1938–54.
3 Andrei Gromyko, Soviet Foreign Minister.
4 V. A. Zorin, Deputy Minister of Foreign Affairs, had been the Soviet Ambassador in Prague during my time there and was instrumental in bringing about the fall of the Beneš regime.
5 Ed Murrow, American journalist and broadcaster.
6 Charmian Douglas had been a prominent social figure in London when her father was Ambassador.

called Scott. I talked after dinner to Mrs Tree, who is attractive and intelligent. She is a rabid Democrat and does the line of the left-wing rich woman. When I asked her whether she attended the endless conventions and luncheons that American women seem to enjoy so much she said, 'I get out of them by saying that I will not join unless they will admit negroes.'

Some relief from the tensions of the United Nations was provided by a visit with Eden to Ottawa on 15–18 November. I had served there on the staff of the British High Commissioner in 1940–42. The relief was short-lived.

18 November

After lunch flew back to New York. Very tired. Great fuss on arrival, where we were met by Gladwyn. Both A.E. and I seemed to be in rather a nervous state. Acheson still resisting Indian resolution.

Eisenhower rang up within an hour of our arrival to argue against the Indian resolution which it turned out he hadn't read. We wondered whether he had been put up to it. Must have been. We sent him round the text.

Returning by sea is off. We are torn between wanting to be in New York to solve Korea and wanting to be in London for Parliament.

19 November

Felt better after some sleep. Morning spent discussing Korea. The Indian resolution was tabled yesterday. Krishna Menon to speak this afternoon. Mike Pearson and Selwyn have been coaching him to be reasonable but fear he may not be as he speaks without notes.

Two visits to Acheson, but got nowhere. I went up for the second meeting and sat in bedroom outside with Hickerson (State Department expert on United Nations matters), Gross and Selwyn. The last two went for each other in semi-bantering way which I thought rather surprising. Selwyn said the Americans had completely ruined the propaganda effect of the Indian resolution by their hostile press conference which had given at least one American journalist the impression 'that the Russians were right and that the US did not want an armistice'.

K.M.'s speech very reasonable, well argued. A good effort which impressed many but Gross very critical in the Committee of Eight (representing the sponsors of the twenty-one-power resolution which the Americans want us to support against the Indian resolution). The climax of the unpleasantness with Acheson took place this evening in A.E.'s room when

Acheson and Hickerson came down from a cocktail party and, after asking me to mix 'a real martini, meaning mostly gin', proceeded to make a most extraordinary scene. Selwyn Lloyd was there. Half-bantering, half-serious, Acheson said S.L. was not to be trusted. Had misled and twisted the Americans for weeks. Was a Welsh lawyer, etc., etc. Selwyn gave as good as he got and A.E. seems to have sat back astonished. Acheson said that unless the US and UK were in line over this Korea resolution (i.e. unless we agreed with them) there would be no NATO, no Anglo-American friendship, etc. Which side were we on? Hickerson actually said: 'Anthony, which will you choose: the United States or India?' They were probably both a little tight. Also chagrined by the general support of Krishna Menon's resolution and the way it has been improved to meet every objection they have raised. Acheson called Pearson 'an empty glass of water' and said that Canada should be brought to heel by the United States. He said that in his speech next week he would tear the Indian resolution apart. He also used the phrase 'debagging that Swami'.

Acheson admitted for the first time that if the armistice talks failed the Americans had plans for a major offensive. A.E. : 'But you haven't enough troops!' A: 'We have four divisions we could send.' A.E. : 'Why didn't you tell us this before?' No answer.

As he left, A. said, 'Don't you ever appoint a Welsh lawyer as your Minister of State again!' He then added, 'All lawyers are failures in foreign policy. Look at myself and John Simon.'[1]

I heard all this from A.E. and S.L. when I got back from dinner with Aunt Louise[2]. . . .

Sat up for hours discussing the day's events and A.E.'s speech for tomorrow. He is going ahead despite Acheson.

20 November

A successful day for A.E. Acheson's position virtually collapsed. A.E. spoke strongly in Committee One for the Indian resolution. He had previously seen from the American press that he was on safe ground and had shown relevant parts of his text to Ike over lunch. Ike said he was only concerned that the prisoners of war left over should not be indefinitely imprisoned. That is the essence of A.E.'s speech and implicit in what Menon said yesterday. All gratified by the speech. French delighted. British and US press correspondents seemed pleased. K.M. himself quite accepts the two criticisms:

    (i) on the Empire (a detail);

1 Sir John Simon, lawyer; Liberal MP and Foreign Secretary 1931–35.
2 See list of family members.

(ii) on future care of POWs who do not go home.

Went with A.E. to Condor Hotel to lunch with Ike. Barrage of cameramen. I stayed in outer office with Edward Green, 'personal assistant' to the General. Various big shots wandered in and out, including Stassen,[1] and all talked American politics to me as if I was a member of the party. Green asked me to lunch and then brought two girls from his staff. One of them, a Mrs Murray, promised me tickets for *Guys and Dolls* for Monday. Took text of A.E.'s speech into Ike's room where they were having lunch. Ike said, 'so pleased to see you *again*'. (I met him at Fontainebleau a year ago.) His staff say he has an extraordinary memory. Fantastic set-up in his hotel. Secretaries, aides, advisers, lovelies, cameramen: total confusion. All his staff had labels on their lapels. One woman had hers on the left side of her girdle: 'I make them look for it!' Babel of pressmen. Ike looked very healthy and unchanged. A.E. tells me conversation very satisfactory. 'You and I, Schuman and Adenauer can work together. Who is the Canadian?' Then A.E. : 'Mike Pearson.'
Ike: 'I thought he was UNO '[2]
A.E. : 'Only temporarily.'
Ike: 'Good, we can work it all out.'
No mention of Winston at any point.
A.E.'s comment: 'It is rather like Queen Mary. Glad she is there, dear old thing.'

Dulles is to be Secretary of State. Ike apparently unaware of his reputation on Far East. Almost apologetic about the appointment. Says it is for a year anyway. Very interested in Persia and well informed.

Interview with Acheson turned out to be not for a wigging on Korea as we expected, but on Persia. (? Coincidence that Ike had mentioned it.) A. says there is 'not enough cheese' in our offer to Persia. Byroade[3] present looking grim. A.E. conciliatory to Acheson. I was very angry and refused to smile when he said, 'I don't want you people to think, as the French do, that the Americans are impossible.' A.E. noticed this and approved. We are both fed up of being lectured by Acheson, but Anthony very warm-hearted, wants to write him a nice letter because he is beaten. He is now pretending to like the Indian resolution.

21 November

Terrible wind all night. Slept very badly on the twenty-third floor, exposed to the hurricane. Out before breakfast to look for toys. Failed to find any.

---

1 Harold Stassen, Director of Foreign Operations, State Department, 1953–55.
2 Pearson then held the Chair at the UN General Assembly.
3 Henry A. Byroade, American diplomat, later Ambassador in Cairo.

Got two ballpoint pens of a new kind which do not smudge.

The struggle continues. The old Commonwealth delegates, including the PM of New Zealand (Holland), came to A.E.'s suite for consultation. Spender had refused to come and the Australians were poorly represented. But all were against the idea that Spender should table a lot of amendments to the Indian resolution at United States behest.

Then British press correspondents. A.E. rather over-eager and over-emphatic, I thought. He is nervy and excited. From there down to a meeting of the '22' (sponsors of original resolution) with Spender in the Chair. Gross tried to force the Committee to take a position on the United States amendments. Selwyn spoke against, so did Turkey, France, Canada and New Zealand. Gross insisted. He said Acheson was to speak on Monday and must have a decision at once so that his speech could be prepared. This was thought very tactless by everyone. Spender moved adjournment to Monday. Honduras and Nicaragua then supported Gross, who very sulkily said, 'OK. Then we will meet on Sunday.'

From there in a rush to meet twenty top radio, television and newspaper commentators at lunch. A.E. again greatly over-excited, in my judgement, and Rids[1] agreed. But I don't think it was noticed by the others. Very frank and outspoken replies to difficult questions. A distinct tendency among the Americans to ask whether it is safe to have an armistice. They are obviously very worried and afraid they may have to get further into the Far East war. Disquieting.

Back in a rush to United Nations to hear Spender speak, and then two hours closeted with Krishna Menon trying to get him to volunteer amendments which will meet the United States points. All exhausted. Back to hotel and A.E. to bed, where I cleared a number of FO papers with him.

I received tonight from Byroade his version of what Acheson had said to A.E. on Persia. He had slipped in a remark implying that if we do not do something soon the US Government may buy oil from Persia regardless of the fact that it is our property. I have to get this withdrawn.

22 November

The battle continues. The Americans have insisted on a meeting of the '22' on Sunday night. Acheson was heard saying to his staff that they will have to 'fight their way out', which gives a pleasant picture of the American tough guy shooting his way out of an awkward position and scattering his friends on every side. The fact is that, when you scratch this elegant and

1 William Ridsdale, Head of the News Department.

civilized Acheson, he turns out to be just another tough guy.

Another meeting with Menon at Mike Pearson's hotel, where we lunched. ... Menon has agreed to put forward amendments to his own resolution which entirely meet our two points and we propose to stick to them, but the Americans are declaring to all that they will kill the Indian resolution by forcing the '22' to *demand* amendments.

Gross asked to come and see A.E. Before he had arrived, the AP [Associated Press] had the story that he was coming to tell A.E. from Acheson where to get off. We confronted him with this. He was speechless and spoke of pressure upon him from the Pentagon and from Washington.

Lew Douglas came in. He is 100 per cent on our side and will, I think, speak to Dulles. He advised A.E. not to budge an inch. The Russians are beginning to say that the Indian resolution is no good so that the Americans are mad not to support it. We are determined to do so whatever happens. A.E. is feeling 'as he did about Mussolini' and says he would not mind if he had to resign over this.

Surprisingly enough, Winston is sending telegrams which indicate no doubts about the line we are pursuing.

Dined alone with A.E. at Le Gourmet. He told me about his Cabinet intentions. S.L. to Ministry of Labour, Walter Monckton to Foreign Office. He is very upset by the Cabinet changes of which Winston has just informed him. Swinton is to go to the Commonwealth Relations Office [CRO], and for the rest it is little more than a juggle with the old-stagers. I told him I thought this was just as well. The more Winston ignored the younger men in the party the sooner they would develop pressure for a change at the top. ...

23 November

Open attacks on us in the American press – put out by the US delegation after Gross's interview of yesterday. Some nervousness on our side, but Lew Douglas telephoned: 'stand firm' after seeing Dulles, though he did suggest a possible alternative – to postpone the issue until January. This would never do.

We summoned Selwyn, Gladwyn, Rids, etc., and drafted a press statement of our own. This reaffirms that we favour no forcible repatriation but consider the Indian resolution preserves this. It points out value of an Asian initiative.

Then we escaped as quickly as possible from New York, Acheson being due back from Canada and we not anxious to meet him.

Lunch with Mrs Ogden Reid in her country house. It is her birthday. Children, birthday presents all over the floor. At lunch she gave me a copy of *The Old Man and the Sea* by Ernest Hemingway. A.E.'s mind is absolutely full of the issue. He lobbies Helen, Whitie and Brownie Reid – with great success, as we later discovered – for consistent support from the *Herald Tribune*. Then we went off to Ophir Farm to stay with Whitelaw Reids. A.E. to sleep. I read my new book.

A surprise party that evening for Mrs Ogden Reid. About fifty people, including all the Reids, Hoffman,[1] Dulles, Trygve Lie, the Jebbs and a quarter of an hour later, as a final surprise, the Eisenhowers.

The house was decorated with enlarged photographs of Mrs Reid at all stages of her career. An hour and a half of speeches after dinner all about 'our little mother' or 'this little woman who made the paper', ending up with ten minutes from Ike about himself. After this, A.E. drew Ike aside for a few minutes. I had taken the precaution of slipping in my pocket the text of our statement to the press. The first thing A.E. did on sitting down with Ike was to call out for me and say, 'Evelyn dear, you could not possibly find, amongst all your papers upstairs, could you. . .?' So I pulled it out of my pocket, and Ike said, 'Say, you're fortunate in your Private Secretary!' This is the sort of story which diplomats put in their published memoirs. I hereby swear never to include it!

Ike was on our side over the Korean resolution. 'So long as we don't have to send them back, the ones we have converted, I don't mind what happens to them.' He spoke of the importance of conversion in the struggle against Communism. We must encourage people coming over. 'We cannot win in the Far East without Asiatic support. That is why the Indian initiative is good. Tell Nehru from me I think it is fine.' (It later turned out that A.E. did not hear the last sentence of this quoted passage and we had to confirm from Eisenhower that he wished a message sent. He did, so it was sent.)

Dulles joined the conversation at the same moment as I did and Gladwyn Jebb too. He was much slower and more legalistic. Ike seemed several times to cut him short.

After the main party broke up we went on singing and dancing with the Reid family until very late. Rather a lot of whisky.

24 November

Hangover. Drove into New York with A.E. and Joan Reid. A.E. nervous. But the British press is behind us. Some curious features in the American press. Good editorials but the news 'United Kingdom blocks American efforts for cease-fire in Korea'. I think these are signs of retreat.

1 Paul Hoffman, President of the Ford Foundation 1951–53.

A.E. saw Cooper (*The Times*) and Alistair Cooke.

William Elliot[1] to lunch. He has seen Bradley[2] and denies that there is any thought of an all-out attack in Korea (Acheson's hint that there might be – in one of his less lucid moments – had caused us to bring Elliot down to New York for this purpose). Bradley thinks the only possibility is to go on as we are, training up more and more Korean divisions and reducing our commitment. But the US Chiefs of Staff are afraid of the Chinese prisoners who do not want to go back being left within reach of the fighting area. They fear cutting-out expeditions, excuses for a breach of the armistice, etc. Elliot is quite sure, however, that they want the armistice.

Bradley has agreed on Mediterranean and Iberian Commands to our satisfaction. This is a gesture and a statesmanlike move on his part, which contrasts very well with Acheson.

A.E. spent the afternoon in Committee One. Vishinsky made an all-out attack on the Indian plan, but despite this Acheson made the same legalistic speech he had prepared in advance. They seem incapable of manœuvre. One gets a terrible impression of the United States and Russia as two unwieldy, insensitive prehistoric monsters floundering about in the mud.

A.E. decided, after Vishinsky's speech, not to try to see him.

Took Catherine Leach[3] to *Guys and Dolls* and found our seats in the second row. Dined afterwards at a restaurant for actors and artists, with signed portraits of every famous person you can think of round the walls. Walked up Broadway to look at the lights in Times Square. Back about midnight and did half an hour's work with Freddie.

25 November

Krishna Menon called at 9.15. The idea was to see whether he would be disposed to meet Acheson's points of yesterday in any way. But he was in no mood for it, and Selwyn advised against trying. Selwyn then saw Gross, who produced the very modest amendments which the Americans now want. They are coming round and perhaps realize what an opportunity they missed yesterday.

Down to the UN with A.E. for the First Committee and left him there. Went shopping to Saks, 5th Avenue. Got back to find A.E., Selwyn and Gladwyn with Acheson, Hickerson and Gross. Joined them. The position is now as follows:

(1) United States requirements now reduced to one very small

---

1 Air Chief Marshall Sir William Elliot, Chairman of the British Joint Staff Mission in Washington and UK Representative on the NATO Standing Group 1951–54.
2 General of the Army Omar Bradley, Chairman of the US Chiefs of Staff 1948–53.
3 See list of family members.

amendment in paragraph 17, viz., those who are not repatriated or whose future is not otherwise determined by the ninety-day procedure shall after thirty days (not sixty) be passed to an agency of the United Nations for care and disposition (not maintenance).

(2) All will try to persuade Menon to accept that.

(3) If he accepts or does not violently object, all will vote for his resolution.

(4) If he objects then will the United Kingdom promise now to vote with the United States for the amendment? If we will, the United States will vote at tonight's meeting of the '22' to give priority for the Indian resolution.

This is clearly another effort to pin us down. We could not do it. A.E. said he would have to tell Menon if he gave any such promise. Acheson agreed. Selwyn asked whether it would be really so terrible in those circumstances if the United Kingdom abstained while the United States voted for the amendment? Hickerson replied, 'It would be terrible.' 'Then can the United States abstain?' Acheson said, 'Absolutely impossible'. But we got out of the meeting without any commitment. Later, in a supreme effort to persuade us, Hickerson said to Selwyn, 'You know the United Kingdom will suffer much more than the United States from any split between us.' It is hard to imagine an argument less likely to move us.

A brief mention by Acheson of Trieste and by A.E. of Egypt. Cannot the United States give economic aid and leave arms aid to us, Egypt's normal source? Acheson said he would telephone Washington. He was all honey, but there is trouble coming over Trieste. He is quoting Mallet[1] against us to the effect that de Gasperi can be relied upon not to leak if we privately offer him Capodistria.

We took off at Idlewild for the United Kingdom at 5.20 p.m. After about two hours' flight, No. 4 engine over-heated and we went down at Gander. We were told there would be an eight-hour delay while they changed the engine, so A.E. and I slept in our berths while the rest were put up in an hotel. Not a bad night.

26 November

We spent the whole day in Gander. Very cold outside. Very exasperating within. Menzies [Australian Prime Minister] lunched with us up at the bar and I sat next to him. He is not at all keen on what we have been doing in New York. Australia is evidently obsessed by the need for a dollar loan

---

1 Sir Victor Mallet, Ambassador to Rome.

and does not want to offend the United States in any way. Speaking of the Commonwealth Conference, he said the objective should be to increase 'the flow of United States capital'. That is the main advantage he sees to be derived from convertibility. He thinks Winston's Cabinet changes give inadequate scope for younger men. Said he personally likes Swinton but thinks he will give great offence to other Commonwealth leaders. He is 'arrogant'. Menzies said to me he thought Winston was too old to be Prime Minister. He described the disastrous effects last year of very high prices for Australian wool. Farmers cut down dairy and wheat production to get quick wool profits. They spent the money on luxury imports, thus upsetting the economy. The Government tried to take it in tax but this was very unpopular. Then the prices collapsed and thousands were ruined. All this seemed to be an effort to justify the Australian cuts of imports from the UK. Menzies asked Anthony to send a telegram to Churchill asking that the Commonwealth Conference in London be postponed one day. We sent the telegram off and felt slightly relieved.

Eventually we got off just before dinner. A.E. talked over dinner in the aeroplane about his intentions when he takes over from Winston. He said he would want a Foreign Office Principal Private Secretary. I spoke rather dubiously. Said Whitehall would not like two Foreign Office Private Secretaries at No. 10. 'They can do what they are told. I am not going to be run by Bridges[1]!'

I am left wondering whether he was thinking about me. He is becoming very impatient to get his hands on the control of the Government. He says that the Chief Whip and the previous Chief Whip (James Stuart) have both told Winston to retire, but do not think he will do so.

I sat in the cockpit and saw the northern lights. I was also in the cockpit while we landed by radar. Very impressive.

27 November

Arrived at No. 6 early in the morning and found Nancy there asleep. Very tired all day after a completely sleepless night in the aeroplane.

---

1 Sir Edward Bridges (later Baron Bridges), Permanent Secretary to the Treasury 1945–56.

Chapter Three

Churchill and Eden, 1952–53

Anthony Eden had long been generally recognized as Churchill's successor, and he held the title of Deputy Prime Minister. But as time wore on and Churchill showed no signs of retiring he became impatient to get his hands on the reins of government. His hopes received a set-back in 1953, when the death of Stalin gave Churchill an additional motive for staying on; as the only survivor of the three great war leaders he felt that he had a mission and a duty to 'unfreeze' the cold war.

The diary illuminates the growing strain which these delays placed upon Eden's nerves.

28 November

PM has told Clarissa he wants to give up. She says he is looking for an opportunity and Anthony must be gentle with him. Must let him go to America. Today he begged Anthony to let him go 'as privately as possible'. 'Only one speech.' A.E. is tempted. It might be the way out. But Winston is worried that A.E. is so deep in foreign affairs and not preparing.

29–30 November

Slept all Saturday at home. Started work again on my corner cupboard. Robin[1] delighted with the Canadian cowboy hat and pistol which I bought him in Ottawa. N. and I played the recorder and piano for the first time for a year.

1 December

The Catholics making a great fuss over Tito's forthcoming visit to England. Evelyn Waugh has written a violent article in the *Sunday Express*. Efforts to pacify them. PM 'anxious to defend A.E. It was my decision.' I don't think this good. We are not ashamed. They are now keen on inviting

1 Our younger son, then aged four.

Salazar as a counter. I am not sure about that either. It would be better if we could get Tito to do something for freedom of worship in Yugoslavia.

Meanwhile, the Americans are beginning to talk to the Italians about their Trieste plan.

2 December

Slept badly and became very depressed about the world in general. Our economic situation, German and Japanese competition, destruction of British influence in the Mediterranean and Middle East (after Persia and Egypt, the sheikdoms on the Persian Gulf are now being absorbed by Saudi Arabia). The Americans not backing us anywhere. In fact, having destroyed the Dutch empire, the United States are now engaged in undermining the French and British empires as hard as they can.

I was therefore rather grudging when I found A.E. keen and optimistic about Europe. The vote in the Saar has helped the French and he thinks he can get it settled. 'I am excited. I think I am on to something.' He wants to do it in Paris next week and thinks this the key to European problems. Frank Roberts is dubious about this and thinks it is better to leave it to Adenauer and Schuman.

I recognize the strength of this strain of optimism in A.E.'s character, though I have difficulty in sharing it.

Meeting with William Strang, Roger Makins and Anthony Nutting about the future approach to the United States after the Commonwealth Conference.[1] Should Rab do it? Commonwealth would oppose this. Should PM do it?

Salisbury thinks A.E. should ask Winston his intentions for the future, when they meet this weekend. He has suggested that, if this fails, senior members of the Cabinet might meet, without Anthony, to discuss an approach to the PM. Last night at a reception for the Commonwealth Prime Ministers, he made it quite clear that he could not follow the business of the conference. Holland: 'It is pathetic.' William Strang does not believe anything will make him go. I feel that the main Foreign Office interest is that he should not go to the United States to try to establish a 'Churchill–Roosevelt' relationship with Eisenhower.

Massigli[2] told A.E. at lunch today that the late Italian Ambassador in London, Gallarati Scotti, told him that the Vatican was doing all it could to prevent any improvement in Yugoslav relations with the West because they fear Titoism in Italy more than they fear Soviet Communism. A.E. was shocked by this.

1 A Commonwealth Prime Ministers Conference was held in London, 27 November–11 December.
2 René Massigli, French Ambassador in London 1944–55.

Went for a moment into the Commonwealth Conference and was greeted by Meyer, formerly South African High Commissioner in Ottawa.

Eisenhower has nominated Winthrop Aldrich as Ambassador in London and published the fact without asking for *agrément*. This is awkward. Gifford will be very disappointed. He had been given to understand by Ike that he would be left in place. I know he does not at all want to leave.

3 December

A woman in the train coming up from Henley saw my copy of David Kelly's book[1] and said that she knew him in Buenos Aires. Then she said, 'You look so like Shuckburgh.' I said, 'That's what I am.' She was a Mrs Goodwin and her husband had been, I think, with the Frigorificos in Buenos Aires.

A.E. was at the Commonwealth Conference all day. Impossible to get any Foreign Office work through him. Very difficult situation. Michael Wright[4] called on me. Delighted with Oslo and the Norwegians. He says they consider themselves to be Britain's best friends but expect the Conservative Government to be less friendly to them than the Labour. He wants a British Minister to visit Oslo and suggests Selwyn Lloyd, Monckton or Jim Thomas.

Drove with the Edens to the Royal Institution, Albemarle Street, where he addressed the Franco–British Society. Lord Bessborough, Massigli and Lord Brabazon also spoke. Dropped A.E. at the House for a Cabinet at 6.00 and Clarissa back at No. 1. On the way she asked me how she should comport herself tonight at the Queen's dinner for the Commonwealth Prime Ministers. I told her she should not ask questions or initiate strange topics. Otherwise be natural and courteous.

4 December

George Middleton in the Office back from Persia.[3] Described his evacuation from Tehran with whole staff, including twenty children, their luggage, etc., the refusal of the Air Officer Commanding to take them out by air to Habanya: 'FO should have foreseen this. Your mess.' But when their convoy went through Habanya he supplied them with everything, sixty chickens.

---

1 *The Ruling Few* (Hollis & Carter 1952). Kelly was my Ambassador in the Argentine in 1942.
2 Sir Michael Wright, British Ambassador to Norway; later Ambassador to Iraq.
3 When Mossadeq broke off diplomatic relations with Britain at the end of October, George Middleton, Chargé in Tehran, had the job of organizing the hasty withdrawal. He left Tehran with the last road convoy of Embassy belongings on 1 November.

Commonwealth Prime Ministers present in Cabinet. A.E. gave them an hour's talk on foreign policy and they all expressed confidence in him and issued a communiqúe saying so. He is delighted, but the effect spoiled by a piece in the *Star* obviously put there by Leslie, the Treasury PRO, saying that 'though Mr Eden is in the Chair, it is Mr R. A. Butler who does most of the talking for Britain'.

I called on Lascelles to clear a telegram about Ike's indiscretion in naming a new Ambassador to London before seeking *agrément*. Took the opportunity to ask why Clarissa was not taken up to the Queen last night. Also tried to sound him about PM but got no encouragement and did not proceed further. I made two points:

(1) Ike and Dulles 'want to work with' A.E., and asked how this fits in with PM's visit to the US. Lascelles said that the PM has told the Queen he wants to go before the hand-over 'to say goodbye to Truman and show him that he is not going out friendless'.

(2) Impossibility of being Foreign Secretary and an active Deputy PM. I mentioned the alternative of giving up the FO and leading the House. This would not be acceptable 'unless there were a term upon it'. Asked whether L. thought that A.E. ought to stay at home more. He did not think so. Doing such a good job abroad. Seemed unconscious of the growing unhappiness in the party. Said he wished Winston would make more use of Crookshank![1]

Gifford came round with Courtney [of the US Embassy] to try the Trieste plan on A.E. again. They claimed he had said in New York that it was 'worth thinking about' and he called me in to witness. In the discussion I asked why, if they thought their plan more favourable for Italy but still possibly acceptable to Tito, they did not sound Tito first instead of sounding de Gasperi first? A.E. took this up and they are going to put it to Washington.

5 December

Commonwealth Conference took a jolt today when India, Pakistan and Ceylon said that if sterling became convertible and fell vis-à-vis the dollar they might want to stick to the dollar. Australia said they preferred to maintain the sterling area, but if others were to make reservations they would have to do so too. In fact, the convertibility plan threatens to disrupt the sterling area. A.E. had asked for a Cabinet on Monday. He thinks he may have a dispute with the Treasury advocates of convertibility, especially

1 Captain Harry Crookshank (later first Viscount Crookshank), Conservative MP and Leader of the House of Commons 1951–55.

Rowan and the Chancellor.

Dined with parents. Thick fog. Walked half-way home and almost choked.

6 December

Spent the morning in A.E.'s bedroom going through papers with him. Tony Nutting joined us to clear PQs for Monday. After A.E. had got up Roger Makins came and we went through Rab's draft statement for Monday's Cabinet on the convertibility trouble. We sat in the small study, now well carpeted, with Chippendale bookcase and Sir William Eden's watercolours all round the walls. I thought of it as it was when Ernie Bevin had it, bare with a safe and several busts of him and trades union memorials on the walls.

Thick fog, train to Reading and nearly stuck there. Managed to get taxi to Henley where N. was meeting John, Paddy and [their daughter] Carolyn.[1]

8 December

Asked A.E. how he got on over the weekend at Chequers. He said to Winston that he must know something of his plans. PM made a solemn Winstonian speech to the effect that his intention was, when the time came, to hand over his powers and authority with the utmost smoothness and surety to Anthony. A.E. said, yes – but the point was when would that be? A whole minute of silence, then, 'Often I think there are things I could say, speeches I could make more easily if I were not Prime Minister.' Then another long silence. A.E. said the position regarding leadership in the House could not be maintained. Crookshank not competent. But the net result was no clear indication.

9 December

Ferocious letter from Clarissa occasioned by an article in the *Sunday Times* praising the 'quality of thought and expression' of Rab and saying that 'his mind has dominated all the economic conference'. The letter said that 'everybody round Anthony' was responsible for his bad press, ought to pull their socks up, were too gentlemanly, etc., etc. After consulting William Strang, I went over to explain that the FO cannot conduct propaganda for one Cabinet Minister against another and that if they want a better press they had better cultivate press magnates, the Camroses, Kemsleys, Astors, etc. Later I felt I had not reacted strongly enough to the letter. I rang up and asked if A.E. had seen it; if so I should have to

1 See list of family members.

offer to resign. Categorical denial. Assurances that I was not meant. Matter closed. But a very bad day in consequence.

11 December

A.E. very tired and very impatient. Thinks we are giving way too much to Neguib over the Sudan; also thinks the Office being casual and inactive over the Persian Gulf sheikdoms in which our position is being undermined by Saudi Arabia. This mood reflected down into the Office. W. Strang says, 'Don't you see why I am thankful to be retiring?'

A.E. depressed this afternoon. In the car he said, 'The world is going in giant strides to its ruin.' This must be something to do with the lunch.

12 December

Flew early to Paris.[1] Very angry to find we are on a tourist aircraft. No room to do our work; read telegrams with other passengers cribbing.

Lunch at the Embassy, then to OEEC meeting at Château de la Muette. A.E. in the Chair. Dinner at the Embassy for the Athlones. Talked about Ottawa to her and to him about the Marlborough Club and wandered vaguely over the world, remembering no names and forgetting where we had started from. After that we sat till 1 a.m. going through A.E.'s speech for tomorrow.

13 December

OEEC morning and afternoon. Slept in the meetings.

Duke of Windsor called to see A.E. A.E. was rather touched by the little man. He seemed well informed and serious. He had come to show A.E. his draft statement explaining that he could not come to the coronation. He asked after Beatrice.[2] 'She and I both hated officialdom and the official social life. I often told her, you may hate it, but you have got to do it.'

14 December

A.E. has a cold and stayed in all day. Result: the *New York Herald Tribune* blamed him for not seeing Acheson about Persia and said he had been 'picking posies in the country'.

1 For meetings of OEEC, 12–13 December, and North Atlantic Council, 15–18 December.
2 Eden's first wife.

Roger Makins and I lunched with the Hayters[1] but I was summoned back by A.E. because he had been rung up in a rage by Winston. Nothing to be done. Walked round the shop windows and into the Tuileries Gardens among the Sunday afternoon crowd, and watched the children sailing boats. Then to a party at Rosamund Benson's.[2] The whole delegation, typists and all. Very well done on slender means. She has a flair for entertaining.

15 December

At the NATO meeting this morning, General Ridgway [Supreme Allied Commander, Europe] made a long statement complaining that the governments don't supply him with adequate forces. This was followed by a slightly less aggressive speech by the Supreme Allied Commander, Atlantic, the American Admiral Fechteler. At the end the Chairman announced that the Allied Commanders wanted these speeches published. This was just about to be accepted when A.E. asked whether it was correct and whether these military points of view should not be offset with political considerations. Ridgway then arrogantly demanded that his statement should be published, while the sailor said nothing was further from his thought. A.E. was particularly incensed (and so were other Foreign Ministers) by the implication that in a confidential report to the Ministers General Ridgway should say no more than what could be published.

I went to lunch alone at a restaurant but met Ted Achilles [a US diplomat] and fed with him. Afterwards called with A.E. on Acheson at the United States Embassy about Persia. I had a talk with Jeff Kitchin, his Private Secretary, who talked of the need of a change of Administration in America. He said that the exclusion of the Republicans from office for twenty years had had damaging effects on the whole political system. That was the cause of the bitterness at this election and would explain much Republican inexperience. One has to forgive Acheson some of his bad temper and cautiousness in supporting us when one considers that he may have to spend the next year or two defending himself before Congressional Committees for his action as Secretary of State. Ike will no doubt try to curb these vendettas, but it will not be easy.

16 December

Lunched with Bob Dixon at La Truite. He said: 'I suppose you are aware how strongly Winston and all his entourage feel against Anthony getting

---

1 William Hayter, Minister at the Embassy; later Ambassador in Moscow and Warden of New College, Oxford.
2 Rosamund Benson, Third Secretary on the UK delegation to the OEEC.

the succession?' He thinks if it does happen I should go over to No. 10 as Private Secretary. Then he added that in 1944 A.E. had asked him to do the same in the event of his taking over! Then he took me to a bookshop where he tried to obtain texts of the Byzantine writer, Procopius.

Dined with Tony Rumbold[1] and a Mr and Mrs Franklin, the Assistant Naval Attaché (Air) who has been working on the naval side of the EDC. He thinks nothing will hold the Germans who are all set to build a navy the moment they get the chance. He has been declared redundant by the Treasury, and is returning to farm and shoot in Notts.

We went to a farce at the Théâtre Montparnasse then to their flat where we talked about the French without much profit.

Rang Nancy this evening.

This NATO conference was marked by the following incidents:

(1) Last appearance of the Acheson, Lovett, Harriman *galère*. A curtain-fall speech by A. with a message to continental Europe to 'Unite and you will attract power to yourselves.' Unfortunately, he used the words 'centrifugal' and 'centripetal' in opposite senses. Anthony replied with a tribute to Acheson, written by me, after I had borrowed a lot of his old speeches from Ted Achilles. Main point: his invention of the theory of creating 'positions of strength'.

(2) Ridgway introduced Admiral Carney and Lord Mountbatten to the Council in a very ridiculous ceremony where they trooped in looking sheepish, each said a few words into a microphone, then trooped out. Stony silence. We could all do with less Ridgway.

(3) The French (Letourneau and Schuman) made a great appeal for more help over Indo-China and impressed the Conference. Our Chiefs of Staff very worried about the effect of French failures on Malaya, Burma and Siam.

(4) A lunch at the Embassy for Segonzac.[2] Interesting talk about the different kinds of light in France; the particular value of the Seine atmosphere for the Impressionists. S. said Utrillo was the son of a woman who modelled for Degas and Puvis de Chavannes, and of an unknown Dr Utrillo. May therefore have been Degas' son. He is now an old man with a fanatically possessive wife and Segonzac described the break-up of his character.

22 December

A.E. now in a very bad way about:

(a) the attacks of Beaverbrook which grow ever more violent and which

---

1 Sir Anthony Rumbold, Counsellor at the Embassy. In 1954 he took over from me as Eden's Private Secretary, and was later Ambassador to Thailand and Austria.

2 André de Segonzac, Impressionist painter and etcher.

Winston does nothing to control;

(b) the evident unwillingness of the Old Man to give any encouragement about the future. He wants the Order of Merit and cannot have it because, as the Palace rightly point out, it is not meant for politicians.

Winston going off to the United States and Jamaica for a month. At dinner for the Bianchis [Chilean Ambassador] William Strang spoke to me about this. He thinks Winston is goading A.E. Latter should show calm and confidence instead of this jumpiness. I drove back with James Stuart, Secretary of State for Scotland and a friend of A.E.'s, who says the same thing.

Sat at dinner next to General Salisbury-Jones,[1] Marshal of the Diplomatic Corps, who refused to speak at all to Mrs Kenneth Grubb on his right and pestered me about the need for foreign Ambassadors to wear uniform when presenting their credentials. He took this up subsequently with A.E. . . .

25 December

Four days home at Christmas. Diana and Harold[2] to stay. N. gave me a weathervane which I fixed on the highest point of the wall. Catherine and Robin both ill over the holiday with bronchitis leading to ear-ache. I was feeling low and irritable on return and took two days off for the New Year. Worked on my corner cupboard and calmed down.

5 January 1953

Back to work and spent the whole day working with A.E. on his broadcast for tomorrow night. Dined with him and Clarissa, who told me that Mrs Butler is going round saying that A.E. cannot be Prime Minister because of his marriage to Clarissa 'whom the Archbishop would not marry'. Walked back in the snow to No. 6, where Jennifer [our au pair], Catherine and Julian were just back from *Figaro* at Covent Garden.

6 January

Another day on the broadcast. Went early with A.E. to Broadcasting House to rehearse it with Archie Gordon. Nancy in town and we went to the First Night of the Old Vic production of *Merchant of Venice*. Various celebrities there, including Margot Fonteyn, sitting next to us, Violet Bonham Carter,[3]

1 Sir Arthur Guy (Guido) Salisbury-Jones, Marshal of the Diplomatic Corps 1950–61; distinguished viticulturist.
2 See list of family members.
3 Lady Violet Bonham Carter, daughter of the Liberal Prime Minister H. H. Asquith by his first wife; President of the Liberal Party Organization 1945–47.

Sheppard the Provost of King's[1] and Eddie Marsh,[2] each with a young man in tow. (This was only about ten days before Eddie Marsh's death.)

7 January

A.E. decided today to overrule the Governor-General of the Sudan about certain safeguards for the South. It has taken him a month to get to this point, time which we badly needed. I take a poor view of the advice he gives us. I am sure he and his officials are trying to make every obstacle to an agreement with Egypt. Decided also tonight to arrest certain Nazis in Germany.

Lunch for Ruegger, President of the International Red Cross, and his wife. The Rob Scotts and Lady Limerick. He talked of Chou En-lai,[3] whom he had seen recently. A decent man, a friend of General Marshal, now, in his view, a prisoner. When he visited him, Chou En-lai would not speak English because his interpreter could only speak French. Ruegger maintains that the Chinese are far too civilized to get on for any length of time with the Russians and that our aim must be to increase their independence of Russia by every method. He had a plan for dealing with the Korea POW question – to get the Chinese to declare acceptance of the Geneva 'Sick and Wounded Convention', then the men who want to go back could be tacitly regarded as covered by this. I don't believe it would work because there is no evidence that the Chinese want an armistice.

There is evidence that Caffery, the United States Ambassador in Cairo, is actually working against us with the Egyptians over the Sudan question.

I ended today extremely gloomy about British prospects everywhere. In Kenya: the Mau Mau. In Egypt and Persia: the Americans refusing to support us. Even Iceland in process of destroying our deep-sea fishing industry. I see no reason why there should be any end to the surrenders demanded of us. International law and the temper of international opinion is all set against the things which made us a great nation, i.e. our activities outside our own territory. Bit by bit we shall be driven back into our island where we shall starve.

8 January

Rab's Private Secretary, Armstrong,[4] came to see me to talk about plans for going to Washington in February. He appeared anxious to impress on me

1 J. T. Sheppard, Provost of King's, Cambridge, 1933–54.
2 Sir Edward Marsh, Churchill's Private Secretary.
3 Chou En-lai, Chinese Minister of Foreign Affairs and Vice-Chairman of People's Revolutionary Committee 1949–58.
4 William Armstrong, Private Secretary to the Chancellor of the Exchequer; later Lord Armstrong.

that Rab regards A.E. as entirely in charge of this trip, arising as it does out of the Commonwealth Conference. We had some talk about the rivalry of our respective masters and Armstrong assured me that Rab, though anxious to be Prime Minister, had no wish to do so yet. He had long-term plans for reforming the Tory Party. He thought it was very hard on A.E. that Winston should remain so long in the saddle. He wanted to serve first under A.E. . . . and more to this effect. I said it would be nice if he could say some of this a little more publicly.

9 January

P. Dixon complained to W. Strang about my record of my talk with Armstrong and because I had spoken to Norman Brook about the trip to Washington without consulting him first. I was summoned down. Was sorry.

10–11 January

Weekend spent moving a beech hedge from the formal garden down to the field. The all-ages dance at Phyllis Court, Henley, where I danced for the first time in my life with my own daughter. She is an excellent waltzer and very good at the foxtrot. We were in a large party with Celia and Peter Fleming, Lady Brunner and her sons, the Bretts and various children. Most enjoyable evening.

13 January

Dined with the Edens for Gifford. Ill-fated evening. First Campbell Stuart [Chairman of the Pilgrims], who must have been half-drunk when he arrived, consumed brandy throughout dinner, clapped too loud during the speeches and then staggered out of the room looking as if he would die. I followed him, got him his coat and steered him to Selwyn Lloyd's car. All he could say was, 'get me home', and I thought he was seriously ill. It turned out his home was in Highgate and when he got there he could not remember where he lived. A quarter of an hour later, Mrs Selwyn Lloyd had a migraine and had to be sent home in a strange car, hers being still in Highgate. We were all just recovering from this when there was a crash and William Strang, who had been standing by the fireplace talking to Julius Holmes [US Minister] and Nancy, lay full length in the fireplace. He got up briskly, then was seen to have blood all over his collar and over his shoulders and to be as white as a sheet. Julius took him out and we found a two-inch gash in his scalp. Doctor sent for. Two stitches. William bright as a button, obviously suffering from mild shock.

After the party had broken up, Nancy and I stayed for the operation up in the flat. Only thing to be said about this party was that on the *last* occasion when the Foreign Secretary gave a dinner for the retiring United States Ambassador, one of the guests died.

Tonight we arrest seven Nazis [in the British zone in Germany] if we are lucky enough to catch them.

15 January

Arrests went off well last night. Adenauer, warned a few hours before, was favourable. A.E. very keen to take responsibility for the action, more so in fact than last night, before the results were known. He was extremely testy with me when I did not guess how his mood had changed and complained because I had told News Department to make clear that 'HMG were responsible for Kirkpatrick's action in arresting these men'. In fact he was very rude and accused me of wanting to give the credit for his work to Butler and co. I was furious at this and would not speak to him for some minutes until I left the room. When I next came back we did some business and at the end he said suddenly, 'Are you still angry with me?' which surprised me so much that I burst out laughing. This is typical. He is like a child. You can have a scene with a child of great violence with angry words spoken on both sides and ten minutes later the whole thing is forgotten. This is not possible with grown-ups, but it is the regular thing with A.E.

16 January

All set for signing with Mossadeq – at least, we have agreed with the Americans on a 'package' deal, which since it contains 50m. dollars down and 50m. to come for Mossadeq, we assume he will be disposed to accept. It has to be done by 20 January when the US Administration changes so the heat is on Mossadeq. Question who should go to Tehran and sign. I thought A.E. would want a politician to do it, to wipe the eye of the socialists who sent Stokes on a vain mission in 1951. William Strang wanted Beeley[1] sent from Baghdad. But Pierson Dixon was determined to go and so it is decided.

On the Sudan we are putting an alternative to Neguib, leaving the Governor-General's powers in the South to be decided by the Sudanese

1 Harold Beeley, Counsellor in Baghdad; later Ambassador to Saudi Arabia and the United Arab Republic.

Parliament. But we cannot make up our minds whether a three-quarters or a simple majority would best suit the interests of the South. Meanwhile, there is news of a coup against Neguib which has been suppressed. This no doubt strengthens Neguib and may be helpful to our negotiations with him.

Jock Colville back from Jamaica came to see me. He described the PM's talks with Eisenhower and Dulles and in particular the 'three-pronged plan for the fall' which Dulles outlined for settling the Korean issue. Winston has this in his head and will report to Cabinet on return. Ike asked if Winston saw any objection to his meeting Stalin alone. Winston said, 'I would have objected strongly during the war when our contribution in forces was about equal. Now I don't mind. But don't be in a hurry. Get your reconnaissance in first.' Winston seems to have been unfavourably impressed with the brashness and impatience of the Republican leaders. According to Jock, he spoke once of his own plans, only to say, 'I think Anthony should have it, but I have not decided when.'

17–18 January

Weekend at home. Went riding with the children on a lovely Sunday morning like spring. Went up to London after dinner to the Resident Clerk, to read telegrams about the Sudan which A.E. wants me to discuss in the morning.

19 January

Went to Buckingham Palace to see Alan Lascelles. I was surprised to be told, 'if Winston were to die tomorrow there is no doubt at all the Queen would send for Anthony. But by the end of the year there will be doubt, if present trends continue. There might be at least 50 per cent opinion in the party and in the City by that time in favour of Butler.' Adeane[1] confirmed this. I expressed astonishment and am unconvinced.

A.E. obviously feels that this sort of thing is growing. He is very depressed this evening. He doesn't think the Old Man will ever go. There are more attacks on him by the Beaverbrook press. There is no doubt that Rab is coming along very fast. I myself heard him answering Questions in the House today and was much impressed. I suddenly thought of myself in the character of Griffith (nurse to Katharine of Aragon in *King Henry VIII*) consoling my master in his loss.

20 January

Prime Minister returned from his holiday in Jamaica passionately interested

1 Michael Adeane (now Lord Adeane), Assistant Private Secretary to the Queen; later Private Secretary.

in the Egyptian situation. No one seems to know how he had become convinced, in the depth of his holiday or on the *Queen Mary*, that a great deterioration had set in. Some say Neguib's speeches were reported in the *Ocean Times*; others that Beaverbrook got at him in Jamaica. Anyway, he started telegraphing and telephoning from his ship long before she reached Cherbourg to stop A.E. allowing four jet fighters, now due for Egypt under an old contract, from proceeding. There were Questions down in Parliament about this for the day before his return and he wanted to see the drafts of what A.E. would say. The latter much upset: 'If he has so little confidence in me, I had better go.' Eventually the Questions were not reached and all the fuss was for nothing.

29 January

But when the Prime Minister got back and A.E. went round to see him at noon today, Jock Colville came round to me in a great state of agitation. He said there was going to be a row. He had gone overnight to Southampton and travelled up with the PM. The latter was in a rage against A.E., speaking of 'appeasement' and saying he never knew before that Munich was situated on the Nile. He described A.E. as having been a failure as Foreign Secretary and being 'tired, sick and bound up in detail'. Jock said that the Prime Minister would never give way over Egypt. He positively desired the talks on the Sudan to fail, just as he positively hoped we should not succeed in getting into conversations with the Egyptians on defence which might lead to our abandonment of the Canal Zone. Jock, who has hitherto sided strongly with the PM over this Egypt question, seemed seriously concerned. He said, 'The only hope is that Neguib will behave so badly that our two masters will see eye to eye.' In other words, the hope is that the talks will fail, which is Winston's hope.

I told only William Strang about this and spent the lunch-hour wondering what might have happened at the interview and in the subsequent lunch which the Churchills had with the Edens. In the event, A.E. told me, nothing happened at all. There was no confrontation. The conversation was quite amicable but equally no decisions were taken. These two always shy away from a quarrel at the last moment.

I went home that night, having bought Robin a toy guardsman in scarlet about three inches high, which he immediately christened 'soldier Piperson'.

30 January

A Cabinet in the afternoon on Egypt. Expectation of more fireworks, but none took place. I spent a very uncomfortable half-hour with the Private

Secretaries at No. 10, during which Colville, Pitblado and Montague Browne[1] all attacked A.E. and the Foreign Office for their policy on Egypt. They thought we should sit on the gippies and have a 'whiff of grapeshot'. If it meant letting the British communities in Alexandria and Cairo be massacred that could not be helped. Anyway, the soldiers were notoriously pessimistic and they thought it ridiculous that we should not be able to cope with the Egyptian Army with the eighty thousand men we have in the Zone. The Chiefs of Staff, they said (obviously quoting the Prime Minister), always say that the force available for any emergency is insufficient. You have to prove the contrary. If we go out of the Sudan and Egypt it will be another stage in the policy of scuttle which began in India and ended at Abadan. It will lead to the abandonment of our African colonies. The Prime Minister is trying to arrest history. People said at Munich that Britain was finished and that history was against us, but Winston had proved it wrong. So, now ... etc.

I tried to prove the falsity of this comparison, explaining the need to concentrate our reserves on things which are really of vital interest to us, either strategically or economically. But it was hard to get a word in. Jock tells me that the PM is very bellicose against A.E. 'If he resigns, I will accept it and take the Foreign Office myself.'

I kept no diary during February, mainly owing to my father's death on 8 February and the very heavy spate of business.

The month started with a visit from Dulles and Stassen who made a good impression on our Ministers, rather unexpectedly in the case of Dulles, against whom we had been prejudiced.

On 6 February Nancy and I dined with the Kenneth Youngers[2] where we met Ivrach Macdonald, *The Times* diplomatic correspondent, and had some general talk on foreign affairs of a very light kind, in which Kenneth seemed to go very near a pacifist point of view. After dinner he played the guitar and we all sang very pleasantly till midnight.

On Saturday, 8 February, my father went out to dine with the Dickens Fellowship. It was a very cold night and he came back in a taxi, feeling evidently quite all right for he wrote his diary in bed and went to sleep. He was up two or three times in the night with a pain and had practically nothing for breakfast. Then he went to sleep again and did not wake up. No end could have been more peaceful for him. He was nearly seventy-six and to spend his last evening with Dickens admirers, swapping quotations from *Pickwick*, was all he could have wished for.

1 A. Montague Browne, Assistant Private Secretary at No. 10.
2 Kenneth Younger, Minister of State at the Foreign Office under Attlee.

Joanna was in town and went straight to the flat when he was found, to be with M.[1] But she did not ring me up till about five o'clock, when I had just come in from making two bonfires. I told the others by telephone and came up the next morning to Connaught Street, where I found M. with Diana, John and Paddy. John and I made the arrangements for the funeral and all that business which is not only necessary but does provide action to distract one from what has occurred.

We received many touching letters from people who had known my father and admired him in his career, the best being from Anthony Bevir, one of the Prime Minister's Private Secretaries, Spencer Leeson and Sir John Hall, of the Colonial Office, who also wrote a most sympathetic obituary in *The Times*.

These were the coldest, bleakest days of the winter. A.E. was in the doldrums politically and having a great fight with the party over his Sudan Agreement. Waterhouse,[2] Assheton,[3] Julian Amery,[4] and the Beaver all in full cry.

Whenever I could get home, I played recorders with Nancy, while outside nothing but wind and snow. Eventually, of course, the snowdrops, which we had brought out of the wood and planted in the long grass, appeared encouragingly. We planted the south side of the new wall with about twenty fruit tree cordons and the north side with clematis, honeysuckle, roses, morello cherries, etc.

26 February

My last day in England:[5] the most terrible of the winter. A.E. shattered by the illusion of having been betrayed within the party by the PM and his friends. The PM is still not reconciled to the Sudan Agreement, but he has suddenly become keen on evacuating the Canal Zone (for very much the reasons I had used with his Private Secretaries – see above), because it has become in his mind a military operation. He has started sending messages to Eisenhower. A.E. seems half glad, half angry that he should thus be taking the matter out of his hands. A whole series of little bits of information which were brought to A.E. confirmed his belief that he was being betrayed. Someone in the Civil Service Commission told us that the daughter of Robertson, Political Secretary in Khartoum, when asked a question about the Sudan, said that the Agreement was a disaster and had

1 See list of family members.
2 Captain Charles Waterhouse, Conservative MP.
3 Sir Ralph Assheton, Conservative MP.
4 Rt Hon. Julian Amery MP, later Secretary of State for Air, Minister of Buildings and Works, and Minister for Housing and Construction.
5 Before the Eden–Butler visit to the USA.

only been possible because A.E. was away in the country and the Foreign Office were defeatists.

Someone told Clarissa that Christopher Soames was attacking the Foreign Office and A.E. for their policy in Egypt. To cap this the *Evening News* had an article by Melville saying that we have decided to quit Suez. Terrible depression. A.E. said, 'Clarissa is right. I should go at the coronation.' They dream of becoming Lord and Lady Baltimore, after an ancestor of A.E.'s who was Governor of Baltimore.

A.E. was in such a depressed condition that I had to abandon all my papers and my preparations for departure to the US and go with him to the flat where he had a television programme to do. There was more trouble there about the technical arrangements, but eventually it went off all right.

US Ambassador Aldrich on the train with us. When we arrived on board ship A.E. went to bed. Freddie and I worked on papers with him till eleven o'clock.

27 February

We sailed at 10.30 a.m. in the *Queen Elizabeth*. A.E. still depressed. The first day I went for a walk with him on deck and met Kenneth Clark, who is lecturing in the United States on 'The Nude in Art'. He said he felt they had got the wrong idea of what his lectures were going to be like because they had said they could not possibly allow one in Holy Week. I met him twice more on the journey, first at lunch alone and when the two of us entertained Mrs Eden and Mrs Butler to dinner one night. An oddly assorted party. Kenneth said, 'Clarissa likes topics to come up briefly and be dealt with wittily and superficially, whereas Mrs B., by nature a Cambridge don, likes to get hold of a subject and worry it out. Our task will be to make harmony out of these two forms of conversation.'

I did not enjoy the journey. Very few people on board. I had to resist a tendency of A.E.'s to summon me in to their cabin when *both* of them were in bed.

On Sunday I went to the church service with A.E. and sang wonderful hymns and was in tears nearly all the way through. The lesson, beautifully read by the Chief Officer – a thoroughly unsophisticated type with the fine voice and real sincerity of a seaman. 'For I come not to bring the righteous but sinners to repentance.'

4 March

Arrived in New York and flew straight to Washington in a special plane. Meeting straightaway with Dulles, Stassen, Humphrey, Lew Douglas, etc.

---

1 A.E. once mentioned the idea to me as we were flying over Baltimore.

Able statements on the Commonwealth Conference by A.E. and Rab. The Americans seemed impressed. Then we dashed off to the White House. Dulles tried to prevent A.E. taking Roger Makins with him (primarily to avoid having to take Winthrop Aldrich) but I intervened and told him he must take the Ambassador. So he did. I sat in the entrance hall of the White House for over an hour talking to the Secret Service men there, reading and writing my diary under a bad portrait of President Truman.

5–9 March

Useful talks with the Americans about Egypt and we think we have persuaded them to go into the negotiations with us. Eisenhower's one condition is that the Egyptians should be induced to invite American participation. Bedell Smith[1] very helpful but Byroade inclined to talk about American 'mediation' between us in Egypt.

9–13 March

New York. Foreign Policy Association speech the main item. Also a speech on Korea in the Assembly. The United States delegate, [Henry Cabot] Lodge, very eloquent. I thought: 'Why do you slander the United States Army? It was good enough for you in 1944!'

President Tito paid a visit to England in March, returning Eden's visit to Yugoslavia the previous September.

16 March

Arrival of Tito at Westminster Pier. A.E. went with the PM in his car so that a gallant convoy of two large cars with those two in the front one and myself alone in the second proceeded across Whitehall and down to the riverside to the great admiration of thousands of policemen gathered to protect the Marshal. The public nowhere to be seen. This was a desperate week and I did not get home at all.

Nancy came up for the Secretary of State's dinner for Tito and we invited Jo Grimond[2] and Laura back for a drink at No. 6 after dinner. Very pleasant talk about old times and much speculation about Donald Maclean, his character, his motives and his present fate.[3]

1 Walter Bedell Smith, head of the CIA 1950–53.
2 Jo Grimond, Liberal MP; Leader of the Liberal Party 1956–67 and again in 1976.
3 Donald Maclean joined the Foreign Service in 1935; served in Paris, Washington and Cairo; Head of American Department at the Foreign Office 1950; defected to the Soviet Union in May 1951.

One night I sat up late re-writing A.E.'s statement for Parliament on the Washington trip, shortening it, trying to make English out of the Office draft which was about eight times too long and verbose. Then I met him at the House and got my version of the draft approved. Next day it was a terrible flop in the House. It was called empty and platitudinous and the Opposition treated A.E. with a ribaldry to which he was unaccustomed and which greatly upset him. I felt very guilty, but in fact the trouble was that they were annoyed at being told so little about the Commonwealth Conference itself and nothing at all about Mr Churchill's talks with Eisenhower on his way back from Jamaica. Also this turned out to be the beginning of a concerted Labour Party attack on A.E., designed no doubt to make the most of the apparent split in the Conservative Party over Egypt.

This incident was followed by leading articles in the *Daily Mirror* and the *Herald* with titles such as 'Buck up Mr Eden!' and finally by a horrible article by Crossman[1] on the front page of the *Sunday Pictorial* with the banner headline, 'Can we afford a flop at the Foreign Office?'

Needless to say, these attacks did a good deal to rally the Tories round A.E.

20 March

I attended both Tito's talks with the Prime Minister. The first in the Cabinet room where I took the record and later in the Prime Minister's map room at the Ministry of Defence. Tito very sound about Russia. He does not think the new régime will want war any more than the old one. They will have uncertainty at home and a weakening of their influence in the satellite countries. He thinks Malenkov and Beria will stick together and that if there is any split it will be against Molotov. But he thinks it most important we should not talk about preventive war or threaten the Russians in our propaganda. 'Always in history when Russia was in danger she found the necessary patriotism and unity.'

Tito seemed at one moment to make a slight move forward about Trieste; later this proved not to be so.

The PM was constantly bringing the conversation back to war and strategy. Yugoslavia must be friends with Italy 'because then Admiral Carney can strike up with his task forces through the armpit of the Adriatic ... etc.' Pure fantasy.

In the map room, Tito and Winston went up in turn to the map and fought past and future wars with a long stick. 'Here I shall strike!' said

1 Richard Crossman, Labour MP 1945 until his death in 1974.

Tito. 'I shall not retire to the mountains, I shall defend all our territory. But I cannot do that by sitting still. We must have an offensive spirit.' Then Winston would get up again, take the stick and indicate where a hypothetical twenty Allied divisions could be landed in the soft under-belly of Europe and strike up through the valleys, etc.

Outside the window, at the edge of St James's Park, there was a sizeable crowd of London citizens waiting to see Tito come out, faced with a thick veneer of policemen. If they had known which window to look at they could have seen these stubby figures taking turns at the map. Others present were A.E., Alexander [Minister of Defence], General Brownjohn, Mallet and Harrison.[1] One of the maps on the wall was covered with a discreet curtain, which A.E. attempted to draw aside thinking that some point could be more clearly illustrated there. The consternation on the faces of the Ministry of Defence officials made it evident that it was some top-secret map.

21 March

I went again to see Tito off. I had not intended to go with A.E. but he said at the last minute he wanted a Private Secretary, so I borrowed a top hat from the Resident Clerk, a stiff collar from John Priestman, a black tie from somebody else and presented myself just in time.

22 March

Flew to Paris after a nice sunny morning pruning roses at High Wood. Feeling much better. Dinner with the Harveys, A.E. and Bob Dixon. Very friendly and cosy. A.E. talking about his father but, to our surprise, has not read Sitwell. It always seems to me that their fathers must have been very much alike.

Marjolin[2] came in after dinner and put us through our statements for the morrow. His questions clearly exposed our dilemma, namely that the 'Commonwealth plan', about which there has been so much mystery and which everyone is so angry with us for concealing, has really got nothing in it and therefore there is nothing to say. Marjolin says Europe will be bitterly disappointed, just as the House was last week.

23 March

Things turned out quite differently. The Europeans were highly pleased with our statements. They were relieved at the increase of travel allowance

---

1 Geoffrey Harrison, Assistant Under-Secretary at the Foreign Office 1951–56; later Ambassador to Brazil, Persia and the USSR.
2 Robert Marjolin, Secretary-General of the OEEC 1948–55.

and with our modest liberalization measures. The Germans immediately followed up with more liberalization themselves and once again the French were left in the dog house. All eyes turned on them, even Marjolin, the Secretary-General, calling upon France to match the British and German measures with her own. A.E. delighted. He thinks it will have a good effect on the EDC ratification, where it is the French who are delaying.[1]

Unfortunately, the death of Queen Mary while we were in Paris prevented any of this getting headlines in the English press. It also caused me an anxious evening when A.E. instructed me late at night to telephone to Kirkpatrick at Wahnerheide from Paris to stop the statement which was to be made next day about the transfer of Naumann and the other Nazis to the Germans for trial. He is determined to be able to announce this to Parliament because he thinks it will be well received and Parliament will not meet tomorrow in view of Queen Mary's death.

Leslie, the Treasury Public Relations Officer, flew back with us and talked with me a great deal about A.E. and the Prime Minister. I thought his comments on my master very derogatory.

24–30 March

The Labour Party attacks described above brought the PM and A.E. closer together. The latter is getting tougher over Egypt. Both are impatient with the Americans because, Neguib having refused to invite United States participation in the Canal Zone talks, the Americans are saying that in that case they cannot participate. But in fact that is no more than what President Eisenhower told us in America must be his position. The PM is sending quite needlessly offensive messages to Eisenhower suggesting that if they do not support us better in Egypt we shall take away our troops from Korea.

Josef Stalin died during this month.

On top of this came a flood of minor Soviet concessions and an apparently new policy in the Kremlin. First General Chuikov suggests talks about air safety in the Berlin corridors. Then they withdraw the notice to us to quit the Embassy in Moscow. Thirdly, they agree to the appointment of

---

1 The EDC (European Defence Community) Treaty, which had been signed in Paris the previous year, as described by me in the last entry in Chapter 1, provided for the creation of German armed forces as part of a supra-national force. It had originally been proposed by the French Prime Minister, M. René Pleven, in 1950. The Treaty required ratification by the signatory powers and it soon became clear that approval by the French Parliament was by no means a foregone conclusion. Much of Western diplomatic activity in this period was directed towards helping the French Government to achieve ratification. This included American pressure on Britain to join the EDC, which was resisted by Churchill and Eden. In the event, the French National Assembly refused to ratify the Treaty and the project collapsed.

Dag Hammarskjöld as Secretary-General of the United Nations. The politicians' noses sniff the air. Away from the ungrateful snares of the Middle East into the purer realms of peacemaking. The PM suggests there should be a Molotov–Eden meeting. A.E. is attracted. Gascoigne[1] is sent for. Past troubles are forgotten in a new atmosphere of optimism. I am very disturbed about this. The Russians have not made any concession which is more than a trifle, but they look as if they were going to adopt a much cleverer policy for dividing and weakening the West than Stalin ever did. If so, we should be cautious and not rush in.

But the idea of a meeting with Molotov becomes exciting. Winston said, 'If it is Mol, you go. But if it is Mal, it's me.' More punning of this kind appears in minutes from the PM about Ike and Egypt. Something about 'unwise counsels moving in by the Byroade'.

I am instructed to obtain the Office view on a possible Molotov–Eden meeting. I do so through William Strang who organizes a meeting with Bob Dixon, Paul Mason[2] and Harry Hohler.[3] All are against the idea but of course prepare the necessary material, viz. a list of Anglo-Russian issues which might form the subject of such a meeting.

1 April

Gascoigne arrives. A.E. not well and the meeting takes place in his bedroom. Strang, Mason, Hohler. A.E. very keen. 'What are the prospects of a meeting? Could it not take place in Vienna?' Gascoigne says he is not at all certain that Molotov would accept but it is worth trying. Much discussion about the topics which should be put to Molotov. It is proposed we should add after the supremely unimportant list, 'and a general exchange of views'. This was clearly the main purpose – to make contact and to discuss peace moves. Nobody suggested that the idea had any dangers. I was horrified. I passed Hohler a little note: 'I strongly oppose the whole idea. Do you mind if I say so if I am asked?' Harry wrote back: 'We are, too, but we think the Secretary of State wants to do it.' So I began by asking 'When do we tell our allies?' Apparently William Strang had thought, 'just before the meeting' or anyhow after preliminary soundings of Molotov by Gascoigne. But this led to some second thoughts. Surely we ought to tell the Americans before we made any move with the Russians? But A.E. replied that they would certainly oppose it, which would be a

1 Sir Alvary Gascoigne, Ambassador to the USSR 1951–53.
2 Paul Mason, Under-Secretary at the Foreign Office; later Ambassador to The Netherlands.
1 Henry Hohler, Head of the Northern Department of the Foreign Office; later Ambassador to South Vietnam and Switzerland.

pity. After more discussion, it was agreed that A.E. should see the Prime Minister. I rang Jock to make an appointment. As the meeting was about to break up, I asked again, 'Have we really thought of the effect on our allies, on the EDC, on Germany, on Tito and on the French? Is not this the sort of action which we should think wrong if the French tried to do it? Are we not trying to jump in ahead of our allies?' They said there was something in this, but that the difference was that we would not be suborned from our allegiance, whereas the French might. After the Ambassador, Paul and Hohler had left, I started again on A.E. and Strang. I said I thought Molotov would only come to the meeting if he thought he could thereby divide us from our allies. I thought it would be equivocal for us to meet him. Moreover surely we could wait and let the Russians pay a little more. They have been kicking us in the stomach for five years; should they not pay a higher price for our smiles? William Strang, coming round, said, 'But I see the need to show the British public that we are not missing opportunities for peace.' I deny that. I think the public are perfectly satisfied with what is already going on. There are moves for peace in Korea. Let us get our civilian prisoners and wounded prisoners of war back to begin with. Then perhaps an armistice and perhaps an agreement on air safety in Germany. But if we go whoring after the Russians like this we get led into subjects where we have no right to be talking to them alone and where, so far as I can see, we have nothing to gain by early talks, e.g. Germany. Moreover, I pointed out, we have a NATO meeting at the end of the month and it would hardly be conducive to a productive common defence effort for 1954 if Mr Eden were gallivanting with Molotov in Vienna immediately before or after. I tried to illustrate the truth that this hankering after a meeting with Molotov is equivalent to a willingness, for the sake of popularity, to abandon policies hitherto pursued: running after the Russians in case our allies do it first. And fancy not telling the NATO powers! A.E. was much impressed by all this and agreed with a lot of it. Eventually William said, 'Let us then just *consult* the Americans.' That is certainly better, but A.E. knows they will oppose it.

2 April

Next day I urged A.E. to wait until he returned from Greece and Turkey. I did not see that there was any hurry. The Russians were coming along nicely. Every day there was some new small sign of a change for the better. Meanwhile, William Strang had a meeting at which Bob Dixon and Frank Roberts expressed the same doubts as I had expressed yesterday. These they expounded to A.E. at the flat. He seemed quite convinced and agreed that we should:

(1) Tell Gascoigne to take up the minor Anglo–USSR questions with Molotov on his return;

(2) Tell Eisenhower we were doing this and consult him as to whether any more direct contacts seemed advisable.

Then came over the Prime Minister to see Anthony and I met him at the top of the lift. He was dressed in a blue boiler suit with an open collar. Instead of being made of a stiff material suitable for a boiler suit, it was of a rather flimsy pin-striped flannel and looked quite ridiculous. He at once agreed to the line proposed and said the situation had changed since he first mooted a Molotov–Eden talk. This is true. There has been progress in the Korea talks. The Soviets have made an offer of disarmament. They no longer need drawing out. So it was agreed.

Then A.E. went off to be X-rayed and I to search for Easter presents on my bicycle. Bought Julian a jet helicopter and Robin a diminutive electric Hoover at Hamleys, and Catherine a miniature cup and saucer. On getting back bad news of A.E.: gallstones. Operation probably necessary. Should they cancel the trip to Turkey and Greece? Should he give up the Foreign Office? I sat late at the bedside discussing these gloomy projects and then had supper with Freddie.

This was another heavy week, working late each night and not getting home at all. But everything was tolerable with the prospect of a fortnight to myself while they were away in Turkey and Greece. (I have got A.E.'s permission not to go.)

4 April

Visit to Cothill for Julian's Sports and Concert. He ran third in the quarter mile and played a Brahms minuet quite perfectly; but very bad reports of his work, and grave doubt whether he will get into Winchester.

5 April

Drove up to London with Julian, he to shop, I to 7 Upper Wimpole Street where A.E. is being X-rayed for the second time. Five doctors huddle round the case history and the photographs, eventually concluded there would have to be an operation. Evans made the remark: 'It is hard to assess the degree of pain when dealing with a highly strung thoroughbred.'

7 April

The Prime Minister had been told the news over the weekend and came up on Tuesday after Easter to visit A.E. at No. 1 Carlton Gardens. He arrived before A.E. and Clarissa had got back from a drive to Kew and I entertained him for a few minutes. He was raging against the Americans. He said, 'If they give lethal weapons to Egypt I shall take the British brigade away from Korea.' They then discussed the next move in Egypt. The PM wants to call Robertson home. He thinks of him as an alternative to Slim[1] to conduct the negotiations. But we say he must be under Ralph Stevenson. As he left, the PM said to me, 'You must come and see me. We will decide what to send Anthony.' He also made it quite clear to me that he intends to run the Egyptian negotiations in his own way when A.E. is safely tucked out of the way.

Then William Strang came to see A.E. and I was sent out of the room. Afterwards A.E. could not refrain from telling me that he had told William that he would like to get me the CB[2] when I cease to be his Private Secretary in the autumn. This all seemed rather 'Last Will and Testament', as did a letter from Selwyn Lloyd which included the phrase, 'I have so enjoyed working with you.' Added to this, a messenger from A.E.'s solicitors arrived with a little note pointing out that his Will was not in proper shape.

I had supper alone that evening in the White Bear restaurant where I smoked a cigar given to me by Mr Churchill, and induced some rather good Spanish musicians to sing and play to me.

1 Field Marshall Sir William Slim, Chief of the Imperial General Staff 1948–52.
2 Companion of the Bath.

Chapter Four

Eden Out of Action, 1953

The ill health which had dogged Eden since his return to office came to a head in March/April 1953, when he was obliged to undergo a series of internal operations, first in London and then in Boston, USA. He was away from work until October. Lord Salisbury acted as Foreign Secretary in his absence. During that summer, in July, Churchill himself had a stroke from which, however, he made a surprisingly quick recovery.

Churchill's desire to conciliate the Russians after the death of Stalin caused Eden and the Foreign Office some alarm. A speech which he made on the subject in the House of Commons on 11 May aroused particular controversy. President Eisenhower proposed an early meeting in Bermuda with the British and French Prime Ministers in order to try to co-ordinate policy, but this had to be postponed until December on account of Churchill's stroke.

In the meantime, I was working for Lord Salisbury and keeping in touch by correspondence with Eden during his convalescence.

Wrote no diary throughout April and May. A.E. being in the London Clinic having two operations, I had little work to do and no contact with the current papers, all of which went through William Strang to the Minister of State. Our main activity in the Private Office was arranging the Foreign Secretary's dinner party for the Queen at the coronation. The Churchills took over as host and hostess from the Edens when it became apparent that A.E. would be too ill.

5 June

I went down last night to Chequers for last talks with A.E., who left for America today. Had dinner with Sir Horace Evans and Dr Blackburn, who explained to me why the American Dr Cattell has so much more experience of gall bladder operations than any English doctor. It seems that since the war the English suffer more from ulcers owing to lack of fats while the Americans are constantly having gall trouble.

A.E. insisted on getting up and dressing to drive from Chequers to Heathrow and was photographed, despite all our precautions, as he drove up to a back entrance to the aerodrome. Prime Minister and Lady Churchill were there to see him off. He still looks extremely thin but much better than a fortnight ago when I saw him carried in a stretcher from the London Clinic to his car looking like a skeleton.

Drove back to London in convoy behind the Churchills and met Lady C. at Lancaster House for a last look at the arrangements for the dinner. Her daughter, Mary Soames, is being very helpful.

20 July

Back from a month's holiday in which N. and I spent ten days at Portloe in Cornwall with our new Riley. On the way back we passed through Winchester and watched the boys coming out of school. Julian goes there next term. Lunch with Bill Armstrong at my club. He told me all the gossip. W.S.C. has had a stroke. It happened after his speech at a dinner for de Gasperi. All his left side, leg, arm and face, affected. At first they thought he would get over it quickly, but then for a week it got worse and there was serious concern at one point. Plans were made (largely through Jock Colville and Alan Lascelles) for the Queen to summon Lord Salisbury, who would form a Government on the understanding that he would hand over as soon as A.E. returned. In the process of reaching this decision it seems to have been firmly established that A.E. is the only possible candidate for the succession. The generally accepted view of the last ten days has been that W.S.C. will hand over to A.E. in October, but within the last forty-eight hours he has much recovered and seems keen to fight on.

Bill evidently anxious to impress on me Rab's absolute loyalty vis-à-vis A.E. But he said there is some intrigue on the part of Harold Macmillan,[1] who I learn sent A.E. a disturbing letter about conditions in the party, this being partly responsible for the latter's decision to return rapidly by air instead of sailing home quietly. (Actually, I gather Clarissa hates ships.) Bill evidently likes Rab very much indeed and told stories of his considerateness. But the same does not seem to apply to Mrs B. She has been telling her friends that A.E. ought to take two years off at least!

1 Harold Macmillan (now the Earl of Stockton), Minister of Housing and Local Government 1951–54; later Minister of Defence 1954–55; Foreign Secretary 1955; Chancellor of the Exchequer 1955–57; Prime Minister 1957–63.

After a few hours in the office, set off by train to Southampton and met Lord Salisbury, now Acting Foreign Secretary, on return from his talks with the Americans and French in Washington. A lovely sunny evening through Hampshire – Winchester Cathedral and St Cross in their green valley. Smoked salmon and roast beef on board the *Queen Elizabeth* with the Salisburys and Freddie Leishman and then straight back by train. The boat train stopped at Micheldever, having 'lost steam'!

21 July

First morning with Lord Salisbury in the office. A very calm and aristocratic atmosphere. Spent most of the day drafting telegrams to A.E. about the arrangements for his return. He had instructed me to lay on television, radio, etc., at London Airport but Mark Chapman-Walker of the Conservative Central Office thinks this a mistake and dangerous in view of A.E.'s probable appearance and the fact that he is going off again a week or so later. So I got him round and we consulted Salisbury. A.E. is clearly thinking of making a triumphal return and even giving views to the press on foreign policy, which will be hard on S. and wrong in principle. We are trying to discourage him. S. is faced with quite an awkward position as a result of the agreement at Washington to invite the Russians to four-power talks on Germany at Foreign Secretary level. The PM in a speech on 11 May excited everybody very much by proposing top-level four-power talks 'without officials and without agenda'. This provoked a wave of wishful thinking and optimism in England and elsewhere and proved highly embarrassing since Eisenhower is determined not to attend any such conference. Owing to the PM's illness he could not argue the case out with Eisenhower himself (as he had intended to do at the cancelled Bermuda conference) and Salisbury was left to do the task in Washington. He is now being attacked by the Opposition and all the optimists for having whittled the glorious initiative of 11 May down to a mundane and routine meeting of Foreign Ministers confined to the topic of Germany. In the FO we all think first that this is the utmost he could have got and second that it has in fact brought us back to realities.

Eisenhower's position seems to be quite firm. He is determined not to attend any meeting with the Russians himself at least until some settlement is within sight, because he conceives it to be derogatory to his position as Head of State to get involved in bargaining and negotiations. He is therefore embarrassed by our Old Man's constant return to this theme. But he loves the old fellow and it has been whispered to Roger Makins that he might be prepared to come to London to see him. S. is embarrassed by this suggestion and does not want to pass it on until A.E. is back. He seems conscious of the difficulty he is going to have in the next three months in running foreign affairs with two other Foreign Secretaries in the background. But he looks upon this as merely a technical difficulty unmixed by any questions of personal ambition or pride. We are all enjoying having the Foreign Secretary in the House of Lords, where there is less politics and a calmer and more objective attitude.

*   *   *

During my leave I practically completed work on my corner cupboard except for polishing, and have been experimenting with some designs of coronation scenes to paint on the panels. We also had a tennis court installed during our absence in Cornwall which is a wonderful asset for the children.

22 July

Jock Colville came round to see me to express his anxiety lest A.E., when he returns on Sunday, assume too much readiness on the PM's part to retire shortly and hand the baton to Anthony. It seems the old man has made a miraculous recovery from his stroke and is far from thinking of throwing up the sponge. Yet A.E. has been led to believe the end was near. Jock said it would be better if he did not even mention any question of a hand-over when he first meets the PM. I am not sure what I can do about this hint, or how far it is disinterested.

Foreign Affairs Debate today about Washington visit and the invitation to the Russians for a Foreign Secretaries' meeting on Germany. The Opposition made great play with the contrast between this and the Churchill proposals of 11 May. The debate was opened by Rab in a rather pedestrian speech written by Frank Roberts and did not go very well for the Government. Violent personal attack on Salisbury by Kenneth Younger.

23 July

After consulting William Strang, decided to write A.E. warning him of PM's mood and condition and am rather apprehensive of the result and see impatient days ahead.

N. and I to Buckingham Palace for the Garden Party. Met Norman Brook who approved of my action in writing to A.E. and asked me to tell him when I meet him on Sunday that the PM feels he is doing very well by A.E. in managing to tide over the period between now and Parliament's return in October, when A.E. will be fully recovered. So he won't like to be asked when he is going to die.

Telegrams coming in daily from A.E. about arrangements for his reception at the airport. Many of his political friends here and Conservative Headquarters think he ought to land secretly in a field and escape all publicity, or not come to England at all. This is obviously impossible and Salisbury is against it in any case. He [Eden] hankers after making a statement on the Washington meeting and the PM's speech of 11 May, but S. is begging him not to.

24 July

S. spent the day preparing his speech for the House of Lords debate next week, when he will be able for the first time to defend his Washington agreement himself. Great argument between him and the rest of us as to the line he should take. He wants in effect to say that he tried to get top-level four-power meeting on the Churchill recipe but that his allies would not have it. We think this wrong, (a) because it suggests he was unsuccessful in his mission, (b) because it gives the impression that Winston's great initiative has been smothered by the Americans, and (c) because it is negative and apologetic in regard to the offer which *has* been made to the Russians. We want to suggest that the three powers considered how best to forward Winston's initiative in the light of the actual situation (including Winston's own illness, the French political crises, the fall of Beria and the riots in Eastern Germany) and came to the conclusion that the meeting now proposed was the best first step, a top-level meeting later on being not excluded; that this is a test of whether the Russians want accommodation and that we should now await expectantly their reply. Admittedly S.'s version is more straightforward, but less politic and characteristic of him.

The more I think of it, the more I disapprove of W.S.C. fostering this sentimental illusion that peace can be obtained if only the 'top men' can get together. It seems an example of the hubris which afflicts old men who have power, as it did Chamberlain when he visited Hitler. Even if you do believe in the theory, surely you should keep this trump card in your hand for emergency and not play it out at a time when there is no burning need, no particularly dangerous tension (rather the reverse) and your opponents are plunged in internal struggles and dissensions. It is hard to avoid the conclusion that W.S.C. is longing for a top-level meeting before he dies — not because it is wise or necessary but because it would complete the pattern of his ambition and make him the Father of Peace as well as of Victory. But it would do no such thing unless he were to make sacrifices and concessions to the Russians which there is no need to make, in return for a momentary and probably illusory 'reduction of tension'. After that splendid achievement he would die in triumph and we should all be left behind in a weaker position than before. I also object in principle to the idea that when a particular negotiation does not succeed or a particular problem proves intractable it must be because your negotiator or Ambassador is not senior and important enough. All through the birth of NATO this doctrine had full rein. Every time the Foreign Ministers met and failed to agree on how much money to pool for defence they turned with relief to the appointment of a higher-level committee or a more powerful superman who, they hoped, might make the decision for them.

26 July (Sunday)

A.E.'s aircraft from the United States due at 11.30. Rang Heathrow from High Wood at 9.30 to make sure all well and was told ETA 10.20. Leapt into clothes and our new Riley and made the trip Henley–Maidenhead–Slough–Colnbrook–Heathrow in almost exactly half an hour. Very little traffic on the road fortunately. A.E. very bronzed and well, but thin. Greeted by S. with news that Korean truce is to be signed tomorrow. He thanked me for my letter which had helped, though he had 'sensed' some of it. I advised him again not to raise the question of the hand-over when he first meets the Prime Minister. He agreed but he is clearly anxious to force the issue before October. In fact probably before he leaves in mid-August. He said that unless the PM's doctors can guarantee that he can carry on until Christmas he must give up or agree to give up well before Parliament meets so that A.E. can face Parliament with a new Government. I foresee quite a clash on this.

27 July

Visited A.E. with William Strang. Told him about the PM's vagaries in foreign policy, his hankering after a neutral, unarmed Germany and agreement with the Soviets at high-level talks. William half defends the speech of 11 May – 'He had to say something like that. The public expect it.' Both think public opinion is being led into wishful thoughts about the USSR.

Lunch at Lancaster House for Adlai Stevenson. Sat next to Oliver Franks, who gave me his views on the qualities required for the successor to Gladwyn Jebb at UNO. We were rather fencing round the subject as he does not know that Dixon is to get the job. He says it is not necessary to have the particular aptitude for publicity which Gladwyn brought to the job. Stevenson made a very good impression on all of us with a witty speech and friendliness. S. finds him far more sensible and level-headed about foreign policy than Eisenhower. Julian was waiting for us at the entrance to Lancaster House after lunch, and had his hand shaken by Stevenson.

To the House of Lords for S.'s statement on the Korean truce. Esher engaged me in conversation while I was sitting on a small stool behind the Chair but was so deaf that my stage whispers drew a look from the Lord Chancellor on the Wool Sack. I took it at the time to be a smile of recognition and nodded back gaily. Afterwards someone said, 'Your peer friends should really not be quite so deaf', and I realized to my acute embarrassment that I had attracted the unfavourable attention of the Lord Chancellor.

28 July

N. and I gave a cocktail party for Freddie and Frances Leishman in the Ambassadors' Waiting Room. When the other guests had gone, John Priestman climbed to the top of the windowsill. He was an expert roof climber at Oxford. Afterwards N. went off with the Leishmans and John for dinner and then drove home to the children, while I went to Lord S.'s house in Swan Walk to run through his speech for tomorrow's House of Lords debate. Stayed with him until after midnight. Talked about A.E.'s ambitions and his intention to beard the PM about the hand-over at Chequers next weekend. (S. will be there.) He seemed inclined to agree with Jock Colville that A.E. would be ill-advised to raise the matter even now. 'I have been through all this a hundred times. The fact is that the PM is much tougher than Anthony. He very soon brings Anthony to the point beyond which he knows he will not go and then he has won the day.' S. does not believe the PM will commit himself to any date for retirement. But he sees that A.E. is justified in wanting an early decision and himself believes that there ought to be one. He said, 'Of course if the Prime Minister asks me whether he should retire I shall say Yes.' I said I was afraid that I had been witnessing in the last two years the slow unfolding of a Greek tragedy; that A.E. would never in fact get the Premiership, which has so often seemed so near his grasp. S: 'Perhaps his real role is to be a great Foreign Secretary.' I: 'But that is not how he sees it.' S., the aristocrat: 'That is the trouble with them all. They are so ambitious.' He asked me whether I thought Clarissa was a sound adviser. Beatrice had always given Anthony good advice. She had been tough, energetic, sensible, but too soon bored by the life of a politician's wife.

29 July

Foreign Affairs Debate. Went to George Simon's consulting room at 15 Upper Wimpole Street to have my inside X-rayed, having been allowed no breakfast. He found nothing wrong at all.

Got the speech completed by lunchtime. Very simple process with S., who does almost all the work himself. Then went off with Selwyn Lloyd to lunch with the Egyptian Ambassador and Madame Hakki.

To House of Lords to hear S.'s speech. Thought it went down very well: a fighting Cecilian speech, well delivered. Home for the night and spent the evening washing up and doing the jigsaw.

30 July

Private Notice Question about Korea and further debate in the House of Commons. Opposition very worried this last day before the summer recess about the next steps after the Korean truce. Much concern over Dulles's speeches which suggest that the United States 'will pay no attention to her allies and are raring to renew the war for the sake of Syngman Rhee'.[1] Dulles's remarks to the press always seem unfortunate and different from the things he says when seriously discussing problems with us. He has really been very helpful and understanding over the Korean truce and other matters and it is unfortunate that the English press have such a bad opinion of him.

S. very upset because a member of the House of Commons (Woodrow Wyatt)[2] was at the bar of the House of Lords taking shorthand notes of his answers to questions. He called in the Black Rod to ask whether it was in order. We dashed round to Rab's room to tell him what had passed just before he opened the House of Commons debate. Tea with S. in the House of Lords Tea Room. Very cosy. An elderly Labour peer came and told us a not very funny story about Winston.

4 August

S. told me all about the weekend at Chequers. He formed a poor impression of A.E.'s state of health. Thought him 'fragile'. PM in no mood to discuss retirement and they did not raise it. Jock Colville went so far as to speak of Winston carrying on until June 1954 when the Queen comes back from Australia. (A.E. says that the PM himself said he was very tired and feeling worse, but that his 'ménage' [Jock, Soames, etc.] came in like attendants

1 Syngman Rhee, President of South Korea 1948–60.
2 Woodrow Wyatt, Labour MP 1945–55 and 1958–70; author and journalist.

in an oriental court, flattering him and assuring him that he was perfectly all right and fit to carry on for ever.) But S. thinks the situation very serious for the Government and hinted that if A.E. is not well enough to take over in October other arrangements will have to be made. The Opposition will not refrain, when Parliament meets again, from complaining at the part absence and incapacity of the Government's two chief men. He is also disturbed, as we all are, by the interference in foreign policy. The suggestion that Ike might be willing to come to England has now been passed to the PM by the United States Ambassador and Winston has sent an enthusiastic invitation. He realizes now that Ike will not meet the Russians so he will try to get 'authorization' to meet Malenkov by himself in Zurich for an all-round friendly discussion of all questions at issue. Apart from the certainty that Eisenhower could not agree; that M. would not come and that such a meeting would give heart attacks to all the Western nations, it has rather absurd internal implications. It would place the future relationship with Russia on a personal basis between him and Malenkov precisely at a moment when he himself is likely to quit the stage. It would be rather like the speech of 11 May only a hundred times worse. Frank Roberts takes the view that that speech destroyed the first real success we have had in our diplomacy in recent years. NATO policy had produced results, the Russians were disturbed at troubles at home, riots in Germany, and were toying with small concessions. All we had to do was to sit tight and 'believe it when we see it'. Into this the PM, for reasons dictated by the pattern of his own life, threw a life line to the Russians and confusion into our camp.

It seems that the old man is now changing his ideas on Egypt. He has come round to thinking that we must have an agreement to evacuate the Canal Zone and seems to have dropped his previous idea that we could not possibly go until a lot of people had been killed. The main stumbling point now is the period of the agreement. We are asking for ten years. We would take five years with consultation at the end and provision that the agreement would remain in force another five years unless an alternative can be worked out. Most privately the PM has said he would take five years as a last resort, but S. thinks the Tory Party will be difficult over this.

6 August

Drove down to Hatfield House in an FO car with Sir D'Arcy Osborne, who is spending the night there. He now lives privately in Rome, having been Minister to the Vatican for many years. Has practically no money.

The great square terrace in front of the house was full of charabancs and parked cars and visitors, and we entered by an area door and up some kitchen stairs. Our driver said this was the door His Lordship uses. But the plebs go in by the main entrance. Lord and Lady Salisbury live in a very small suite of rooms in one corner of the building and spread somewhat when they entertain.

S. and I did our business in his grandfather's study, which is still filled with very elementary security precautions, such as cupboards near the ceiling only reachable by a ladder which used to be removed overnight, and a desk with slits in the surface through which the old Foreign Secretary put confidential papers into the top drawers, of which his secretary held the key.

Our main business was the Office's first draft of a telegram to Washington saying what we think of the Soviet reply to the three-power invitation to a conference on Germany. It is a very long draft and we shortened it a little. But when it went to Winston subsequently he entirely disagreed with it because it is critical of the Soviet note. He described the draft as an 'ocean of verbiage'. Winston actually wanted us to say to the Americans and French that the Soviets had 'naturally' responded to our invitation with a palpable manœuvre because our invitation had itself been simply a manœuvre. He is still taking the line that nothing less than a meeting between himself and Malenkov, with or without Eisenhower, has any value. He is taking the line that the Americans and French 'got us into this mess' by refusing to agree to such top-level talks and that it is up to them to get us out. Actually, of course, it was his speech of 11 May which got everybody into the mess. He made it without consultation with his allies, who had never thought such a meeting practicable.

S. took me round the public rooms where gangs of visitors were being conducted and showed me many interesting portraits, including excellent ones of the first prominent Cecil, Lord Burghley, his hunchback son who built Hatfield and others down the ages. A lovely portrait of Mary Queen of Scots. Then he took us down into the cellars, stuffed with family documents, and showed us fascinating manuscripts by Queen Elizabeth, Burghley and others; all the state papers, in fact, which Elizabeth received and handed over to her adviser, Burghley. We were particularly fascinated by the note Queen Elizabeth wrote in her aged and almost illegible hand ordering the arrest and trial of Essex. It showed great reluctance and insistence upon due forms of law. Salisbury said, 'that shows you how very wrong that wretched opera of Benjamin Britten's is'. Then there were Mary Queen of Scots' letters written in French begging for release and for her life, Burghley's notebook, or diary, in which he jotted down all his life important events which interested him. There is a fine sentence on the destruction of the Armada. Contemporary maps by Drake and Hawkins, etc., sent to the Queen to show the latest state of their discoveries. The Queen's summer hat, her silk stockings, her gloves. It is a store-house.

7 August

A great fuss today from the PM over our telegram. Rab, too, seems afraid that public opinion demands we should reply favourably to the Russians, at any rate to the extent of ensuring that a meeting of some kind takes place. S. and William Strang summoned to Chequers tomorrow. Great annoyance at PM's interference.

8 August

Saw Anthony and Clarissa off to Nice from Heathrow. He seems to be leaving England with full confidence about his position in the party. Colleagues have all been assuring him that the succession is his. Oliver Lyttelton,[1] Harold Macmillan and the Chief Whip, Buchan-Hepburn,[2] have all told him they feel sure the PM must retire in October.

10 August

W.S.C. has had a thoroughly damp reply to his effusive invitation to Ike to visit the UK. He was evidently most seriously misled by Aldrich, who had told him Ike was ready to come. Great astonishment and bewilderment all round. When you become a sufficiently great man you tend to be told things you want to hear.

11 August

There is a good deal of criticism in the press about the Declaration made by the sixteen powers when the Armistice in Korea was signed, to the effect that an unprovoked breach of the truce by the Communists would 'in all probability' lead to a conflict not confined to Korea. Opposition are saying that Parliament should have been told about this. Unfortunately it could not be done because the sixteen nations had agreed not to publish it until some days after Parliament recessed.

    W.S.C. came up to town for two hours last night and discussed this with Salisbury and Bob Dixon. (I went over for a few minutes and was duly reported in the press as one of the only three people the Prime Minister saw when he came up to London.) He was given quite a good clear draft statement explaining that there is no new commitment in this and why it could not be given to Parliament. He said he would use this, after making some changes in the language. Today, however, Jock Colville came over

1 Oliver Lyttelton (later Viscount Chandos), Colonial Secretary 1951–54.
2 Patrick Buchan-Hepburn, Conservative Chief Whip; later Lord Hailes.

with an entirely new draft prepared by W.S.C. himself, which is wholly wrong both on facts and presentation from A to Z. It actually says that the Americans in 1950 asked us to agree to bomb Chinese cities and rail centres and blockade the Chinese coast, and that we might have been willing to do that but for the risk of running into conflict with the warships of the Soviet Union, with whom we desired improving and friendly relations. It seemed at first sight that nothing could be done with this draft, which was mischievous and wrong-headed in every paragraph. However, it was agreed that John Addis[1] and I should drive down to Hatfield with it and try *en route* to produce a new version using as many of the PM's actual phrases as we could, which Salisbury could then telephone through to Chartwell. This we did. I drove the Riley and John read out the sentences to me as we went along. By the time we arrived we had a not bad text which in the end, after a few minor changes, the PM accepted. This was hailed in the Beaverbrook press as an illustration of the great man's return to public life – his master hand being detected by one and all. . . .

In the course of this hullaballoo, Jock Colville told me the PM was now thinking of carrying on until the Queen's return from Australasia, i.e. about May or June 1954. He thought Eden ought on his return not to take the Foreign Office but to become Lord President, Leader of the House and principal speaker on foreign affairs in the House. I said that I was absolutely convinced this was the one thing A.E. would not agree to do. It would be asking him to do all the PM's work for him for another six months without any of the credit or true responsibility. Jock got rather annoyed and said he thought A.E. would be making a great mistake and that if he took this decision 'the reversion might go elsewhere'. I in turn was annoyed by this and said that I thought it was a terrifying prospect for the country to think that the PM might go on as long as that, when he could produce documents like this one in Jock's hand (his draft telegram) which were so hopelessly misguided and incorrect from start to finish. This was not a happy conversation. I told Salisbury about it at Hatfield. It confirms his worst fears. He is writing to A.E. urging that he come back before the end of September, so as to deal with what looks like becoming quite a serious struggle to get the Old Man to retire.

Meanwhile, Joe Alsop, who spent the weekend at Hatfield not long ago and saw a number of people in London, has reported in an article in the *New York Herald Tribune* that Winston had a stroke, with full details and speculation that he cannot come back. This has caused the *Daily Mirror* to ask what is the truth and the situation may be difficult to hold. Alsop's article, which appeared in the continental edition of the *Tribune*, was read

---

1 John Addis of the Far Eastern Department of the Foreign Office.

by A.E. and, though it clearly designates him as the successor, he was not at all pleased with it. He sent me a long rambling letter complaining that it does not bring out the fact that he is popular in the country and suggests that if he succeeds it will be through the machinations of Sir W. Churchill, Mr Butler and Lord Salisbury. The poor old News Department comes in for some criticism for not having entered more fully into the mind of Mr Alsop before he wrote his article and this has upset Ridsdale. I have written A.E. a soothing letter telling him how strong I am sure his position will be when he gets back, provided he is physically fit.

17 August

There has now been a second note from the Russians about the meeting on Germany before we have replied to the first. We spent the day revising our draft reply for consideration by Cabinet tomorrow. Salisbury came up unexpectedly from Hatfield and I was caught out, having missed the early train.

18 August

Cabinet approved our draft reply to the Soviets; also the Office paper on Egypt suggesting the lines on which we might reach a settlement of the outstanding differences on the Canal Zone. It looks as if there is really a chance we might get an agreement, though I suspect this will gravely upset the Tory backbenchers. I have suggested to S. that if we do we should at once occupy Buraimi to show that we can be tough as well.

There have been mysterious plottings in Persia and a move against Mossadeq on Saturday night failed. The Shah has fled.

With the Foreign Secretary absent through illness, the Prime Minister had taken charge of the Foreign Office, which was the one major department of which he had never been the chief.

26/27 August

All this week we are trying to conduct our foreign policy through the PM who is at Chartwell and always in the bath or asleep or too busy having dinner when we want urgent decisions. He has to be consulted about drafting points in the reply to the Soviets; about every individual 'intelligence' operation (which he usually forbids for fear of upsetting the Russians); about telegrams to Persia and Egypt. We are constantly telephoning minutes and draft telegrams down to Chartwell. After many minutes and arguments he has consented not to insist upon a full-scale naval visit to Sebastopol. This idea occurred to him as a means of offsetting British and American naval visits to Turkey which the Russians have complained about. There are inspired stories in the evening papers that the PM is engaged in forming a new Government for the autumn with A.E. as a sort of Deputy – described in the *Standard* as 'Personal Assistant to Sir Winston' and Leader of the House. Monckton is tipped for Foreign Secretary, mainly because he has recently lunched at Chartwell.

I went over to see Monckton one day this week at the Ministry of Labour in St James's Square to talk about the 'Windsor' papers – captured German documents which show how the Germans tried to get hold of the Duke in 1940 when he was in Portugal. M. described what a terrible time he had in 1940 persuading the Duke and Duchess to get on board ship for the Bahamas, and how she was persuaded that the British would murder him, etc. He said one must always remember how completely at sea a king is, who has always been surrounded with advisers and had the best opinions constantly available to him, when he finds himself alone. . . . M. seems to have an affection for the Duke and none for her. He sent me back to the FO in his car as there was a tropical downpour.

Cabinet decided – feebly and under pressure from the PM – to try to suppress the Windsor papers. There is sure to be a row with the historians who will regard this as tampering with history. The PM and Salisbury are to see the British editor, Miss Lambert, and try to 'persuade' her. She has already threatened to resign if her historian's conscience is assailed. We shall see.

Salisbury very concerned at having to continue as Acting Foreign Secretary for two reasons:

(1) He does not approve of our line in recognizing Red China and will not want to be responsible for pressing for her admission to the United Nations;

(2) he disapproves of the PM's policy of trying to get a top-level meeting with the Russians. He says it is one thing to be a member of the Cabinet and to refrain from opposing such policies but quite another to be the responsible Minister.

Now I see why A.E. gets so little active support in Cabinet when he is fighting the PM's bright ideas.

7 September

Family away in Devon having a rare spell of fine weather. Weekend at High Wood – alone except for the two cats which followed me everywhere.

Finished painting the coronation figures on the corner cupboard. Played tennis with Lionel and then over to Cookley Green for three sets with Captain Reid on his uncle's grass court.

Stayed several nights with Diana and Harold and heard more about their struggles to make a living out of vegetables. Dined with Tony Nutting in Chester Square. Much talk about A.E.'s prospects and it emerged that Nutting's great ambition is to be Foreign Secretary, which I should think he has a good chance of becoming one day.

8 September

David Pitblado showed me the PM's correspondence with A.E. in Athens about Cabinet changes. Pretty cagey on both sides, W.S.C. assuring A.E. that he need not leave the Foreign Office unless he prefers to be Deputy PM, and A.E. replying that he has no wish to do so. David tells me that the odds are on W.S.C. staying on to face Parliament.

Cabinet today more or less decided to reach agreement with Egypt on a seven-year basis. Protests from the aged Lord Hankey.[1]

26 September

To King's, Cambridge, for Old Boys' Dinner, where I made the principal speech. Had tea first with Dr and Mrs Dixon and went afterwards to a party with Patrick Wilkinson.[2] Speech went down quite well. Left Cambridge by car at 2 a.m. with a bright moon but soon got fog-bound and after a miserable drive arrived at High Wood after 5 a.m.

Reports from Athens that A.E. is not gaining strength as fast as he should.

29 September

Clarissa back from Athens. Discouraging news about A.E.'s health.

30 September

Dined with Salisbury and the Nuttings at London Airport to meet A.E.

He looks fit and bronzed; was careful not to commit himself to returning to the FO when talking to the journalists. Drove back with Nicholas Eden and gathered from him that A.E. has been following the PM's Malenkov policy closely and strongly disapproves.

1 Lord Hankey, Secretary to successive Cabinets between 1923 and 1938.
2 Patrick Wilkinson, Fellow of King's, lecturer in Classics and Orator of Cambridge University; author of *A Century of King's 1873–1972*.

1 October

Went to the office very early, making the morning's arrangements for the
Secretaries of State. Called on A.E. at 10.45 at Carlton Gardens and drove
with him to Downing Street for his first interview with Winston. He was
obviously not looking forward to it. His doctor has said he can do any job
except that of Foreign Secretary; yet he knows the PM wants him to do
that and is afraid to refuse in case it looks as if he is not fit. I advised him
not to take the FO, to swallow his pride and to take life easily for a week
or so. But I fear his resolution to confront the PM with awkward decisions
is ebbing.

At 12.30 he was back at Carlton Gardens and summoned Salisbury and
me over there. It was clear he had got no change out of the PM in regard
to the future. The Old Man determined to carry on, first to the Party
Conference speech on 10 October, then to face Parliament on 17 October.
Thinks he can do it, but promises A.E. that if he finds he cannot 'fully do
his duty' he will quit. Does not want A.E. to take a sinecure and act as
Deputy because this would give the impression he himself is being bolstered
up by A.E. Thus, despite his doctors, and at least half his own inclination,
A.E. is confronted with a return to the FO and I do not think he put up
any strong opposition to the idea. But he says they had a row over policy.

After luncheon, A.E. kept Rab, Monckton and Salisbury back and they
had a consultation together on what is to be done. All profoundly disturbed
at PM's determination to carry on. S. offering to resign on grounds of age
(he is sixty) in order to set an example. He is distressed for the future of
the party. Average age is over sixty and if they lose the next election and
are out of office for four or eight years they will come back with no leaders
having experience of office. Rab urges A.E. to leave FO and lead the House.
All agree he has only two choices, to acquiesce in the PM's wishes or to
refuse to serve in his Government and this they do not think he can do.
In short, they are all stymied by Winston as usual.

So it looks as if A.E. will take the Foreign Office. He summoned William
Strang and me to discuss how we might lighten the burden – allocating
work to Selwyn, Tony Nutting (who might be a second Minister of State)
and Reading.[1] I made it quite plain that I did not believe any device of
this kind will greatly alter the position. A.E. will never delegate and I
doubt if it is possible for the Foreign Secretary to divest himself of
responsibility for substantial chunks of the work. Having now seen him
for forty-eight hours, I am strongly against his taking the FO and have
done all I can to advise against, short of seeming to want to be rid of him.

1 The second Marquess of Reading, son of Churchill's friend and former colleague, Rufus Isaacs;
Parliamentary Under-Secretary at the Foreign Office 1951–53; Minister of State 1953–57.

I am sure it will break him. I got him at least to refrain from sending a message of acceptance to No. 10 until he meets the PM again at dinner and talks to the Chief Whip after tea. But I am sure I am losing this battle. I can see the glint in his eye as he thinks of the speech he can make about Persia and Egypt if he is Foreign Secretary. In fact before he went in to PM this morning, when we were sitting in the car at the bottom of the Downing Street steps, one of his main arguments for taking the FO was that 'otherwise I would have nothing to say at the Party Conference'.

2 October

Telephone rang at 8.30 at St James's Street: A.E. wanting to tell me – not what was decided about his future last night or plans for today but – what line he should take at the Party Conference next week on Korea, four-power talks, etc. That was conclusive. He seemed to assume that I would be writing his speech and was quite annoyed when I suggested the party should do it. At the end I asked how last night had gone. He said there had been 'more rows' about policy (speech of 11 May). He had agreed to take over the Foreign Office. In fact he is doing as he is told as usual when Winston wants it badly enough. Announcement to be put out by No. 10 today.

Cabinet 11.30. Both my masters at it. In their absence David Pitblado came over and talked about how to deal with A.E. when he becomes PM: question whether he would want Private Secretaries around until he turns the light out at night as PM does. What would be relations with Clarissa, etc. Rather like dividing the lion's skin....

Salisbury asked me to lunch with him afterwards at Turf Club where we joined (for coffee) Harold Macmillan and James Stuart. H.M. contemptuous of Tito who he says has no courage. Stories of T. being afraid to sleep in a tent and frightened in a rowing boat. H.M. seemed to be using this as an argument for suggesting that T. will give way over Trieste if presented with a firm enough front. Neither S. nor I thought the argument sound. S. went off with Sammy Hood[1] for the weekend at 3.30 and an hour later I saw A.E. and Clarissa off, likewise by car for her cottage in Wiltshire. A perfect autumn afternoon. Cleared up some papers on my own desk and got the 6.58 home for a long weekend.

Finished the corner cupboard and put it up in its corner. Planted a lot of shrub cuttings and drafted a letter to *The Times* attacking the PM's Russian policy just for the fun of it. I feel more and more strongly opposed to his line.

---

1 Lord Hood, Assistant Under-Secretary at the Foreign Office.

Chapter Five

Middle Eastern Storm Clouds, 1953

When Eden returned to work as Foreign Secretary in October 1953 he found most of the problems which he had left behind six months before still unsolved. One of them, the Italian–Yugoslav dispute over Trieste, had reached a dangerous stage. The Italian and Yugoslav Governments had been exchanging recriminations and making military gestures throughout the summer and the British and US Governments were about to make an (unsuccessful) attempt to break the deadlock by announcing their intention to withdraw their troops from Zone A and transfer its administration to Italy. This issue was to exercise Eden's diplomacy to the full for the rest of the year.

Meanwhile talks with Egypt about the replacement of the Anglo-Egyptian Treaty of 1936 had made little or no progress in his absence. The revolutionary government of General Neguib was having grave internal difficulties and Egyptian nationalist fervour was mounting, voiced with increasing violence by Neguib's deputy, Colonel Nasser, who was later to displace him. The main difficulty, as before, was the future status of the Canal Zone base, the Egyptians insisting that it must be their absolute property and under their military command, and that the British technicians who would have to run it for a time must be under Egyptian orders and could not wear uniform. There was also a wide divergence as to the circumstances in which the British might be entitled to reoccupy the base after it had been handed over. Violent incidents in the zone were on the increase.

Nor was the situation in Iran any better. Britain had had no diplomatic representation in Tehran since relations were broken off in 1952. The summer of 1953 had seen the flight of the Shah, the overthrow of Mossadeq, the advent to power of General Zahedi and the Shah's return, but the British oil installations in Persia remained 'nationalized' and out of action and there was growing rivalry between British and American oil companies as to how the Iranian oil fields might be reactivated.

An irritating disturbance in the hitherto friendly relations between Britain and Saudi Arabia had been caused in 1952 by the occupation of the Buraimi oasis (belonging in our view to the Sultan of Muscat) by a Saudi force under an official called Turki. All attempts to secure Turki's recall by negotiation

had failed and the dispute was to fester until October 1955, when forces of the
ruler of Abu Dhabi and the Sultan of Muscat, commanded by British officers,
reoccupied the oasis, incurring Mr Dulles's displeasure (see Chapter 10).

5 October

A.E.'s first day back. Meetings on Trieste (Anglo-US plan just about to
be launched; all wondering whether Tito will go to war over it); Egypt
(negotiations near deadlock. The Egyptians going back on the reactivation
formula and adamant on no uniform for technicians at the Base); Persia
(A.E. wants early resumption of relations[1] and is jealous of US participation
planned by Mr Hoover); Buraimi (no new decisions. We are giving a fair
run to Hafez Wahba's new scheme for withdrawing Turki and leaving
twelve Saudis and twelve British officials in Buraimi and going to
arbitration. If the Saudis don't accept it in the form we propose then the
idea is to tighten the squeeze on Turki and possibly kidnap him. A.E.
seemed to want violent action soon and to complain that we had not got
T. out during his absence. We persuaded him against doing this while we
need so much US help on Egypt and Persia.)

Main thought of the day is that we should call for 'another Bermuda',
i.e. the meeting of three Heads of State to consider next steps with Russia
which had to be cancelled when PM fell ill. Object, to offset criticism in
the House of Commons that the PM's four-power top-level initiative of
11 May is being stifled. Calculation is, nobody can persuade the PM that
Ike won't agree to meet Malenkov except Ike himself, so why not make
the PM and Ike meet? Danger is it gives more currency to hopes of a top-
level meeting and may end by PM going off alone to Moscow. A.E. was
discussing this with Salisbury, Crookshank and Selwyn Lloyd. I reminded
him of Dulles's expressed wish to see him and asked whether a less
conspicuous and less dangerous step would not be to invite D. here for a
three-power meeting at Foreign Minister level. This was taken up. Fact is
A.E. is scared of the popularity of the PM's project and cannot see any
effective role for himself in the House of Commons until it has been
'decently buried'. I fear the burial service may revive the corpse.

Drafted a message to Dulles for discussion tomorrow and hope this may
prove a diversion. Also did some work on the Margate speech today.
Strangely enough, A.E. wrote a lot of it himself. It is crammed with
platitudes.

1 Relations were resumed two months later.

6 October

Walked to the Office and saw a young man in a bowler hat airing his dog as if he had no job in the world. Surprised to find myself assuming it could not be true.

Our plan for Trieste has leaked in Washington before we are ready. Great rush today to get the approach advanced. Another terrible leak over plans to suppress Communist putsch in British Guiana. Troops are on their way from Jamaica. United States Ambassador has told us his Government hope we shall take strong measures to nip in the bud this Communist threat to an American territory. Very different story when we try to assert ourselves in other parts of the British Empire.

Went with A.E. to No. 10 and met the Lord Chancellor to whom I made my apology for the whispering behind the Wool Sack. Alex and Salisbury very bellicose about the Egyptians and think we should stand pat. Row between A.E. and the PM over speeches at the Party Conference. PM seems to have thought A.E. was trying to take over the leadership from him. He is opposing A.E.'s plan to get Dulles over here.

7 October

Rung up early by A.E. about his Margate speech. Am trying to get him to include a passage suggesting that the subject matter of a conference and the willingness to agree are more important than the 'level' at which it is held. He is not showing much fight. He rejected a phrase that 'high-level talks ought to mean talks held with high purpose and skill regardless who takes part' as being too like a criticism of the PM's plan. But the speech is not bad. I have urged him to insist on seeing the PM's speech for the Party Rally on Saturday because the Beaverbrook press suggest it is going to be a major reaffirmation of the top-level idea. A.E. would look very silly if tomorrow he made a speech showing no knowledge of what was to come.

PM asked to see him at 11.30 to discuss the draft telegram inviting Dulles here. I had premonitions about this and, sure enough, he argued in favour of an alternative – getting Ike to a 'top-level' meeting in the Azores.

The Edens lunched at No. 10 and while there A.E. gave his consent to a message to Eisenhower putting this forward. Did not see the text until the afternoon, when A.E. had gone to sleep, and was much shocked by it. I have recorded separately my talk with A.E. about this, when I tried to get him to take a stand against this policy leading up, as it surely does, to a Winston–Malenkov meeting. However, the telegram was gone and that was that. Even Jock Colville astonished that A.E. had given his consent.

8 October

A.E. at Margate. Drove up to London with N. arriving Office mid-day. Quiet day. A.E. and Salisbury summoned to a Cabinet at 6 p.m. to decide whether in the last resort to arrest the Ministers of British Guiana who are to be deposed tomorrow. Decision taken – I should imagine mistakenly – not to do so. So they will be left to stir up trouble against us and, as Norman Brook scribbled in Cabinet to A.E. – 'This will keep our troops there longer and be a Communist success.'

9 October

Woke 5 a.m. with horrible headache to a most exciting day. A.E. rang me early at No. 6 to say PM has had a very dusty answer from Ike. Won't come to the Azores. Offers Dulles for talks in Washington which he himself might 'look in on' at the end. Insists on French being there too. PM very distressed. A.E. says he will certainly not go to Washington in any circumstances. Later it became apparent Winston wants to fight back. Ike has used arguments based on other engagements during the week suggested. Now PM wants to suggest the week after, though this means missing the first week of Parliament. It will put Ike on the spot. We stir up A.E. against it. He is rather gloomy. 'I haven't got a log heavy enough to hold this elephant.' He goes over twice to No. 10 with alternative drafts suggesting we go back to the idea of inviting Dulles here. But PM won't drop it and takes both drafts off to Margate.

In the afternoon the PM rang up A.E. from Margate, who weakly agreed to another shot at the Azores plan. A terrible second message to Ike was drafted and read over to me from Margate. After more argument A.E. finally gave way and I was instructed to send a message to Jock to that effect. I got John Priestman to telephone: 'The Secretary of State concurs in the telegram. Mr Shuckburgh has cut his throat.' Jock replied, 'That seems a little premature. I will do the same in forty-eight hours if Eisenhower gives the wrong reply.' This was 7 p.m. Half an hour later, when the telegram was half encyphered, Margate rang up again to stop it. The old man had changed his mind. An eleventh-hour victory. Back to A.E.'s plan. In fact twelve solid hours of wholly unnecessary labour and pain for many people simply to suppress (momentarily) a fleeting whim of this old man. A.E. was remarkably patient throughout it all. Much more so than he would have been before his illness.

18 October

The Trieste proposal has gone very badly with Tito (though when first told of it he was calm and we were optimistic). It has been taken all too well by the Italians who will ruin its chances of acceptance by throwing their hats in the air. This week has ended with two days' conference between Dulles, Eden and Bidault.[1] Meetings in A.E.'s room. PM not at all pleased with it but he gave dinner to Dulles first night and lunch to Bidault next day. A.E. tells me that at the dinner Dulles told PM that Eisenhower opposes top-level talks with Russia and will not go except to conclude agreement already completed by the Foreign Ministers. Also he would not approve a visit by W.S.C. alone to Moscow. A.E. says Winston is indignant at last point and says he will not allow an American veto on his movements. When I asked Jock what passed I got slightly different account, viz. that Ike has promised to go to a Big-Four meeting as soon as EDC is ratified. Meetings mainly devoted to Trieste which has blown up into a serious row. Tito says he will attack Zone A if any Italian soldiers enter; Pella[2] that he will resign if we falter in carrying out your decision to evacuate the Zone and hand it to Italy. We are trying to bring both sides to a conference, being in our hearts afraid to carry out the 'decision' of 8 October which we now describe as the 'proposals' of 8 October.

Massigli gave big dinner for Dulles, Bidault and Eden to which we were invited. N. cannot come. At last moment I discovered William Strang had been deliberately left out. Reported this to A.E. and on his instructions told Massigli (through Gérard André) that it must be a mistake which Massigli will want to correct at once. Within quarter of an hour an invitation was on its way (declined). I would not have gone otherwise. Excellent dinner, sat between Claud Lebel and Comtesse de Crouy-Chanel. Some talk with Peter Thorneycroft[3] and Noel-Baker[4] before dinner about the conference and afterwards with Duncan Sandys who trotted out all the arguments in favour of father-in-law's scheme for personally saving humanity. I went as far as I could in countering them but with no effect. He, like the others in the entourage, believes in the personal magic of the PM. They regard him as the Greeks regarded the Hero. The technique of the Super-Man. Actions which in anyone else they would recognize as appeasing, impatient or misconceived cannot be wrong when done by the Great Man. I fear that our Trieste venture has been a major error. Both sides are refusing to come to conference and it is hard to see the way out. We ought not to have allowed the Americans to push us into the proposals of 8 October which, though we did not recognize them as such at the time, were in effect no more than the concession to Italy of what she had been asking, viz. complete control over Zone A without giving up her claims on

1 Georges Bidault, Foreign Minister in various post-war French Governments before 1958.
2 Giuseppe Pella, Italian Prime Minister.
3 Peter Thorneycroft, President of the Board of Trade 1951–57.
4 Rt Hon. Philip Noel-Baker, Secretary of State for Commonwealth Relations 1947–50.

Zone B. It might have gone better if we had consulted Tito and Pella first. It was the original intention (when Salisbury was in charge) to sound Tito out before the proposals were put formally to him or published and to obtain an assurance that he would not go to war on account of them. This was changed by A.E. on his return to the office two or three days before the event and the consultation was omitted. I must admit that I thought it rather absurd, if we were purporting to deliver a 'judgement of Solomon' to go round beforehand to Tito and ask him for an assurance not to make war. I do not think the department explained clearly enough to A.E. (who was newly back and not yet a very willing horse) either the pro-Italian character of the proposal or the warnings we had had from Belgrade against presenting Tito with a diktat. One by-product of the change was that poor Salisbury, who did not appreciate that it had been made, put his foot wrong in the House of Lords this week by giving an assurance that Tito had been warned 'two or three days in advance'. All this was, it must be admitted, a bit of a mess but perhaps not surprising as we were changing Foreign Secretaries at the time and, to all intents and purposes, changing Permanent Under-Secretaries too since William Strang has really ceased giving opinions on political matters at all.

During this conference Bidault described PM's speech of 11 May as '*un désastre*'. It had given an alibi to all those in France who wish to do nothing.

November

During this month Trieste is a continuous puzzle, 'a classic diplomatic issue'. A.E. loves it as an exercise but is worried. Personally I am convinced it will not lead to war. A letter from Pitblado, delivered mysteriously at No. 6 St James's Street while I was at the office, and which I opened in the presence of the McLachlans,[1] saying I am to have the CB in the new year. Another excitement this month for me; Harold Caccia[2] to be brought back from Vienna to replace Bob Dixon. Promotions Board recommended Wallinger[3] for Vienna but A.E. queried it and told me, the night before he was to discuss it with Kirkpatrick, that he wanted me to go. Ideal post, just what Nancy always dreamed of, great excitement for twenty-four hours but A.E. was (rightly) talked out of it next day. Deeply involved over tax and super-tax problems and we both feel broke. Death of Dylan Thomas. Have been reading his collected poems and find them most moving, especially the later ones which are more comprehensible.

1 Donald McLachlan, Assistant Editor (Foreign) of the *Economist* 1947–54; later Deputy Editor of the *Daily Telegraph* 1954–60 and Editor of the *Sunday Telegraph* 1961–66.
2 Harold Caccia (now Lord Caccia), British Ambassador to Austria 1951–54; later Ambassador in Washington.
3 Geoffrey Wallinger, later Ambassador in Austria and Brazil.

30 November

A.E. told me last week that the PM said 'I am not regretting what I said on 11 May. It is a cheap way of being popular.' News of Sudan elections having gone against the UMMA,[1] A.E. came into the office with a set face and started writing out his resignation. I quickly got Nutting along in order to try and get some discussion going before he did it, but A.E. said, 'You can say what you like, I am going to do it.' I had to read out the draft while he wrote it out in longhand and was very disturbed because, from what he said, it seemed to me like a pure manœuvre which he had no intention of pressing. Told Kirkpatrick. Went over to No. 10 with A.E. on his way to Cabinet and discussed it with Jock C. and Pitblado. Both indignant with A.E. for doing this on the PM's birthday and on eve of departure for Bermuda. They doubted its sincerity, and thought the PM would have no difficulty in talking him out of it. I could not disagree, and so it proved, but A.E. came out from the interview convinced that the Old Man had said something new to him: 'I am tired, I am not enjoying office. It will not be long now before I hand over to you.' I do not believe he means a word of it. He just hypnotizes A.E. with these stories. However, all is now sweetness and we are not anxious to cross No. 10 on any other matter.

The postponed summit with the Americans and the French eventually took place in Bermuda in December. Writing to me on 16 November 1953, Sir Pierson Dixon, then Deputy Under-Secretary of State, summarized the prospects as follows:

> It is pretty clear that the heart of the matter at Bermuda will be whether the allies are to go serenely on with the Bevin–Acheson policy of Atlantic defence (streamlined) or whether something different is required in view of (a) Russian change of heart or (PM's thesis) the feasibility of seeing if there has been one, (b) American itch to get the boys home (the French fear) and (c) inability of the French to face up to a rearmed Germany (the American pretext for a call for a new policy).

1 December

Another Cabinet and tonight we leave for Bermuda. Character of this meeting has undergone many changes. W.S.C. proposed it simply in order to 'see Ike' and as a step towards his cherished ambition of a meeting with Malenkov. Then the FO and A.E. got to work on it and on him, emphasizing that the main business must be the Far East, not Europe or meeting

1 The People's Party of the Sudan in favour of self-government and separation from Egypt.

the Russians. PM prevented A.E. circulating papers to the Cabinet to this effect – by the usual process of sending for him and talking him out of it. But they seem to have made some impact and we were told he 'would be good'. Then suddenly the Russians accepted four-power meeting for Foreign Ministers at Berlin – to talk Germany and Austria – at which they will raise the question of a five-power Foreign Ministers meeting with China for world-wide reduction of tension. This has changed the character of Bermuda again and the first task will be to agree upon a reply. But I think that (as all three Governments are clearly going to agree to the Berlin meeting) this may bury Winston's top-level idea even deeper. In fact it may remove his last reason for wanting to stay on as PM.

Adenauer is the only person who has expressed serious hesitations and doubts about accepting the Russian invitation to Berlin. (Dulles has done so publicly and clumsily but seems really ready to go ahead, and A.E. is keenness itself.) F. Roberts put up a telegram severely rejecting Adenauer's doubts and Kirkpatrick passed it. The British press are full of blue-eyed enthusiasm for this new turn in Soviet policy (though they say with their lips that it is only a new tactic) and are censorious of the Americans for 'examining the Russian note with a super-critical and suspicious eye'. Since when have we had cause to accept Russian notes uncritically? I went back to Kirkpatrick with the telegram and he saw my point and altered it considerably. He said he felt A.E. was 'out for quick returns', W.S.C. would soon go and A.E. must make sure of his position by some foreign policy success. Sudan was bad, Trieste was bad, the Canal Zone agreement, if reached, would be unpopular; Persia might go sour again. So you could not expect him to think twice about going to Berlin to meet the Russians with the prospect, however faint, of achieving something.

Nancy drove up to town with Robin and put him to bed at Connaught Street, then she came for me at the Foreign Office and had a drink with Stark,[1] Priestman and Grady and we went to Wheelers (St James) where we ate excellent sole. Then up to Connaught Street to say goodbye to M. and on in an FO car to Heathrow at 11 p.m. The Canopus floodlit under a battery of cameras, television, etc. Airborne about 11.40 for Shannon. Sat in the bar first with the others, Brook, Dixon, Lord Moran, Denis Allen, Caroline Petrie,[2] Burroughs,[3] C. Soames, Pitblado and Colville. Christopher was ragging these two as 'joint principal private secretaries to Serial 1' which is how they are described in the Conference Department manual. He had a long talk with me before dinner about W.S.C.'s ideas. He too is

1 Andrew Stark, Assistant Private Secretary to the Foreign Secretary 1953–55; later Ambassador to Denmark.
2 Caroline Petrie, First Secretary at the Foreign Office.
3 Ronald Burroughs, First Secretary at the Foreign Office; later Ambassador to Algeria.

hypnotized. He sees the arguments against what Winston does but concludes with some remarks such as 'He is so much more clever than most people. So often when everybody has said some action is wrong or impossible he has done it and has been proved right.' I spoke against the policy of running after the Russians, describing the terrible falling off of our Western position 'since Stalin died'. He at once assumed I meant since 11 May, so I said certainly I thought that had contributed, but it was only a part. The main thing was a cleverer Soviet policy. Christopher thinks Winston is now off going alone to Moscow but believes he will want the Heads of State to turn up at the end of the Berlin Conference 'just to shake Malenkov by the hand'. This assumes, I suppose, that the conference achieves something or is near agreement on something.

2 December

At Gander snow on the ground and very cold as usual.

Arrived Bermuda in a high wind. Guard of Honour of Welsh Fusiliers with goat. A line of notabilities and their wives, headed by a bishop, in grey top hats and Buckingham Palace garden-party dresses blowing flimsy in the wind. Drive through the winding oleander and hibiscus bordered roads in pouring rain, but the inhabitants, black and white, were standing there waving. Most of them looked as if they had very little to do.

On arrival at the Mid Ocean Club A.E. and I suddenly felt désœuvrés in our bare bedrooms. Why had we come so early, two days before Eisenhower? what was there to do? what was the point of the conference? what was going on at home, in Persia, in Egypt, in Trieste, etc? We went first for a short walk up to Mrs Jimmy Dunne's house and saw a large area of the island with all the dead cedars like a mist over the hills.

3 December

Although we the officials have had an easy day A.E. has spent it trying to get the Old Man's mind into some sort of order on the various topics for discussion with the Americans and French. He starts confused and wrong on almost every issue. He is raring to be rude to the French, to ask the Americans to join us with troops in the Canal Zone, to bring the Germans straight into NATO without conditions, and so on. He hardly listens to argument and constantly reverts to wartime and post-war analogies. I was at part of one of these meetings in his room and was shocked how old, weary and inconsequent he seemed. A.E. finds the impatience hard to bear.

4 December

Drove with C. Soames in a little open car behind the PM/A.E. and

Laniel,[1] Bidault from Mid Ocean to the airport to meet Eisenhower. Sunny morning. The bougainvillaea, hibiscus, etc., shining bright and little groups of waving people. Fine ceremonial reception. Welsh Guards and an honour guard of US airmen. Ike struck me as more ceremonial, withdrawn, royal, than last year. He greeted PM and was then marched smartly off to inspect the guard leaving the old man trotting behind, neglected and pathetic. A really lovely bathe with A.E., after lunch on the terrace with Dulles. First meeting in the afternoon. Opening discussion of Soviet intentions. After a robust speech by Bidault the PM spoke about the 'new look' in Russia, suggesting there had been a change of heart and that we should 'infiltrate' through trade, contacts, meetings. Ike came down like a ton of bricks, very rude I thought and vulgar 'So long as you mean what I think you mean, I agree; – that it is the same old woman of the streets, even if she has on a new hat'. All this was faithfully leaked to the press by the French afterwards. Soames and I went down to the Castle Harbour to hear a calypso band but all we could find was a large empty dance room with six blacks playing guitars and Ned Russell of the *New York Times* sitting at a small table with a colleague, Charles Kline. These two related to us in detail what we had heard in the secret meeting an hour before. The PM and A.E. furious when we reported this to them later that night.

5 December

Swim ?

Not feeling very bright this morning, didn't bathe. Foreign Ministers meeting in the morning when they discussed time and place of meeting with Russians. Americans want it very soon and threaten that if it is delayed they may reconsider their whole attitude to the meeting. They are also determined not to let it drag on. Three weeks, they think, and if no progress made we should go home. I think they are right. They believe the whole object of the Soviets in accepting this meeting is to delay EDC and divide the allies, a trap in fact into which London and Paris both fell at the first word. This irritates the French and us too. A.E. did not like being told he was walking into a trap. More signs that the Americans are very grave about further delay in EDC, threatening a new strategy, etc. 'Will not guarantee where Congress will go.' Cocktail on terrace with A.E. and then lunch with Pit./Col. and F. Roberts who has been busy with a working group on the reply to the Soviets.

Had a swim in the afternoon when we were chivvied on our little private beach by the journalist Brandon. This threatens to be the Achilles heel of our intensive security arrangements by which pressmen and correspondents are excluded by barbed wire from any contact with the conference. Dived down to the coral reef to see fish, but saw none. Afternoon meeting of the

1 Joseph Laniel, French Prime Minister June 1953–54.

Big Three. Winston went into emotional attack on the French for not ratifying the EDC, during which he said that if it is not through in six to eight weeks there would have to be a German army. He said we would keep our forces in there so long as the Americans did so and no longer. Ike followed in like strain and asked what 'we' could do to help. This had obviously been cooked up with the French when they lunched together and gave Bidault a golden opportunity to put all the blame on the British when he makes his reply tomorrow. He made a remarkably eloquent speech describing the psychological and political difficulties of the position for France but he played out time, leaving for tomorrow the specific requests he has to make. A tour de force. We are obviously for it. We walk into every trap and ambush with flags flying, drums beating and the goat marching in front. I watched Eisenhower during Bidault's speech. He has a strangely wild and distraught look in his eyes which darted hither and thither, not focusing on anything and he chews his spectacles. But when he comes to speak he has a forceful, military and rather domineering way but with a quick broad smile. He appears to be making sketches of Winston most of the time. The latter had an electrical appliance today, brought over by Lord Ismay from New York, so I think he heard a little of what was going on. Laniel has pneumonia with 104°. Went to bed without supper after a bath in A.E.'s bathroom. My bedroom is next door to the PM's dining-room and as I write this I can hear Ike, the PM, Dulles and A.E. reminiscing over the brandy. The G-man outside the door can hear every single word and I have just sent in a little note to warn A.E. of this.

We have agreed finally on the new approach to Belgrade about Trieste. Hope it was made today and not contemptuously rejected by Tito. Good news from Persia; relations to be renewed.

After I put out my light A.E. came in very gloomy and concerned from the dinner with Eisenhower. They had been talking about atomic war and the risks of renewal in Korea by China. Ike said the American public no longer distinguished between atomic and other weapons — nor is there logically any distinction, he says. Why should they confine themselves to high explosives requiring thousands of aircraft in attacking China's bases when they can do it more cheaply and easily with atoms? The development of smaller atomic weapons and the use of atomic artillery makes the distinction impossible to sustain. They cannot, for example, have two navies, one equipped with atomic guns and the other with HE. A.E. said 'prospects are too horrible for the human mind to contemplate' and was in a rather dramatic post-prandial mood. For some reason I do not feel very moved by all this.

6 December

This morning PM and A.E. still most anxious about what they have heard from Ike about Korea. A.E. went down to the beach with Dulles having told me (a) to send a telegram to FO cancelling the despatch of a British squadron to Aqaba which I thought rather excitable, (b) to make sure the PM, when he sees Eisenhower before lunch, puts in a reservation about the reference to atomic weapons in his draft speech for next week at UNO which has been shown to us. The speech is not very clever, pretends willingness to internationalize atomic weapons, coupled with the threat to use them. Our object seems to be to get the threat removed. But personally I am more in sympathy with American inclination to say out loud what they may do if the enemy make an aggression, than with our own desire never to say anything unpleasant.

Sat on the beach in the sun writing this while Dulles, in a canvas hat and flowery shorts, talks to A.E. on the sand twenty yards away under a natural arch of rocks. Denis Allen appeared on the cliffs above me, my attention being drawn to him by the suspicious glances of the detectives.

During the course of the day PM and A.E. decide they must dissociate themselves from two passages in the Eisenhower speech, one of which spoke of the escape of colonial states from bondage and the other the threat to use atomic weapons in Korea if the truce is broken by the other side. This seemed all the more necessary when it was found next day that Mr Hagerty, the US Information Officer, had told the press that the British had seen the draft and approved it. Eisenhower willingly made the corrections we asked and it is held that in this we have definitely had a success in restraining the Americans, not only perhaps over the speech but on actual policy.

At plenary this afternoon Bidault continued his speech about his needs for EDC; nothing very specific to our surprise and nothing suggesting that the UK should do more. But Winston attacked him again, taking particular exception to Bidault's references to the Saar in connection with the EDC – 'a few fields'. Ike supported him to some extent, making clear again that the US may change their whole course of policy towards Europe if EDC not ratified. Very bad atmosphere with the French in the dock.

7 December

Henderson (US Ambassador at Tehran) has telegraphed that the Persians do not want Hankey as Ambassador because Mossadeq refused him. They want nobody who has had anything to do with the previous régime. A.E. at once suggested I should go. He thought it might be a gesture to the Persians to send his own Private Secretary. I am not going to be twice bitten and refuse to be excited. He spoke to Bob Dixon about it who thought it 'excellent'. He became quite serious on the subject. Went through the FO list mentioning and rejecting various other names (Ward,[1] Chapman-Andrews,[2] Mason, Wallinger – my choice of course, as that would release Vienna). Still it seemed to be me. But we shall see. Afternoon: two plenaries all about the Far East, security guarantees, and the communiqué. Eight solid hours. Winston made another long speech on security assurances, starting with the statement that he had been 'looking round for something to please the Russians' and by the time we came to the communiqué the atmosphere was again very unsatisfactory. Trouble started at once when the French refused a reference to 'European unity'. When I remember how we clung to the word 'unity' to placate the French who were pressing upon us 'European union' I realize how far we have come downhill in the last two years. Outbursts by Eisenhower and Winston, former left the conference table in a rage, came back, having changed for dinner, sat another four hours. I heard him say to Dulles, 'Never again will I come to one of these, unless it is all prepared and agreed beforehand.' Winston said: 'The EDC is dead. We want a German army.' Bidault tried every means to get us to say in the communiqué that ratification of EDC depends on problems still to be discussed with the allies, i.e. to put the blame on us. We refused. Everybody very angry, appeals, sentiment, Bidault looks like a dying man, Laniel is actually dying upstairs. At 1 a.m. a formula was found which Bidault agreed to try and sell to Laniel. He sent it up. Nothing happened for half an hour. Finally A.E. suggested going himself to plead with Laniel. I went up with him to the bedroom where the Prime Minister of France, totally inexperienced in foreign affairs and new to office, was holding up the entire proceedings hour by hour. The French advisers all in despair: '*Nous ne pouvons plus rien.*' A.E. succeeded in his mission and came down with the text agreed. Everyone worn out and bad-tempered. Later the PM visited A.E.'s bedroom in a single vest, having walked all down the passage looking far from decent.

8 December

Saw Eisenhower off in the morning and Bidault in the afternoon.

Walked up with John Priestman and A.E. to Peggy Dunne's villa 'Troon' above the Mid Ocean Club for a drink. Christopher Soames was there and some minutes later there arrived Mr Cyrus Sulzberger, Ann O'Hare McCormack and Ben Wells of the *New York Herald Tribune*. A.E. sat

---

1 Sir John Ward, Deputy High Commissioner in Germany; later Ambassador in Buenos Aires and Rome.
2 Sir Edwin Chapman-Andrews, Ambassador in the Lebanon.

down on a sofa with them and was highly indiscreet for about an hour. I think he forgot that Sulzberger had let him down last time when he spoke like this in Paris and imagined he was amongst his personal friends in the *Herald Tribune*. Needless to say Sulzberger at once cabled a story including statements that the British had no trust in Byroade, the State Department expert on the Middle East. It is quite true A.E. said this. I spent the evening listening to Lord Ismay and Peggy Dunne comparing notes on cattle breeding.

9 December

Swimming

A free day, spent the morning bathing and lying in the sun. Lunched with Lord Cherwell and Lord Moran. The Prof. [Lord Cherwell] in excellent form, telling us vulgar stories. Dined at 'Out of the Blue' with Soames, Colville, Denis Allen and John. After dinner we went back to the Club to see if the PM and A.E. were all right and having, we thought, satisfied ourselves on this, we all went down for another midnight bathe. On return we found a tremendous storm. PM indignant that none of his Private Secretaries or PAs could be found. A.E. had taken down a telegram at the PM's dictation and we were all clearly in great disgrace. Poor Jane Portal[1] got the brunt of it. The old boy kept repeating to her, 'You left me all alone.'

10 December

Spent the morning shopping in Hamilton where I bought an Italian and two Indian silk scarves for Nancy, a coral necklace for Catherine and some attractive shells, etc. Picked oleander and poinsettia on the roadside on my way back and determined to take them back to England tonight.

11 December

Arrived about 11.30. N. at the airport and drove with her to London in Greeners [my car]. Just in time for lunch at No. 1 Carlton Gardens for the Danish Ambassador. N. next to Walter Monckton which she enjoys and I between Lady Hambro and Mrs Marcus Cheke. A.E. cut it. Straight to work after lunch with the usual topics but could not get A.E. to hold his meeting about whom to send to Persia. Meanwhile Kirkpatrick said to me: 'How would you like to go to Tehran?' I said of course I should be proud to do so but pointed out the snags: (1) I know nothing of Persia; (2) I know nothing of oil; (3) I have not even been a counsellor abroad and am far

---

1 Churchill's secretary.

from sure how to conduct myself as an Ambassador. But I see the point would be that A.E. would seem to be paying a personal compliment to the Shah by sending his own PS. Greatly agitated by all this. Had to unpack all my Bermuda luggage very late. My oleanders are OK.

12 December

A.E. rang early when I was still asleep to tell me more trouble with the PM. Latest idea is to send troops to Khartoum ('to restore order' – though not a dog has barked), so as to offset the disgrace of retiring from the Canal. We would also discontinue negotiations with Egypt and announce that we will leave in our own time, taking away or destroying the base. This is too bad. A.E. has just begun the process of pacifying the party over the Egyptian negotiations and explaining his motives to them. He saw Waterhouse and co. yesterday. Now comes along the PM to undermine his position. A terrible day, spent trying to kill this idea with the result that I could not get home at all. The PM actually wrote a minute (of which we kept a copy) saying that the Governor-General should be asked to provide evidence that order needed to be restored in order that we could send our troops in. I pointed out that this was for the first time an issue between him and the PM on which it would be possible for him to resign; since the PM's policy meant, and could be shown to mean, an unnecessary and gratuitous war. Hitherto (on Russia for instance) Winston's divergencies have always been in the other direction.

In the midst of this an office meeting decided to send Roger Stevens to Tehran. Foiled again! Kirkpatrick very understanding, says he thinks I should have 'something nice', but that unfortunately nothing nice is just yet available. He will consult me whether to take something less nice earlier.

13 December

Slept till 10.15 at No. 6 St James's St and then had A.E. on the telephone again. Still troubled over Khartoum but the PM now proposes to telegraph to Howe for his opinion. He has promised A.E. (a) that his telegram will be fairly phrased, i.e. not 'nonne', and (b) that even if Howe agrees, no action will be taken until A.E. returns from Paris. A.E. has alerted Oliver Lyttelton to hold guard in his absence.

Flew to Paris about 1.30 p.m., driven to the Embassy by Kit Steel[1] and his wife with a debutante niece. Adenauer to tea, with Halstein and

---

1 Christopher Steel, Minister at the British Embassy in Washington 1950–53; Ambassador to NATO 1953–57.

Von Herwarth. The Ambassador, Frank Roberts and I also present. Most satisfactory sensible man. Extraordinary how the Germans should have so far calmed down as to have a Chancellor like this. 'I want England to come as close as possible to EDC in order that France may not fear Germany.' He wants 'British experience, character and way of life' to play a dominant part in Europe. Tony Nutting appeared while I was making my record. He thinks A.E. ought to lead a revolt in the party, but I know that this will never happen. Long discussion with Bob Dixon and Nutting on the way A.E. was treated at Bermuda and then went in to dine alone with Clarissa and took her to a play, *Le Frère Jacques*. Quite funny.

After the play we went back to see A.E. off to bed and then out again to a night-club, 'Le Versailles'. C. talked freely about A.E.'s future and character. No good expecting he will lead a revolt or will confront the PM with firm demands. His character too set and he does not command a majority in the party. C. therefore wants him to find an excuse for resignation and retire to private life. I know that this, too, won't happen. So the Greek tragedy will simply go on and on, until it pleases God to end it.

14 December

Up early, correcting A.E.'s speech for NATO plenary. It is supposed to contain a 'British initiative' but all it is really saying is we cannot spend more on defence, cannot reach our goals, better abandon them and make do with what we have. It is called the 'New look' and the 'Long haul' to make it sound impressive.

Monty to lunch with the Harveys, Deans, Bob Dixon and myself. He is strongly in favour of an agreement with Egypt and evacuation of the Canal Zone. Wants us to put all British troops in the Middle East under the NATO hat. 'Quite simple, quite simple.' Headquarters in Smyrna, base in Alexandretta, troops in Libya, Jordan (Transjordan he kept calling it). 'Turkey is the key!' 'No use keeping troops in the Canal.' He eagerly undertook to teach the facts of life to Waterhouse the moment he gets back to England.

Rest of the conversation very discouraging. Monty says that though there are troops and headquarters arrangements in being on the Continent there is no industrial or manpower preparation for war. None of the continental countries are capable of conducting war. He wants Ismay to try and organize this with the Standing Group. We pointed out the risk of steering the Europeans towards expenditure on civil defence projects. They

---

1 Sir Patrick Dean, Assistant Under-Secretary at the Foreign Office 1953–56; later UK representative to the United Nations and Ambassador in Washington.

would be only too ready to divert to this what they should spend on arms.

In the afternoon I sat in the office reading up Trieste while A.E. went to NATO meeting. Talked to the Chief Whip in London about arrangements to lobby the rebels. PM had sent a message countermanding Alexander's proposed talk to the party defence committee upon which A.E. is setting so much store. This means there will be nobody to explain the military reasons for our Egypt policy. I strongly advised A.E. to fight back on this and handed him a minute while he was in the meeting. He agreed I should again speak to Buchan-Hepburn, who finally achieved a compromise in the form of a private meeting of thirty or forty MPs whom Alexander will address.

15 December

Again escaped the morning session of NATO where I heard Gruenther[1] made a fine speech. Lunched with Dulles at US Embassy with Livingstone Merchant,[2] [Doug] MacArthur, A.E., Bob and me. Pure business. Dulles gave us the full treatment about US policy changing over to 'hemisphere' or 'peripheral' defence if EDC not ratified. Takes a very gloomy view. In five years the Americans may show no more interest in Europe. May think only of Far East. Soon Germany will be fed up waiting and will insist on the freedoms offered to her in the Bonn Treaty. He says he has toyed with the idea of a UK/Benelux/German association of states if France fails. But rejected it 'because Benelux will not have it'. (Can't imagine what he has been up to.) Conclusion: there is no alternative to EDC but chaos. He thinks a special French Government will have to be found simply to put EDC through, because the majority for that is not the same as the majority needed for running the country. D. also very tiresome about Egypt. Caffery now says we must write down what we have so far agreed with the Egyptians, before the latter can be expected to agree to the two outstanding points we want – uniforms and availability. Otherwise the poor Egyptians are not to know that the British will not raise all sorts of new issues once they have agreed on these two. A.E. very angry.

16 December

A.E. called me very early. Worried by this morning's newspapers which show the Government have allowed their motion on TV to be talked out.

1 General Alfred Gruenther, Supreme Allied Commander Europe.
2 Livingstone Merchant, US Representative at NATO 1952–53; Assistant Secretary of State, European Affairs 1953–56.

He was upset that Selwyn Lloyd took a major part in the debate on behalf of the Government 'when he should have been looking after the FO for me'. But Clarissa reminded him he had given his consent to this in the car, returning from London Airport after Bermuda. He had entirely forgotten.

I spent the morning checking more material for his wind-up speech on Thursday, covering Bermuda and NATO meetings and putting the balance between hopes of negotiations with the Russians at Berlin and refusal to be led on to delay EDC and NATO tasks. Then I had to cancel my lunch with Tony Rumbold in order to lunch at the Embassy with A.E., Lord Ismay, Ambassador, Bob and Frank, to talk about what to do if EDC does not get ratified. Most interesting talk. All agreed we must not say a word about alternatives lest we give the French an alibi. But there are three main alternatives (a) UK take the lead and run Europe as the French want. But we must eliminate the federal element in EDC and Schuman plan if we are to do this. I worked this out a little and suggested we build on Brussels Treaty; offer permanent alliance to Germany/France/Italy/Benelux; agree not to take substantial part of our forces from Continent without consent; form them with the other forces into one 'confederate army' under British C.-in-C.; have political HQ of the alliance in London, military HQ near SHAPE. It will need a lot of thinking about. (b) Try to persuade the Americans to take over. This will not be easy and goes counter to Dulles's threats. (c) If Americans remove to hemisphere policy, rescue what we can by gathering Norway, Denmark, Low Countries to our side.

17 December

Whole day on the speech, started in A.E.'s bedroom at No. 1 where he dictated certain passages to a relay of typists. Selwyn, Nutting and Carr came at mid-day, to talk Egypt, and then I lunched with the Edens. C. very cross because we kept the soufflé waiting and because there was difficulty in getting her a seat in the House for the whole debate. But both came out all right. Then A.E. and I went to the House where his room was strewn with drafts and notes and filled with nervousness. I listened to PM, Attlee, Waterhouse and half of Bevan when A.E. sent Selwyn Lloyd to ask what the hell I was doing in the box and why I was not working on his speech. Back at it. About 6.30, PM came in to read the passage on Egypt and made few good suggestions. He liked it but he is longing for a break: 'It has been my constant fear – that the Egyptians might accept.' 'If they attack us, that would be war, and you can do a lot of things then.' He does not change. Always he has wanted a war with Egypt, after which we would march out and leave them.

At 7.30 I dashed back to No. 6, changed into black tie and on to Savoy

Hotel to Christopher Chancellor's[1] dinner for Ridsdale, but was only able to stay for the cocktails as A.E. summoned me back to his room by 8.30. Saw him through his last anxious stages and then sat in the official box and heard his speech. A success. Much support in the party and I think he strengthened his position. Many odd people patted him on the back, including Dalton.[2] I dashed back to the Savoy just in time to hear Ridsdale conclude his speech of thanks, and then after another speech by Hector McNeil[3] I realized I must say something as the senior FO man there. Unfortunately in praising Ridsdale I seem to have slighted John Rob who went to Bermuda instead of him.

18 December

Foggy. Telegrams suggest there is something unpleasant coming in Egypt. Worrying. A.E. went to be inducted as an Elder Brother at Trinity House and lunched there. Winston left his cigar lying under his hand on a box of matches which caught alight and burned him badly in the palm. Nice letter from Oliphant[4] welcoming me to the Turf Club. Back to No. 6 in the afternoon to pack up all my belongings for the lease is up.

Meetings with Jock Balfour[5] from Madrid at which we decided nothing can be done to improve relations with Franco. A.E. had been confirmed in this opinion by Lord Templewood,[6] whom he met at lunch. Jock says Spaniards think we are so weak we shall give way on Gibraltar and he wants the Americans induced to tell them flat that there is nothing doing. But he also wants to assure Franco that the Queen's visit to Gibraltar on her way home from Australia is not a calculated insult to Spain. A.E. very cautious about this. Does not want to make any explanations about the visit.

Roger Makins at last able to see A.E., having almost finished his week's visit to London which we authorized in lieu of his going to Bermuda. I got a late slow train to Henley. Home at last after eighteen days.

19 December

An ideal weekend at High Wood. All the children at home and a faint sun peering through the winter mists. On Saturday we all sang carols in bed and found we had an effective family quartet; N. taking alto, Julian tenor

1 Sir Christopher Chancellor, General Manager of Reuters Ltd 1944–59.
2 Hugh Dalton, Labour MP 1924–31, 1935–59; Chancellor of the Exchequer 1945–47.
3 Hector McNeil, Labour MP 1941–55; Minister of State at the Foreign Office 1946–50.
4 Sir Lancelot Oliphant, a friend of my father.
5 Sir John Balfour, British Ambassador in Madrid.
6 Formerly Sir Samuel Hoare, Foreign Secretary 1935–36; Ambassador in Madrid during the war.

and I bass. Then we had a wild game of tennis in a high wind. On Sunday morning Alfred[1] and I cut down a dead oak forty foot high with the motor saw, sawed it into lengths, split them and had them in the wood shed by lunchtime. In the afternoon we felled another and would have done that too if the engine had not given out. Meanwhile the three Brett boys were indoors singing carols (very poorly) with N. and ours, in preparation for the children's service next week. High tea at 6.30 with sausages and bacon and then off to the new house Lionel has built for his assistant, Bosanquet and his wife, where we practised with the local choir for an hour; then to the village hall and gave a carol concert to about twenty locals and their children. I sang a solo! A full moon in a clear sky and colder tonight. We hear there is some snow in Switzerland at last. When we got home neither N. nor I could sleep and had to take a soneryl each.

21 December

Motored to London with N. and Julian. They went to St James's St to pack up my belongings and move them to Connaught St which is to be my HQ until I can find somewhere else to live. A very full day for A.E., mostly on the Middle East, Egypt, Sudan, Buraimi, Persia. The Tory rebels are still on the warpath and are now trying to catch him out on a legal point as to whether the 1936 Treaty is terminable. Meanwhile the Americans want to give aid to Egypt in the New Year regardless of whether agreement has been reached with us. PM has sent Eisenhower a fervent appeal on this, more or less openly saying 'This will bring my Government down. How would you get on with a socialist Government?' A.E. followed it up with an appeal to Dulles.

22 December

Exasperating day, almost all our troubles acute. Americans insist on aid for Egypt and Ike's reply to PM very unsatisfactory. PM had said in effect, how can you expect us to support you over China if you do not support us over Egypt; to which Ike replies, does that mean you *will* support us over China (non-recognition and exclusion from UN) if we support you over Egypt? Certainly it means no such thing. Went shopping at lunchtime to Fortnum and Mason's and got N. some caviar and toys for the children. Walking back through St James's Square got in conversation with an old man digging the earth. 'I always keeps my eyes open. There's untold wealth

1 Alfred Khas, a former German prisoner of war who settled in Oxfordshire and helped me with my garden.

down there if you could find it.' He had found the butt end of an eighteenth-century clay pipe.

PM suddenly announced intention to invite Malik (Soviet Ambassador) to lunch at Chequers. Suggestion, he said, came from Julian Amery. This not calculated to endear it to A.E. since Amery is leading the Egypt revolt. Both Amery and Robert Boothby have been having talks recently with the Soviet Embassy and are most indiscreet. Home by train and find the children just back from carol singing round the neighbourhood with the Williamsons. First leeks of the year from the garden and excellent small sprouts.

23 December

Drove to town from High Wood and saw a horrible accident on the Northolt road. Over a dozen cars mixed up. Fog most of the way and it took two hours. Big meeting to discuss EDC, what to do if the French fail to ratify. I tried to direct attention to the possibility of doing something to *prevent* an adverse vote rather than waiting until there has been one. Naturally we should not produce any new plan while there is still a chance that the EDC will go through, without more help from us; but we should be ready to do so at the last moment. The experts have various technical things we may be able to do, e.g. put a brigade into EDC; but I think A.E. is looking for something more general and imaginative. I think this is what we shall need even if it is a little phoney, e.g. a 'confederate army' or a 'permanent alliance' between the UK and EDC countries with under-takings to keep our forces on the Continent.

29 December

A Cabinet in the afternoon mostly about the Drogheda Report,[1] over which A.E. had a struggle and seems to have quarrelled with Walter Monckton. After the Cabinet Rab and Harold Macmillan invited A.E. to join them secretly at No. 11, when they revealed their anxiety about the state of the Government, unwillingness of the PM to look ahead or plan party policies; slowness of Cabinets, etc. Both said they had reason to think he might go soon which surprised A.E. Rab wants this year's budget to contain no surprises and to reserve good news for next year; nearer the general election. PM's comment was, 'but I am not sure I can last as long as that'. H.M. is to sound the Old Man out at dinner tonight regarding his intention to

---

1 The Drogheda Report on Overseas Information Services by an independent committee of enquiry chaired by Lord Drogheda (Cmd 9138, 1954).

resign. Feel pretty sure he will get no change.

A.E. seems to be toying with the PM's so-called alternative to an agreement with Egypt, i.e. break off negotiations and announce we will 'redeploy in our own time'. But unless that means we announce that we will start moving our forces out at once, unconditionally, it is surely the equivalent of a straight break and show-down with Egypt and would lead to attacks on our base, bloodshed, the occupation of Cairo and all the rest. Selwyn Lloyd is even more influenced by the Tory rebels' case. His suggestion is that when we speak of 'redeployment in our own time' we should in our own minds intend that we will remain there in some force until 1956 and even after. This is the Waterhouse theory; that you reduce the size of the base and hold on to it with 10,000 fighting men. A.E. sees through this and thinks it dishonest.

30 December

Awoke very cosy at Connaught St. Breakfast with M. A.E. held meetings on Persia, Egypt, Trieste in his bedroom. Nothing sensational on the first two but we decided to go ahead with plan for a confidential Anglo-American approach to Tito with detailed proposals for a settlement. The difficulty is now how to exclude the French (who if they were included would leak everything to the Italians) without giving them offence again. Gave Tony Nutting lunch at my club, the Marlborough, which closes down tomorrow for good. A.E. lunched with PM. All the PM would admit was that 'another stroke' would be an alternative to his continuing as at present. A.E. said Winston had been 'very nice about the FO and entirely agrees we must get the Egyptian agreement'. He had also been strongly in favour of A.E. doing a broadcast on foreign policy in January, only adding 'don't be too rough on my poor Communists; leave the door open for them'. In other words, the charm has been brought into action again and the opposition is stillborn.

31 December

Talked to Kirkpatrick about the present state of our foreign policy. He says the trouble is we have no fixity at any point. In the Middle East A.E. is uncertain whether he does not want to throw over the Arabs altogether and to rely on Israel and Turkey. This is the PM's strong choice. In Europe he is uncertain whether we should not alter our policy fundamentally in order to get the EDC through, e.g. by joining ourselves or undertaking to keep troops permanently on the Continent. On Persia he keeps wavering between a settlement of some sort with American participation (consortium) and the hope of getting the AIOC [Anglo Iranian Oil Company] back in their own right. It is very difficult to have certainty when there are in effect two men acting as Foreign Secretary at the same time.

1 January 1954

My CB in the paper today and received many letters; especially nice note from Kirkpatrick pointing out that only Harvey, Jebb and Dixon have it in the whole Foreign Service. He himself incidentally a KCB and Strang GCB.

Chapter Six

The Elusive Premiership, 1954

In January 1954 I accompanied Eden to Berlin for a conference of the four occupying powers on the future of Germany and Austria. I wrote a full diary recording blow-by-blow the failure to obtain Soviet consent either to the establishment of an all-German Government through free elections or to the signature of an Austrian peace treaty. Most of it has been omitted here, but some extracts are given illustrating the way in which Eden's attention was increasingly diverted from these problems by troubles in the Middle East and the Far East, and by concern over his position in the Government. There continues to be no vacancy at No. 10 Downing Street.

18 and 19 January

Picking up the threads at the FO after a fortnight's family skiing in Switzerland. Everybody getting ready for Berlin. Some doubt whether Tony Nutting will be allowed by the Whips and the PM to go but A.E. is insisting. John Priestman tells a curious story of having been asked to lunch by Montague Browne and given inside picture of the PM's attitude to our Egypt Policy; PM only staying on to save A.E. from discrediting himself over Egypt. Purely disinterested anxiety over his successor. Feels that though his successors are on the whole so feeble, the socialists must be kept out. He never read the original Cabinet paper on Egypt or understood the Cabinet discussion when it was decided to go for a treaty involving evacuation, and has never consciously agreed to such a policy. He therefore seeks now to save what he can from the wreck. Thinks a possible solution is to join Israel in seizing all territory up to and including the Canal and compensate Jordan with a strip of Israel territory the other side. Then hold the Canal and base our Middle East policy on Jordan and Israel. (These happen to be the two countries most likely to go to war with each other in the world at present.) Got John to write this down and showed it to A.E. very confidentially. After lunch at the Turf Club (my first appearance as a member) I walked back with Jock Colville who told me a very different story. PM now seriously resolved to retire when the

Queen gets back in May. Very tired, depressed but more likely to do it if A.E. is 'kind' (because every time A.E. is rough the PM says this is a proof he has not yet matured enough to be left in charge). I told A.E. this (except the bracketed part) when I heard he had asked for a talk with the PM, for fear he might intend to make a scene about the Priestman story. It seems the Cabinet colleagues are for the first time seriously concerned – to the point of wishing to take some action – by a lack of leadership. About seven of them met today under A.E. with Norman Brook to discuss industrial situation, strikes, etc., and I think that it was without the PM's knowledge. (Not sure of this.) Some of them want to leave the Government.

Kirkpatrick told me today he is working on a new plan to release me from Private Secretary. Jack Ward would take Paul Mason's under-secretaryship in May; Roger Allen would go to Bonn and I would succeed Roger in charge of the Middle East Departments. After a little thought I asked him whether I would not be better in Mason's job. He said 'no'; that was the easiest under-secretaryship, Middle East the most difficult. But if Roger really wants to stick to his present job (he is now away honey-mooning) then I would certainly be a candidate for Bonn. However Kirkpatrick said I should be quite able to do the Middle East job and that if I did this for a short time 'he thought he could assure me the Office would find me a really nice post next time'. So perhaps I would be well advised to wait.

Our policy for Berlin seems at present to be quite sound. We are ready to give way over trifles, e.g. siting of the meetings (under Dulles's guidance we abandoned the three-to-one principle), but show every sign of firmness on essentials, e.g. free elections in Germany before any peace treaty. But the weakness of our position is that we are in a hurry. We must either get results or break off in a matter of three or four weeks, for after that every day spent undecided will obstruct the passage of the EDC and of American congressional votes for defence aid to Europe. The Russian game will be to keep us there as long as possible. On the other hand G. Harrison thinks that Molotov will not want to be out of Moscow for longer than three weeks on account of his own position at home. Our other weakness is the PM's determination to get a top-level meeting and the atmosphere of expectation he has created. Much of the press, with the honourable exception of *The Economist*, is already showing impatience with any firmness on our part and suggesting dangerous compromise solutions. *The Times* leader today is particularly weakening.

22 January

Perfectly smooth flight to Berlin, stopping half an hour at Düsseldorf, where A.E. was presented with a little white equestrian statue of

Nymphenburg china. When we started coming down over Berlin A.E. seemed convinced that the bank of cloud we passed through was fog, and got rather apprehensive. I had to express a jolly confidence which I had no reason to think justified. But it was. Great ceremony at Tempelhof – bitterly cold. Derick and Bunchy,[1] with daughter, General and Mrs Coleman,[2] Michael Rose[3] and others there to meet us.

23 January

Lunch with François-Poncet.[4] About thirty persons. Marvellous lunch. '*Oui, mon chef est bon quand il n'est pas ivre. Vous mangez mieux le matin que le soir. Si on commande un savarin il vous fait une éponge.*' Table cloth covered with white muslin with printed flower decoration, very modern and chic, by a woman Paula Marron and said to be terribly expensive.

25 January

First meeting with Molotov in Allied Control Commission building at 3.0 p.m. Drove with A.E. and Tony through the empty Berlin streets, with our escort wailing discreetly and the odd Berliner waving his hat.

Molotov arrived with a close bunch of followers, like a bodyguard, about twenty strong. Prominent among them Gromyko, Malik, Zaroubin, Semeonov. He was smiling and greeted A.E. very cheerfully. Yellow, oriental face with white moustache and pince-nez. The room is smallish, and the square table cosily arranged, five on each side. Not over-crowded, once the cameramen had gone.

28 January

Spent the morning pushing papers to A.E., who remained in bed. Main excitement the discovery that a draft Cabinet Paper on Egypt, prepared by Selwyn Lloyd, seemed to suggest that 'arbitration' would be a fairly satisfactory alternative to an agreement, and that we might therefore set the Egyptians a time limit of twenty-eight days in which to accept or reject our terms. A sharp emergency telegram sent home.

More talk of resignation when he gets back, unless the Old Man will go. Oliver Lyttelton is resigning.

A Russian called this morning and handed me two black tin boxes

---

1 Mr and Mrs Frederick Hoyer Millars. He was High Commissioner in Germany; later Ambassador to West Germany and Permanent Under-Secretary at the Foreign Office.
2 General Charles Coleman, General Officer Commanding the British sector in Berlin.
3 Michael Rose, Deputy to the General Officer Commanding the British sector in Berlin 1952–55; later Ambassador to the Congo.
4 André François-Poncet, French High Commissioner in Germany.

containing a Russian film *Heroes of the Ballet*, lent by Molotov to A.E. We shall have to show it to ourselves somewhere, and think of sending him the Everest film.

I went with A.E., Tony and General Coleman to a boxing final between the Royal Irish Fusiliers and the Royal Scotch. Hated it. The Irish boys all bigger, better boxers. Tremendous cheering of all ranks for A.E., which elated him greatly. He is worried lest no journalists witnessed it!

29 January

I spent an agreeable morning shortening and sharpening A.E.'s speech on the plan for all-German elections with the aid of Michael Palliser[1] who had originally drafted it. Found him very clear-headed and easy to work with. We eliminated a lot of lawyer's nonsense and jargon.

30 January

Evident from press summaries this morning that our plan for Germany has gone well at home and in Germany. Widely described as 'the Eden Plan', which gives much satisfaction but is really a little hard on the others, since the plan was worked out in all its details by the tripartite working group in Paris.

A quiet morning dealing with the FO bag. A.E. says he has been thinking about Egypt, and wondering whether he ought not to have reached an agreement long ago, regardless of uniforms for the technicians, etc. A telegram from Cairo showing that the Egyptians might add Turkey and perhaps Persia to the list of countries an attack upon which would bring about our right to re-enter the base. If so, this greatly improves that position, and only uniforms remain. He thinks of taking a stand with the PM and party, and insisting on an agreement whether we can get uniforms or not. Thinks we could perhaps get 'NATO status' for our technicians even out of uniform. But I have an idea on this, which I shall discuss with Tony [Nutting] and Fitzmaurice.[2] If the Egyptians were to recognize, in the agreement, that these men are soldiers, belonging to recognized units, though not wearing uniform, would we not have as good a right to insist on their protection as if they wore uniform?

Talked to Tony and Fitzmaurice about my Egypt (uniform) plan. Tony thinks it impossible for A.E. to make any more concessions, especially on a matter of symbolic character like uniforms which he has publicly declared to be a breaking point. I see this, but cannot help feeling it is a tragedy.

1 Michael Palliser, Private Secretary to the Permanent Under-Secretary; later Head of the Foreign Office.
2 Gerald Fitzmaurice, Legal Adviser to the Foreign Office 1953–60; later Senior Judge of the International Court of Justice.

Fitzmaurice confirms his opinion that technically my point is a valid one, so I have drafted it as a telegram to Kirkpatrick.

31 January

We all went off to see a horse-jumping competition, part of the Grüne Woche exhibition. A.E. presented General Coleman's prize to the winner, a French officer. Very cold. Back for tea and a quiet evening, rather disturbed for me by the arrival of boxes, summonses to A.E.'s bedside and conundrums such as 'Why is Lord Killearn[1] allowed to broadcast about Egypt?' (Clarissa had reported this) – 'Why hasn't the *Manchester Guardian* arrived? Why don't I have the headlines in all the papers every day, instead of being pushed into the background by the death of seventeen children falling through the ice?' Having seen A.E. a great deal this week at non-official mealtimes and just sitting in the drawing-room with the family, I am afraid I realize more clearly than before how terribly vain and egocentric he is. He can't really bear any conversation to take place which does not in some way bear upon himself, his politics, his popularity, his successes in the past or present. Yet it is such open and schoolboy vanity that one cannot find it detestable.

3 February

A.E. notices in *The Times* that Selwyn Lloyd yesterday gave a luncheon for the Persian Ambassador to which he invited Ralph Assheton, who is one of the leaders of the 'rebels' against A.E.'s policy in Egypt. A.E. suspects Selwyn Lloyd is playing against him.

A.E. is getting into rather an unhappy frame of mind. His earlier successes at this conference, and the good press he has had, blinded him to the certainty that it must fail; and Molotov's conduct yesterday and today is bringing him back to reality. All the charm and the sweet reason are going to be of no avail. Molotov cannot afford to allow free elections; the point is coming when we shall have to admit that publicly, and then the deadlock will be there for all to see. No triumph for A.E. ... only the question whether we 'can get anything out of it at all' – a conference on the Far East, an Austrian settlement, some form of relaxation of tension. And the Old Man hovering in the background, waiting to fly out here and wipe our eye. Not pleasant.

4 February

A big speech by Molotov, which marks the turning point of the conference,

---

1 Formerly Sir Miles Lampson, High Commissioner in Egypt and the Sudan 1934–36, Ambassador to Egypt 1936–46.

and ends all hope of agreement on Germany. 'There are two Governments in Germany, each with own police, currency, administration. Interests of both must be taken into account. The differences between them are too great for unification to be brought about by technical means. The Eden plan dealt merely with constitutional technicalities; we are concerned with the substance. His plan by-passes the need for a peace-loving Germany.'

7 February

A rude message to A.E. from the PM about the Israel–Egypt dispute on the Suez Canal. It is very clear that the PM is doing all he can to thwart agreement with Egypt over the base, and that Selwyn Lloyd is not playing straight with us. I really do not know what A.E. can do, short of flying home and having a scene.

8 February

Drafted telegrams to the PM and to Lord Salisbury about Egypt, making sure A.E.'s views are properly laid before the Cabinet.

9 February

A.E. arose this morning feeling strongly that the time has come to break off the discussion on Germany. Our position with German and European opinion, which is satisfactory at the present moment, can only suffer with every day that that argument continues. Molotov will find new ways of diverting attention from the clear issue of free elections, and opinion will be confused. Clearly this is his purpose, for he showed every determination yesterday to delay starting on Austria and to postpone the next restricted session on the Far East. From A.E.'s morning telephone call to Clarissa I got the impression that he is beginning to think in terms of getting home.

However, we still have to deal with Austria, and must not break up the conference as a whole before that. It is going to be difficult to live through the next few days.

News from Indo–China is very bad, and some think Molotov has been stalling on the Far East item until the Viet Minh gain some great success. They are closing on Luang Prabang.

11 February

A.E. is annoyed with Dulles this evening for wanting to put a fixed term on this conference (today week) and for not wanting to give way over China. He thinks Molotov is really trying to negotiate helpfully over this item. Very different mood from last night. I think Dulles is in an extremely difficult position for negotiating on this. American public opinion might easily turn on him for agreeing too readily to sit down with the Chinese Communists.

17 February

I am worried about A.E.'s attitude towards the Far East business. He is so keen to get a conference, so as to have some 'success' to go home with, that he seems to forget how terribly dangerous this topic is for Dulles. Dulles has come a very long way in agreeing to meet the Chinese at all. I urged this on him after lunch today. We, too, have to be careful not to give a boost to the Communist Chinese – Malaya, etc.

18 February

Tonight the conference is over, and no feathers lost, to my great surprise. At least I think not. Great pallyness when we broke up. Molotov came round through our seats at the head of all his gang, and shook us all by the hand. It must be admitted that after being shut up all day with these people for nearly a month one has a sort of fellow-feeling for them which was absent before, and I suppose this is all to the good.

Rather surprised this evening that we have heard nothing from London since we told them of our success with the Far East. Might have expected a word from the PM. We all dined again at the Ritz (A.E.'s party for the Hoyer Millars) and at 10 o'clock he and I drove over to Bidault's house to clear the tripartite declaration. Both Ministers very tired, and the advisers too. But we got it done, and then home to bed.

19 February

Foreign correspondents at 11.0, and then I got an hour to drive through the Stalinallee. Ugly. Extraordinary silence from London, except we hear the PM is proposing to speak in the debate on Berlin, and is already writing his speech. Selwyn Lloyd, true to form, is not going to be in town when we get home.

Last-minute flurry because the Viscount which came to fetch us all landed on three engines, and is not serviceable. So we decided to come in Derick's Dove, in which I am now writing, over the Air Corridor, with A.E., Bunchy, Tony and Con O'Neill. Very comfortable and smooth so far. When we arrived at London Airport, lots of anxious faces – Lord

Salisbury, Kirkpatrick, John Priestman, etc. – did we have a terrible journey? Couldn't understand. Apparently our wireless was not working (outwards), and they nearly diverted us to somewhere in Kent for fear we run into other aircraft!

Strange stories from John Priestman and John Killick[1] about Selwyn Lloyd's conduct in our absence; suppressing our telegrams, intriguing over Egypt, and refusing to be present when A.E. returned. He is evidently most unpopular in the Private Secretary world.

Dined with N. and Pinkie,[2] then to Connaught Street for the night. Gave N. seven yards of Chinese silk from East Berlin – 50 RM, and M. a bottle of gin from the NAAFI, 7/6!

20 *and* 21 *February*

Weekend at High Wood. Robin is coughing a lot, but not yet whooping. Brought him down a box-kite, which we flew in the field in rather inadequate wind. I finished my little matchbox and gave it to N. Am considering what to make next and thought of some quite abstract construction, a sort of miniature tower of Babel, if only I could design it. Shall probably compromise and make a chair. The shrubs have survived the frost pretty well, but a rabbit has been doing damage.

22 *February*

Tiresome day. A.E. didn't come in until nearly noon, and then was in too much of a rush to deal with our business – except to be briefed for Cabinet on the percentage shares in the Persian oil consortium (very ably, by Harold Caccia). However, the PM rang up during that half hour and said we must be nicer to the Russians. It was a mistake to ask them to talk about Germany and Austria – 'putting them on the spot'. What should we have talked to them about, one wonders, just peace and loving kindness, presumably, without hordes of experts or specific agenda. He thinks they could be persuaded to sign an Austrian treaty though what evidence he has for that none can tell. A.E. wonders who got at the Old Man since last night, when he was on quite a different tack. Frank Roberts has been asked to go over and run through his (PM's) speech with him.

Very trying afternoon, mostly in my black hole of Calcutta in the House. A.E. in Cabinet, where he tells me there was a row about housing costs between Harold Macmillan and Rab. It was to do with the carry-over from one budget year to another, and the PM backed H.M. though in private he had previously given Rab assurances of support. Hopeless.

1 John Killick, Private Secretary to Selwyn Lloyd; later Ambassador to USSR and to NATO.
2 See list of family members.

Rab offered his resignation in a fit of anger, and the Lord Chancellor said there was 'no need to go up in the air'.

Frank Roberts brought back the PM's speech, which is terrible; full of every solecism. Germany 'our sword on the Continent'. 'The five-power conference.' 'Top level.'

Was sitting quietly at 10.0 p.m. with M., just finishing *The Waves*, when the telephone rang and A.E. summoned me back to the House over his beastly speech, and I sat there with him until midnight going through it. I am once again reminded what a dog is a private secretary. '*Es möcht kein Hund so länger leben.*'

23 February

A.E. did not come to the office in the morning, but kept ringing up and sending for papers. I went steadily through the speech in my small room, ignoring all. Andrew [Stark] and I had the sad task of explaining to the beautiful Jacqueline that she is being transferred to Harold Caccia's office. She was in tears; loves us all; what has she done wrong? We think we comforted her.

Norman Brook rang to ask if A.E. will take Cabinet on Friday – television – as the Old Man has too much to do. It seems, also, that the row in Cabinet between Rab and H.M. is wider than that, and involves a great issue between the Treasury and the spending departments. Woolton[1] rang A.E. in a great state – 'one might just as well not be a member of the Cabinet if one is not allowed to discuss financial matters.' I don't think A.E. can quite make up his mind which side he is on. The fact of the matter is, there is no PM worth the name and they are all at sixes and sevens.

Frank Roberts seems to have had some success, or so he thinks, over the PM's speech, and got the worst features removed.

Through the speech again with A.E. in the afternoon. I had slipped in the sentence 'We sleep more safely in our beds in Europe tonight than at any time since the war' and am now a little worried because A.E. jumped at it, and won't hear of it being taken out again. Not sure if it is true, but on the whole I suppose it is. Berlin certainly showed the Russians in no forward mood here in Europe. But one tends to forget the atomic bomb and the piling up of arms in the background.

Home by the 6.15. Robin still coughing, but had a fine day flying his kite. Today Roddie told me I should take over from Roger Allen about 1 May. This means *not* going to Geneva as Private Secretary. But A.E. may have other views.

1 First Baron Woolton, Chancellor of the Duchy of Lancaster 1952–55.

24 February

A day dominated for me by A.E.'s speech in the Foreign Affairs Debate, which went down well but was eclipsed, as a spectacle, by Herbert Morrison's attempt to explain away the divisions in the Labour Party. I thought it a good effort – bland, humorous, and on the side of the angels – that is, on our side.

Had time to get my hair cut and got away on the 6.58. Pinkie staying the night.

25 February

Pinkie drove me to town. In Kensington Gore I saw a poster 'Egypt sensation; Neguib out' – first I had heard of any trouble. Seems there has also been a revolt in Syria. In the afternoon, during the debate, I met the PM coming into his room in the House, and he drew me in – 'Splendid news from Egypt. Neg-wib's gone.' 'Well, sir, I don't know that Nasser is much better.' 'No, no. Much worse. That's the point. Perhaps he will bring it to a head. I have been afraid they might agree. I have been afraid [chuckling] they might bring it to our tail.' I despise myself for not having asked what he means by Nasser 'bringing it to a head'. He can only mean attacking our troops, so that we have an excuse for fighting. His speech in the debate was pathetic; generalities, no fire, and he was in tears about Austria. Kenneth Pickthorn[1] was looking at me with an expression of disgust at the speech, and left the chamber when the PM began telling us how many historical precedents there are for having conferences with the enemy while fighting is still going on. He quoted the 'International Council' of 1814. This is all to justify talks with China about Indo-China, I suppose. A.E. wound up the debate, and had a success. He only really attacked one opposition speaker – Harold Wilson – and it was I suppose typical of the British Parliament that H.W. came up to him afterwards and congratulated him on a fine speech!

27 and 28 February

Long weekend at home. Catherine home for half-term. Gardening and tidying up the wood, with bonfire. John and Paddy dropped in for tea, in their best attire, having been to a wedding in Marlow. N., C. and I went off to sing madrigals at a small house at Cuxham, belonging to a Dr and Mrs Skottowe. Delightful evening, with several new songs. We sat round a table. Someone had heard on the six o'clock news that Neguib is back in power, with Nasser as his No. 2. On Sunday we had a short brisk knock-up

1 Kenneth Pickthorn, Conservative MP and Junior Minister.

on the tennis court between snow-storms, but the rest of the day I spent with my bonfire, and clearing leaves. We are considering colours for redecorating our bedroom and various other rooms.

1 March

Bad news from Khartoum. Riots on Neguib's arrival, by the supporters of the Mahdi, shouting anti-Egyptian and anti-British slogans. Twenty-one killed including the British Commissioner of Police. A.E.'s first reaction, why did Howe allow this to happen? Have we not troops there? Second thought – the PM will be wanting to send more at once, and to occupy the country. Private Secretaries at No. 10 can scarcely conceal their *Schadenfreude*. The more chaos in Egypt and the Sudan, the more they can say it is no use trying for an agreement.

Lunch at Carlton Gardens. Senators Bridge and Symington. They have been visiting France, Italy, Germany. Their conversation, showing impatience with Europe's progress and pessimism about France and Italy, came pat upon our fears that the US Government is going in for another bout of high-pressure selling, to force through EDC and to have a 'show-down' with the Russians. Aldrich has come forward with a 'timetable' for French ratification, which they want us to force down Bidault's throat. Also, the PM has now revealed to us the message which he received from Eisenhower while we were in Berlin, dated I think 9 Feb., in which he talks very broadly and grandiloquently about the great responsibility he and Winston hold, to protect civilization against atheistic materialism, and of 'sharpening our swords for the struggle which cannot be avoided'. Personally, I don't think he means inevitable war; I think he is talking about the spiritual struggle; but it is disquieting, and Salisbury thinks it most sinister. We must certainly query that sentence, if only for the record. A.E. spoke sharply to the Senators about American impatience, but he is worried. They said America cannot go on bearing this burden, without obtaining 'results' and their implication is clearly a 'show-down'.

Cabinet on Egypt at 6.30, and after it A.E. rang me up to say he had a very bad time. Just as we expected, the PM is raring to occupy Khartoum. Says we should have listened to him a year ago and sent troops there after the election 'when Howe asked for them'. (This is quite untrue. Howe in fact begged us *not* to send them; we must prove this to him in the morning.) But it does seem as if everything is breaking up in Egypt; Neguib and Nasser are only ostensibly reunited, according to our reports, and the army deeply divided. Maybe we shall end by occupying Egypt again. It will be a terrible affair.

Kirkpatrick offered A.E. Tony Rumbold an alternative to Colin Crowe,[1] as my successor. I told him I would gladly stay on until after Geneva Conference if he wishes.

A.E. pressing us to put a division into EDC. I think we can find some way of 'placing a division at the disposal' of EDC – without actually joining it, or causing them to cease to be British troops.

A.E. had a talk with Butler today about Budget prospects, election prospects and the prospects of the Old Man retiring. They both think he will do it on the Queen's return, but don't seem very optimistic. That would enable them to have an autumn election after a few months with a new and younger Government.

2 March

Neguib has left Khartoum, having in effect been warned off the course, and if we play our cards right we could score heavily in the Sudan. Long telegram from Selwyn Lloyd; A.E. anxious to make a statement in the House, but we (Tony Nutting, Kirk, Dodds-Parker,[2] Roger Allen) persuaded him to wait until tomorrow when we can see more clearly what is happening. PM still hankering after despatch of troops and aircraft. 'You will never have such an opportunity again.' He is also furious with the Chiefs of Staff for having written a paper urging agreement with the Egyptians and evacuation of the Zone.

On my way to Paddington tonight I stopped at 45 Park Lane, for a cocktail with Roger Allen and his new wife. His description of the life of the Under-Secretary in charge of the Middle East made me realize suddenly what a scurvy trick has been played on me, in snatching Paul Mason's job (which had been promised me) away for Jack Ward[3] and giving me Roger's. Easily the nastiest Under-Secretaryship in the FO. I ought to have objected long ago – when Kirk first mentioned it to me before Berlin. I shall speak sourly to Roddie Barclay when he lunches with me tomorrow. Quiet evening at home. N. is on a two-day diet of milk and bananas only, hoping to lose nine pounds.

3 March

Up to London by train. I was just getting into my usual carriage – the first non-smoker in the second coach – where I travel with Pat Rathcreedan,

1 Colin Crowe, Head of Far Eastern Department; later Ambassador in Jeddah.
2 Douglas Dodds-Parker, Conservative MP; Joint Parliamentary Under-Secretary at the Foreign Office 1953–54 and 1955–57.
3 John Ward, later Ambassador to Argentina and Italy.

Dick Troughton, their friend whose name I forget and occasionally a Mrs Makins,[1] when I was hailed by Charles Steele (Head of Conference Department, FO) to talk about plans for the new FO building, about which he was to see A.E. this afternoon. Personally I can work up no enthusiasm for the plan to convert Carlton House Terrace into a new FO, for three reasons – (a) it will be too far away from 10 Downing Street and the House of Commons, and may thus detract from the central importance of the Foreign Secretary and the Foreign Office, (b) it will not be satisfactory for the Foreign Office itself, because it has to be a horizontal lay-out, with hundreds of yards between one end and the other, (c) I do not approve of building a new, utilitarian structure within a classical façade. It would be much better to pull the whole thing down and start again. Rathcreedan and Troughton collected me when we arrived at Paddington and gave me a lift to the Admiralty Arch.

A.E. was nervous about Egypt and the Sudan this morning, being faced with a Cabinet on the subject in the morning and a statement in the House on the Sudan riots (against Neguib) in the afternoon. We had a meeting with him, after which I walked with him to Cabinet and urged that above all he should not allow himself to seem to be changing policy or hesitating in any way as a result of events in Cairo and Khartoum. As it turned out, Cabinet was easy, and the PM, he says, was 'all milk and water', and said he was convinced of the need for a settlement with Egypt. No talk at all of sending troops to Khartoum. This seems to be the result of a grim discussion of our financial position, which shows a higher estimated expenditure than ever in our history and no possibility of making substantial savings – except by evacuating the Canal Zone. There is much agitation today amongst members of the Government on this question – because it seems the plan they are being forced to work for – to please the PM – is a 'respectable' Budget this year, meaning a popular Budget, which will lead inevitably to a very bad Budget next year, with *increased* taxation, and that in the year they'll have to hold elections. This is another case of W.S.C. hoarding up successes in his own lifetime and the devil take thereafter. Woolton wants elections *this* autumn, but that would only be possible if W.S.C. resigns pretty soon, because they need six months of the new Government to prepare. A.E. is not sure about it – thinks the public would not like an unnecessary election. But Labour are so split, and the effect of a new, younger Conservative administration might be so

(x)

1 Lord Rathcreedan, solicitor, Master of the Founders' Company. He and Dick Troughton had both served in the Oxford and Bucks Light Infantry and were prisoners of war together 1940–45. The latter (now Sir Charles Troughton) was Chairman of W.H. Smith & Co. 1972–77 and Chairman of the British Council 1977–84. Mrs Makins was for many years the author of the column 'Ask Evelyn Home' in *Woman* magazine, and described herself as the original Agony Aunt. She is a Quaker.

favourable, that he is tempted. Chief Whip, Chancellor and Leader of the House are so worried by the state of opinion in the party that they are begging A.E. to talk to the 1922 Committee, not on Foreign Affairs but on all the financial and home questions which are worrying members. Tony Nutting advises him strongly not to do so – says he would merely pacify discontent which ought to be allowed to grow until it pushes the Old Man out. And what is the PM for, if he can't give leadership and reassurance to his own party?

I told Roddie Barclay I was disappointed to have been given the Middle East Under-Secretaryship instead of Paul Mason's. He said he thought A.E. had suggested it; but seemed uncertain of this.

Statement went well – and no awkward questions on Egypt. There was a great row in the House while I was there about the raising of the telegram charge to 3/- for twelve words. A statement by the Under-Secretary for the Colonies, John Foster, about possible end to Mau Mau, negotiated through 'General China'. John Foster seems a very good and effective Minister, and should get a better job.

4 March

Telegrams this morning from Howe and Selwyn Lloyd in Khartoum saying we must have a 'show-down' with the Sudanese Prime Minister and his Government; otherwise the Governor-General cannot maintain law and order. The effect of these throughout the day has been to get everyone into the mood of sending troops to Khartoum. This is a very hard decision, and it may be they are all right. If we don't make a stand against Egyptian intrigue, and if the Sudanese Prime Minister is allowed to alter the composition of the Governor-General's Advisory Council by removing the SAR[1] man on the pretext of the 1 March riots, no doubt our position will collapse and the party feeling in the UK will be so strong that a Canal Zone treaty will be impossible. On the other hand if we are forced to send troops, the row with Egypt will be such as to make an agreement impossible that way, and maybe Neguib's Government will fall and worse betide. We are hoping to cow the Sudanese Prime Minister by the *threat* of declaring a Constitutional Emergency and of sending troops. If it works, OK.

This all led up to a Cabinet at 6.0, at which our telegram to Selwyn was approved. A.E. could see I was not happy about it, but he said 'if it is any consolation to you, Bobbety [Lord Salisbury] thinks we have no choice'. While we were discussing the draft with A.E., Bobbety and the Lord Chancellor, the PM came in, in a great state of excitement, saying, 'Just one more thing; when the blood begins to flow, it is essential to have

---

1 Sayed Abdel Rahan el Mahdi, the party of the Mahdi.

adequate force. Everything can be forgiven except failure to have enough strength at the vital moment. So please send two battalions rather than one; it costs no more.' As soon as he got back to No. 10 he was ringing up the FO to ask when the telegram would be in the Governor-General's hands, and to say that he 'assumed the FO would not go to sleep tonight'. He sniffs exciting scraps, movements of forces, emergency operational messages, etc. He said to A.E., 'The last time we did this sort of thing together was Greece.' Personally I feel sure (and Roger Allen agrees) that it won't come to this; for either Howe will get cold feet when he sees that his moaning telegrams have been taken *au sérieux*; or the Sudanese Prime Minister will find ways of preventing us having the excuse to act. I hope so.

I had a long talk with Jane Portal, the PM's secretary. She now admits that the old boy, whom she loves dearly, is getting senile and failing more and more each day. She says he is open to constant influence and is easily stirred up by his entourage. On Egypt and the Sudan it is Christopher Soames who is egging him on. Life is a misery to him; he half kills himself with work, cannot take in the papers he is given to read and can hardly get up the stairs to bed. Yet he thinks he has a mission on three subjects – Russia, Egypt, and the atomic bomb. It is impossible for him to resign, because he can no longer write, dreads solitude and oblivion, fears rest. But he will soon die.

I talked to Tony Nutting about my future, and I get the impression there may be some change in the offing. Perhaps Frank Roberts will be sent abroad, and I shall get some of his present (German) work, and be rather a regular adviser to A.E. on European matters. That would be better than the Middle East.

5 March

Today A.E. decided (with Kirk and Tony) that Anthony Rumbold shall be my successor, and that I shall hand over *after* the Geneva Conference.

Main concern today – our association with EDC and how to present it so as to give maximum boost to French ratification.

Ridsdale looked in and told us a story: Two fleas, coming out of the cinema. 'Oh, it is raining. Shall we walk, or take a dog?'

Private Secretaries' cocktail party in the Cabinet Offices. Talked to Norman Brook, George Mallaby[1] and Bligh (Bridges' Private Sec.) and they all complained about the Chancellor. He is moody and impossible to deal with, having his Budget shortly ahead. Norman attributes his character to the fact that Mrs Butler ought to have been a man – is a man – so that Rab has become a woman. I said, pity both Chancellor and Foreign

1 George Mallaby, Under-Secretary in the Cabinet Office; later High Commissioner to New Zealand.

Secretary should be women. It seems that there is much concern over the Budget, and that Rab's hopes, so high when he returned from the Sydney Conference, have been sadly dashed. Bligh seems to be implying that A.E. ought to take a hand.

6 *March*

The telegrams from Khartoum this morning (Saturday) show that Roger and I were quite right in supposing that Bob Howe would have cold feet. He does not propose to have a real 'show-down' at all. He is not going to do what the Cabinet told him he should (could) do – demand an assurance in writing from the Sudanese Prime Minister that the UMMA member of the Commission shall not be replaced and declare a constitutional emergency if he does not get it. Instead, it seems, he is going to 'ask the PM to postpone any action regarding the composition of the Commission for a fortnight'. He is going to make the non-return of Neguib for the postponed opening of Parliament on 10 March the main plank in his demands. Selwyn agrees with him, and I think this is probably right, but it is quite different from what he was bleating for three days ago. These telegrams had been read to A.E. in the country by the Resident Clerk before I got to the office, and he had only mildly commented that Howe did not seem to be carrying out the Cabinet's instructions. But at 10.30 he rang me up, and expected us all to be busy working out a new policy for Egypt and the Sudan and was very difficult to handle. I called Roger Allen and Con O'Neill into consultation and was able later in the morning to persuade him that there is nothing to be done until we hear how Howe's interview with the Sudanese PM (this morning) goes off. Clearly there is great disappointment down at Chequers that no blood has yet begun to flow. Howe is even declaring that he does not want any fresh troops, and will not want them unless there are fresh outbreaks of disorder.

Heard from my old club that they are selling off gin and whisky at 15/6 a bottle and wines of excellent quality at between 7/- and 12/-. Put in an application for £52:5:0 worth at once.

7 *March*

Sunday. After a stormy night, it became a sunny, early-spring day, and the few first crocuses opened up. I spent the morning pruning and tying up the fruit trees on the south side of the new wall, while Robin played with Helen Khas. In the afternoon, Alfred, N. and I cut wood and organized the compost heaps, and the Eshers came in for a drink. They said they had 'business' to transact, and it began with a bill for £35 for arrears of rates on High Wood, and ended with a cheque for £10,000 for N. to spend on 'luxuries and enjoyment' over the next twenty years; not to be invested or saved! All we can think of at the moment is a cello for Julian (Christopher Cowan[1] has written saying that he is a very promising pupil and needs one), new curtains for the drawing-room and a summer holiday. Dined at Watlington (Eshers too) and heard about Lionel's visit to India, Taj Mahal and all.

8 March

The nett result of having run into ten thousand pounds last night is that this morning I had to borrow 2/6 from an almost-stranger, Mr Wyck, a friend of Rathcreedan's, at Henley station, in order to get a ticket to London. Travelled up with him, and heard a sad tale of his house in the country which the local authorities wish to overrun for the widening of a road.

Calm in Khartoum, matched with much excitement here because the PM, in the night, caused a telegram to be sent to the Canal Zone ordering (or very nearly so) aircraft out to evacuate the women and children from the Sudan. A.E. had not been told, and I had that pleasant task. He stormed over to No. 10 and got a 'chaser' sent – 'no movement of any sort except at the direct request of Governor-General'. That held the matter until the evening, when we learned at 7.30 p.m. that on *someone's* authority thirty-three men, seven Jeeps and bren guns are being flown to Khartoum tonight. This could trigger off a lot of trouble.

Lunch for the retiring Afghan Ambassador, a polite, shy Royal Highness. Fitzroy Maclean[2] and John Tahourdin.[3]

Nothing much happened today, but it was sunny and spring-like. Supped with M., and read some more about the idyll of England in 1820 (*Age of Elegance*, Arthur Bryant).

Bob Dixon looked in – he is off in a few days to take up his UNO post in New York. He has been doing some TV tests, and they seem to be quite favourable. Perhaps he, like Gladwyn, will become the idol of every American home – but I doubt it. He seems thoroughly re-established in self-confidence and looks well.

Received this evening from No. 10 a sealed envelope addressed in W.S.C.'s hand to President Eisenhower, for despatch. A covering note

1 Christopher Cowan, the Director of Music at Winchester.
2 Fitzroy Maclean, former diplomat; Conservative MP; Parliamentary Under-Secretary War Office 1954–57; traveller, author of *Eastern Approaches*, etc.
3 John Tahourdin, First Secretary in the Foreign Office; later Ambassador to Bolivia.

said A.E. had seen it, but FO is not allowed to! Yet it contains a reply to
the high-policy message Ike sent last month, and is all about the risk of
war, the responsibilities of the Great Powers, etc. In fact, it almost certainly
contains, and certainly should contain, a passage drafted by me commenting
on Ike's sentence about 'sharpening our sword for the inevitable struggle'.
I really think I shall have to get Roger Makins to send us a copy! Ike is in
low water in everybody's esteem at present, for not standing up to McCarthy.[1] Dulles seems to be the only hero on the horizon at present, having
recently demoted the man McCarthy put into the State Department to
control personnel and check security. Stevenson, as usual, has voiced the
mass of decent feeling in the US against the McCarthy threat.

9 March

Selwyn Lloyd back. He sent for me and I went with Tony Nutting.
Interesting account (repeated more fully later to S/S) of his experience in
Khartoum. He justifies having postponed the issue over the Governor-
General's Commission on the grounds that the UMMA and others will
come to see more clearly the significance of a change in the present balance.
The trouble, he thinks, will come over the intended arrest of Saddik, the
Mahdi's son, for his part in the riots of 1 March. Then there will be danger
of UMMA riots which the British-officered police will have to quell. He
is very discouraging about the Sudanization committee's activities, the
state of morale of the British officials (thinks HMG must assure them of
pensions) and the quality of Howe himself. Said not a single Sudanese
was invited to the Palace to meet him the whole time he was there; that
Howe has no 'feel' for the situation whatever, and the Cabinet under
Sir W. Churchill is rapid and businesslike compared with a meeting under
Howe. This picturesque simile gave us some idea of it. Selwyn thinks our
real weapon in the Sudan is the threat to withdraw the British officials
altogether, and that, if only we had a skilful man on the spot, the situation would have distinct possibilities.

10 March

At lunchtime I walked to Withers in Wardour Street and chose a cello for
Julian: £23, including canvas case and bow. Had it put aside. Also got
some strings for my violin and think I might take it up again. Paid Wyck
back his 2/6 in the train this morning and talked to him and Rathcreedan

1 Joseph McCarthy, US Senator known for his witch-hunt against American Communists in the
1950s.

about Egypt. Cabinet today approved our plans for association with EDC and A.E. tried out on them a new idea for a treaty with Egypt without leaving technicians in the base. We would just leave it to the Egyptians to run – through civil contractors. A.E. very angered by a story Basil Boothby told him (quite wrongly) about Amery and Fitzroy Maclean having boasted last night that the PM was behind the 'rebels'. He raised it in Cabinet and the PM denied it. Then later he wanted me to go over to No. 10 and ask Jock to tell the PM to send Christopher Soames round to the rebels and tell them where they got off. I refused to do this, and persuaded him that it was idiotic. Wait until the Cabinet decide a policy: then force the PM to support that policy publicly.

Spent the evening with M. reading a lot of letters written by me from Winchester twenty-eight years ago. Did not feel that it was me.

11 March

Lovely spring morning and I walked to the office from Connaught Street – just over half an hour. Crocuses in full bloom in St James's Park.

A.E. was summoned to PM at 12.0, to talk about 'the future of the Government'. Great excitement. He said he had been expecting it, because Rab has at last succeeded in getting the Old Man to see the Budget problem, and the need for a plan for elections, etc. On return, he told me as follows, strictly in secret and no one else to know. PM said he had decided to resign in May – or end of summer at the latest (depending on his health). His only concern is to hand over as smoothly and effectively as possible to A.E. He will not resign his seat in the House, but remain as a backbencher. As to timing, Harold Macmillan had told him it would be awkward for Ministers now steering Bills through the House if the change came before the summer recess. He recognized that this was nonsense when A.E. said so. They then discussed the question of the Budget and elections. PM asked A.E. whether he thought election should be this year or next. A.E. replied (as he had said he would) that he would like to have the option. PM had seemed impressed by this 'which showed that I had thought the matter over'. They both agreed that it was better not to decide until much nearer the autumn; it would not do to appear to be taking a snap election before the economic difficulties of next year set in; but perhaps the socialists would demand an election in the event of a change from Winston to Eden, in which case A.E. might well decide to have one this autumn. But that means W.S.C. must go in May at the latest, so as to give him six months in office.

Drove with A.E. and Robert Carr to the Savoy for lunch with the American Correspondents Association. Sat between Drew Middleton and

Charles Kline. M. as usual very understanding of our difficulties. Said two things which he knew we had to do worried him in his bones – German rearmament and evacuation of our garrison from Suez. Kline talked about McCarthy: said one of the elements in his position is the fact that he is a Catholic. Jews and other 'minorities' are afraid to attack him for that reason as well as others. This argument seemed rather loose, and Drew Middleton intervened to say he did not think much of it. He pointed out that several Catholic papers regularly attack McCarthy.

Decided to buy the cello, and had it sent up to the FO, where John Priestman played it, in the afternoon sunshine in the Private Secretaries' room.

Meetings p.m. about EDC with Kit Steel and on Egypt. Long argument on Egypt/Sudan policy in which Selwyn Lloyd showed strong inclination to subordinate our major interest (getting out of the Canal Zone) to the lesser need to ensure true freedom for the Sudanese. He has much sympathy for the rebel case. Kirkpatrick strangely silent – but he is in favour of an agreement. Roger Allen and Tony Nutting also very much so, but R. does not think it reasonable to start negotiating again with Egyptians *now*, owing to the Neguib/Nasser changes and their behaviour in Sudan. A.E. was coming very near saying that we should break off the negotiations 'until they behave better' and towards the very end I suggested turning this to a positive approach. Let us say to Neguib: you want an agreement. We note you have offered Turkey. Good. We think the remaining problem – uniforms – can probably be overcome (under our new plan, if Cabinet accept it) but we cannot renew talks or conclude agreement unless they will do certain things to restore confidence – e.g. stop Salah Salem,[1] stop ministerial speeches and radio attacks against us, undertake not to upset the Governor-General's Commission in Sudan, etc. This was accepted as basis for a Cabinet paper which the Department will now draft. I was feeling very active and clear-headed over all this, for a change, and know exactly how it should all be put to Cabinet. It has a chance, if Neguib really wants an agreement, as he seems to.

12 March

Most of the day discussing policy towards Egypt. A Cabinet paper in draft – changed about many times, and finally about 5.0 p.m. I took it into my small room and re-dictated it entirely anew. A.E. and Kirkpatrick accepted it and told me to have it printed for Cabinet without further argument. Roger very doubtful if the policy has any future: but there is

1 One of Nasser's leading supporters, responsible for propaganda.

no other. We are to try to persuade Neguib to 'create conditions of confidence' by his behaviour towards Britain, especially over the Sudan, which will enable us to offer him a settlement on the new lines.

N. and I drove up to NW8 to lunch with the Israeli Minister and Mme Elath. We had rung up to say we should be late, but when we arrived Mme Elath said, 'Now we can eat,' and neither gave us a drink nor introduced us to anybody. N. furious. I sat next to Lady Semphill, who was in a great indignation against David Eccles for cutting down the elms in Kensington Gardens. Said elms are the least dangerous of all trees, especially when hollow and these ones good for another 200 years. She used to glide from Watlington Hill.

This morning I went to see Jock Colville about a letter from Prince Bernhard to W.S.C. about EDC. At my request he showed me the PM's reply to Ike, of which however we are not permitted to have a copy in the FO. It makes the point in which I was interested, but it is mainly about the horrors of the hydrogen bomb, and whether the black heart of Man cannot be touched before use is made of this calamitous weapon. It is a powerful and dramatic letter, which I admit only W.S.C. could have written. Ike has called it 'thoughtful' and promised a careful reply, which I suppose may come our way eventually.

13 March

Saturday. Got away from A.E.'s bedside by 11.30, picked up the cello at the FO and Nancy at Connaught Street and drove down to Winchester for 'Hatch Thoke'. Found Julian on his bicycle a few hundred yards from Hopper's and took him to lunch, a cinema and tea up town. He seemed cheerful and looked healthier than usual. I think he was thrilled with the cello, but he never reveals himself much. After leaving him up to House we drove home to High Wood in the dark, where the cats and a liver casserole were ready to welcome us.

14 March

Sunday. Ingrams came in for a drink before lunch. He will gladly plough up the lower part of our field (in which the thorns are beginning to take hold), but is short of labour at present. Sad usual story of his staff leaving him in the lurch. Sawed logs in the afternoon with Alfred and set some rabbit snares.

1 David Eccles, Minister of Works 1951–54.

15 March

Travelled to town with Rathcreedan, who talked of his experiences as a POW, especially towards the end of the war, when they were marched south-east ahead of the victorious American army, and bombed and machine-gunned by their friends. Picture of him in a large railway shed with masses of POWs and German children, comforting the children when American rockets were zooming overhead and the children quite calm until their mothers panicked. Dick Troughton gave us a lift to Admiralty Arch.

A. E. still showing signs of indecision over Egypt, with Cabinet discussing his paper this evening. He is like a sea anemone, covered with sensitive tentacles all recording currents of opinion around him. He quivers with sensitivity to opinion in the House, the party, the newspapers. Fortunately the *Sunday Times* came out very strongly for an agreement now. Chiefs of Staff like our new plan: Salisbury likes it but thinks it more difficult to sell to the party. Monckton likes it. But Butler is very dubious, and thinks all the stores will be stolen by the Egyptian Army. Very likely: but they are obsolete anyway. Dead silence from No. 10, which means the PM does not approve. Cabinet was still sitting when I left tonight for supper with George and Joanna,[1] so I don't know what was decided.

16 March

Left my violin at Withers to be repaired, and had that feeling which I remember so well from school days – how lovely to have a beautiful instrument, a bow, rosin, a case and music – only one detail missing, the ability to play.

Message from the PM that an emergency Cabinet is called for noon, to consider advice to the Queen about the risks of polio in Australia. A.E. very busy and reluctant to go – thinks it is a matter for the Australian Government. Also, the PM wants to talk about the Sudan, for which A.E. is not ready. But he went.

Yesterday's Cabinet on Egypt went badly, he says. All his colleagues, led by Salisbury, favoured his new plan (Rab not helpful, however, and he was disturbed to hear the PM and Rab had had a long discussion together beforehand), but the PM gloomily opposed, and wanted all the usual things – a brigade to Khartoum, 10,000 men on the Canal, etc., and a break of negotiation. But he is to see if the Americans will join with us in providing civilian contractors to look after the base.

Plans to go ahead for declaration of emergency in the Sudan if the Sudan Government upset the balance of the Governor-General's Commission by removing the UMMA man. Selwyn a great protagonist of it. I consider it

1 See list of family members.

a great mistake, but cannot very well say so, as Cabinet have approved and there are already enough uncertainties for A.E. to cope with. I don't think *any* consideration ought to induce us to be so foolish as to reoccupy the Sudan, which is no use to us, and may be a bloody and laborious commitment. It is all sentimentalism, pride, folly. And of course it will put an end to any possibility of agreement on the Canal Zone. The latter anyway set back this evening by news of more British soldiers murdered there. We seem to be caught in the *engrenage.*

17 March

With N. to Barker's to look at curtain material for the drawing-room at High Wood. Most of the morning spent on the Persian oil consortium, still subject of high-level financial haggling between AIOC and the American companies. Fraser[1] called – a dour, dictatorial Scot. At lunch, went with N. to see room I am to take in Albany, and to Harrods to buy shirts and underclothes. When I got back, found A.E. upset that he had been 'deserted' over lunch.

Jock Colville came round to tell me that the Soviet Chargé has passed a cryptic message to the PM through Soames that Malenkov 'would be willing to consider meeting him'. Jock was anxious I should make it clear to A.E. (whom PM would inform shortly) that this was *not* Christopher Soames' instigation or initiative. Roger Allen says, too, that the Chief of the Imperial General Staff, after one and a half hours' grilling by the PM last night, has turned his coat on Egypt and is now ready to advocate Course 'C', plus occupation of Khartoum by a brigade. This is a serious but probably not final and certainly not fatal defection. Meanwhile, more murders in the Canal Zone, and grave warnings from Paris about the situation in Indo-China, and the probable effects on French policy at Geneva if they suffer a severe military reverse. A day of disquieting reports and worry.

A.E. was duly summoned by the PM and told the story about Malenkov. He says he told the PM it was 'most insulting message ever conveyed to a Prime Minister of this country' – for it said, in effect, 'If Mr Churchill wishes to propose a meeting with M. Malenkov alone, the matter will be considered'. He found Winston quite sound on the subject – excited but not optimistic. Realizes it would be fatal to do it before Geneva, but thinks if Geneva fails – or succeeds – then he might. Trouble is that this mirage may give him an additional excuse for not resigning.

PM also spoke to A.E. about his new idea for Egypt (in which the CIGS

1 Sir William Fraser, Chairman of the AIOC.

is now giving him some half-baked support) of leaving 15,000 men there, to do God knows what. A.E. said he would not have it.

Hair-raising comment by Dulles and Bedell Smith (through Roger Makins) about the iniquities of Sir W. Fraser and the AIOC. If this consortium breaks down owing to his greed and folly, USA will leave us to stew in our own juice, abandon co-operation with us throughout the Middle East, etc. Everyone here, too, is scandalized by Fraser, who seems to be quite unconcerned with the national interest, and anxious only to squeeze the utmost out of Persia for his already bloated company. A tough nut.

Luncheon for Hamarskjöld, Secretary-General of UN. All-male – in fact all-FO except him. Very boring and too much food.

This morning the Chief Whip started to warn A.E. that the policy of reaching agreement with Egypt is doing him harm in the party; that the rebels are again on the warpath, plan to refuse the whip, are putting down another motion, 'go round looking as if the world were on their shoulders'. James Stuart (S/S for Scotland and a personal friend) is singing the same song. There is a definite increase in the pressure – abetted of course by the PM – and A.E. is beginning to be worried. In the car on the way to lunch he asked me whether we could not find a way of delaying the issue for three or four months – until the Old Man is out of the way – because he 'does not think it can be done while the Old Man is there'. He begins to see it as a clash which, if faced now, can only lead to the resignation of the PM or himself with great damage to the party. More murders in the Canal Zone, arrogant speech by Neguib, and leaks to the British press about Winston's 'robust' intentions, add to the dismay. Kirk, Roger and I had a long talk with him in which we tried to work out a line to hold matters. At any rate we can make the PM await the result of our approach to Washington. My strong feeling is that we *must* make some move which will show Neguib confidentially that if he behaves – in Canal and Sudan – there are prospects of agreement. In other words, show him the carrot. The trouble is the Cabinet never agrees to anything at the critical moments – the PM prevents it – and then some new scandalous event intervenes to thwart us. I very much fear, today, that we are moving towards a costly and ridiculous policy of 'deeds not words' in Egypt.

19 March

A.E. left early for his constituency bearing a speech written (as to the Foreign Affairs section) entirely by me, so I stayed at home until after lunch, and started to strip down the walnut chest of drawers from my room. The whole top will be re-veneered. Drove to London with N.

through very heavy traffic, and had two and a half hours in the office, during which I had to ring A.E. twice in Warwick and got sharply answered for my pains. We dined with Laura Grimond – Ernst[1] and Ilse Gombrich and their son, Laura's little daughter and the little daughter of Con O'Neill.

20 March

A.E. returned about mid-day from Warwick, having apparently had a bit of a flop in his constituency – half-empty meeting and not a word about his speech in any paper this morning except the *Manchester Guardian*. He was in a bad mood, irritable and impatient, and thoroughly jittery about Egypt. There has been more terrorism in the Canal Zone – a major and three others killed – and it is certainly impossible to go ahead with a negotiation at this moment. But A.E. seems ready, on internal political grounds, to go much further and quicker than is necessary in declaring negotiations 'out of the question'. The fact is, he is beginning to find the unpopularity of his Egypt policy in his party too heavy a burden, and is seeking ways of abandoning it. He is also insisting on our being tougher than anyone else in UNO about the resolution on freedom of navigation through the Suez Canal – not because we can influence the event, but because it will show we can be 'tough' against Neguib. This is all very distressing, and we drift away from any chance of agreement. But if the US will support our 'civilian contractor' scheme, and Neguib will keep order better, there is still a chance.

A.E., Woolton and Macmillan today put more heat on Willy Fraser and the consortium is still not quite dead. Took a 4.0 p.m. train home (sunny Saturday afternoon, quite spring-like) and went in the woods with Robin looking for catkins.

21 March

Sunday. I was thinking today of the flatness and lack of interest of A.E.'s speeches, most of which I write myself. Oliver [Esher] told of meeting a man three days ago coming from Central Hall, Westminster, where they had been electing A.E. National Chairman of the Conservative Party. The man said A.E. made a speech containing not a single idea or a single piece of information that had not been in the papers for three weeks. Oliver asked if I had written it: I had not, but I wrote the one he used on Friday in Leamington, which was so dull that not a single paper reported it. Perhaps I am at fault in pandering to him – by turning the FO drafts

1 Ernst Gombrich, Slade Professor of Fine Arts, Oxford, 1950–53.

which he hates so much (but which contain no doubt plenty of matter and some edges) into Edenese. But I know what he likes, and give it to him – with occasionally a turn of phrase which he would not have thought of, but which strikes him as a possible headline. Oliver was also lamenting that no one in the Government thinks ahead at all – he had in mind the total abandonment of all attempt to plan for London – and when he asked me whether A.E. ever looked beyond the immediate problems and the political concerns of the day, I had to say no. Yet I think he is better than other members of the Government. (Many people have the idea, which I am sure is not right, that Rab is a great thinker and leader.) I would say Macmillan is nearer being a big man. At least A.E. can *see* a little ahead; the trouble is that he is too keen on popularity to push far-seeing measures through.

This morning I went 'hunting' in the wood with Robin, but was immediately called back to the telephone – A.E. to tell me that the Americans are ready to co-operate over the base. This is very good news – and gives us something to work upon in moving back towards an agreement. What we need now is no more murders and some real effort by Neguib to behave himself.

Robin broke one of my drills. When I found it later, I asked him if he had done it, and when he readily confessed I said he should have told me at the time (I had been in the workshop with him). He seemed to take this quite calmly and with understanding, but half an hour later came in saying, 'Daddy, you have upset me' and began crying. He has much feeling and a fine character in the making.

23 March

To Buckingham Palace with N. and M., to receive my CB from the Queen Mother.

25 March

A.E. stayed in his flat this morning and was extremely difficult to deal with. Early on, I warned him that Reading would be ringing him up about arrangements for negotiating with Stassen about East–West trade. I said the FO view was that Reading should lead, with assistance from the Board of Trade and the Treasury. He indignantly denied the Treasury interest, accused us of selling out our independence to the Treasury, and said he would never preside over a Government in which the Treasury bossed everyone. (Rab declared in Cabinet recently that he would not have Treasury [Budget] business discussed in Cabinet.) I had great difficulty in calming this down, and warned Reading about it. But when R. later rang him, he was equally indignant that FO should be taking the lead, and said it was a matter entirely for the Board of Trade. He blew poor R. into the air, and then rang me. Most unmanageable. The point is, he thinks people regard him as opposed to trade with Russia, and does not want to take the blame for the concessions we must make to American opinion on the subject. Eventually he agreed to discuss with Norman Brook, to whom I was able to have a word beforehand. A compromise was found. Meanwhile, the PM has sent a rather splendid message to Ike about all this, urging that the main hope in the world's predicament is to encourage the Russians to buy and enjoy the amenities and luxuries of the West, and to penetrate them with trade connections. Beside this, he said, the supply of some goods indirectly valuable to their defence effort is a negligible matter. The ban won't stop them continuing to develop their hydrogen bomb. This haunts him. But Ike has again insisted, in a message to him, that he sees no advantage in a meeting with Malenkov.

At lunchtime I signed the Queen Mother's book at Clarence House, collected the gin I have bought from the Marlborough Club and cashed a cheque at the Turf. There I heard that there is martial law in Cairo again. Met Christopher Hawkes[1] in Pall Mall, but he was with a woman and refused to stop and talk.

Poor A.E.'s tantrums of this morning were entirely due to worry over his TV appearance tonight. He rehearsed the foreign affairs peroration (about peace) with me. His object is to show that the hydrogen bomb may be the only effective deterrent to war, and is not something to be thrown away because it is so horrible.

Spent some time in the afternoon preparing my 1951, 1952 and 1953 diaries for binding by the FO printers. The news today, apart from Egypt, is that the Government's 'commercial TV' bill got a majority of twenty-seven and that the latest US hydrogen bomb explosion had far wider effects than the scientists expected. Went to Tony and Jill Nutting's house in Chester Square to see A.E. on the TV, and dined with them after. Thought him effective, but the questions too diverse and not enough continuity in the discussion. Sat late with the Nuttings and an artist friend called Brian.

26 March

The newspapers today say that the H-bomb explosion on 1 March was three times more powerful than the scientists themselves expected. In other words, it was out of control. Very great excitement everywhere about it,

---

1 Christopher Hawkes, Professor of European Archaeology at Oxford 1946–76.

as if people began to see the end of the world. A.E. went over to talk to the PM, who was on the whole quite sensible – unlike *The Times* leader of this morning which proposes an immediate Churchill–Malenkov meeting as a sort of desperate throw. A.E. saw Sir William Haley, editor of *The Times*, and tried to instil some calm into him. He also had a very unsatisfactory interview with Massigli, and his contempt for the French grows daily, as they twist and wriggle in the inexorable toils of EDC.

27 and 28 March

Saturday and Sunday, A.E. and Clarissa drove to John and Liza Hope's[1] house at Grey's, near Henley, for the weekend, after giving me quite a bit of trouble over the telephone about the UK 'declaration' on EDC. All is now ready for signature of our agreement with the six EDC powers, and A.E. took that occasion (from the bed) to complain about the language. I followed three hours later in an FO car, eating a sandwich lunch on the way. Lovely spring afternoon, and they were cutting the cricket field at Grey's Green.

Found many of our roses have been killed by the frost.

A.E. came over with John and Liza Hope for a drink, just in time to see the view and a moderate sunset. He seemed relaxed and friendly (Becketts and Lionel were here too) but we thought the Hopes looked as if they might have been having a strained weekend. Lent the Becketts my Berlin diary. Read Lionel's diary of his trip to India. Very well written, colourful descriptive style, but lacks human interest. Nobody ever *said* anything. Came to the conclusion that the main purpose of a diary should be to record what other people said. Mine is not literature, but might serve as material for someone writing a life of A.E. or W.S.C. in thirty years' time.

29 March

Big issues today, the H-bomb and East–West trade, with a background of trouble in Cairo. A restricted Cabinet to discuss what the PM shall say on the bomb tomorrow. Main points: it is not out of control; we cannot stop the Americans experimenting; it remains our only safeguard. Incidentally, they let off another on Friday, but nobody knows yet, except our scientists and watchers on and above the ground. Another, bigger one to come. Christopher Soames said, 'The Prof. assures me that the scientists are *not* in a position to blow up the world.' Thank you very much, and for how long can we rely upon this assurance? Theoretically, if they used all the

---

1 Lord John Hope (later Lord Glendevon), Under-Secretary of State for Foreign Affairs 1954–56; his wife Liza is the daughter of Somerset Maugham.

material available to the Western Powers at one go, they could make a very big bang, i.e., one hundreds of times greater than 1 March. But they never would; it would be wasteful! The great question is how to make it manageable in size, and how to deliver it to the right place. This is where British ingenuity is expected to make a contribution beyond what the Americans have so far achieved.

Then as to E–W trade, Stassen is here and there is a first-class row. Thorneycroft, who is leading for us because A.E. wouldn't take the responsibility, has already got across Stassen by adopting a purely *trade* attitude, and is supported by the PM, who wants to loosen up the Russians by trade and penetration. A.E. much concerned, for we stand to lose £20 million of off-shore purchases if we upset the Americans too much by insisting on reductions of the strategic controls list; while we can never get more than £2 or 3 million with Russia. After A.E.'s lunch with Stassen, Aldrich sent over a little note pointing out how much better we should do if we discussed the patient and piecemeal reduction of the present list, instead of insisting on a brand new 'short' list, and warning us of the congressional dangers. After dinner at Carlton Gardens, Thorneycroft produced a note showing results of the day's discussion. We are beginning to compromise, but the PM, according to Jock on the telephone late at night, is 'hopping mad' with the Americans.

Rioting in Egypt. Looks as if Neguib is losing out to Nasser, and the attempt to get back to parliamentarism has been dropped. British troops in the Zone put at seventy-two hours' notice, in case there is threat to British lives. This of course has excited No. 10, who think we might find an excuse soon to occupy Cairo. Meanwhile A.E. and Dodds-Parker are coming to the conclusion that Nasser is the man for us, together perhaps with Ali Maher, and that we ought to be ready for a quick agreement with them if they emerge on top, and help them to keep power while we remove ourselves from the Zone. Not a bad programme either. But the PM will sabotage it I expect.

A.E. says the party are coming strongly to the idea of an election this autumn. (Kenneth Younger is reported as saying they would be mad if they didn't.) But of course he is counting on the Old Man retiring between May and July, as promised. The only trouble is, the old boy is feeling rather well at the moment. Jock says 'he has never been better since his stroke' (though it seems he sleeps most of the day). Tony Nutting is laying fifty to one that he will lead the party right up to the election.

30 March

Announcement in *The Times* today of my transfer and promotion. A.E. came in early, having had a long telephone conversation with the PM about the H-bomb which he said was most unsatisfactory. 'He is trying to blow his statement up into a great international event, and ignoring the realities entirely. Do you think I should advise him to fly to the USA and see Ike?' I thought this hardly a straightforward suggestion, since obviously the Old Man cannot fly the Atlantic, and anyway what would be the point? I think A.E. felt it might help to 'expose' the situation. Anyway I advised against it, and I think it has been dropped. In talk with Kirk and Pat Dean about the unsatisfactory set-up for controlling some of our Whitehall work A.E. said it was no use asking the PM to undertake any administrative reforms – he simply would not take it in, and would never interfere with the 'old faces', so could it not wait 'two or three months'. He seems quite certain the change is coming.

Great excitement in the House of Commons after the PM's statement on the H-bomb. Backbenchers of the Labour Party duelling with the Speaker on points of order and trying unsuccessfully to adjourn the House. Thoroughly enjoyed the sport.

A.E. made a nice little speech to me about being 'a very good Private Secretary and I shall miss you'.

Home by the usual train and found Julian back from school. He has got his remove and ran fourth in junior half-mile. He had brought back two pieces for violin, cello and piano which we played after dinner with great success, N. playing the piano. Great fun, and resolutions to get a lot more.

31 March

Glorious spring morning. Julian came to London with me, and we travelled with Pat Rathcreedan and Mrs Makins. Conversation about Shakespeare's tragedies. Why is Othello intolerable, Lear not so? Mrs M. thinks because jealousy is so much more unpleasant than ambition, pride. I thought it was because Othello's jealousy was misplaced. It seems the Elizabethans did not see the same objection as we to unexplained, unreasonable intervention in man's destiny by outside forces. We want to introduce reason always, and put things right 'with a few well-chosen words'.

Left Julian at Marble Arch to walk down Oxford Street shopping, and I to the FO where I had a terrible day. A.E. highly irritable over everything. PQs all wrong for him, and a lot of trouble with Arthur Lewis [Labour MP], who seems to have got hold of a letter from Lady Churchill to Frau von Neurath mentioning *me* (!) as saying that if it were not for the Russians, Neurath would be freed.

Then came messages from Paris that the French do not want us to announce our new measures of association with EDC as planned on 5 April. A.E., furious, kept saying they are such a miserable contemptible

Government they cannot even say 'yes' when we offer them help. He was minded to reject their request, and publish on 5 April, but we shall have to stop him doing that. Selwyn and Tony agree; the whole point of our measure is to help, not embarrass the French. A.E. said, 'Evelyn, put it in your diary; never in all my experience have I known such conduct.' But poor Bidault is doing his best; he wants to get his Parliament into recess before he signs the agreement with us. A.E. should understand that – and will.

A terrible Cabinet, slow, waffling and indecisive, which had to be continued in the afternoon. W.S.C. sending messages to Eisenhower every half hour about the hydrogen explosions – not with the object of stopping them, or affecting them in any way, but in order to be able to give the impression in the House that he (or, to be fair, this country) plays a large part in arrangements for these tests. Even Soames is exasperated with him, and the disclosure that we have had facilities to watch the explosions may mean the end of the co-operation we have had, sub rosa, from Strauss. No arguments of this sort affect the Old Man, who vents his feelings by sending peevish telegrams to Roger Makins. A.E. says, not for the first time, 'This simply cannot go on; he is gaga; he cannot finish his sentences.'

Lunch at No. 1 for some Iraqi politicians. Was rather impressed by Heathcoat Amory, Secretary for Overseas Trade, expounding on trade policy to my Iraqi neighbour. A.E. in an exalted frame of mind, trying to persuade the Iraqis to do more useless propaganda, to offset the Egyptians.

To cap the day, Molotov has now asked if he can join NATO! Suitable news for 1 April (tomorrow).

Took Julian to dinner at the Turf Club, and we walked back across the park to Connaught St.

1 April

Attlee put down a PNQ to the PM this morning, about Molotov's note. A.E. determined to take it himself, and had me send a message to No. 10 to that effect. Result – a message that the PM thinks 'as it is addressed to him, he should answer it'. This news, telephoned by me to A.E. as soon as he came out of his bath (11.45), caused an outburst – 'my nerves are already at breaking point', and he rushed over to No. 10 to beard the PM in person. Won his point, but after he had got back to the FO, the PM sent a message that he would rise himself and say 'I will ask my Rt Hon. Friend to reply'. This caused another fury – 'treating me as if I needed a nurse' – and I succeeded in getting Jock to have it withdrawn. By that time, Jock was saying the PM never wanted to make the statement, couldn't care less, etc.

Bad start to a bad day. Spent until 2.30 over the statement, ate a slice of pork pie and a boiled egg in my 'cubicle' in the House, and then heard him make the statement. Not much opposition. Most people clearly think Molotov's note is a phoney. A.E. left early with John for Belfast, and N. collected me for dinner at the French Embassy. Honour of Jebbs.

N. looking lovely in her new Chinese silk dress. After dinner, I talked for hours to Pamela Berry, who seems to have something stinging her, and does not like the FO. Nancy with Salisbury-Jones. Then we drove home to High Wood, arriving 1.0 a.m. – all three children safely tucked up in bed.

2 April

Spent the morning at High Wood mostly in bed, partly practising the violin. But was then summoned to London and drove Julian and Sebastian Brett there.

5 April

As soon as I arrived this morning I was given to read the PM's draft speech for this afternoon's debate on the hydrogen bomb. It appeared he was still determined to publish the Quebec agreement, despite the efforts of Cherwell, Norman Brook and other advisers to dissuade him. It seemed obvious that Attlee would then demand publication of his own 1948 agreement, and I went round the office discovering whether there would be serious objection to that. Apparently not.

A.E. had read the draft speech and seemed reluctant to interfere. (He had been away in N. Ireland and Broadchalke for the last three days, and was a bit out of touch.) I said I thought it a pity the PM was going to make a party matter of this, and he said, 'I don't see how he can help it; they have been attacking him.' So the Old Man made his speech the way he wanted it, and brought the House down on top of himself. I have never seen such a row. Attlee red in the face, quivering with rage, 'I was too loyal', the backbenchers shouting and booing, the Tories glum and silent (Mrs Braddock, like a London fishwife, shouting over and over again 'Look be'ind yer; look be'ind yer'); all the tough guys putting on shocked expressions and yelling 'disgriceful'; 'shockin''; 'another red letter'; 'resign'; and the Old Man looking utterly dumbfounded, plunging further and further where he had not intended to go, and making it seem as if he blamed Attlee for the fact that McMahon had not known of the existence of the Quebec agreement. A most entertaining spectacle, but grim from the Government's point of view and no good for anyone. Great excitement afterwards – Norman Brook and Edwin Plowden came round to A.E.'s room to advise what he could do to save the situation. Both very wise and calm, but Christopher Soames and the PM's people in high excitement, sending for Fife Clark[1] and trying to influence the press. In all this it became apparent that Attlee, in the heat of his anger at being accused of 'abandoning' the British right of veto on the use of the bomb, had made use of a false argument. He had said that the McMahon Act (1946) prevented the US Administration from carrying out the Quebec agreement, and that is why it was dropped. But the McMahon Act did not deal with consultation on the *use* of the bomb; it affected merely exchange of information about the manufacture of the bomb. So here was something for A.E. to say in winding up. But I was very keen he should not over-state the case, because as a matter of fact Attlee did get, in 1950, assurances of *consultation* (not prior consent) out of Truman, and these have been steadily whittled away since, not only under the Labour Government, but under the present one too, and more particularly at Bermuda, where Eisenhower went so far as to say it would be 'treasonous' of him to promise to consult us before using the bomb. (He added that it would be 'treasonous' of him *not* to consult us, if there were time.) So I was very cautious about the fighting line which Selwyn Lloyd was advocating, and Edwin Plowden clearly agreed with me. There is absolutely no point, anyway, in this inter-party wrangle about the past, and my sympathies are entirely with Attlee, who was not warned that this attack would be made.

A.E. was rather difficult to handle in preparing his speech (he apologized later for being so tiresome – said that it was because his heart was not in the issue for which he had to stand up). My worst trouble was this: the whole justification for the PM's action was supposed to be that the Labour Party had been attacking him for not any longer possessing power of veto over US use of the bomb. But the quotation (from the socialist Michael Foot) which he had himself used in his speech related to something quite different – viz. getting information from the Americans about the hydrogen bomb (Hansard, col. 49). So – I was to find some good quotable attacks on the right point. Tried Central Office, tried FO, tried Edwin Plowden's staff – nothing to be found, except very general nasty remarks about the PM in the *Daily Mirror*, with which A.E. had to be contented. When eventually he made his speech, it was masterly. Morrison's wind-up had been very piano, playing down the issue and merely scolding Winston for playing party politics. As he sat down, the Leader of the House whispered to A.E. that he should say nothing more about the controversial point – which A.E. felt would have been the easy way out, but would have left the

1 Fife Clark, PR adviser to the Government.

PM out on a limb. (For everyone thought Attlee's remark about the McMahon Act had completely refuted the PM's charge.) So, instead, he dealt with the point, corrected Attlee and sustained the Old Man, but managed at the same time to soothe the House and reduce everyone to calm. A great personal triumph. Clement Davies[1] told Dodds-Parker it was the best parliamentary and debating speech he had heard for twenty-five years. Overwhelming impression that the PM has made a real bloomer and exposed his aged feebleness to the House.

6 April

The whole press reflects the opinion we formed last night – Granny *Times* very cross and spinsterish with Winston. A.E. told me he has now decided (and his colleagues agree) that W.S.C. can in no circumstances be allowed to attend a top-level conference. He wishes to speak to Lord S., Norman Brook and the Chief Whip – and has already spoken to Rab – and then 'someone' has got to beard the Old Man and tell him. No enthusiasm for this task apparently! A.E. seemed to be suggesting Norman should do it! Meanwhile it seems to be thought that his failure in the House yesterday may have the opposite effect on the old boy – make him want to cling on to repair his reputation.

Very excitable messages from Ike today, about immediate action by the six powers in Indo-China. The Department and Reading most hostile to any joint action before Geneva; but Kirk, Selwyn and I, from rather different points of view, looking for some *political* move, such as a Far Eastern Pact, which might stiffen the French, overcome for us the Anzus trouble (in which the UK are not represented) and impress the Chinese with the seriousness of further aggressions.

A.E. saw the Chief Whip and Norman Brook this evening, about how to bring the governmental issue to a point, and seemed quite satisfied. Both of them think the PM must be made to resign at latest by Whitsun, and some sort of meeting of Ministers is to be arranged at which W.S.C. will be pressed to that. Before dinner (with Woolton, doubtless on the same subject) A.E. said, 'Here is something I want you and Anthony [Nutting] to think over seriously. Do you think I should encourage the Old Man to propose a top-level meeting straight away, so as to get it over and done with, and so that I shall not be perpetually plagued with it when I take over? You see, it cannot possibly come off, because even if Malenkov agreed, Ike would refuse.' I said I was against such a step. First, it would be terrible if M. did accept and Eisenhower refused (we should then be aligned with Russia against the US); secondly I did not think the Oppo-

1 Clement Davies MP, Leader of the Liberal Party 1945–56.

sition would run this hare once Winston ceased to be PM. Half the fun of it for them was that Winston himself had produced the idea, and that he was obviously incapable of carrying it out. A.E. certainly agrees with this. He says that in no circumstances will he attend an international conference at which Winston is present; that he is incapable.

8 April

Two terrible days, in which I have been completely exhausted and out of temper. The Eisenhower plan for the Far East worrying everybody and Dulles is to visit us next Monday. The question is, can we 'go along' with him at all on his project? Certainly we are all thinking that an anti-Chinese 'declaration' immediately before Geneva would be regarded by Western opinion as a poor contribution to the success of the Conference. But maybe we can announce some line-up in support of the French, to strengthen our bargaining position at Geneva. The only trouble is, the Americans don't want to bargain and think any division of Indo-China would be disaster.

Ike has announced that he will not make bigger H-bombs than he needs!

Saw Winston in the House this afternoon, during speeches in aid of the Entente Cordiale, and thought he looked terribly old. A.E. says he thinks the poor old boy must be going to have another stroke quite soon – that he is ashen grey and taking nothing in. He said to A.E. wasn't it 'splendid news' that *Izvestia* has called for a cease-fire in Indo-China, to which A.E. says he replied: 'Don't you see it is a trap; there is no line there; it is a trap and they would overrun the whole place' – and the old boy was quite crestfallen.

Philip Noel-Baker, who seems to be more anti-Communist than the Tories, came up in the House and asked A.E. why we don't publicize Chinese breaches of the armistice in Korea. A.E. said we would and I must arrange it. Lunched alone with A.E. today and one American journalist who is doing a profile of him and is supposed to be a great expert on Russia and a great wit. We found him superficial and dull, though friendly disposed and rather nice. He talked a great deal about Stalin, whom he described as a paranoiac, and said that everyone loathed him and was infinitely relieved when he died. He illustrated his themes with 'displaced persons' stories' – the sort of jokes that go around in dictatorships, against the dictator. 'Stalin couldn't be buried in Palestine, because once a man rose from the dead there' – that sort of thing. He never asked A.E. any questions and didn't really let him do much reminiscing on his own. After he had gone, I had to stick around while A.E. had an after-lunch nap, so I read *Country Life*.

9 April

Another Comet has disappeared. Had my hair cut by 'Peter', a Welshman who told me how much he disapproved of Bevan, and how the Welfare State (except for the old) deprives men of their manhood. Said he was brought up in a strict presbyterian home and was a miner in the Rhondda Valley. 'David' my usual man, has taken over the business from 'Alfred', and had it all repainted.

The Chief Whip has heard through round-about sources that the Labour Party are going to stage a demonstration against the PM in Parliament on Tuesday. A.E. fears this will be very unpleasant; he is asked to be there (despite Dulles talks) and will presumably have to rise and defend the Old Man again. PM today agreed to have a meeting with a few colleagues about 'plans' (this should be next week), which means about his retirement and elections; but he added that if Geneva is a complete failure he might go alone to see Malenkov. A.E. says the trouble is, how can he retire without apparent humiliation, unless he can find some gesture to perform? But there is no possible gesture, and I fear the incidents will multiply and get worse. If he were wise he would announce now that he will be placing his resignation in Her Majesty's hands upon her return to England.

Preparations for Dulles – but it is still not certain he will come, and meanwhile Roger Makins has infuriated the S/S (and us) by appearing to share the State Department belief that we are responsible for the many leakages about Dulles's plans. Drafted a sharp reply. The Soviet Ambassador (Malik) asked to call, and A.E. expected some communication about Geneva, or something, but it turned out to be purely 'courtesy, on his return from leave' (most unusual) and he had nothing whatever to say. The Soviet Ambassador in Paris, on the other hand, Vinogradov, has twice been to assure Bidault that the Soviets truly want a settlement in Indo-China, and we had been inclined to think this was probably true. But Malik couldn't be drawn to say the same.

Tony and I spent an hour together in his room cutting down the Office's draft of the S/S's statement for Wednesday next, about UK relations with EDC. On this being effective may turn the French ratification – and hence the future of Europe.

10 and 11 April

Glorious spring sunshine and our daffodils, forsythia and border white in full glory, covered with 'hover bees'. Mr Coles got all the seeds in, and has broad beans and peas three or four inches high.

Catherine and Julian to their first dance – at the John Hopes (Grey's Green) – she in a new evening dress of pale mauve net and he for the first time in a dinner jacket. N. and I went to Watlington Park after dinner to see Lionel's coloured photographs of India, and then on with the Bretts and Ronaldshays to see the children at the dance. Both of ours obviously happy, and Catherine a great success – quarrelled over by Christopher and Mark [her cousins], she says. Danced with her and N.

On Sunday afternoon I had to go to town for a 5.30 meeting about the Dulles visit (he arrived earlier in the afternoon). N. drove me up, and we brought Julian back, who had been to the *St Matthew Passion* with the Eshers. Dined on the way back at the Bull, Gerrards Cross, rather expensive and full of rich but completely cockney guests – the new middle classes, with bank notes in every pocket.

12 April

In the train I read a complaint by the Ramblers' Society about a keeper in the Pennines who found some of them walking on his moors and 'cursed them in the unrestrained style of pre-war days'. As if game-keepers, too, were supposed to have lost character and smoothed themselves down to the golden age. This led to a discussion with Pat, Wyck and Mrs Makins on whether we are bloodless and effete. We do not appear to work, curse, fight or hold convictions with any of the tenacity of a great age – or even to admire those who do. At lunch for Dulles and was quite ashamed to discover how much less hard any of us work in the FO than people like Doug MacArthur and Livingstone Merchant. 8.0 a.m. they begin, and off at 7.30 p.m. and only occasionally a Sunday free. So they say, and I expect it is so. Also Livingstone Merchant says that apart from his normal work as Assistant Secretary he is obliged to appear constantly before Congressional Committees to explain State Department policy, and even to be 'quizzed' by Senators on the TV for hours on end. When I expressed horror at this, he and Butterworth[1] said that undoubtedly Foreign Policy could no longer be a matter handled by experts in secret, but must become the subject of continuous scrutiny by the masses. Even the English would have to give up the 'old-fashioned' idea of entrusting these vital matters to experts. They said the US was getting back to the concept of the Greek City–State – but in a mechanized form for the leaders were once again in direct contact with their electorate. I said I feared that democracy could not survive if *issues*, as opposed to personalities, were to be put before the public for judgement. This was the fascist referendum idea. You can fool the public about issues, but not so easily about the character and quality of leaders.

Harold Macmillan is a splendid Tory: he was at lunch too and spoke well in favour of stopping 'progress' wherever possible. Dulles has a dreadful man called Robertson, his expert on the Far East, who told me he was an intimate friend of Chou En-lai and Mao Tse-tung, but that

---

1 Walt Butterworth, Minister at the US Embassy in London.

neither he nor Dulles had any intention of taking a whisky with the Chinese at Geneva. 'You do not take a drink, when the court rises, with the criminal at the bar'. I said but you are meeting them at a conference. 'No, we are not,' he said, 'we are bringing them before the bar of world opinion.' 'I beg your pardon,' I said, 'but you are not bringing them; they are coming.' 'Yes,' he said, 'but you do not sit down and drink with ... etc.' What a fool. When I told Harold M. this he said, 'Tell them, when they are in Switzerland to do as the Swiss do.' No doubt that is just what Foster Dulles will do – for he is not half so stupid as some of his advisers. I asked this Robertson whether Dulles had entirely given up any idea of trying to play the Chinese off against the Russians at Geneva. He scorned such a thought, said it was no use, never would be, what good had it done you (British) to recognize China, they just spurn you. A wholly inelastic and opinionated man.

The talks with Dulles went quite well, and he settled for a much milder statement on S.E. Asia – *not* committing us to fight in Indo-China – than we had feared. We are 'ready to take part, with other countries concerned, in an examination of the possibility of establishing a collective defence. ...'

13 April

Meanwhile Dulles has produced some interesting ideas about the H-bomb, which were committed to paper by Denis Allen, to the alarm of the atomic experts, who called the lot in. So far as I can make out, nobody has been told – not even No. 10, except in very vague terms. A.E. announced his agreement with Dulles in the House this afternoon, and it caused the Labour backbenchers to shout at him before they had really listened to what he was saying, and Nye Bevan to weigh in, leaping to the despatch box, in a bid for leadership against his own Front Bench. But the actual agreement is so favourable to us, and so far from what Dulles's speeches before he came here led everyone to suppose he would demand, that the extremists were quite discomfited, and the opposition cloven in half. A.E. enjoyed this very much. After it was over, as they streamed out of the chamber, I heard the PM say to Christopher Soames, 'Of course I couldn't hear; this thing [his earphone] is turned off'! A.E.'s only fear is that the handling of the Indians by the CO and Clutterbuck[1] in Delhi may have been bungled, and that they may claim not to have been kept properly informed. He is most keen to carry them at least tacitly with him in the new 'Far Eastern NATO' idea. He fussed all afternoon about this – but I think it is all right.

A.E. told me that ever since he had to do with the FO he had admired

---

1 Sir Alexander Clutterbuck, High Commissioner to India.

each spring a certain tree in St James's Park, just behind the Horse Guards memorial, which comes out yellow–green in bud. So I went up to a gardener there, an old man with a birch broom and a bowler hat, who told me it was a golden sycamore. Realized that the bowler hat is Edwardian uniform for a park gardener.

There has been a spate of defections from behind the Iron Curtain lately, culminating today in one Petrov, head of the NKVD in Australia, who has given us some news of M[aclean] and B[urgess]. As I always imagined, it began at Cambridge.

14 April

Catherine's report came this morning. Excellent. She has been working hard, and of course they all love her. We had a great argument in the 8.48, in which Mrs Makins maintained against us all the quietist, pacifist thesis, and I did not realize until told afterwards that she is a Quaker. It all turned on the 'exposure' of Oppenheimer, the American atomic scientist.

Today A.E. made his statement about our putting an armoured division into EDC. It went well and he was pleased. Had to entertain Eric Berthoud and Brosio (Italian Ambassador) for some time in the House of Commons, while A.E. dashed in and out for divisions.

15 April

A.E. says the PM produced an idea in Cabinet about Egypt. Hard to see exactly what it amounts to – but the gist is that if Dulles would agree to an Anglo-US 'statement' expressing joint interest in Middle East defence, freedom of the Suez Canal, maintenance of the base, etc., rather on the lines of the S.E. Asia statement of this week, then it would serve as sufficient 'cover' for us to 'scuttle' from Egypt. This, apparently, could be combined with our plan for Anglo-American civilian contractors running the base itself. There may be something in this. But it will mean inducing Dulles to slap down Caffery once for all, who continues to urge that there must be no 'ganging up' between US and UK over Egypt.

Lunched at Claridge's with the Burmese Foreign Minister, a nice short friendly man. A.E., Alex and Attlee, [Lord] Listowel, Tahourdin and I the only Englishmen, matched by five Burmese. A.E. made a great point of wanting the Burmese to be represented at Geneva when Indo-China is discussed, on the grounds that they are a 'neighbouring power'. Some talk about the Chinese, Chou En-lai, etc., but the Burmese didn't seem to know anything about them, how much influence Chou En-lai has, or what line they are likely to take in Geneva. But he was stoutly anti-Communist, and told how the Chinese Ambassador in Rangoon refuses ever to speak. Then Attlee talked of the Russians and how the only human experience he ever had with them was when he spent an afternoon playing table-tennis with Litvinov's children. He also told how a stranger came up to him in the London Underground and said, 'Are you not Mr Attlee? How is it safe for you to be here? I do not understand.' To which Attlee replied, 'Yes, I am Mr Attlee, it is quite all right. Why are you so worried? Where do you come from?' 'Romania.'

Alex, who is a sweet, simple soul, proceeded to argue that having no police protection at all is in some ways more protection than being surrounded by police. When he was Governor-General of Canada, President Truman came to stay with him. Despite the splendid Mounties, the G-men 'came pouring into my house. It was most annoying.' He told this so simply and touchingly that we all laughed.

Attlee surprised us by making a joke about Bevan, who has today challenged his leadership and resigned from the 'Shadow Cabinet'. A.E. had been studiously avoiding any mention of the name.

Discouraging accounts of Nehru's attitude towards our S.E. Asia collective security plans. He says the Americans are trying to 'hem in' India! A.E. was furious, said Nehru is blind beyond the end of his nose, whose only interest is bagging Kashmir and Pondicherry. 'Within your lifetime, India will have either broken up into little pieces because of this man, or gone Communist while he fiddles around, complaining about the Americans.' Nevertheless, he asked me to draft a message to Nehru, which I did, trying to keep him on the rails about the pact.

Had a long, long letter from Violet Bonham Carter, complaining that A.E. does not answer her letters.

Home for four days' Easter holiday. New curtains in the drawing-room.

16–19 April

Easter weekend. Four clear days at High Wood. Redecorated my room, finished polishing the new top on my dressing-table, and built a brick border to the beds in front of the house. A picnic with the Bretts in glorious spring sunshine (aided by a bonfire). We dined at Stonor, and Julian Stonor told us he had that day discovered an inaccessible room at the back of the house, where perhaps will be found the illegal Catholic printing press of the sixteenth century, and the hidden chalices and reliquaries which anti-Catholic governments came time and again to look for. A nice farmer called Birkin was also there with his actress wife; he farms on the Thames banks near Henley and told us that on Bank Holidays the trippers come armed with wire nippers to cut the fences of his fields and let his cattle out.

I was not disturbed by the office, but A.E. tells me he had 'a bloody weekend' because of various telegrams from Washington and the fact that he could not get hold of the right Under-Secretaries at the right time to advise him. Kirk was away ill, Denis Allen rightly inaccessible in Devonshire and the office in the charge, by rotation, of Harold Caccia, Frank Roberts and Roddie Barclay. No continuity.

The telegrams related to the Dulles plan for S.E. Asia security, and revealed a divergence of opinion as to whether A.E. had agreed to the first meetings taking place before Geneva. Roger Makins seemed to be taking the American view that we *had* agreed, and received sharp reprimands, drafted by A.E. himself round the edges of his telegram copies.[1]

21 April

Luncheon for Casey and Mike Pearson, with Norman Robertson,[2] at which we went over the Geneva problems and found Canada and Australia absolutely in agreement with us and ready to work very closely with us at the Conference. They are to send a representative to our delegation meetings each morning.

Went over to see Jock Colville about a peerage for Oliver Harvey. He told me the PM is *not* now thinking of retiring at Whitsun (!) but 'might go at the end of the session *provided* he is not given any impression that he is being pushed'. In other words, no one is to say a hard word to him, or speak of his retirement in any way. Jock also said that the PM had been impressed with the way A.E. had faced a hostile House in defending him (W.S.C.) over the Quebec agreement, and was more disposed on account of this to consider him fit to succeed. I expressed astonishment at this, and Jock added, 'Oh, but he has not been at all sure that the Government could hold together if he were to retire.' A.E.'s comment on what I told him of this was that Whitsun is the last date his colleagues will stand. If the Old Man doesn't go then, the Government will break up – several of them will resign. We shall see.

Nancy came to town and we dined at the George and Dragon, Brompton Road.

Mike Pearson's definition of a fanatic ... 'one who redoubles his efforts after he has lost his aim'.

---

1 See facsimile on page 21.
2 Canadian Ambassador in London.

Chapter Seven

The Geneva Conference, 1954

One positive achievement of the Berlin Conference of January to February 1954 was an agreement to summon a five-power meeting, including the Chinese, to discuss the situation in Indo-China.

The French were losing the struggle against Ho Chi Minh and the Viet Minh, backed by the Russians and the Chinese. By early April the French Army at Dien Bien Phu was surrounded; its surrender would be a resounding set-back to the attempt to contain Communism in South-East Asia. It was partly this which brought Dulles to agree to American participation in the Geneva Conference despite the fact that the US did not recognize 'Red China'. The Conference presented a dramatic challenge to Eden's negotiating skill, with the French in a tight corner needing encouragement, the Americans concerned above all to 'contain Communism' and the Commonwealth (by whose approval he always set so much store) uncertain and divided in its attitudes. As co-chairman with Mr Molotov he played a dominant role in the Conference.

I handed over the duties of Private Secretary to Sir Anthony Rumbold half way through the Conference, and returned to London to take up new work in the Foreign Office.

22 April

Day started badly, with A.E. impatient that we were not in the flat early enough to clear him of papers before departure. A wild drive to Heathrow, N. driving and Andrew Stark in the back, trying to keep up with the Humber. Usual TV and radio session, but indoors this time. I felt very much out of sympathy with the keen mood. Lovely smooth flight – met by Bidault, Gladwyn and Cynthia, Kit Steel, Michael Wilford and others. G. put me in his car with him and A.E. and he took advantage of the drive into Paris to give A.E. a long account of the latest position on the Saar. I was unfortunately in such desperate need to relieve nature (having had a large gin and It in the plane) that I could think of nothing except how brave it would be to stop the car and the cortège and all the police motorcyclists, in order to pay a short visit to a Parisian pissoire *en route*. I recall, however, that the French have made some concessions and there is still hope.

Straight to lunch, with the Dulleses, Doug MacArthur, Livingstone Merchant and Walter Robertson as guests here.

A depressing and bewildering day. Bidault is right back to his Bermuda form, worn out, garrulous, ironical and obscure. The French papers headline calamity in Dien Bien Phu, and Bidault is hysterical about it. Dulles having irritated B. beyond endurance this morning, and provoked an excessive reaction, came to us with stories of complete French moral surrender, which are much exaggerated I am sure. Nevertheless we feel sure that the fall of Dien Bien Phu will occur at the worst possible moment, as Geneva opens, and the question will be, how far does it shake the French will to resist anywhere? The general British view seems to be that there are compensatory factors which would make possible a negotiated settlement with the Chinese – e.g. we do not know how much they themselves are being hurt, how far they are keen to stop the fighting, how far they may be scared by Dulles's 'noises off', with air lifts, security pacts, threats of atomic war. In other words, the Americans and French are being excitable and depressed, and the British, we think, steady and dour.

We met '*à trois*' (if that is the way to describe a meeting of about thirty persons) at the Quai d'Orsay in the afternoon, and poor Bidault was scarcely making any sense at all. Some thought he was drunk, but I doubt it very much. He made a great fuss over agreeing to the joint reply to the latest Soviet note, and said that he was casting himself to the wolves, into the waves, under the train, but we could not quite make out which wolves, waves, train. He also read out a curious 'declaration of French intentions' in Indo-China, which seemed admirable, in that it announced their intention to defend the Associated States at all costs, but which he seemed later to explain away as merely '*une tendance*' which he did not intend to publish, and of which we could not extract a text afterwards from his delegation. Dined late with the Steels, and met the *New York Herald Tribune* European diplomatic correspondent, Cook (and his wife), who is going to Geneva, and Con O'Neill. I drank no wine, and went back early to be available when A.E. returned from a Brussels Treaty dinner. Could not get to sleep when I eventually got to bed, and had to take a pill at 2 a.m.

23 April

Papers full this morning of the new defection of a Soviet agent in Berlin. Impression that the Soviet Secret Service are undergoing grave malaise, resulting perhaps from the disgrace and fall of Beria.

Today is devoted to N A T O. Full (public) session at Palais de Chaillot at

10.30, where I met many old friends from my NATO days. Bidault in chair, and seemed to have recovered himself from last night. A.E. gave lunch to the 'non-Brussels NATO representatives', including the new Italian MFA Piccioli, to whom Gladwyn talked fluent Italian all through luncheon, and the Norwegian (Lange) and Greek (Simonopoulos) whom A.E. regaled with accounts of his own political prowess. I sat between the Turk and the Icelander and did not enjoy myself much – perhaps because, though the lunch was excellent, and quite up to Harvey standards, I again drank no wine.

It was a glorious, warm spring afternoon, and I did not go at first to the NATO meeting, but wrote some telegrams about Egypt instead. When I got down to the Palais de Chaillot I was told Bidault had been drunk again, and had kept the Council all afternoon doing almost nothing. I joined the meeting for a bit and it was pathetic to hear him, loquacious, sentimental, brittly ironical and weary, weary. Frightful impression of mental collapse, coupled with a histrionic show of courage and morale – '*Aujourd'hui les châtaigniers sont en fleur. Quand nous nous réunirons encore, en Octobre, qui sait? J'espère qu'elles ne seront pas tout à fait défleuries.*' The news from Dien Bien Phu must be pouring in, and all bad. He made a great speech about French failure to ratify EDC, thanking US and UK for what they have done, which made us all uncomfortable. Our experts here are all of the opinion that EDC will not go through and that it is high time we stopped basing ourselves on the belief that it will. They say we ought to be working out alternatives with the French.

When A.E. and Gladwyn got back from the NATO dinner with Bidault they had grave news (all admittedly through Dulles, not the French) about the imminent fall of Dien Bien Phu. French say nothing can be saved unless there is a 'massive air strike' by US within the next seventy-two hours. Dulles apparently quite accepts the view that this would be wholly ineffective, but is so gloomy about French will to resist at all, anywhere in Indo-China, that he may urge Eisenhower to take steps which would lead to all-out American intervention. This could lead to US war with China and incalculable consequences. A.E. has got his promise to do nothing without consulting us. A.E. wrote out a telegram to the PM in his own hand, while Gladwyn and I and the Military Attaché, Lamb, made suggestions. A.E. seems to discount any further French resistance in Indo-China at all, and fears that this collapse will mean the end of the French Government, and perhaps the sliding of France into neutralism. He is therefore urging the PM that we should agree to military talks with the Americans about a guarantee for Siam. But Lamb and I argued that the Chinese are not likely to attack Siam now – possibly they will try to infiltrate and communize it over the next six months – and that our first task should be to stiffen French morale so that they do not throw in the sponge altogether, just because of the loss of one fortress. They must be made to resist at least until the Geneva Conference. For a posture of continued resolution in the Delta coupled with American 'noises off' is the only card the French have to play in getting a settlement with the Chinese. And the French who have to be stiffened are the politicians in Paris, not the soldiers in the Delta. This is very grim. Dulles says the French leading politicians are completely demoralized, and even General Gruenther says he has never known their morale so low. Certainly Bidault seems on the verge of collapse. Everyone is talking of 1940. We, however, went to bed determined not to despair until we hear the news *direct from the French* in the morning. Gladwyn is to see Parodi.[1] The Americans may be exaggerating. However, despite a half pill, I only slept from 1.30 to 5.30 and awoke very tired.

I spent an hour with Tony Rumbold, telling him the secrets of the Private Secretary's trade. He seemed to be pretty well informed about the personalities concerned. He seems to take comfort in the thought he is not likely to have A.E. for more than a few months, and that he knows and likes Harold Macmillan.

24 April

Another glorious day, but not for us. In the morning A.E. received first Marjolin, Catani and Harry Lintott,[2] to hear about the forthcoming OEEC exercises; then Casey and Mike Pearson – in the courtyard of the garden in the sunshine. Casey and Pearson very much in agreement with us about the impossibility of agreeing to joint air action in Indo-China, and also on the need to bring Asian countries in to any defence organization. A.E. told Casey we would look after Australian interests in the USSR if asked to do so. Then came the Portuguese MFA (de Cunha) to ask for our help with the Government of India over Goa. We think we might be able to say something to Nehru, but have not yet decided what and don't believe it will be effective. Nehru is on the grab.

After lunch, serious things began to happen to our day. A.E., Harold and I went to Ambassador Dillon's house in order (we thought) to discuss a number of assorted and harmless questions with Dulles. When we arrived we found Dulles and Mrs Dulles in the garden, with an array of top-level army and navy officers, including Admiral Radford, and the wife of one of them playing with some dogs. Dulles took us into the study with Radford

---

1 Director-General at the Quai d'Orsay.
2 Harry Lintott, Deputy Secretary-General of the OEEC; later High Commissioner in Canada.

(×)

and Livingstone Merchant, and proceeded to tell us, in effect, that the US Government are ready to give immediate military help to the French in Indo-China provided we will do so too, and subject to Congress giving the President the necessary powers. Radford, whom we did not think very intelligent, and who is obviously raring for a scrap, said that the only thing to do, to stop French and Vietnam morale collapsing when Dien Bien Phu falls (as it must in a day or two), is for US/UK more or less to take over the conduct of the war, push the French into the background and hope that the locals will be so inspired by this spectacle that they will rally against the Communists. He was not specific as to the military action required, but it involved sending RAF squadrons from Malaya to Tongking and an aircraft carrier if we can. We were deeply disturbed by this. It seemed, moreover, to be based on an estimate of French morale and prospects which differed greatly from what the French had said to Gladwyn this morning.

I should have said that before setting off to this meeting (and while A.E. was engaged after lunch with the Italian MFA) Winston rang up and said that he thought of flying over today (moved by our telegram of last night) to see Laniel and Bidault and consult with us. Needless to say, this prospect did not please. So when Dulles produced all this, A.E. said he could not commit himself in any way but would fly home to consult. All our plans changed. I spent the afternoon dashing by car between the Embassy and the Quai d'Orsay, drafting telegrams, getting them approved and taking them back for despatch. We had a serious consultation – again in the garden – about our position (A.E., Gladwyn, Harold Caccia, Con O'Neill, Denis Allen and I) and all agreed A.E. must go home. We also found ourselves pretty well agreed how far we could go with Dulles, and what we could not do, and Denis reduced this to a bit of paper with eight points. This we carried back to London for discussion with the PM and the Cabinet. We, the three travellers, had supper at a small table in one of the drawing-rooms, going through records of the day's events with Gladwyn, while the guests collected for the nice friendly dinner party we were to have attended. (Mr and Mrs Patton, the Reillys, the John Hopes.)

We are much pressed by the dilemma. If we refuse to co-operate with the US plan, we strain the Alliance. If we do as Dulles asks, we certainly provoke the bitterest hostility of India and probably all other Asiatic states and destroy the Commonwealth. Also, a war for Indo-China would be about as difficult a thing to put across the British public as you could find. We are quite clear we can not undertake any commitment in advance of the Geneva discussions, and so far as we personally at this moment (in the air) are concerned we are sure it would be folly to try to save Indo-China by force of arms – especially air and navy alone. Even Radford says it could only be done by hitting 'the source of the trouble', i.e. China, and then what about the Soviet–Chinese alliance and what price the third world war?

We landed about 10.20 p.m. and got straight into two large cars (A.E. and Harold in the front, me in the back one) and drove down to Chequers. A nightmare drive for me, following the large Humber in a rather loose-about-the-joints saloon which reeled from side to side, and took awful risks to keep up. But we arrived safely, about 11.30 p.m., and were received at the door by Montague Browne. In the large hall was the PM in a kind of silken two-piece suit, covered by a silk dressing-gown – no collar or tie – also Sarah Churchill and her husband and Mrs Duncan Sandys. We were given a drink, and A.E. showed the PM the eight-point policy which we had brought with us. He seemed to like it, but his comments were of a somewhat reminiscent and apparently inconsequent character – 'We have thrown away our glorious Empire, our wonderful Indian Empire, we have cast it away' – the thought being, I suppose, why should we fight for the broken-down French colonial effort after that? He took us in for a cold supper, served by WAAFs, just the three of us with the old boy sitting with us smoking a cigar. There he read some of our telegrams, but again he was talking more of other things. 'Of course when I go to see him, I shall talk atomics' came suddenly in, when I thought we were on the subject of Ho Chi Minh – for he had just received Ike's answer to his telegram suggesting that he go over again to Washington in May. The answer says yes in principle, but does not fix a date. Winston said, 'Do you think it is discouraging? Clemmie thinks the words "of course" indicate that he is annoyed.' The phrase was 'of course you are welcome' or something of that sort. He said to A.E., 'You must naturally come with me', at which A.E. looked very sour, as he does not at all approve of the trip. PM also said that he is going to meet the Queen at Gibraltar on her return, but nobody is to know until he actually lands. Then he started bemoaning everything that has happened recently to upset the Russians. 'Things have turned sour – I have that feeling.' The Petrov case in Australia, the defection of the Soviet agent in Berlin and the 'insulting' note which the Americans have sent to the Soviet Government about that, were the cases he mentioned. He said that after all the Communists had made very little use of assassination as an instrument of policy – ever since Trotsky they have behaved with remarkable restraint in that regard. (I was told afterwards that he was thinking primarily of the surprising fact that he himself has never been assassinated by Communists!) None of us dared contradict all this – only A.E. looked weary and eventually said he would like to go to bed. So the old boy toddled off, looking like an old granny of about a hundred smoking a cigar, and Montague Browne fluttered about, visiting my bedroom in the far recesses of the house several times with messages. I slept very badly – perhaps because I was in 'the prison room', where Lady Mary Grey, sister of Lady Jane Grey, was incarcerated for two years by Queen Elizabeth. There are some scribblings on the wall, said to have been made by her.

25 April

I woke very early and wrote out the following notes, which I used on A.E. later in the day:

1. There is no hope of preventing large portions of Indo-China from remaining under Communist control.
2. If anything is to be saved, a negotiated settlement involving partition is the only way.
3. Our object should therefore be to provide the French with sufficient bargaining power to negotiate a partition settlement at Geneva.
4. Every day in which the military situation deteriorates reduces the bargaining power of the French. Therefore we should consider the possibility of a cease-fire. To this end we should:

(1) Increase to the utmost Chinese uncertainty and apprehension as to what might be the consequences of failure to make a settlement and encourage any tendencies that may exist in the Chinese to want an end to the fighting.
(2) Encourage the French to feel that a negotiated settlement is worth holding out for – i.e. that it will preserve something for the French Union and be guaranteed by the Great Powers.

These objectives are not served by actual military intervention before the negotiation. In present circumstances the threat of such intervention is more potent than the reality. The Chinese, and even more certainly the Russians, do not want this conflict to develop into a major war with no certainty that non-conventional weapons will be barred.

Up very early to telephone our eight points to London, so that they would be duplicated for Cabinet at 11.0. Then we drove in convoy to London, Harold and I in the second car with Montague Browne, who told us a good Winston story: 'If I was God, and mankind blew itself to bits with H-bombs, I should not give them another chance. I should be afraid they would get *me* next time.' On arrival at No. 10 I took A.E. in, explained to him some notes which Harold and I had prepared in the car, and then launched him into Cabinet. Back in my office, it was quite a shock to discover that despite all our activity this was a Sunday morning; no one about, no usual facilities. Rang N. at High Wood, and all well there.

Our plan had been to fly back at 5.0 p.m. to Paris, see the Ambassador and then fly at 8.0 p.m. by Air France to Geneva. But the PM insisted we should have a special RAF plane, which upset all our arrangements, and got us into a terrible muddle with Paris, especially over Clarissa who had by that time changed her own plans (without telling us). However, it was a good thing we were in a special plane, because our departure kept being put off by new developments in the crisis, until eventually we left at 6.0 p.m.

The trouble was this: no sooner had the Cabinet unanimously endorsed our eight points, and supported A.E. in all his actions, than M. Massigli announced that he must come and deliver an important message from Bidault. A.E. had by then gone off to lunch at the Carlton Club with the PM and Oliver Lyttelton (and been occupied, he says, in a dour struggle to keep O.L. from resigning from the Cabinet – on some personal grounds, I think). So Massigli came at 2.30 – we being due to leave for the airport at 3.15. A.E. kept him waiting half an hour but got a bellyful when he came. Massigli produced the text of a letter from Bidault to Dulles saying Dien Bien Phu could be saved if there were a massive 'air strike' by USA in the next few days. State Department (Bedell Smith) had told their Ambassador that US was willing to do this, and the President would obtain the necessary powers from Congress next Wednesday – *provided* that HMG would at once join in an undertaking to 'resist communism, by force if necessary' and build a common front in Indo-China. In other words, all the blame being put on us. Nothing had been said to us, and we were furious at having ourselves used as whipping-boys in this way. The PM had to be called back to No. 10, and the Chiefs of Staff collected all over again, and again they refused to be committed to action in Indo-China. Everyone quite clear that it would be folly, ineffective, fatal to our relations with Asiatic opinion, fatal to the Geneva Conference and liable to rend our own public opinion in half. A.E. thought the UK Government would fall if it tried to agree.

Having got this firm opinion from the Cabinet, the question was how to convey it to the French. I urged that he should not say anything to Bidault until we had discovered *direct* from the Americans what it was they were prepared to do and what they really thought the prospects of success. So we gave Massigli the slip, swept off to Heathrow and got into our shining Queen's Flight Hastings. Unfortunately we had to stop in Paris to pick up Clarissa, and there was Bidault on the tarmac, waiting for our reply. So we went into a waiting-room and there, over a pot of hydrangeas, A.E. gave B. the negative decision. Deep gloom; but Bidault obviously understood and even (I think) agreed with our decision, though he lamented it. A sort of 1940 feeling – yet none of the Sunday crowds watching these goings-on at the airport seemed conscious of tragedy. So we left poor Bidault, and got back into our aircraft. Harold and I sat at a table writing records of the day's events, and we had a moderately smooth journey to Geneva. One big bump which upset the tea-pot, and a warning of lightning storms over the Alps, but that was all. Cold supper on board. Arrived about 9.45 p.m. at the Beau Rivage, where I last stayed in 1935, on Sam Hoare's staff for the Abyssinia Assembly. Immediately Dulles came round to see us (we were not very welcoming) to hear the result of our journey to London. We had a disagreeable session – Dulles and MacArthur, A.E., Harold and me – in which A.E. put very firmly the Cabinet's line. D. seemed to have no explanation for having failed to tell us what he had told the French, but he did say (thereby in effect denying Bedell Smith) that he was against any air strike to save Dien Bien Phu. He thought it would be ineffective and that 'we do not yet have the political basis for taking military action'. So the whole Bedell Smith incident was little more than an attempt to bounce us, and to shift the blame for the fall of Dien Bien Phu on to us.

Wrote the record and got late to bed, where I set down my reflections, as follows:

1. Dulles is after all *not* advocating an 'air strike'. He admits that Dien Bien Phu must fall.
2. He is concerned with the effect of this on the French.
3. He does not rule out the possibility of a partition settlement but sees that no such settlement can be reached if the French collapse entirely.
4. Therefore he wants to give the French 'expectation of help to come' sufficient to make them carry on.
5. So do we. We have offered to guarantee any settlement reached.
6. Must more be done to bolster French morale?
7. This depends on how effectively and speedily we can get to grips with the Chinese on the Indo-China negotiation. If we could start the negotiation at once, put forward a solution and back it with every poker trick we possess, even including alarming American atomic moves, we might well find the Chinese ready to talk.
8. It will be a game of poker. We may have to take extraordinary measures to keep the French face straight – e.g.:

Action:
(1) Determine our own idea of a reasonable partition based on Bidault's ideas, whatever they are. Find these out urgently.

(2) Try to start discussions with Chinese/Russians at earliest possible moment on Indo-China.

26 April

Feel ever more strongly this morning that my reflections of last night are correct. We must get the conversations on Indo-China going *soon*. There is no time to waste, for every day which passes weakens us in *two* respects – (1) Dien Bien Phu gets nearer capitulation, (2) the natural reaction in the West against foolish American proposals weakens the deterrent effect of the fear that they might act. Already Cye Sulzberger has leaked the story that the French have asked for an air strike and that it has been refused. Thus the Chinese get daily more assurance that nothing will happen to them.

A.E. is so anti-American today that it is hard to get him to look for positive ways of bringing Dulles to a more patient frame of mind.

In the morning A.E. went with Denis Allen twice to see Molotov, as a result of which they reached agreement on all the procedural questions for the Conference. The Chair is to rotate between the Siamese, Molotov and A.E. This is rather a satisfactory solution, though I fear it will give more burden and work to A.E. Dulles was rather put out when he first heard of it – but played up well.

We had the three Commonwealth Foreign Ministers to lunch, and found them still entirely in agreement with us. Mike Pearson and Webb [of New Zealand] particularly firm against any military commitment, and against any move to call a public meeting of the ten countries (US, UK, France, three Associated States, Australia, New Zealand and Philippines) proposed by Dulles for membership of the S.E. Asia Security Pact, until the Geneva Conference has had a chance to show its paces. Casey agrees too, but put in a reservation about Australia having to be careful not to discourage this new US interest in S.E. Asia and Pacific security, which is so much a matter of life and death to them. They read all our telegrams, and took away copies of our 'eight points'.

We all went up at 3.30 to the United Nations building for the first meeting of the Conference. First time I had seen this very fine building. Most of the delegations were assembled, when we arrived, in the Council Chamber with striking murals by a Spanish painter (Serle?). A sort of double horseshoe arrangement of seating, in which we found ourselves within about six yards of Chou En-lai, on our left a little in front, and of Molotov the same distance to the left, a little behind. Molotov and his cronies – those who were in Berlin, i.e. Gromyko, Zaroubin, Troyanovski etc. but *not* Malik – exchanged friendly nods with us all, and one almost felt a common feeling with these white men amongst all the little yellow fellows who teemed on every side – Burmese, North Koreans, South

Koreans, Siamese, Philippinos, Chinese. The Chinese all seemed to be dressed the same – in blue high-collared suits – but apart from that, how is one to tell friend from foe? Prince Wan, of Siam, took the Chair, let in about 200 cameramen for ten minutes, made a pretty speech, read out a telegram from the President of the Swiss Republic, and got through all the procedural business in forty minutes. Then we trooped out again. A.E. went up to Molotov and asked him to present him to Chou En-lai, who looks a pretty serious and businesslike chap, and there was a deal of hand-shaking.

But all this while, A.E. was in a very excitable and increasingly impatient mood. He kept complaining about the procedure, wanting things to go faster, and making me and Denis Allen, who could of course do nothing about it, very uncomfortable. Then unfortunately the car was badly held up, on departure, by a fleet of Chinese cars, and everyone was roundly cursed, the driver, the detective, me, Lord Reading, the United Nations and the entire Swiss people. It was a glorious sunny day, so I said why don't we walk, and Reading said why don't you come and see the villa where the delegation works? Both these suggestions were unfortunate, for when we got to the villa A.E. was enraged to see the delegation offices surrounded by green grass, chestnut trees and sunshine, while he was forced to live and work in 'a filthy hotel, noisy, smelly, uncomfortable, insecure etc. etc.' All sorts of unfortunate people who were not responsible in any way got blown up, and the whole organization of the delegation was condemned from top to bottom. Reading and I were rather upset, especially Reading. Eventually I got A.E. away, and he calmed down in the car. I even managed to say a word about the dangers of too great a split with the Americans. I pointed out that though it was true that the British public would thank him for not letting them get into a war for Indo-China, they would not be best pleased if they woke up to find the Communists rolling into Malaya, and all American sympathy and support withdrawn from us. They would wonder why they had not been warned. This seems to have 'taken' to some extent.

I was much concerned over this episode. I am wondering whether I have enough confidence in Clarissa, and enjoy enough of hers, to say can't she stop him from drinking wine at luncheon when he is under such great strain. It makes him too elated, and I am sure it is a mistake.

After this we drove out to Bidault's villa seven kilometres out on the Route de Lausanne, to discover from him if we can what he means to do about Indo-China. It was rather a more promising meeting. I travelled there with A.E. and Reading, and managed to put in a word to the effect that he should try to probe a little the prospects of a negotiated settlement, and thus get us away from Dulles's perpetual clamouring for military action and 'declarations of joint intention'. This also 'took', and we got down to quite serious talk about the possibilities. It is true that A.E.'s remarks annoyed Dulles, who subsequently said he thought we were trying to press the French into a cease-fire; but I don't think Bidault thought so. De Margerie[1] was helpful, and there are glimmerings of a constructive approach – though maybe this is due merely to the fact that for some reason the expected final assault on Dien Bien Phu did not take place yesterday. It is not easy always to remember, in these sunny Geneva surroundings, the ghastly horror of Dien Bien Phu, with the wounded being driven out from the flooded cellars into the gunfire above.

After this, and when I had done all the records, the strain relaxed. A.E. and Clarissa went out together to dine in a restaurant, and I went similarly with Con O'Neill and Humphrey Trevelyan,[2] and unwisely ate a huge plate of boiled bacon, frankfurters and cabbage, with beer. Bed early for the first time for a week, and got a good night's sleep without a pill. But somewhat overeaten and must avoid getting fat again.

27 April

The weather had broken a bit today, and the mountains are no longer visible at all. We have not yet seen Mont Blanc.

Having at last slept rather well, I slept a bit late, and was cross to be interrupted dozens of times while I was dressing by John Priestman and others. However, it was a good morning, with no meetings until 12.30 when Dulles came, and Bidault to give us an account of his talk at 11.0 with Molotov. The only real excitement of the morning was a series of telephone calls to Chequers and No. 10, about the P M's answer to Attlee in the House this afternoon. The first of these calls produced the information that Massigli was calling on the P M, which made A.E. very suspicious, and I was instructed to say that if this sort of thing went on, we should come straight home. As it turned out, the visit *was* rather improper, for it was to convey an appeal for help from Laniel, about which Bidault knew nothing. A.E. and Bidault agreed they must put a stop to 'back-seat driving'.

Bidault's conversation with Molotov seems to have gone moderately well. They are within reach of agreeing who shall attend on Indo-China, and kindred technical points. Bidault wanted the four Berlin powers, plus China, plus the three Associated States. Molotov wants Viet Minh added.

1 Roland de Margerie, Directeur General adjoint at the Quai d'Orsay since 1950.
2 Humphrey Trevelyan (later Lord Trevelyan), High Commissioner in Germany 1951–53; Chargé d'Affaires in Peking 1953–55; Ambassador to Egypt 1955–56.

Bidault might do this – and we and Dulles are pressing him to – if he can get a 'price'. A.E. suggested that he try to get the evacuation of the wounded from Dien Bien Phu. That would indeed be something. He will try it on Molotov tomorrow.

Lunched with Harold and Livvy Merchant downstairs – a very light meal (*truite au bleu*), and while waiting for it to come had a talk with Reading, who is not enjoying himself and thinks he has in some way 'got across' A.E. I assured him it was not so, and told A.E. he must be nicer to him. Result – they had him alone to supper this evening. But he *is* rather a fifth wheel, and A.E. speaks scathingly of him and does not help him much.

Sent off my diary to N., complete up to last night.

28 April

Poor A.E. was in a dreadful state this morning, having been unable to sleep owing to the traffic outside his window. It starts about 5.30 a.m. – mostly those horrible little motor scooters which abound here, and Volkswagen too. He was indignant at having been put in this beastly hotel, where he can't speak without being overheard by Chinks, sleep, get food without endless delay. He is blaming poor Reading who came out in advance and recommended this hotel. I went to Reading, in order to convey tactfully that A.E. would not want him to travel down with him to Bidault this morning, and found he had a quiet room, not looking over the main road, which he readily offered to the Edens. But this was not accepted, and will hardly do because R.'s room is adjacent to the Chinese office, and Chinese are constantly up and down the passage! It seems to me incredible that we should have taken hotel rooms all cheek by jowl with the Chinese, but so it is. I called for the Conference and Security officers and found they had no plan for daily inspection of security, and did not even know who was responsible for it. Meanwhile, we are looking for a villa for the Edens to live in, and I shall consult Madame Morier.[1]

A.E. went off with Harold to meet Bidault (with Dulles) before B. goes in to bat again with Molotov. The idea was just to show solidarity, and not much was discussed. The only event seems to have been that Dulles lost his temper when A.E., just as they were leaving, showed him what the PM said in the House yesterday, and stalked out of the house without a word. Our relations are very bad, and we shall have to be very careful.

After that we had Casey, Pearson and Webb again, and then a press

---

1 Wife of a Swiss banker whose family I had known in London and Geneva before the war.

conference in A.E.'s dining-room. Our press seem fairly solid behind us, though of course pretty gloomy. The Edens then went off to lunch with Dulles, and I ate an omelette with Harold and Denis. Our concern today (A.E. being in the Chair at the Conference) is how to handle Korea. Only Dulles is inscribed to speak this afternoon, and the question is, whether to break off the general debate and go into subcommittee and, if so, what subcommittee? Harold favoured a 'restricted meeting' – i.e. *all* the Foreign Ministers with one adviser each. Trouble about this is, it is really just as unwieldy as the whole, and suffers from the disadvantage that it is *supposed* to be secret, and certainly will not be. Denis and I think it would be better to try for some more limited membership.

I attended the plenary today and heard Dulles's speech. Disagreeable, but not over-violent. His proposal – to reactivate the U N Neutral Nations Commission for Korea, and try to unite the country – by withdrawal of Chinese troops from North Korea. It won't go – but it covers the South Korean proposals of yesterday with a UN look. His highlight 'We know that those who live by faith prevail over those who live by calculation' – whatever that means. There is buzzing and rustling among the Chinese, and I am sure that Chou En-lai is going to make a speech.

Yes, he has taken off his headphones, and started reading in a high, singing, bird-like voice from a long written speech in Chinese script. Starts with unexceptionable sentiments about reducing tension, but is soon attacking the 'influential circles in the United States'. Praise for Soviet Union. A very severe and arrogant false history of the Korean aggression. I am upset – what is it? – frightened by the violent self-confidence of this man speaking for hundrds of millions of yellow men who, for some reason which we did not will, have become our enemies. We, the British, were never hostile to the Chinese; yet here they are preaching hatred of the white man and confident in the massive forward march of their nation, and reckoning to throw us out of Asia altogether. One feels, in a way, that it is the fault of the Americans not recognizing them; not letting them in to UNO; marching up to the Yalu; being so damned contemptuous of them. At this conference, unlike Berlin, we seem to be hopelessly on the defensive, despite the moralistic denunciations of Foster Dulles. One has only to look across the room to poor Bidault, pale, apprehensive, doomed, to see how far we have fallen back since last year. I think I have been over-impressed by all this – the serried ranks of yellow faces and blue suits, the confident handshakes between Molotov and Chou En-lai after the latter's speech, the ashen anger of Dulles. But Molotov sees it better than I, for he said to A.E. afterwards, 'Two very wise speeches' (Dulles's and Chou En-lai's). 'After all, it is just as well that two different points of view should be clearly expressed.' One is in danger of thinking of Molotov as a sort of benevolent middle-man – 'Auntie' – he smiles so nicely and talks so gently to us.

I rang up Madame Morier and went round to see them. She was lively as ever, friendly, cosy and he very much aged, looking most frail. I asked them about a villa for A.E., and immediately they had all sorts of ideas, sent for [her younger daughter] Eliane (Barbey) who lives in the same house and promised me something. Eliane came straight away in my car, we picked up the Conference officer (Col. Vergin) and went to see their two villas, one a smallish, ancient villa on the lakeside, closed for the winter and covered in paper – would do at a pinch but would take forty-eight hours to prepare – the other Le Reposoir, where I stayed twenty years ago, now in glorious condition, packed with superb furniture, pictures and books. This belongs to Madame Morier's brother, M. Pictet, and after a few telephone calls he agreed to lend it to A.E. for three weeks. Triumph. I took Eliane out to dinner on the strength of it; then returned to tell the Edens, who are thrilled. Am to ring Pictet in the morning.

29 April

As far as Indo-China is concerned, we are rather in blinkers this morning. No news from Dien Bien Phu, and Bidault's discussion with Molotov (who has incipient flu) last night over dinner led nowhere. A.E. is concentrating on Korea, being concerned at the fact that no reasonable proposition has yet been put forward from the Western side – nor can be, because the Americans feel obliged to give a further run to the ridiculous S. Korean proposal of elections in N. Korea only. So we are thinking of suggesting that the Conference go into restricted session, limited to the five big powers and the two Koreas. Apparently Dulles (surprisingly) would accept that.

This morning the Edens were snapped on their balcony with long-range cameras by two German pressmen. This made them all the keener for a move!

I spent almost the whole day negotiating with M. Pictet about the loan of Le Reposoir. Visited it with him and Mrs E. twice, and got it all fixed. In the afternoon, having missed the Conference, I sat for a while in the sun on the lakeside, watching the Swiss playing about, children on scooters, old couples on benches, men painting the boats for the summer.

At 7.0 we moved into Le Reposoir – Harold, Denis and I, with Miss Winder. The Edens came after dinner, and we had got their rooms all ready for them, their bags unpacked, fire in his bedroom. He was delighted with it.

Tomorrow I am to go with him, Harold and Denis, to lunch with Molotov to meet Chou En-lai. This will be a highlight I hope.

30 April

Awoke to the singing of birds in the chestnut trees – especially a small tit-like type with a loud voice. There is a cow with a bell in a field behind the trees; I cannot see her, but hear that gentle, egg-shell sound in the night.

We all took stock of our new surroundings, and were overjoyed. A.E. had slept soundly – after a poor start, caused by their lighting a fire in a closed fireplace and smoking them out. Nice French breakfast in the dining-room, with cherry jam.

Dulles came round for 'half an hour alone' with A.E. before lunch, and was extremely grim. Said that nobody was supporting the US; nobody had said a word to defend them against Chou En-lai's attacks; the alliance was nearly at an end; Asia lost; France finished, etc. 'We have seen the best of our times ... and the bond cracked between father and child' (*Lear*). It emerged later that he had sent emissaries to say the same thing to Mike Pearson and to M. Spaak.[1] He wants someone to make a speech, like his, attacking Communism. I think one of us had better do it. A.E. says, 'They would think in London I was mad.'

After that, we set off to Molotov's villa for lunch. The Chinese had arrived before us, so as we entered the room the only 'friends' we saw were the Russians – Auntie Mol himself, Zaroubin, Gromyko, Kuznetzov, Troyanovski. They were all beaming with hospitality and introduced us to the grinning Chinese with host-like care. I cannot distinguish the recollection of one Chinese from another – except for Chou En-lai himself, a little ugly one called Se and the sinister-looking Chinese Ambassador in Moscow.

A.E. started with some business straight away, and Molotov agreed to a meeting of seven on Korea. Then we drank. Then we went in to lunch, where we ate about twenty courses, rather well cooked and served by extremely hygienic-looking Russian maidservants with 'comely' rustic faces. I tried some conversation with Se, who was opposite me, but discovered little more than that he was *not* the same Se as was up with me at Cambridge. Molotov in excellent form, always popping up to propose toasts, and all the chairs scraped loudly each time on the parquet floor. Caviar, duck, eels, chicken, meat, ice cream.

First topic – why is Dulles leaving on Sunday? A.E. hard put to it to answer. Second, why have you not brought Mr Nutting? Third, A.E. to Chou En-lai, 'You were very rough to us yesterday. You call us a wicked Colonial Power. Look what we did for India, Burma. We recognize you, I sometimes wonder if you recognize us.' Chou, 'You don't recognize us

---

1 Paul-Henri Spaak, Belgian statesman; I served as his political adviser when he was Secretary-General of NATO 1957–61.

in the U N.' Molotov – 'That undermines the U N.'

Fourth topic. A.E. – 'I have brought my Mr Trevelyan, from Peking, to Geneva. You never see him in Peking. Can he talk to one of your people?' Chou – 'Certainly, I have my Director of European and African affairs.' (And before the vodka was dry on our lips, Trevelyan had been invited to a meeting!) Fifth topic, what to do on Sunday if it's a fine day. Someone mentioned Chillon, and Gromyko at once spoke of Byron's 'Prisoner of Chillon'.

Zerda?

After we rose from the table the party was divided between two rooms. Molotov put Chou En-lai down on a sofa with A.E. at his side, and sat himself in an armchair alongside. The Chinese interpreter and Troyanovski were also there, and for a moment it looked as if A.E. would be left alone. So I pushed in, took a chair boldly and (assisted by Gromyko who saw the point and joined us too) joined the party. Thus I was able to make a record. Topics here: first, A.E. raised the question of the wounded in Dien Bien Phu. Both Molotov and Chou (but Molotov more warmly) agreed it should be possible to arrange a truce to get them away, but it must be done 'between the two parties concerned' – i.e. we must first agree to have Viet Minh at the Conference. Second – started by Molotov – how useful are conferences like this, for personal contacts (meaning A.E. and Chou En-lai). A.E. – 'Certainly, I am glad to meet Mr Chou En-lai. Of course, Mr Molotov and I know each other well. I always know when he is cross with me and when he is pleased.' Molotov – 'In that case, I am a bad diplomat. I should conceal my feelings.' We all laughed at this, and I, leaning back, cracked my chair. A.E., 'That is a bad diplomat, to break his host's chair.' Probably its structure had been weakened by the insertion of microphones. Next topic, the Americans. Chou En-lai very bitter against them – 'Helping Chiang Kai-shek to kill Chinese.' 'They hate and are jealous of China.' A.E. – 'On the contrary, they have loved China, and when their relations went wrong it was an emotional disappointment. Their vast new powers and responsibilities. Their honourable intentions. Ask Pearson, he knows them. Canada close to US but independent.' Molotov – 'Is Canada so independent of the US?' Molotov also said that the UK underestimates its power and influence with the Americans.

Throughout this, Molotov made the running, rather like an anxious mother bringing a farouche daughter out into polite society. Not much response from Chou En-lai, who however looked thoughtful from time to time and may have been imbibing something. His voice is quite different when he is talking privately; none of the hypnotic sing-song. Like (I am told) all Chinese, he bursts out laughing when there doesn't seem to be a joke around, and this is said to be to cover embarrassment. He has a small thin hand but a very firm handshake. His hangers-on all wear spectacles and look very young.

When we rose to go, Molotov somehow arranged for Chou En-lai to go out first, and when he had seen them to the door he came back to A.E. and said, 'That was a useful lunch, do you not think so?' almost as if he and A.E. had been dealing together with a strange fellow. We must not build too much on this impression. I think they had clearly worked out together beforehand what they were going to say – at least Chou En-lai, whose translator always seemed a little behind-hand, never showed any surprise at the change of topics. It may be that he understands more English than he admits. Neither he nor Molotov seems to know anything of each other's language.

The Americans are insisting that we should adopt, as a first bargaining position, the demand of the S. Koreans for elections *in N. Korea only* – i.e. elections to the vacant seats in the S. Korean Assembly. A.E. refuses to give his support to this proposal because he thinks it will seem to the world unreasonable, and he does not agree with putting forward mere bargaining positions publicly. But if we could get into secret session this might not matter so much.

A quiet evening. The Edens had their supper in bed, while Denis, Angela [my secretary] and I ate downstairs. We thought the Edens were safely ensconced together, but no sooner had they finished their supper, it seems, than she retired to her room and he started sending for me. I found him surrounded by newspapers, elated by the success of his message to India, Pakistan and Ceylon (which incidentally was my idea and wholly drafted by me, though it has now become one of his major personal coups) and wondering whether he should not send some more messages to someone – *n'importe à qui*! Denis and I managed to stave this off. We had better wait for replies to the first before sending more. I think A.E. is right to be pleased by the way he has handled things so far; we are widely supported, and have prevented the Asiatics from breaking away. Only two worries – one major, one minor. The first is the almost pathological rage and gloom of Foster Dulles, which we must really do something to allay. (Not easy; A.E. is fed up with Dulles, refuses to make concessions to his feelings, and almost resents seeing him.) The second is the thought that Nehru must be getting very impatient at being out of the picture, and annoyed at his failure to stampede the Colombo Conference into condemning the 'Colonial Powers', and is likely to try to send Krishna Menon here in some form or another. That nobody could stand.

1 May

The weather has turned again and it is a lovely day, of which I spent a proportion sitting on the terrace in the sun working, and even walking round the estate. I did not attend the meeting of 'the sixteen', but drove there with A.E. and saw it sit down.

At 12.0 we went to Bidault's villa, where we were kept waiting a long time by Bidault and Dulles but eventually heard a depressing account of Dulles's interview with Molotov about pooling of atomic materials. There is a wholly negative reply from the Russians. Most of the talk was about who should take the Chair when 'the nine' meet on Monday to discuss Indo-China. A.E. is advocating the Premier of Ceylon, so as to bring in the Colombo Conference of which he was Chairman. But the most notable thing about this talk was that Bedell Smith, who had just arrived from Washington, greeted A.E. effusively and said he was 'not to pay too much attention to some of the stupid things being said in USA' – thereby suggesting that perhaps he had come out with instructions which differ from Dulles's. We speculated in the car going back whether Eisenhower perhaps was more in sympathy with the line we have taken. He is very close to Bedell Smith. Both of them, being soldiers, might well differ from Admiral Radford in their judgement of the effectiveness of air/sea intervention in a campaign of this sort. As a result of this, A.E. is now hoping Dulles will go away as soon as possible, and longs to start talking to Bedell Smith. I have told him he really cannot do so until Dulles is out of Geneva and I suspect we shall be disappointed if we expect much difference of policy. But there is no doubt that Dulles and A.E. have got thoroughly on each other's nerves, and are both behaving rather like prima donnas. Dulles is said to be irritated by the 'imprecision' of A.E.'s mind.

We had the Turk (Acikalin) and the Siamese (Prince Wan) to lunch – just A.E., Denis and me, and took our coffee on the terrace in the sun, where I nearly went to sleep. This afternoon A.E. went off with Reading, Harold and Denis to the first seven-power meeting on Korea. They say it was an extraordinary affair – these bitter opponents, N. and S. Korea, Americans and Communist China, sitting round a table in a very small room and making sharp speeches at one another. Foster Dulles, sitting between the N. and S. Koreans, not knowing where to look, his mouth drawn down at the corners, and his eyes on the ceiling, sucking his teeth. Not much sign of any possibility of agreement, but still it is a beginning to have got the relative positions clear.

A relatively quiet afternoon and evening for me.

2 *May*

Woke at 5.30, but got a bit more sleep. Have got a tiresome catarrh, which causes me to swallow continuously and thus wakes me up in the mornings.

A.E. had a terrible dinner with Dulles last night. After the ladies had left the table, he and Reading were left with Dulles, Bedell Smith, Merchant and Robertson. He is not sure whether it was premeditated by them, or whether it was his own fault that they got into a prolonged session on Anglo–American relations. They all went for him, saying U K had let U S down, etc. Their new line is that they do not want us to put a single aeroplane or a single man or a single pound in; they know we are fully stretched (rather contemptuous, he thought). All they want is that we should give our moral support to whatever they think it necessary to do to save Indo-China, and to agree to a 'declaration of common intention to combat Communism in the Far East'. But what it is they propose to do, that we cannot find out. They say it is simply to train Vietnamese armies, and build up resistance in Hanoi and Saigon over the next two years. But that must mean in effect taking part in the military operations; also it seems to mean (A.E. and Reading certainly are convinced it means) taking over the direction of the war from the French. If we were to give our moral support to a programme of that kind, without knowing what they are going to do exactly, should we not be in effect approving the first steps to a third world war? That is what A.E. thinks. He foresees having to get up in the House of Commons, after American forces have landed in Indo-China, 'to direct and train the Vietnamese', and answer the question 'Did you know of and approve this move?' My own feeling is that we should be very cautious before we again turn down an American proposal. We should find out precisely what it is we are asked to give moral support to. I have strongly expressed this view to Reading, Harold, Denis and A.E. After all, we *want* the French to stand somewhere in Indo-China. Anything which the Americans can do to help and encourage them to do so, short of open and direct military intervention, ought to please us, e.g. lending them aeroplanes, even perhaps training their ground forces. These forms of assistance would not be different in character, or more likely to promote massive Chinese intervention, than the help the Americans are giving already. So do not let us turn down, blind, anything which *could be reduced* to these proportions. I wish we were in the mood to produce a set of ideas of our own for this – and put them to the Americans as an interpretation, or definition of what we would regard as action we could 'morally approve', then we might get somewhere. Unfortunately we are all steamed up against the Americans. Another thing: A.E.'s conviction is that all the Americans want to do is to replace the French and run Indo-China themselves. 'They want to replace us in Egypt too. They want to run the world.' Well, if that is the case, let us expose it, and make the French share some of the odium of opposing it. Personally, I doubt it very much, but let us find out. I hate these posturings, this taking up of rigid positions. Perhaps I will put this down on paper.

Alan drove me back at 4.30, and I tried (it being Sunday) to get a little sleep, but was interrupted first by A.E., who having been in bed all day was 'wondering whether we had any work for him', and then by a series of summonses to the telephone or to see the cook or to get drinks for the Vietnamese Minister for Foreign Affairs, who called. I am beginning to find that I am expected to be a sort of housekeeper for this entire menage. Clarissa just writes out, on pieces of paper put under her door, elaborate menus for lunch and dinner, and expects the whole thing to run itself – with two German-speaking maids and a ritzy chef who are assumed to do the catering, the shopping, the accounts, the laundry, the housework, the cooking, pressing A.E.'s trousers, answering Clarissa's bells etc. etc. Everyone comes and asks me questions – who is in to dinner? – what is to be done about wine? – is Mrs Eden having lunch in bed? – and Clarissa herself sends me notes saying '*Please*, where is the Evian water?' I am going on strike. I told A.E. this evening I propose to bring in a conference officer, Miss Brand, to run the establishment. He said I must consult Clarissa. I will send her a note.

Supper with Harold and Denis – an exquisite meal, far too much, far too rich and elaborate, cooked by our chef. After dinner we drafted telegrams, and a letter came in from Dulles which shows a great advance on his previous attitude. Also, Webb's account of the Anzus meeting shows that the Americans are becoming much more realistic. They now want discussions in Washington of the five-power staff agency (US, UK, France, Australia, New Zealand, I think) plus Siam – that is, no longer 'the ten' countries of the original Dulles SEA pact, to discuss SEA defence problems. Denis and I think we should go along with that. In that context, I don't think the presence of the French would imply any obligation to go to their aid in Indo-China, and it might give them some courage. A.E. had gone to sleep by the time it arrived, so I am keeping it till morning. Hope he will regard this as an opening to restore his relations with Dulles and get back to Anglo-US co-operation.

3 May

The Dulles letter did not go at all as we hoped. A.E. saw in it a trap; thought it no advance on Dulles's earlier position; sees no need to 'hold out a lifeline' to Dulles, as we were urging. He takes his stand flat on the Cabinet's decision which said that we are not committed to start discussions in advance of Geneva on the subject of action in Indo-China. But Harold, Denis and I still argued that there was a difference. Why should we refuse even to discuss military co-operation in SEA (provided we make clear

Eden and I enter the United Nations Assembly in Paris, November 1951

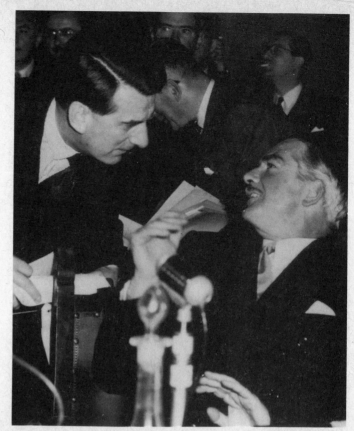

Right: On the job at the
United Nations

Below: In the library at the
British Embassy in Paris

Above: Eden, Robert
Schuman (*centre*) and Dean
Acheson, June 1952

Left: King Hussein of Jordan
(*centre*) 1953

Eden with Eisenhower, Washington, March 1953

Return from convalescence: 'A.E. very bronzed and well, but thin', 23 July 1953, with Clarissa and Lord Salisbury

Photographs of Nancy and me at High Wood by Francis Russell

The corner cupboard

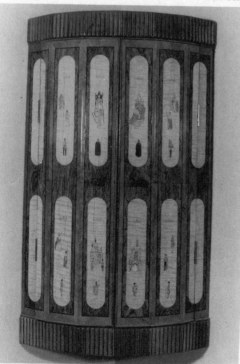

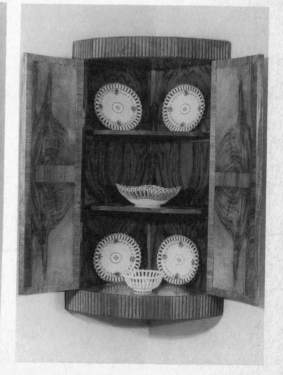

Francis Russell of the US State Department

Eden with John Foster Dulles, October 1953.

Downing Street

The Prime Minister with his
Foreign Secretary, 1954

Being met at Tehran airport by the Ambassador and Lady Stephens, 1954

The Conference of Middle East Ambassadors, Beirut, 1954. *Left to right, front row*: Sir John Nicholls (Tel Aviv), Sir E. Chapman Andrews (Beirut), Sir John Sterndale-Bennett (British Middle East Office), Sir John Troutbeck (Baghdad), myself, Sir Bernard Burrows (Political Resident in Bahrein), Horace Phillips (Consul in Jeddah), Sir Roger Stephens (Tehran), Sir James Bowker (Ankara); *back row*: John Richmond (Counsellor in Amman), Sir John Gardener (Damascus), Ralph Murray (Minister in Cairo).

Anthony Nutting and Colonel Nasser sign the Anglo–Egyptian Agreement, October 1954

Music-making at home

Brief amity: Eden and Nasser in Cairo,
21 February 1955

Harold Macmillan at his desk at the Foreign Office,
April 1955

With the last British and the first Sudanese Sudan Agent in London, 1955

Eden with John Foster Dulles at No. 10 during the Suez crisis, August 1956

Dulles, in London for a meeting of the Suez Canal Users Association, September 1956, walks from the Foreign Office to lunch with Eden with (*left*) the Foreign Secretary, Selwyn Lloyd, and Winthrop Aldrich (*right*), the US Ambassador

Above: Rough going: the Prime
Minister broadcasts to the
nation on the Suez crisis

Right: Calm waters: a boat trip
up the Thames with the
Imperial Defence College

there is no commitment to fight in Indo-China)? The argument that it would prejudice the success of Geneva is a pretty feeble one, considering what the Communists are doing in Dien Bien Phu. As a sort of wedge into the argument I have suggested that we could agree to military talks on the lines Dulles suggests provided the subject matter was declared to be to concert the action to be taken *in the event of a settlement being reached*, in accordance with the commitment which we have already publicly undertaken, viz., jointly to guarantee any such settlement. This seems to have struck a slight spark; at least A.E. has sent a telegram to Selwyn Lloyd asking for his views and saying 'perhaps I am seeing things out of proportion'.

While I was arguing this I also told A.E. about my housekeeping troubles, and he had a word with Clarissa, after which I did too. As a result, she has seen Diana Brand and has started taking an interest in a big way. The first result of this was that we were all excluded from luncheon and from the drawing-room where we have been sitting. But never mind; I am to have no more domestic responsibilities!

We persuaded A.E. to see Dulles off at the airport. There he was far from attempting any 'reconciliation' on the basis of the Dulles letter. On the contrary, he went out of his way to point out that his own 'memorandum' of 30 April, which Dulles had quoted, was merely his personal thoughts and in no way committed HMG. I warned him in the car not to do this in such a way as to suggest that he was going back on this memorandum, but I fear it was not successful. According to what Denis says, we are getting very near having cheated the Americans on this question of starting talks on SEA security. Denis told Harold and me at lunch today that when Dulles was in London A.E. *did* indicate that we should be willing to start such talks at once, provided we were not committed to any action in Indo-China. The American record showed that, but ours was obscure on the point and A.E. has always denied it. Ever since then we have been refusing to move in any way in the matter, and I am much concerned at our refusing even this latest and much less objectionable version. But A.E. says his instinct is all against the slightest concession to Dulles.

Later, we had Mike Pearson, Webb and Watt (Casey being gone away) to discuss Dulles's letter. A.E. trotted out the idea described above – let five-power staff agency meet to discuss how to guarantee, or police, a settlement. Mike Pearson saw it at once, and liked it. It is now going to become The Idea, and I am going to be unable to remember whether in fact it *was* my idea, as recorded in this diary earlier this morning. I suppose all one's ideas in a party like this are really the product of the situation and of the combined thought and talk of the group of us.

I went off, when we got back from the meeting, to cocktails with

Laurence Lemole.[1] A large party of Geneva smarties, and I was the 'lion' of the party, 'M. le Ministre', to whom all the women were brought up in serried ranks. I was naturally in terrific form and talked French like nine o'clock. After, Laurence and Eliane and their two husbands and another pair, related to them, took me out for supper at a nice cosy restaurant, where I ate a most delicate steak and then left them about 9.45. Lemole drove me back to Le Reposoir, and I found Bedell Smith had just left after dining with A.E., Harold and Denis. As soon as I walked in on them I saw there was better news. Bedell seems to agree entirely with the British attitude on Indo-China. He thinks air/sea action futile to affect the present campaign and says American ground forces will go into Indo-China over his dead body. He was surprised and delighted when A.E. produced 'his' new idea (see above), and has asked us to put it on paper; which we did there and then in front of the fire, dictating to Angela. We will sleep on it and give it to him in the morning.

This conversation was very satisfactory, and we look like being able soon to heal the rift in the Western ranks. There are three elements in this – (1) the plan discussed this evening for calling together the five-power staff agency to discuss the military implications of our promise to 'support a settlement in Indo-China', (2) agreement, which both Bedell and we think we must really get out of the French, to send off the reply to the Soviet note on NATO, (3) a real plan for Korea (elections throughout, withdrawal of troops, etc.) which Bedell now seems ready to try and swing on Syngman Rhee. A.E. shows a tendency to want to put this forward as an 'Eden plan', which Denis and I disapprove strongly of his doing. We have had enough Eden plans.

4 May

A fairly quiet morning, though A.E. was cross with me because I drew his attention to the *Journal de Genève*, which says he is 'mediating' between East and West, and told him that Con is worried about this impression. His mood is that he is not shocked by being told that he is mediating, and rather resents our suggestions that it is wrong. He said, 'I am inside right, the Americans outside right. Molotov is inside left, Chou outside left.'

Nevertheless 'the idea' has been put into final shape and was shown to the three Commonwealth chaps who liked it, and afterwards to Bedell Smith who at first was lukewarm but later said it was good. Meanwhile our main preoccupation of the day was the discovery that the French, having got Molotov to agree to the nine-power concept for the Indo-China

---

1 Madame Morier's elder daughter.

conference, are not in a position to produce their three Associated States until Friday at the earliest. They have let the Vietnam man, who was brought here with such difficulty, go off again to Paris; while the Laotian and Cambodian have not yet arrived in Europe. Thus the conference is stalled on both counts, Korea and Indo-China, and in both cases it is the fault of the non-communists. (On Korea, the Americans have not yet induced Syngman Rhee to agree to any plan remotely acceptable to the rest of us.)

After good speeches by Mike Pearson, the Ethiopian and the Dutchman the plenary adjourned for two days this afternoon. I was very exhausted for some reason. I had lunched alone with A.E. here – a most exquisite meal by our new chef – and then sat through the speeches, so I ought to have been all right. Rang N. in the evening.

A quick bite with Angela at the village bistro, while A.E. and Denis entertained Bidault and Chauvel.[1] Then a bath, re-dressed and had a post mortem after Bidault's departure. It seems he was half in despair, half courageous; half helpless, half vigorous. Terrible descriptions of Dien Bien Phu, followed by remarks like '*Mais enfin, ce n'est pas sans intérêt.*'

Winston rang A.E. up this evening, to urge that Bedell Smith should fly over to see him on Saturday. A.E. very rightly demurred. It is a ridiculous suggestion – Dulles has gone, and if Bedell Smith goes too, Bidault will go and A.E. will have to go, and the Communists will be left in full control. The Old Man is simply trying to draw the limelight back to himself. And imagine the public speculation, if the US representative flew to England to consult the PM. Everyone would think that pressure was being put on us once again. Also, it emerged that the PM had not even read A.E.'s telegrams about his talks with Bedell.

5 May

Today should by rights have been tolerable, as there were no meetings of the conference and it was gloriously sunny. But in fact it turned out very badly and I was in a rather hysterical condition by the evening. It started by my being constantly summoned to the bedside throughout the morning and fussed about this and that. The main cause of the trouble was a telegram from the PM. Last night the PM rang up A.E. and said he wanted to invite Bedell Smith over to Chequers this weekend. A.E. advised him against it, seeing that such a visit would look either as if Bedell were going to the PM over A.E.'s head, or as if there was renewed American pressure on UK to do something about Indo-China. He thought the PM had agreed. It seems that Bedell must have been given some pretty bad news by his doctor yesterday; he was feeling very low. Anyway, he entirely

1 Jean Chauvel, French Ambassador in Berne.

agreed that if he went to England A.E. must go too, and that there could be no question of their going this weekend.

John and I had lunch with A.E. at home, and I was overfed and overstrained by the end. I told A.E. that we thought of trying to get a game of tennis during the afternoon, and that was quite enough to cause him to make sure that I was never let out of his sight for the rest of the day. Even *two* attempts to get a stroll in the sun in the garden, to read and think over a disquieting letter from home were thwarted with precision just as I was rounding the corner of the shrubberies. The trouble all relates to the offer we are making to have five-power Staff Agency talks. Bedell wants to expand and generalize the terms of reference, so that they are not limited to 'the support of a settlement if reached in Geneva', but cover the situation now and after Geneva, whatever it may be. A.E. agreed a text saying this, and then got cold feet after reading the *Herald* and *News Chronicle*, and we all had a horrible time. Vallat,[1] Con, Denis summoned. I think it is quite all right, though the American press will certainly try to present it as a victory for Dulles. But why be so sensitive? However, A.E. thinks he has thrown away today the whole popular position he has established since he came here. Well, he does not really think so, but he says so. I was so exhausted and stuffy by the time this was over that I was quite unable to face the prospect of our dinner for Molotov. At the last moment I asked if I might be excused, and got Vallat in to replace me. By this means I avoided eating any dinner, and spent the time instead visiting Mike Pearson, Watt (Australian) and Webb in their hotels, and going through the text of the five-power Staff Agency plan with them. The first two gave me whisky, so I was adequately sustained. Found them quite convinced that A.E.'s concessions to Bedell are necessary and right, though Mike warned that the Americans will distort it in public presentation in order to save Dulles from the attacks of Congress. Watt of Australia, who had Keith Officer[2] with him, was positively in favour of the new text, and little Webb, in a silk dressing-gown and half undressed, raised no difficulties.

I then took a tiny little Volkswagen taxi, and bounced back at high speed to Le Reposoir. It was 10.30 and the Russians were still there – their detectives and motor cars crowding the entrance, and our detective, Dyer, whom I do not like, came up in a familiar manner and said, 'We have all been drinking whisky, we are quite happy.' But within a few minutes the party broke up, and I joined A.E., Reading, Denis and Vallat for the post mortem. They were in a state of some excitement, the dinner having been, they said, a great success and quite fascinating. I began to be sorry

---

1 Francis Vallat, Deputy Legal Adviser at the Foreign Office; later a member of the Permanent Court of Arbitration.
2 Frank Keith Officer, Australian Ambassador to France 1950–55.

I had missed it until I realized the sort of success it had been. For Denis was clearly shocked by the way A.E. had talked, and A.E. equally obviously knew it. He was in an *exalté* frame of mind, having had plenty to drink, and being excited about the 'frank' talk with Molotov. It seems A.E. talked the whole way through dinner and for an hour afterwards, keeping up a most brilliant entertainment, they all said; but the theme was the middle position of USSR and UK, with an implication that we deprecate the wildness of the Americans (and Chinese), the hopelessness of the French. Rather an admission, it sounded, of the divisions in the Western alliance. A.E. recounted all this to us with the utmost satisfaction (though with frequent interjections like 'Have I done wrong?', 'Denis thinks me a bad Foreign Secretary', 'The Foreign Office does not approve; you are so severe, dear', 'I really enjoy talking to Molotov; he has mellowed').

I myself, grumpy spoil-sport, could not really bear the mood, quite apart from what had been said at dinner, so I manœuvred hard to get the others away and him to bed. Having achieved this at last, I went to see Denis in his room, to ask him what had really happened. He said it had been pretty terrible. A.E. had certainly played up to Molotov, mostly upon subjects which, though they seemed 'frank' and daring to embark upon, were in fact easy for Molotov to agree with. I expect there will be some remorse in the morning.

Of course, I daresay there is something in the idea that Molotov wants peace in Korea and a settlement in Indo-China. But why does he want it? I asked A.E. that, and he replied, 'Because he is afraid what the continuation of this fighting may lead to. It may lead to a world war.' All right, then our policy should surely be to encourage that fear in Molotov's mind, not to allay it by exposing our determination to do nothing? There is another theory emerging – that Russia is now a 'satisfied power', anxious for stability and repose, and therefore likely to be apprehensive of the activities of unsatisfied adventurers like Chou En-lai. A.E. cheerfully told Molotov his joke about Russia and UK being 'inside left and inside right', and says he enjoyed it very much. I'll bet he did: but he did not criticize *his* outside wing, or show any divergence from them. A.E. seems now to be accepting the 'New Look' idea which he has been so roundly abusing in the PM ever since 11 May. When it is a question of Winston wanting to throw his arms round Malenkov, it is one thing. But when we ourselves are involved, and playing the beau role, it is a very different matter. These politicians are two-thirds prima donna.

6 May

Reading and Vallat gave a rather more favourable account to me of A.E.'s talk with Molotov last night. They thought he made it pretty plain that there were grave dangers in Chinese policy, and did not too much dissociate himself from the Americans. I expect it was all right.

I was still feeling very stuffy today, but managed to get a game of tennis with John in the afternoon, which helped. We played at a nice little UN club, on red courts.

7 May

Feeling a little tender this morning, and got sharply reprimanded for inattention by A.E. when I used a false argument in defence of Lord Swinton, who has sent us a telegram about telling our Staff Agency plan to the Commonwealth. Not too busy a morning, but gloomy because the news from Dien Bien Phu is very bad overnight. Bedell came round, and he and A.E. drove together to see Bidault with Reinhardt (US Ambassador to NATO) and me in the second car. We stood talking in the garden while the three ministers were within trying to agree upon getting the Indo-China talks started. Bidault seemed quite unable to decide anything – was awaiting instructions from Paris, had to ring Paris for confirmation before he could even agree to say that there might be a meeting tomorrow. Eventually that was agreed, and I had to suggest to Molotov, today's chairman (through ringing up Troyanovski) that he should announce it at this afternoon's plenary. This made me very late for A.E.'s lunch with selected US correspondents at the Beau Rivage – Stoneman, *Chicago Daily News*; Frank Kelly, *New York Herald Tribune*; Marquis Childs; Shackford; Ben Welles, *New York Times*; Ward; Don Cook; Thomas Hamilton; Chalmers Roberts, *Washington Post*. He gave them a quite brilliant exposition of our policy over Indo-China – the reasons why the British, having had the sense to give up India and Burma at much cost and pain to themselves, did not feel disposed to go to war to hold down Indo-China for the French – our belief that it is a struggle of ideas, not of armies, and therefore we must have Asiatic opinion on our side: hence his efforts with the Colombo Conference powers: hence his reluctance to start on South East Asia pact talks until you have *first* brought in the Asiatics to play some part in underwriting a settlement: hence his anxiety to get negotiations started and a reasonable French proposition tabled. I think they were much impressed. Unfortunately we had to break short for a talk with Molotov before the plenary.

I cut the plenary and spent the afternoon in the sun going through the Foreign Office bag stuff. Huge demands from the Income Tax and a lovely long letter from N.

When they came back they had the news that Dien Bien Phu has fallen. Poor French, poor chaps there. Very gloomy. Drafted message of sympathy to Bidault, which B. answered in exquisite moving words. Bedell went to see him, and came unannounced, just before dinner, to tell A.E. what he had found. He brought Ted Achilles with him. Bidault had been in a very bad way, 'weaving about wringing his hands', but still, he thought, doing his best to keep a firm policy. Bidault was expecting – fearing – instructions from Paris which he himself would deplore, and which would amount to his having to propose a cease-fire or some such arrangement which he knew the US could not accept. He was afraid of the influence of some of his defeatist colleagues in Paris. Bedell concluded from this that we must try to encourage Bidault as much as we can, and at the same time strengthen his position in Paris. He asked A.E. to ring up Bidault telling him what a fine fellow he is, butter him up a bit. A.E. looked rather glum, being in a rather anti-Bidault mood on account of all the hesitations and delays which the poor man has imposed upon us during the last few days. Bedell said, very nicely, 'Oh, come off it, Anthony; you can bring yourself to do a little of that stuff, can't you?' A.E. said he would. Bedell Smith himself seemed very tired, and said, 'I am getting too old for this.' After they had gone I asked A.E. why he should not get the PM to send a message to Laniel urging him to give Bidault the instructions he needs to get on with the negotiations here. He thought this a good idea, and I quickly dictated a telegram to Winston, with a suggested draft message. Harold and Denis were both out at a concert, so I could not consult them. After a nice dinner alone with A.E. and Clarissa, A.E. approved the drafts with some changes and I sent them off. I thought I had achieved something quite useful but it turned out in the end to be in vain, first because the PM sent a sulky reply back in the middle of the night, to the effect that having been compelled to tell Massigli (for Laniel) last week that all this was in A.E.'s hands and that he could not intervene, he did not see why he should now take a hand; and second, because Bidault in the event got the instructions he wanted from Paris without any intervention on our part.

After A.E. had gone to bed early, I sat before the fire reading *Madame de Pompadour* (Nancy Mitford) with John and Angela until Harold and Denis returned.

Just before I went off to sleep (about midnight) I heard a shot in the garden, and going to the window saw soldiers searching the bushes with a torch. It seems one of them had 'heard a suspicious noise in the bushes', and had fired at once! I must warn the staff not to go philandering after dark in the shrubberies.

8 May

The *bise* continues and the sunshine is glorious. In the fortnight we have been here the trees have burst full out, the lilac, chestnuts in flower. A most wonderful profusion of young greens and pale copper colours in the park around our house and the lake and mountains beyond. This morning the French finally agreed to have the Indo-China meeting in the afternoon, and we duly passed this to Molotov. He was displeased that it could not start until 4.30 but agreed. Meanwhile we discovered that the French had not even invited Laos and Cambodia to come to the Conference until, I think, the day before yesterday, so naturally their representatives were a little resentful and suspicious. But they came.

A.E. had a luncheon for some people, which I did not attend. Instead, I swiped two delicious eggs cooked with cheese out of the kitchens, and ate them on the terrace in the sun. After that Harold and I tried to get a game of tennis, but there was no court. So we came to 4.30, and the first of the meetings on Indo-China.

This was a dramatic scene, for there is after all a war going on between these people, and the whole thing seemed infinitely more alive and explosive than the Korean talks. The Americans and French were there when we arrived, Bedell looking drawn and grim, Bidault quite perky considering yesterday's events. Then came some little Vietnamese and then suddenly, through the two doors, the Russian and Chinese delegations, five minutes late, with the Viet Minh in tow, having obviously been having a last-minute pow-wow together. Molotov looked quite benign as usual, and his people friendly to us, but Chou En-lai looks more and more like a monkey to me, with probably a nasty savage bite. For one awful moment we thought Viet Nam was going to fail us, but eventually they came and photography began. A.E. in the Chair. He had previously agreed with Molotov how to handle the opening phases, procedure, etc., so all that was plain sailing except for one point. Molotov had said that he assumed A.E. would give an opportunity for 'any other points' to be raised on procedure, before the real discussion began. Everybody knew this meant that they wanted to propose that the puppet 'free governments' of Laos and Cambodia should be invited to join the conference in addition to the three real Associated States and Viet Minh. But though A.E. acted perfectly fairly, and gave the opportunity, nothing was said, and he passed to the general discussions, inviting Bidault to speak, as agreed. I never saw such terrifying raised eyebrows as those Molotov directed towards the Viet Minh delegate, who had obviously missed his cue through sheer over-confidence and inattention. His unfortunate assistant got a rocket from the Chinese, too, and looked as though he would die. This was a good start. Bidault sailed on with his speech, tabled his proposals, and thus obtained the initiative from the outset.

We adjourned for a drink, and then the poor Viet Minh man, having received a drubbing from his superiors, made his speech. It was entirely devoted to the request that these two puppet stooges should come to the Conference. Bedell Smith rejected it flat, said it was the business of the four inviting powers to decide who should come. Chou En-lai, very arrogant, insolent, answered him back sharply. Then Auntie Mol supported the proposal, but rather more gently, which is not surprising as in all the discussions with A.E. and the others which led up to this meeting of nine powers on Indo-China, he never even hinted that these two non-existent regimes should be admitted. Some think he may have been taken to task by Chou En-lai for not having insisted on this earlier. But the general opinion of our snoopers is that Molotov is very much in command of the Communist team, and treats the others cavalierly.

9 May

Sunday. Up early, and was on the tennis-court by 9 o'clock with Harold. He was far *far* too good for me, and I played very badly. Realize that N. and I are living in a fool's paradise, beating the ball back and forward between one another, always the expected stroke. But wonderful exercise. After that, a bath, and then realizing that A.E. was going out for the day and would be working in the evening I rang up Jill Hare, who had invited me to dinner, and asked whether I could come to lunch instead. They at once asked me to join them in a family picnic across the French border, on the Rhone, at the mouth of the Belfort Gap. Glorious sunshine, lovely picnic, played with the children, face sunburnt, paddled, back in time for a nice cup of tea. Then a little work preparing telegrams and speeches for A.E., dinner with him, Harold and Denis, and got through a lot of work, and so to bed. A glorious day, made better by the knowledge that it is the beginning of the last week I ever serve as Private Secretary. Am going to get Tony Rumbold out on Tuesday; then with luck we can persuade A.E. to go home on Friday, for a few days, and I shall *not* return with him.

Roger Makins has sent us an embarrassing telegram. Dulles came to see him about the PM's projected visit to Washington, which he thinks ill-timed and awkward. He has to discuss it with the President on Wednesday, and wanted to know A.E.'s opinion. How can A.E. express his real opinion? We have given Roger a *hint* that we do not think the moment ripe. But I wonder whether this is not to be the PM's swan song – and if we do not let him sing it he may refuse to die. A.E. talks of going home to demand a meeting of Ministers to force a decision out of the PM. But he will not do that. On the other hand he *ought* to be there when the Queen returns, i.e. go back on Friday instead of waiting until Sunday, as he inclines.

During this pause of Sunday we have no idea whether the Communists are going to discuss seriously on Monday the problem of stopping the war in Indo-China, or whether they will insist on their proposal to invite the stooges to the point of breaking up the Conference. My bet is that they will talk, but one can have no certainty. If it were not for the very nasty faces which the Americans are making, I don't see why the Communists have any incentive to talk, or to stop the war. It is going so nicely for them. But Molotov is more afraid of a world war and atom bombs than Chou En-lai, partly because Russia is more open to attack, partly because she is more of a satisfied power and has a lot to lose, and partly because he is a wiser and calmer man. One has a feeling that the Chinese are in a reckless and self-assertive mood. But I am bound to say, Chou En-lai has been polite to A.E., deferred to him twice as Chairman on Saturday without a protest (when A.E. had to tell him he could not speak because another was inscribed), and has allowed the trade talks with Trevelyan to go quite far. Oddly enough, before we came here I should have wanted to use all this to get close to Chou, and try to detach him from Molotov. As it turns out, we are more in the mood of getting close to Molotov, to help him control Chou.

10 May

Bedell Smith came up in the morning, full of grave prognostications about the political situation in Paris. There is fear that the Government will fall, and we shall get either General de Gaulle or a neutralist Government. Either would be fatal to EDC, co-operation with the US and a settlement in Indo-China. We are very gloomy about the situation, and wonder how it can be made sound enough to prevent the Americans abandoning us all, or alternatively losing patience and starting World War No. III. I must say I understand the temptation. I just have a feeling that the Russians are afraid of a world war, and may do something to prevent it getting to that. Bedell was most sensible and helpful about the five-power Staff Agency, and he and A.E. agreed about a public statement on it. We are getting into line again.

Then Molotov came, as today's Chairman, to consult A.E. about the deadlock over admission of the two stooge Governments of Laos and Cambodia. He first tried to sell a Chinese compromise – that they should be invited to come and make known their views (not as members of the Conference) but when we turned that down he seemed quite willing to agree to our formula – 'that both sides should maintain their point of view, and the Conference get on with its business'. This is of course equivalent to a defeat of the Viet Minh proposal. So again Molotov has been reasonable and helpful over a procedural matter.

Harold and I lunched with the Edens. Clarissa had been advising A.E.

against going home this weekend and we both argued the other way. I think I have made him feel that he ought to be there when the Queen arrives. He authorized me to find out if there is any part he can play in the welcome to the Queen, and I have got No. 10 to lay one on. So I think with luck Friday will stick. It was wonderfully sunny and hot today, and we did a lot of our talk and work outside on the terrace, with Mont Blanc visible.

Meeting on Indo-China at 3.0 p.m., Molotov in the Chair, and the question of the stooge Governments of Laos and Cambodia was duly passed over in silence. The debate began with a long, insolent and bloody-minded speech by the Viet Minh man, a thin-faced, thick-lipped bespectacled little bastard who hurled every insult at the Americans, but produced a counter plan most skilfully 'baited' to appeal to French opinion. The plan means in effect the total communization of Indo-China, and withdrawal of all French forces. But then they offer to remain in the French Union, trade with France, develop cultural ties, etc. I only hope the trap is apparent enough to the war-weary, divided, defeatist French. Bidault seems very worried about its effects at home.

After tea the Cambodian and Laotian answered him, and then A.E. made a short speech in which we induced him to defend the US against some of the iniquitous attacks of the Viet Minh man. He was not enthusiastic, and cut out a good deal of what I had quickly written for him in the tea interval; but he said enough. Bedell Smith followed, very well, and we felt that Anglo-US unity was being restored. But behind it all are the reports of steady military deterioration in Indo-China, hopeless French generalship, disorder and defeatism in Paris.

11 May

When I told A.E. he had been asked by the Lord Chamberlain to be present on Westminster Pier when the Queen arrives on Saturday (as a result of my telephone call to Pitblado yesterday) he was outraged, and said I had done all wrong. Nothing would induce him to cadge an invitation. He had only asked me to find out yesterday whether, assuming that the PM was going on board the yacht at Dover, he should receive HM (as Deputy PM) on behalf of the Government. I explained that the PM was indeed getting on at Dover, but he was getting off later and would be there to receive her at Westminster Pier. 'Yes, he is taking all the limelight, making it a stunt.' Then I said – as was true – that I had only asked David to find out if it would be in order for A.E. to excuse his departure from Geneva on the grounds of the Queen's return (which would be a reason well understood by the other delegations here), and had not asked for him to be given any special ceremonial function: nor, I understood, was he being given any such function. Eventually, by dint of ringing up London twice, I got him calmed down, and he is going to talk to Roger Scarbrough[1] on the telephone tomorrow. Harold and I both decided that we must continue to press him to go home. He really must keep good relations with the Queen, for his own sake. Also, the public will not be in the mood to tolerate any slight, however indirect, to the Queen on her return. Perhaps we can get him an audience on Monday.

Meanwhile letters keep coming out from home (Tony Nutting and Robert Carr, inter alia) telling him how wonderfully popular he is for standing up to the Americans, and that he should stay in Geneva carrying on the good work. This is short-sighted in my opinion.

Harold, Denis, John and I lunched in the little restaurant at Versoix, on a terrace under some clipped lime trees, but were somewhat disturbed and made dusty by road-menders. When we got back there was Tony Rumbold, my relief! Already I feel a burden lifted off my spirit.

Four-hour plenary on Korea. Long speech by Molotov, full of Communist propaganda but no noticeable contribution, either good or bad, to the negotiation. The line is that only the Communists champion the national freedom of Asian peoples. Then a short, snappy and effective speech by Spaak, and two hours of boredom from the South Korean. First he made his speech in Korean and we all read newspapers; then his interpreter, a horrible sententious American-educated smoothy, made it all over again in American, not quickly as if it was a translation, but as if it was his own speech, with a lot of heat, dramatic pauses, etc. Most irritating to all.

Tony and I dined with the Edens, who then went straight to bed. A.E. is cutting up rough (and I'm not surprised) at the idea of Harold going home this weekend. H.'s departure and mine will leave him with no really familiar face on the level he needs except Denis, who is so busy all day running the delegation that A.E. hardly sees him.

Against all this background A.E. has decided *not* to go home to greet the Queen. We all think this is a mistake, but the Conference is in a bit of a mess and he feels he ought not to leave it. He rang Lord Scarbrough, who says he can do just as he wishes about being on Westminster Pier. Question now is, can I go home on Friday? Tony is being most efficient and inspiring confidence so far as I can see. I am standing back so far as I can, and letting him take A.E. over. Keeping my fingers crossed.

12 May

M. Pictet and Mme Morier came to lunch, and we sat out after in the glorious sunshine. He told me that the big chestnuts by the house are 200

1 The Earl of Scarbrough, a close friend of Eden.

years old, and a double line of younger ones eighty-five years. Before lunch I had gone with Clarissa to see the villa where the delegation offices are, and where it is proposed to make a suite for A.E. to live in next week when Le Reposoir is no longer available. To my surprise she liked it very much, and so did I. So I think that will be arranged. There is a little room for the Principal Private Secretary (not me!) next to his, very cosy. After lunch A.E. had to go off to the meeting on Indo-China, and I had the delight, for the first time, of not having to go in the car with him, but being given instead a job of my own to do, in my own time, viz. help Reading write a speech. They sailed off in the convoy, Tony Rumbold on the strapontin, carrying the necessary papers. I took my time, and then drove down to the UN building, where I found Gerald Reading only too anxious to be left alone while he wrote the speech, so I came back and spent the afternoon reading telegrams and the bag material in the garden. Don't know what they did at the meeting, except that Chou En-lai was very rude to the Americans. Harold is much alarmed at the liberties the Chinese are taking with the Americans, and thinks they are playing with World War III if they try to take too much advantage of their temporary military position in Indo-China.

Harold consulted Kirkpatrick by telephone and the result is I can go home as arranged and he is to stay out here. He is rather distressed, I fear.

Speech-making all evening, until midnight. A wonderful letter from N., saying how beautiful is the spring at High Wood which I shall see in a day or two. A.E. had a telegram tonight from the PM which shows plainly that he has no intention whatever of resigning at Whitsun, but proposes to visit the USA in June.

13 May

Up early to get the speech typed out, and then snatched an hour while A.E. was at a meeting of the sixteen, to play tennis again with Harold. I was a little better this time and we had three-quarters' of an hour hard exercise in the sunshine. Just back in time to slip into a bath when A.E.'s car drove up, and I had to dress hurriedly to be on tap to go through the speech again. Just before lunch, when all seemed quiet, the PM rang up, and said he wanted to make a statement this afternoon on the SEA pact. The text was telephoned through and it was very long, all wrong and a quite unnecessary raking up of the issue. A.E. had to ring him up in the middle of his luncheon for the Philippine, Colombian and Tom O'Brien,[1] to remonstrate with him. He argued back, and A.E. ended by saying, 'All right, if you make it, I shall take no responsibility for it, and shall have to

1 Tom O'Brien, Labour MP.

say so.' He really spoke quite angrily to the old boy, but still did not get him to agree to drop it. Then he told me to ring the Chief Whip and say that he may have to resign this afternoon. Fortunately I couldn't get him. At about 2.30 we got the message (after about ten telephone calls to London) that the statement is postponed to Monday. Tom O'Brien was highly entertained and said that Aneurin Bevan would be horrified if he knew what trouble his questions were giving to A.E. The latter said, as Tom O'Brien left, 'I would not have pressed it so hard if I had not known that you approved.'

Then down to UN to hear the speech. I sat, not in the UK seats behind A.E., but a little behind, within about three yards of Molotov and just behind him. Watched him as A.E. made a few digs, and noticed how Troyanovski (translating for him) looked up at him and smiled on these occasions. Molotov too. The speech seemed to go down quite well, and the South Koreans said afterwards that they were ready to work on A.E.'s 'five points' – not five very interesting or significant points, I fear, and of course there will be no agreement.

After this meeting, Bedell Smith and Bidault came to A.E.'s room for a talk. Bidault was quite recovered in spirits, and robust about the French Government's future. He said *'On n'osera pas me chasser'* – meaning that the Government will get a majority in this afternoon's vote of confidence because of the importance of not letting Bidault down at Geneva. Let's hope so. He said he had telegraphed Laniel that if there are 313 votes against him he should carry on, if 314, resign. Then A.E. asked the other two if they thought it a good idea he should go and see Chou En-lai and 'ask him his intentions'. Object would be to tell him in all seriousness that if he goes on coming to the Indo-China meetings merely to make rude speeches about the Americans, he is playing with fire. Both agreed it would be an excellent thing; also that A.E. should subsequently see Molotov and tell him what he had said to Chou En-lai. Bedell Smith said he had himself seen Molotov yesterday, and that M. had been very frank. He had said that he was not so worried about Korea 'because there at least we are not shooting one another'. But in Indo-China, Bedell had said, there was a situation full of gravest danger, which might lead anywhere. Molotov had appeared to agree, and had given the impression that he was holding Chou En-lai back. It was agreed that Bidault shall speak on Indo-China tomorrow (Friday) and that there shall be a recess on Saturday. This rather upset A.E. who has told the PM he cannot possibly get away for the weekend!

Went with Harold to look at the botanical gardens near the UNO building, and then on to buy a cuckoo clock for Robin and other objects. A cocktail party for the staff at Le Reposoir, during which M. Pictet came to see me, and offered to let A.E. have the house for as long as he needs it.

14 May

Woke with a sore throat, early, but had little work to do and anyway was going home. Went into town with Jill Hare to get her a few plates of a new dinner service, in return for their kindnesses to me. Then, after sitting for half an hour on a pavement terrace drinking *jus d'orange nature* in the sun, drove back to Le Reposoir in time to go with John to A.E.'s press conference at the delegation villa. He did not handle this one very well, being put off by the presence among the pressmen of Bob Boothby and Dick Crossman. The latter always acts like a snake on a rabbit to A.E. – hypnotizes him and renders him incapable of firm action. Trilby Ewer and some of the others were worried about the results of this press conference and wanted me to get A.E., at the end, to issue an extra warning about it being 'off the record'. But I was quite unable to detach him from Boothby and Crossman. When this was all over, I walked with him across the fields to Le Reposoir – my last time with him as his Private Secretary. He said he was depressed about the state of the Conference and not enjoying himself at all. He had told the latter to some of the pressmen. I do not think it is really true. He is enjoying it in the fullest sense, because he is really running it, and recognized to be 'the King of the Conference' as the Chinese said. Nor do I think he really believes that World War III is at hand. He said that he had never been to so difficult a conference, and that he felt the situation was very dangerous; but when I said that I could not get the *feeling* of acute danger, he agreed. He thinks the Russians do not want war, and will have to prevent the Chinese from bringing one upon their heads. Of course he is influenced by the *universal* praise he is getting from the British press for standing up to the Americans and keeping us out of war in Indo-China. The British people regard Indo-China as something remote and nasty, like Czechoslovakia; they would react very differently, I daresay, if it were Egypt or Afghanistan. I have done my best in the last few weeks to paint in the other side of the picture, and to bring him back into relations with our only effective ally in the world. We had a late cold collation – A.E., Clarissa, Harold, Denis, Tony Rumbold and me, and in the middle my car arrived to take me to the airport. A.E. very friendly, came out to the front door to see me off. In a way, was sad to leave the scene: but relieved to be away from the personal connection. Comfortable flight home and N. met me at Heathrow. We drove to London, where I called on Kirkpatrick and packed up the contents of my desk against Tony's return. Then supper with M. and Diana at Connaught Street, and drove home late to High Wood.

In spite of some of the harsh words contained about him in the diary, I admired

Eden and had enjoyed the experience of working for him. But it had been a tiring job and I was glad to move. Eden wrote on 3 June 1954:

I should have written long since to try to thank you for all your wonderful help and kindness to me. I can only say that I enjoyed every hour of our work together, and that I could not have survived physically or politically without your wisdom and guidance.

We have all missed you very much since your departure ... I do hope that you like your Eastern Empire, I have little doubt that you will....

But once more, dear Evelyn, thanks and yet more thanks,

from yours most gratefully,

Anthony Eden

Part II

Middle East 'Expert', 1954–56

This second part of my diaries, from mid-May 1954 to their gloomy end in 1956, is of a different nature from the first. No longer am I attached to an individual minister. I am now an Under-Secretary in the Foreign Office dealing with Middle Eastern affairs. I have re-entered the regular Foreign Office hierarchy and am fully subject to its rules.

The dominant unit in the Foreign Office is the department (often written with a small 'd' to distinguish it from the Department, which could mean the Foreign Office itself or the Home Office or the Department of Overseas Trade). There were between fifty and sixty departments in my time. An Under-Secretary 'superintends' a group of departments on behalf of the Permanent Under-Secretary, Head of the Office. He is not directly involved in the business of his departments but he acquires an almost parental feeling of responsibility for them and lives or dies by their success or failure. If his departments are efficient, with good Heads, the Under-Secretary can let them run themselves and is free to concentrate his mind on problems which they have in common and on issues which have sufficient general interest to warrant the attention of the PUS and of ministers. I was very fortunate. I had excellent Heads of Department and I was able to give nearly undivided attention to the major Middle East issues of that time. These must be briefly summarized if any sense is to be made of all the activity described in these diaries.

The British position in the Middle East in the early 1950s is unrecognizable in terms of today. We were the dominant power throughout the area. We had a huge military base on the Suez Canal, a naval base at Aden, air squadrons stationed in Iraq, rear bases in Cyprus and Malta. We paid for and provided the commander of the Arab Legion in Jordan. We had Protectorates over the Persian Gulf sheikdoms, whose foreign relations we conducted through a Political Resident in Bahrein. We had enormous oil investments in Iran and a growing interest in Gulf oil. All these positions and interests, however, were under threat in one form or another. Mossadeq had nationalized our Iranian oil; the Canal Zone base was under growing harassment by Egypt; the treaty with Iraq, under which our squadrons were operating there, was about to expire; Saudi Arabia was threatening

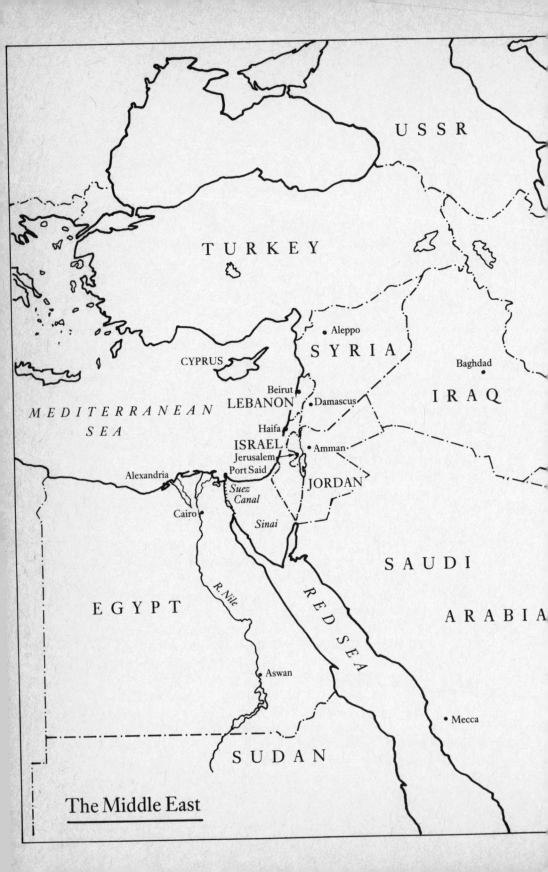

The Middle East

USSR

Tehran

IRAN

AFGHANISTAN

PAKISTAN

P E R S I A N   G U L F

WAIT

BAHRAIN

QATAR

Abu Dhabi

Buraimi

Muscat

OMAN

TRUCIAL
OMAN

Riyadh

| 0 | 100 | 200 | 300 miles |

| 100 | 400 km |

MEDITERRANEAN
SEA

Haifa

ISRAEL

Tel Aviv

R. Jordan

Jerusalem

Dead
Sea

Gaza

Port
Said

Port
Fuad

El Arish

Beersheba

Alexandria

Suez
Canal

Gaza Strip

Negev

Ismailia

JORDAN

Cairo

R. Nile

Suez

SINAI

Eilat

Aqaba

EGYPT

Gulf of
Suez

Gulf of
Aqaba

SAUDI ARABIA

Straits of
Tiran

| 0 | 150 |
| miles |

Sharm-el-Sheikh

| 200 km |

RED SEA

our Gulf Protectorates; Jordan was weak, penniless and threatened by Israel; Communism was seeping into Syria; Arab nationalism was rising everywhere, stimulated largely by the common hatred and fear of Israel. The question was, how much of all this apparatus of British power and influence, relics of the Empire, could we expect to retain? How much did we *need* to retain? Such questions rarely obtain clear answers.

Since we have now lost all these positions in the Middle East and yet are still alive the subject may seem academic. But as part of the process by which this country came to terms with its reduced status after the war it is historically interesting. Most people could see at the time that we were overstretched. But that is about as far as the consensus went. Some saw no reason why Britain should not continue to be one of the Great Powers if only our people would show the will, whilst others thought that the capacity as well as the will was lacking. The Prime Minister, Winston Churchill, who twelve years before had 'not become the King's First Minister in order to preside over the liquidation of the British Empire',[1] lamented the throwing away of the Indian Empire, and, as we have seen in Part I, was constitutionally and emotionally opposed to any further withdrawals. The Foreign Office view, on the other hand, and Eden's up to a point, was that our interests in the Middle East area and notably our growing need for Middle East oil would have to be protected in the future by agreements with the Arab states rather than by holding on to positions of strength; and that consequently we must eliminate unnecessary irritants in our relations with those states. The Suez Canal base was the prime example of an irritant which, with no clear benefit to ourselves, was poisoning our relations with the most influential Arab nation. The first objective of our policy therefore, at the point where these diaries begin, was to reach an agreement with Egypt which would enable us to evacuate that base. For the defence of the area and the oil against *outside* threat the idea was that our bilateral treaties with countries like Iraq and Jordan should be replaced by multilateral mutual defence arrangements (Northern Tier, Baghdad Pact, etc.) which would have a less 'imperialistic' connotation for local opinion and which would spread the burden more evenly amongst allies. That was our second broad objective. As for the greatest irritant of all, Israel, our thought was that we must work for a settlement between the Jews and the Arabs which would give peace and security to Israel and which could be guaranteed by the Great Powers. We reckoned that Egypt was the only Arab country with sufficient strength and detachment to give a lead towards such a settlement. Hence our great efforts to establish a working relationship with Nasser.

1 Speech at the Lord Mayor's banquet, 10 November 1942.

It is possible to trace in these diaries the record of our partial successes and of our ultimate failure in the pursuit of these objectives. We achieved agreement with Egypt on the evacuation of the Canal base and the diary for 27 July 1954 describes Antony Head (the Secretary of State for War) and me, under the shadow of the pyramids, rejoicing with Nasser and his henchmen that a 'new era' of co-operation between our two countries had begun. It was short-lived. In bringing about the Baghdad Pact and in inducing Jordan to join it we aroused the fierce opposition of the Egyptians, who saw the whole thing as divisive of the Arab world and as a threat to their leadership. Thus our concern for area defence came into conflict with our concern for a Palestine settlement. We did not face up soon enough to this basic contradiction in our strategy. As late as September 1955 and even beyond that we were still hoping to get Nasser's co-operation in reaching a settlement with Israel.

From my own point of view as expressed in these diaries the most lamentable aspect of the whole period was this failure to make a dent in the Arab–Israeli confrontation. Eden and Dulles had deputed me and Francis Russell of the State Department to work out a plan whereby in return for minimal Israeli concessions and with various forms of economic and material assistance from the West the Arabs might be induced to make peace with Israel and the US and UK would guarantee the settlement. After innumerable meetings in Washington and in London we produced a detailed plan which was given the code-name of 'Alpha'. It was accepted by our two Governments as a reasonable proposition to be put to the two sides. It was first broached to Nasser by the American Ambassador in Cairo (see diary, 5 April 1955) and not badly received. We had hopes that he would give the necessary lead. The plan was under discussion and revision throughout the summer, and I see that on 15 July our two Foreign Ministers agreed that they would launch it publicly in September. But events were overtaking it. By 30 August, according to the diary, 'Alpha seems like a beautiful dream'. Russell and I were still working on it when the news came of Nasser's arms deal with Czechoslovakia (22 September). I must say, however, that at no stage was there any indication that the Israelis would make any concessions whatever, even for a guaranteed peace on their borders. Much the reverse (see my diary entry of 2 May 1955). It seems more than probable that even if Nasser had been co-operative no settlement would have been reached.

Palestine was the burial ground of our hopes for maintaining the British position in the Middle East. I suppose this was inevitable from the time of the Balfour Declaration and it may have been naïve to suppose that we could do anything about it, such were the pressures, the passions and the prejudices involved on all sides. But since it is still unsolved today we need

(*x*)

not be ashamed of our efforts thirty years ago.

Palestine played a painful role in my life from very early days. My father, having begun his career in the India Office, was transferred after the First World War to the Colonial Office where he became responsible for Palestine in the 1920s. All through my teens I was aware that he found this an almost unbearable burden and it brought him to nervous breakdown. I doubt if I should have entered the Foreign Service at all if I had imagined for one moment that I should one day have to become involved in this same insoluble problem.

My posting to Cairo in 1937, described in Part I, brought me close to it. Palestine seems to have been the only international problem (apart from the impending Second World War) which caused me any serious concern in those halcyon days. I wrote no diary then, but letters to my father and to my father-in-law, which were kept, reveal my early thoughts on the subject:

1. Letter to my father, June 1938: 'We are beginning to get very worried about that question here – for there can be no doubt that the Arab world in general is getting slowly but surely excited about it.... How can we risk prejudicing our whole position in the Arab world for the sake of Palestine?'

2. Letter to my father, 12 July 1938: 'I regard the grant of a Jewish National Home as a *separate* thing from the grant of asylum to the poor devils from Germany, Austria, Poland, etc. You have given them ... a place where the Law can be preserved, a safe place for a religious centre, a "Rome" to which all Jews can look. Very well, keep it as it is; stabilize immigration at the existing (or an agreed) percentage – as Lord Samuel has urged, and the Arabs will accept it – a Jewish minority.... Give them ... a place for settlement elsewhere.'

3. Letter to Lord Esher, December 1938 (after Munich, passions rising): 'Would you not suggest to some of these people [i.e. those who, he had said, were "hanging their heads" over Munich] who talk so morally and with such assurance, that what the House of Commons is forcing the Government to do in Palestine is ruining the reputation of England throughout the East. Mr Herbert Morrison, I see, urges an almost completely pro-Jewish solution of the problem. This can be achieved by ... blowing up Arab villages one after the other because they are compelled to harbour rebels. When order has been restored, Palestine can be held against the entire Arab world by a ring of British troops round the frontier. This will look well for the champions of self-determination, and for all those whose heads are hanging. The fact is that on any except an intellectual reckoning, the Palestine policy is *infinitely* shame-making compared with the refusal to go to war over Czechoslovakia. In Palestine we, with our own

hands, are having to burn and explode villagers out of their villages for the sake of what is, as usual, a *theoretical* obligation, an interpreted, often misinterpreted, text of twenty years ago, of which no one knows the meaning.[1] And why are we doing it, considering that even the Cabinet know it is unjust and suicidal? Can it be that Gollancz, and Laski and Kingsley Martin, and Weizmann,[2] have got Liberals and Socialists so much in their pockets? Forgive all this – it is very near us here, and apparently very far away from those at home.'

All this was before the Holocaust and before our judgement had been entirely warped by shame and indignation at the treatment of the Jews in Europe. It should still have been possible then for Britain to impose a settlement compatible with the two-sided aims of the Balfour Declaration; after Dachau the whole affair went out of our control. The only people from then on who could have brought it to a peaceful conclusion were the Jews themselves. All through my years of involvement in their affairs I was, as the diaries show, seeking for conditions which would enable them to promote a settlement and hoping they would do so. But they would not.

On one major point, I may say, we miscalculated: we thought that Communism was the fever which would inevitably seize hold of Israel's Arab hinterland if she did not come to an understanding with her neighbours. The Jews were always telling us that we exaggerated this danger. Perhaps they were right, for, as it turns out, a different and more complicated virus has arisen to dispute this field with Communism, a blend of Muslim fundamentalism and Palestinian terror. But this is likely to prove no less deadly, for Israel as well as for the Arabs – and perhaps for us too.

My father and I between us spanned some thirty years as participating spectators at the Palestine tragedy, and I must come back to him at the conclusion of this introduction to the second part of my diaries. He brought very different qualities to bear on the problem; he was modest, fair-minded and above all discreet. He entered a few lines in his diary every day of the year but he would never have dreamed of writing about his work so freely as I did. As children we used to peep into his large Letts diary when he was out of the house, and so far as I can remember it never contained anything more revealing than that he walked to the Office in the sunshine through Hampstead Heath, Primrose Hill, Regent's Park and St James's Park or, if the weather was bad, took the No. 24 bus all the way, riding if

1 The Balfour Declaration of 2 November 1917 said that HMG viewed 'with favour the establishment in Palestine of a National Home for the Jewish people ... it being clearly understood that nothing shall be done which may prejudice the civil and religious rights of existing non-Jewish communities in Palestine. ... '

2 Dr Chaim Weizmann, then President of the World Zionist Organization; later the first President of Israel.

possible on the uncovered top deck. He was a supremely honourable, scholarly and able civil servant who had earned the respect and friendship of Curzon at the India Office and of Churchill at the Colonial Office. In dealing with Palestine he sought to bring about what the Balfour Declaration was supposed to have foreshadowed, namely a Jewish National Home without prejudice to the rights of the local population. Both sides, in his day, purported in their saner moments to regard this as an attainable end, and my father kept friendships in both the camps, notably with Dr Chaim Weizmann and with the Emir Abdullah of Transjordan. I cannot remember that we ever regarded him – or heard him described – as pro-Arab or pro-Jewish; my mother received crates of oranges at Christmas from both parties. But he saw, I think, that the 'remit' was an impossible one and he became profoundly depressed by it, not really being able to enjoy any peace of mind until he had retired from the public service. If there was one positive consequence for me of my sufferings in the same cause it was that they enabled me to understand my father better.

When one has worked so closely with a minister as I had with Eden one tends to form, or believe one has formed, a clear understanding of his *real* opinion on various problems, as distinct from the views he may be heard expressing under day-to-day pressures. I always believed, and still believe, that Eden meant to base his Middle East policy on co-operation with Egypt (by far the most influential country in the Arab world, dominating Arab press and radio, providing the teachers in so many Arab universities and schools) and that his determination to reach agreement with them over the Suez Canal base was motivated by this. The fact that it all went wrong in the end does not invalidate the thesis; it merely illustrates how much more there is in foreign policy than just having the right long-term ideas. This particular idea became submerged and ruined by such factors as personal animosities, the weakness of friends and the steady, grinding march of Britain's decline. There is always the factor of pride. Great nations, no less than individuals, must have pride, and never was British pride more sorely tested than in those years after victory when we found we were not victors at all. It is no use blaming individual leaders for having overestimated our strength and our importance; the whole nation, indeed half the world, did so too. And it is perhaps something of a consolation to think that half the world is in many ways sorry that it was wrong.

Chapter Eight

Anglo–Egyptian Agreement, 1954

From June 1954, I was the Under-Secretary in charge of Middle East affairs in the Foreign Office and thus directly involved in the events which were to culminate in the Suez crisis of 1956. The diary gives an inside view of the gathering storm.

In this chapter, the focus of attention is on the re-negotiation of the Anglo-Egyptian Treaty of 1936, and the chapter ends with the successful conclusion of an agreement with Nasser over the conditions of British withdrawal from the Suez Canal zone base. But at home the Prime Minister could not be reconciled to what he considered a policy of 'scuttle', and the 'Suez Group' in the Conservative Party, led by Julian Amery and Captain Waterhouse, taunted Eden with appeasement.

15–30 May

A fortnight at High Wood, during which I eventually threw off dreaming about Geneva and A.E., and enjoyed an unworthy sense of relief at being no longer concerned. We did a great deal of work in the garden and decorating the house; also played recorders with a group of six or seven others from Benson and Britwell, gave a dinner party for the Troughtons and Colin Mackenzies [our neighbours], lunched with the Eshers, invested in eight geese and made runs for them, had M. to stay one night and Pinkie (with Lucy and Jeremy) [her children] another for our joint birthday.

31 May

Up to town with Dick Troughton, Pat Rathcreedan and Wyck, on 8.48, the strike of Western Region footplate men on account of lodging turns having been called off just in time. Found that I have a very nice room on the second floor, with view over St James's Park, and a wide ledge on which pigeons strut, with afternoon sunshine. A blackbird, too, which sang there. Lunched with Selwyn Lloyd at the House of Commons to meet Kern,

European editor of *Newsweek*, just back from the Middle East. He was rather run down, had lost his voice and did not help us much over Egypt. Said Nasser needs agreement desperately but stands only a 50–50 chance of remaining in power. Painted black picture of conditions in Cairo – hooliganism only held in check by the barest margin, law and order deteriorating, Egyptians who won't let their wives walk alone in the main streets in daytime. On the Far East he expressed the conviction that the US will intervene alone in Indo-China if the Geneva Conference fails to produce a settlement and will 'hit China to hurt'. When questioned he said this meant bombing their new industries, mining the Yangtze, 'putting back their industrialization plans, which are their main pride, by ten years', but *not* using atomic weapons. He thought they would come quickly to heel. Moreover, he said if US do *not* knock China about in some way, and let the Indo-China situation go sour, 'Japan will go Communist within twelve months'. As he is said to be close to Dulles, these views have a rather grim sound.

In the afternoon I saw Bromley, Head of African, Fry, Head of Eastern, and Falla, Head of Levant departments, and got an account from them of the work of their departments.

1 June

Lunched again with Selwyn Lloyd at the House of Commons, to meet Zafrulla, the Pakistan Foreign Minister. Other guests – Lord Salisbury and the Pakistani High Commissioner. On the way there I met Rab Butler, who astonished me by saying 'You have been very courageous in taking over this new job. It is full of difficulties, but my belief is that you have picked a winner. Of course I know that is not why you chose it – you took on this duty with great courage – but I think we may get somewhere.' I could hardly imagine what he was talking about, but assume it is the politician's flattery line. However, very nice of him. I asked after Mrs Butler, and he sounded most gloomy about her.

2 June

A discouraging day, during which I was introduced to the horrors of Persian oil, the Trucial Coast dispute with Saudi Arabia and other current issues of Eastern Department. Fry knows his stuff. Lunched with Mr Guy Prince, of Lebegue and Co., wine importers, where I met his principal tasters and assistants and Reggie Secondé, and had the most exquisite wines to drink. Home early and played recorders with N. I have bought her a new Dolmetsch descant and a Schott tenor. Her present to me – a leaden urn with decorative handles – was standing on its pedestal in the garden, making the whole difference to the walled garden. Shall put drooping geraniums in it.

3 June

We are expecting a party of Saudi Arabians with some American members of the 'Aramco' Oil Co, to make an incursion into Abu Dhabi territory any day now – about a hundred strong. All plans had been made to eject them by force, but on Monday (my first day) the PM sent down an order that firearms are not to be used except in self-defence. This caused Bernard Burrows[1] in effect to say that nothing can be done except a purely formal protest by a District Officer which will probably be ignored. Yesterday I persuaded Selwyn Lloyd[2] to go back to the PM and seek a reversal of his decision – but the reply came last night that he stands by it. However, I have done my best to encourage Bernard – told him to gather as large a force as possible, and said we 'hope' it may be possible for them to make the raiders' position untenable within the limits of the PM's instruction. But it will be heart-breaking if we again fail, as we did when Turki entered Buraimi, to defend our position.

4 June

Ethiopian Ambassador, Wilson of US Embassy (Middle East expert) and General Benson (C.-in-C. Canal Zone) called on me. Benson showed me recent paper by Chiefs of Staff saying that we don't *really* need to keep more than about one-tenth of the facilities and equipment in the base that we have hitherto been arguing about. This has greatly encouraged him and he thinks we could get an agreement on that basis. I would like somehow to slip out of the condition that American contractors should come into the picture with us and the Americans too have the right of re-entry. This merely complicates the issue and adds an unnecessary pill for the Egyptians to swallow.

5–7 June

Whitsun weekend. Catherine home. Poured with rain. Played a lot of new recorder music with N., and went through Keats' odes with C. Flew the kite in the field with Robin, dined with the Bretts (William Clark[3] of the

---

1 Now Political Resident in the Persian Gulf 1953–58.
2 Minister of State in charge of the Foreign Office while Eden was still in Geneva.
3 William Clark, diplomatic correspondent of the *Observer* 1949–53; adviser on Public Relations to Anthony Eden 1955–56, resigned over Suez; worked with Robert Macnamara at the World Bank; author of *Cataclysm: The North–South Conflict of 1987*.

Observer and an attractive couple called Street) and refused to fill a gap in Peter Fleming's cricket team. Not feeling very well, and not liking the prospect of Middle East problems.

8 June

Persian oil. Question whether the 'operating companies' should be Dutch or some outside neutral. We would have agreed to their being Persian (under a British holding company) but the American companies won't have this. They suggest Dutch, but we know A.E. has always been afraid of this – as difficult to defend in the House. All the technical arguments are in favour of it, so we have submitted the matter to him. He will agree – if some of his political colleagues will assure him that the House will take it as well. So we are calling a meeting of Ministers. Willy Fraser opposes Dutch, because he hates Shell. But I think we'll get it.

Meanwhile it looks as if the Aramco party are withdrawing. No contact yet.

Dined at Claridge's with all the oil people. Long talk with Leslie Rowan about Indo-China. Gloomy.

9 June

Selwyn Lloyd received Sayed Saddik, son of the Mahdi, and Ibrahim Ahmed. Both complaining bitterly about Egyptian intrigues in the Sudan and both doubting whether the Sudanese will be able to preserve their independence. But whereas Saddik was completely negative, without any proposals except that the British should step in, tear up the agreement, turn out the Sudan Government and hold fresh elections under international supervision, Ahmed was more tough. He agreed that if we did any such thing we should have the whole Sudan against us, including the UMMA themselves. He also agreed that the only card we can now play is to get ourselves, our soldiers, our officials and our technicians out of the Sudan as soon as possible, so that the Sudanese can see clearly that it really is an issue between independence and domination by Egypt, and not between British and Egyptian domination. This is the policy Selwyn outlined to him – and we might announce willingness to advance the date of self-determination (and of our departure) and set up the international supervisory commission at an early date. An interesting interview, which Selwyn handled very well.

Then the Saudi Ambassador called on me – very friendly: wished his Government would not keep putting out statements attacking HMG – was sorry he had had to do so himself. Went over the Buraimi question with him – neither of us pessimistic about possibilities of a settlement – or at any rate agreement to go to arbitration.

After lunch, a meeting of Ministers under Lord Salisbury in the Lord President's office, to talk about the nationality of the operating companies in Persia. [Walter] Monckton, the Home Secretary, and Geoffrey Lloyd. Unanimously in favour of Dutch nationality, so I rang Geneva to get A.E.'s clearance. Then to Chiefs of Staff for a discussion of the Suez base – what do we *really* need to keep there? Chief of Air Staff (Sir William Dickson) ridiculed the War Office demand to keep hospitals, cookhouses, Jerry-can factories in cotton wool for years against a major war in which UK would be subjected to hydrogen bombs. I hope we may end by having a very modest requirement, which could be easily looked after by civilian con-tractors, and the rest perhaps by the Egyptian Army itself. Determined to press for an agreement soon.

Gather from Kirkpatrick this evening that A.E. is showing the utmost reluctance to go to Washington with the PM, who has 'ordered the aeroplane for 17 June'. Some think it is simply a farewell visit, a swan song, and that there is no need for A.E. to go too. Others feel it is too dangerous to let the Old Man go alone. A.E. is beginning to talk of having to break up the Geneva Conference – presumably on a failure, which will produce a grave situation. Can't help thinking the Russians will prevent a complete break.

10 June

Iraqi Ambassador called on me in the morning. Very friendly, but he never looks you in the eye. He spoke vehemently against the Egyptians and said that Iraq, Syria and Lebanon should eventually join together, and get close to Turkey or Pakistan, to produce a really sound Middle East defence system. Contemptuous of the Arab League. Said that the Yemeni Chargé had asked him to join in a common *démarche* of protest to UK for not handing over some Aden tribes to the Yemen. He had answered that he did not take his orders from the Arab League.

11 June

Dinner tonight at Lancaster House for the whole diplomatic corps. Wore my CB for the first time and was glad that there was this small distinction between me and the other FO Secretaries, who without exception wore St Michael and St George. Salisbury the host. Some talk with him about A.E., whom he thought very thin, though bronzed, when he came back

1 Geoffrey Lloyd, Minister of Fuel and Power 1951–55.

from Geneva for the weekend. S. said he thought it high time A.E. came back; he might soon begin to look ridiculous, talking in Geneva to Molotov and Chou En-lai while the French are chased out of Indo-China. Before dinner I went up to Malik, the Soviet Ambassador, very friendly. But after we had got on to the subject of Geneva he said, smiling as if I would agree, 'But while in Geneva they talk peace, in Washington they talk war.' I said he was forgetting the Far East, where his friends are *acting* war. He seemed a little nonplussed by this. An excellent dinner, during which I sat between the Venezuelan Chargé and the Hungarian Minister. Lots of ex-Ambassadors there – Leeper,[1] [Sir Neville] Bland, [Oliver] Harvey, Victor Mallet, Cadogan[2] – and most of the Cabinet. After the party, drove in the Rolls-Royce of the CAS (Dickson) to his flat with Leeper, Mallet and Frank Roberts, where we drank whisky until 2.0 a.m.

12–13 June

Weekend of continual rain. Robin pulled out a tooth, and expected the fairies to replace it (beneath his pillow) with a sixpenny bit. Unfortunately they forgot to do so, and had a hard time recovering their reputation.

14 June

Spent most of today at meetings over Persian oil; first among ourselves (John Maud,[3] Eddie Playfair,[4] etc.), then with Snow and Gass from AIOC, and then (in my room) with Butterworth and Hoover from the US Embassy. I find it a great intellectual effort to follow the argument, and am wholly inexperienced in the art of negotiating things of this kind. Have never done it. Fortunately, though I am in the chair, Maud does all the talking.

Settled for the first time into my new room in Albany. Not fully furnished yet, but attractive and wonderfully quiet.

For the last few weeks it has been authoritatively held within the FO that the PM is retiring at the end of July. But tonight I saw a letter from A.E. saying he has had 'a very depressing letter, looking well beyond July'!! A.E. is being dragged *most* reluctantly to Washington in a fortnight's time

---

1 Sir Reginald (Rex) Leeper, former Ambassador to Greece (1943–46) and the Argentine (1946–48).
2 Sir Alexander Cadogan OM, Permanent Under-Secretary at the Foreign Office 1938–46 and British Representative at the UN 1946–50; Director of the Suez Canal Company 1951–57; Chairman of the BBC 1952–57.
3 Sir John Maud (later Lord Redcliffe-Maud), Permanent Under-Secretary at the Ministry of Fuel and Power.
4 Edward Playfair, HM Treasury 1947–56; later Permanent Secretary at the Ministry of Defence.

with the Old Man. I thank God I have no further part in these death-bed agonies.

19 June

To Hatherop for Catherine's confirmation. Moving address by the Bishop of Madagascar, a picturesque Irishman. C. and [her friend] Hope Canfield sang duets in the drawing-room, very sweetly – 'Lost is my Quiet'. C's teacher says she really has a talent for singing and could be very good. Greatly surprised. C. obviously loved by all mistresses and girls and very happy. As we drove away, five little girls crowded round her to photograph her in her white dress. She has determined 'to be good all her life'. N. gave her an ivory-backed prayer book.

29 June

Meetings all this week about the Suez Canal, the Egyptian negotiations, etc. The Americans have agreed to give us the support we need, and the PM and A.E. have told us from Washington that we can go ahead with the negotiations as soon as they get back. Selwyn Lloyd now a strong convert, and arguing for almost complete abandonment of the base facilities.

5 July

Andrew Stark showed me to my consternation a message which the PM has sent to Molotov from the *Queen Mary*, suggesting he go to Moscow with Anthony for a top-level meeting, *without* the Americans! Telegrams show that he completely ignored the Cabinet over this; sent the text 'private and personal' to Rab, saying 'I hope you will agree', and just as Rab (advised by the FO) was about to reply suggesting that he wait to discuss it with colleagues at home, followed it up with another saying 'presume you have sent on my message, it does not commit the Cabinet'. So Rab (feebly in my opinion) proposed a few minor changes and sent it on. So it is done. Anthony Eden 'agrees in principle'. Fancy A.E. allowing himself to be talked into acquiescing in this! It looks as though there was a compact – 'You let me go to see Malenkov and after that I will resign.' What is to prevent everyone else – Adenauer, Tito – running after the Russians in Winston's wake?

6 July

Found in the FO that everyone who knows about the PM's message is outraged. F.K.R. [Frank Roberts] and Harold have written to A.E., who returns tonight, setting out the likely consequences and making clear where the FO stands. Selwyn Lloyd and Tony Nutting talk of resigning. I am told that one of the reasons why Rab did not argue back was that he assumed this was A.E.'s way of holding the PM to his promise to retire, and did not feel he could interfere with that, lest he seem to be intriguing against A.E.! A.E. always swore to me that the *one* thing he would not allow was a visit to Moscow without the Americans. None of the Cabinet knows a thing about it yet.

I wrote A.E. a note tonight, for his return, begging him not to go to Moscow with the Old Man. 'The future PM should not be mixed up in any way with it.' I know it will do no good. Tony Nutting encouraged me to send it. Can it possibly happen that the Russians will make excuses? No, they will jump at it, this golden opportunity to divide the Western world.

7 July

First thing, A.E. rings me up at the Albany, thanks me for my note, says it was 'very difficult' and goes into a long discontent about our Cabinet papers on Egypt. As soon as I got to the FO I went to see him about Egypt, and he talked at once about the other thing. He tried to put the blame on Rab for not consulting the Cabinet colleagues. He also said he had been to see Norman Brook, who had 'agreed that no power on earth will stop the Old Man doing this'.

Molotov has replied – very welcoming of course, but correct, and not doing more than say that if the suggestion is put to the Soviet Government, it will be received with understanding and favour. Also he says it might lead to a 'wider' top-level meeting – meaning he wants the Americans there too, eventually. This has evidently awakened the faintest stirrings of conscience in the PM's mind, for he has telegraphed the exchange of messages (carefully bowdlerizing his own to leave out the bits about America) to Eisenhower and asking him what he thinks. So there is a hope still that Ike will bring us to our senses.

This was the story told to the astonished Cabinet at 11.30 this morning. I am told there was 'some hesitancy and shock'. Bobbety is said to have said that he would await Ike's reply before forming an opinion but that if Ike shows doubt or dislike of the project, he will be against it. I expect everyone is doing the same. But whatever Ike says, we are surely hooked; we cannot get out of it.

But the Cabinet did find time to agree to go ahead with the Egypt negotiations – with the unusual proviso that we should delay action forty-eight hours in case any member of the Cabinet has second thoughts on reading the minutes!

12 July

Lectured to Joint Services Staff College at Latimer about the Middle East. Eisenhower's reply was about as scathing and negative as it could be without actually being rude. 'You have not let much grass grow under your feet.' 'I thought you were going to think this over and discuss with me again before taking action' – (these are not the exact words). PM then sent another shame-making message – 'I hope you are not vexed with me.' To which Ike replied, 'Of course not; know you too well for suspicion; only amazement.'

Now the PM is beginning to put water in his wine. His message assures Ike 'I will not go to Moscow. We must meet as equals' – and suggests Stockholm or Berne. This is the FO's (and A.E.'s) belated influence. But I do not see how he can possibly get away with this, because his message to Molotov quite plainly implied that he was going to Moscow. 'I hope to see all your people, including Comrade Malenkov', or words to that effect. F.K.R. remarked a day or two ago to the Soviet Ambassador that 'time and place were still open', to which Malik replied 'time, yes, but the place is Moscow'. Now Harold Caccia thinks the main danger is that we shall offend the *Russians*! He takes the view that whatever follies we commit, our yea must be yea and our nay, nay. Therefore, having said he will go, he must go, and having said A.E. will go with him, A.E. must go ... but *not* to Moscow, he says. They are in a thorough mess.

Tonight I could not bear any longer to do nothing about this, so I rang Salisbury to ask if he would see me. He asked me to his room in the House of Lords at 8.30 p.m. They are sitting late. Found him indignant, not so much on the issue itself as on the PM's underlying claim that he has the right to take major decisions of this sort without consulting Cabinet. S. says this is contrary to our constitutional system. The *final* decision lies with the PM (unlike the Australian Cabinet) but this implies prior consultation with his colleagues. This and the 11 May speech are the two cases which S. would quote if he resigns. Both were done without consultation with Cabinet. He wants to do it soon, because he feels that if you wait, you get into a position of acquiescence in which it is impossible to resign, though the policies you are supporting are repugnant to you.

After getting all this off my chest with Salisbury I went round to see George Simon and Joanna; found them both in bed looking at TV with the children, so far as I could make out. Talked for an hour with them, drank a glass of beer in a pub opposite their street, and home to Albany.

13 July

First reports from Cairo show our proposals not too badly received, but little sign of compromise by the Egyptians on length of the agreement or air force rights.

14 July

We have a formula for the air force rights and there are signs the Egyptians may extend the period during which we withdraw; but no prospect that they will give us longer duration than seven years for the agreement. Sent Ralph Stevenson a stiff message for them. But I feel we shall have to take what we can get. PM spoke strongly to the party last night, but privately is saying that he hopes there won't be an agreement; he would prefer to march out fighting. This means we should get *nothing*, and lose everything we have in the base. He said to F.K.R., 'Well, I did your dirty work for you.'

Met Jane Portal in the FO courtyard, and said what I think about PM's message to Molotov. She agrees it is terrible, but blames all the colleagues for not standing up to him – in fact applauding him to his face and then abusing him behind his back. Special contempt reserved for Salisbury (who she said had resigned) and Macmillan, who is 'playing a double game'. She says that the PM has now abandoned all thought of retiring, and that this is partly A.E.'s fault for 'pushing him too hard.' He now has his tongue in his cheek.

I gather that the Persian negotiation is going very well, but some doubt whether compensation for AIOC is not getting left behind. Sent a telegram to Roger Stevens warning against this. Negotiations for arbitration with Saudi Arabia also going well.

15 July

Today Selwyn Lloyd and I had a long interview with Nuri Pasha about his plans for the future of Iraq. The Crown Prince (whom he does not trust) came over to Paris to meet him, and gave him carte blanche to form any Government he likes, and restore stability. He wants to make a treaty with Pakistan and then bring in Syria and Lebanon 'but without touching their sovereignty or independence'; and hopes we will join the group too. This would split the Arab League 'and leave the Egyptians out in the cold'. Thought him a clever and a strong man; but a bit full of bright ideas and extremely reactionary so far as social and land reform is concerned. He intends to sustain the authority and power of the Sheiks, and to 'dispose of the Communists'.

Dined with the Lebanese Ambassador and Mme Khouri. Sat between a crazy Tory fanatic, Lady Dalrymple-Champneys, who said I was not a loyal Englishman because I advocate a treaty with Egypt, and the nice wife of Evan Wilson, Counsellor at the US Embassy. Dinner was in honour of the ex-PM of Lebanon, Saeb Bey Salaam, who knew my father and was very friendly. I nearly put my foot badly in it by suggesting to Khouri that the waters of the Litani river might well be added to those of the Jordan for distribution to all the Jordan valley states. He said, 'If I were to report home that you had said that, the Government would fall.' Must be more careful.

16 July

Robert Howe, Governor-General of the Sudan, came to see Selwyn and me and gave us a more encouraging account of the situation there than I had dared to hope for. He confirms absolutely that our policy of getting the British officials out is right; already the Sudanese are more friendly, less keen on Sudanization, more suspicious of Egyptian intentions, more on the look-out to preserve their independence. Soon we shall be their best friends again. Howe himself has excellent relations with the PM, Azhari, which will be useful so long as he does not resign, as he threatens.

17–18 July

On Saturday before leaving the FO I launched a minute on Selwyn Lloyd, to the effect that we are unlikely to get more than seven years for the Egyptian treaty, but must have the agreement none the less. I urged him to summon a meeting of his colleagues on Monday and extract authority from them to conclude. He seems to have accepted more or less my view, but decided to send Ralph Stevenson instructions to make one more great effort to get more. That is all right; but we probably won't get it and our own policy is not determined.

19 July

A.E. is being rather clever about the Malenkov visit. He is sending telegrams from Geneva, based on talks with Molotov, putting little grains of doubt and difficulty into the project. In particular he is stressing that there must be full Cabinet discussion (influenced no doubt by a long letter from Salisbury, who has made this issue grounds for resignation but is being persuaded to hold his hand until A.E. returns).

A hitch over the Saudi agreement at the last moment; but I saw Hafez Wahba and he seemed willing to try and persuade his Government to get round it.

20 July

Selwyn Lloyd told me this morning that he had spoken to A.E. over the telephone about Egypt, and mentioned my advice about accepting a seven-year agreement. To this A.E. had replied, 'Evelyn always wants to give everything away.' It was only a matter of time before he started saying this sort of thing about me, as he always used to about others who gave him unpalatable advice. It is like the ancient kings who slew the bearers of bad news. This has made me determined to be as difficult as I can possibly make myself over this Egypt issue. I am *certain* that we have to get agreement on the best terms available, and that A.E. has to be forced to get that accepted by Cabinet. He will get furious with all who press him into so disagreeable a task, and will call us all sorts of names. But he won't like it if we do not appear to be convinced; he hates to think of us against him. Meanwhile, I had a useful talk with Selwyn Lloyd, who though he pretends to think we are all wet and weak negotiators, really agrees that we must have the agreement. I showed him another minute I had written on the subject, 'explaining' my position.[1] My idea is now to send Antony Head, the Minister for War, to Cairo this week to make a last effort to get what he can. But he *must* have authority in his pocket to settle if necessary on seven years and fifteen months for evacuation. Needless to say we get

1   MINISTER OF STATE

May I please explain my position on Egypt?

2. I do not want to give anything away which we have the remotest prospect of keeping. I am entirely in favour of hard bargaining up to the last moment.

3. The question is, what is the last moment? I have a strong belief that the present favourable (or shall I say tolerable) conditions for an agreement both in England and in Egypt cannot last very long and may never recur once they are lost. Broadly speaking I would define the period we have to play with as being between now and the rising of Parliament. I much fear that if the nettle is not grasped before the Recess the opportunity will be gone.

4. If we can get ten years in return for accepting fifteen months that would be fine. Let us send a Minister to Cairo to try and get that by a last effort of bargaining.

5. *But* if that fails the whole thing may be lost *unless* that Minister has authority in his pocket to conclude on seven years. In other words, I do not think there can be another inconclusive session in Cairo on this topic without risk of a total breakdown.

6. I adhere most firmly to the view that to lose the agreement because of the duration would be sacrificing a major and immediate British interest for the sake of appearances. I believe we are at a moment in our Middle East affairs where an act of boldness and imagination is required.

no help from the PM, who said in Cabinet this morning that we must 'stick on twenty years'. But at least it seems that he thinks that we could (physically) move out of the base in six months if we tried. What he wants of course is no agreement and a 'fighting withdrawal'.

21 July

Lunch at Jordan Embassy for King Hussein, Selwyn Lloyd, Salisbury-Jones and Marcus Cheke. In the evening I went to Geoffrey Furlonge's[1] house where I met all the Middle East diplomats and had an argument with Hakki about the Canal, in which I mentioned a fourteen-year agreement as possibly more acceptable to them than twenty. Then drove out to the Charteris'[2] house in Hampstead where N. had been playing tennis, and heard at dinner all about the Queen's tour to the Far East from the Private Secretary angle.

23 July

To the Dorchester after lunch to take leave of King Hussein. Felt sorry for this serious, lonely boy surrounded by gross uncles in a pompous hotel. He gave me coffee and talked about the Middle East. Speaking of Saudi Arabia he said 'The trouble is not King Saud, but his advisers. That is what happens, these Kings get bad advisers.' He did not seem to be joking, or really to be thinking about himself. He said that if we reached agreement with Egypt our prestige would go up all over the Middle East.

There was a flaming row in Cabinet today about the PM's projected meeting with the Russians and in the dust caused by that our recommendations on Egypt went through. These are that Antony Head is to go out and get what he can. Long session with him, explaining the matter.

At 6.0 p.m. Selwyn, Head and I went to see A.E., who was in bed at No. 1 Carlton Gardens. Quite like old times. Before we went in, Selwyn asked whether it would not be a good idea for me to go to Cairo with Head. I said I would do what I was told, and thought perhaps it was a good idea. Head said he would like it, because he expects to find Stevenson and Co. rather weary and depressed. A.E. at once agreed, so I am to go – tomorrow. Great rush, collecting papers, etc. with Tom Bromley and Guy Millard[3]

1 Geoffrey Furlonge, Ambassador to Jordan 1952–54.
2 Martin Charteris (now Lord Charteris), Private Secretary to the Queen.
3 Guy Millard, Counsellor in the Foreign Office; later Ambassador to Hungary, Sweden and Italy.

until nearly 9.0; then a glass of milk and toast in the Albany flat, and read the briefs. Our trip was announced on the radio at 9.0 p.m. and I woke up in the night wondering whether anyone told the Egyptian Ambassador first. Should have thought of it myself of course.

24 July

Up early and bought a tropical suit at Austin Reed's. Saw Harold Caccia and Frank Roberts and made sure they agree that we are not likely to get much out of the Egyptians. Said I thought we should add the seven-year period to the evacuation period, thus getting, say, eight and a half years and calling it seven. They both thought we should have done very well if we got that. Talks with Tom Bromley and Guy Millard too, getting the brief right about the consultation clause at the end of the period, which may cause trouble. The Egyptians have been wanting to put in a sentence to the effect that if no agreement is reached to extend the treaty we shall be obliged to withdraw or otherwise dispose of our remaining property. This will in fact be the case, but A.E., with his infallible nose, has picked on this phrase as humiliating to us. Quite clear I must in no circumstances agree to it.

Caught the 12.45 home and spent the afternoon in the garden watching N. weed. Roses on my new wall are at their most perfect. Robin went to the Nettlebed Fête, where he won a prize, but Catherine stayed at home 'because she sees her father so little'.

Fetched by FO car at 6.45 and driven to London Airport. Somewhat delayed on the road by an accident, not to us, under the bridge at Maidenhead, but arrived in good time. Airborne 8.55 and discovered not a drop of liquor on board of any sort. Milk with our dinner. Not a good effort by Transport Command and insult added to injury when we were told that it is always thus except when the Air Council travel, when there is 'carte blanche'. Good flight with a long talk on tactics with Head. He is worried by the fact that we offered seven years last year and are now trying to get more. I gave him reasons for justifying this (need to hand over to civilian contractors; disorder; sorting; only get effective use for about four years). But he is not keen to bargain. Is looking for a take-it-or-leave-it position.

25 July

Early in the morning I woke to see the coast of Africa from the window of my berth. Brown and flat with occasional lumps that might have been Roman or Crusader castles. The bright green rim of the sea. View over Alexandria in early morning sunshine and up to the Delta where one could see large new irrigated plantations sticking out into the desert. Met by Ambassador, Ralph Murray,[1] etc., and Ralph drove me to his house, where I am to stay. It is the house the Kellys[2] had in the 1930s and in which N. and I went to our first diplomatic lunch abroad a few days after our arrival in 1937.

After a bath and change into my tropical suit we had a meeting at the Embassy. HE, General Keightley (GOC, Middle East Land Forces), General Benson, Murray and the admirable Second Secretary Drinkall, who has been acting as Secretary to the UK Delegation. The following is the way our thoughts developed.

Our instructions were extremely flexible. We were to do our best to get an improvement on the Egyptian offer of a seven-year duration and a fifteen-month evacuation period. In the last resort we were authorized to accept Egyptian terms.

My own thought on leaving London had been to work for a solution based on an eighteen-month evacuation period plus a seven-year duration, i.e. eight and a half years. This was on the assumption that the Egyptians were wedded to seven years as a symbol and might not be so particular about when it began. Head seemed to be quite receptive to this plan but he could not see what valid arguments we could use for saying that seven years had been enough in 1953 but not enough in 1954. My arguments in the aeroplane yesterday really led to the conclusion that we needed more time for evacuation rather than a longer duration. If we suggested adding seven years to the evacuation period it would harden the Egyptians against any increase of the latter above fifteen months. We both came very soon to the conclusion that advocacy of this solution would have resulted in an agreement of eight and a quarter years' duration with a fifteen-month evacuation period.

Meanwhile Head, looking at his mission as a whole, saw that it ran a risk of appearing like the last stage of a piecemeal surrender. The fact that we had mentioned twenty years was already widely known. He felt, and I agreed, that if after a great struggle we were to turn up with eight and a quarter years it would not look like a very creditable approximation to twenty. Moreover, it would involve a period of evacuation which was almost certain to lead to a chaotic hand-over, with great loss of stores and probably much friction and ill will. Were the extra one and a quarter years worth it?

Here it was evident, and I pointed out to Head, that we had a possible conflict between the alleged political advantage of getting a longer duration

---

1 Ralph Murray, the Minister at the Embassy in Cairo; later Ambassador to Greece.
2 Sir David Kelly had been the Minister in Cairo in the 1930s; later Ambassador to Argentina and the USSR.

and the practical military need for more time to effect a hand-over. Head might be supposed to be influenced by the military arguments and I might be held to be the guardian of the political, or Foreign Office, case for a longer duration. We discussed this fully and tried to judge by ourselves, without too much consultation either with the Ambassador or with the Generals, which was the greater interest of HMG. I became very doubtful of the real value of an extra one and a quarter or one and a half years as compared with the value of a smooth hand-over. Head was always sceptical of the importance of a long duration and so, as a matter of fact, had I been.

Head wanted if possible to produce a solution which could be made to look like an act of will on the part of HMG. Therefore he was most disinclined to go in for a bargaining process in which he would be driven gradually from one position to another, possibly ending up at the bottom of his instructions with fifteen months and seven years running concurrently. Instead, he wanted to determine in his own mind the maximum the Egyptians might really be expected to take and lay that before them on a take-it-or-leave-it basis. He would try to explain away our earlier mention of twenty years by suggesting that there had been a further review in London of our whole strategic position in relation to the base (and the H-bomb) and that we had decided that a short duration with good evacuation time and a friendly Egypt was of more importance than a long one bargained out of them. I thought this sensible and right and in any case felt that Head, having been asked to undertake this mission, was fully entitled to take that line. The question then was, what was the best the Egyptians might take?

At our Sunday morning meeting the Generals argued for two years' evacuation period but Keightley said he could make 'a more or less tolerable job of eighteen months'. Anything less would be a shambles. All present were convinced that the Egyptians would never budge above seven years but might meet us over evacuation. When we asked the Ambassador whether 'seven years added on to the evacuation period' would have any chance of acceptance, he thought it most doubtful. He would put it at 50–50 but the evacuation period in that case would be the minimum, i.e. fifteen months.

Head and I therefore reached the conclusion that the combination we were looking for was seven years' duration and an evacuation period of twenty or twenty-one months. Twenty-one was the maximum within the life of the 1936 Treaty and we were told this was a point with the Egyptians, but we decided after much thought that twenty had a better chance of immediate acceptance. Head accordingly sent a personal message to A.E. saying that he proposed to put this to the Egyptians as HMG's last offer in a genuine spirit of confidence and good will, etc. His message quoted me as agreeing and he asked me to confirm this in a telegram to Kirkpatrick, which I did. The Ambassador was not shown these messages and was a little plaintive in the morning. But I think that he was very pleased with the decision itself, and in due course we got a most welcome telegram that the Cabinet approved our line.

26 July

Drove with the Murray family to the Gezira Sporting Club, where the children dived into the pool. They have a sort of lady nurse, a relative of Mrs Murray, called Countess Neipperg, an attractive red-head of twenty-three, who is descended from the man who seduced the Empress Marie Louise when Napoleon was in Elba. Then on to another meeting at the Embassy, where we prepared our case for this evening. Lunched with Stevensons and Head and afterwards went round the garden to see what will happen when the Egyptians drive the riverside road through it. In my view it will completely ruin the Embassy and we ought to get another. The house is already too big for present purposes. Had my siesta on a sofa there, then we received Fawzi,[1] returning our call of the morning, and had some talk with him about this and that, carefully avoiding the subject of the negotiations.

We all set out for King Farouk's new rest-house under the Pyramid for dinner and for the first meeting. It was dark when we got there and the flood-lighting of the rest-house faintly illuminated the Pyramid which, as usual, struck one dumb with its size. A good dinner, with the top Egyptian leaders, Nasser, Fawzi, Salah Salem, Bogdadi, Amer (the Commander-in-Chief), Shukri. Very friendly but a bit tense and suspicious. Then we adjourned into a smallish room with bad but seductive murals all round it, and Head made our proposition in a brief, soldierly and effective statement. The Egyptians did not bat an eyelid when he announced our concessions, but when he had finished and suggested we might adjourn till tomorrow, they at once said they would prefer to retire for half an hour and give their answer tonight. We had expected this and agreed, though we were anxious not to get into detailed argument about any except the main points. While they were out I walked up and down outside the rest-house under the Pyramid with Head. Dark night, sky full of stars and the lights of Cairo away down on the plain. We thought they would accept.

When they came back it was clear they were looking cheerful. Fawzi began humorously, 'You will not be surprised to hear that we accept seven years. Furthermore, though we are sorry not to have the presence of our

[1] Egyptian Foreign Minister.

friends the Persians, we accept your omission of Persia. We also accept' – and here I was quite sure he was going to refer to our new formula about consultation, thus leaving the essential issue of the twenty months for haggling later – 'we also accept twenty months.' Great relief on our side. It is in the bag. Fawzi went on to make one or two minor conditions including one which Head turned down flat, viz. that we should agree to remove the fighting troops within the first fifteen months and the ancillary personnel thereafter. CIGS had been emphatic before we left that he could not agree to any evacuation plan which did not give him a balanced force capable of defending itself right up to the end. The Egyptians dropped this without a further word. We handed them a new formula for the consultation clause which they did not seem to mind. At this stage Head mentioned that there were some minor drafting points on our side and doubtless on theirs, and suggested we should deal with these in the morning. The Egyptians wanted to deal with them straight away, so we then suggested that our side leave behind an official or two so as to exchange suggestions and clarify the issues for the morning's meeting. This was agreed. Head and I then left with Baker, and rather to our regret the Ambassador stayed behind with Fawzi, to go through the minor points. Head was afraid this would lead back into the atmosphere of haggling between the two Delegations which had come to an impasse before his arrival, and in the car going back to Cairo we were quite annoyed with Ralph Stevenson for having in effect prevented a break-off of the talks for the night, after the successful disposal of the main points. Our fears turned out to be quite unjustified, for after three hours the two Delegations cleared up all the points outstanding and in the process of doing that the Ambassador succeeded in knocking down a complete redraft produced by Fawzi at the last moment. They returned in triumph about 2 a.m. I had already gone to bed in Ralph Murray's house but heard him arrive home and got the news from him. It was a nice cool night and I wrote up my diary, now some three days behindhand, in bed.

27 July

Early to the Embassy to join Head, and then to the Pyramids again at 10.30 a.m. in a convoy of cars, with heavy police escort. When we arrived we asked for a quarter of an hour for the Delegation to prepare some documents, and while this was being done Head and I stood talking with the Egyptians in the main room at the top of the stairs, a view eastwards over the Nile Valley, with a fresh breeze. Very friendly and confident atmosphere. Nasser raised the question of arms for Egypt and they all urged us to release some Meteors which had been stopped after the breakdown of negotiations a year ago. They also spoke of Centurion tanks and urged us to make a gesture of confidence in Egypt. Just before we moved into the meeting Salah Salem drew me aside and said he had a declaration to make in connection with our agreement last night. He had not slept, he had instructed his broadcasting stations to stop anti-British propaganda. He, who had made so many speeches against us, would become our best friend in the Middle East. His speeches in the future would prove it. In particular he wanted no Anglo-Egyptian quarrelling over the Sudan. The Sudanese must be free over the next two years to decide their future, etc. He was in an excitable state of mind and I am sure meant every word he said – for the moment. I said this was an important statement which I was very glad to hear, and that we certainly wanted friendly relations with Egypt and between Egypt and the Sudan. This could be a new start. I was about to make some reference to Egyptian support for Mau Mau but we had to join the meeting.

This meeting was most amiable and easy, everything having been pretty well agreed. They accepted at once my draft of a communiqué containing reference to 'no aggressive purposes' which is intended to mollify the Israelis. We asked them whether attack by 'any outside power' included Israel and they said, 'Thank you, no. If we are attacked by Israel we shall ask you for help in any case.' Head made them a speech about not crowing over us as a result of this agreement. Nasser replied very straightforwardly and honourably, we thought, saying he had no desire to do this but we must remember how difficult it would be for them to change their tune overnight. We had been the main target; now they must find another. He would do his best (and Salah Salem confirmed this) to stop anti-British propaganda, but we must not expect miracles. We thought this a satisfactory reply. We agreed to say nothing to the press about our agreement, but merely to announce a further meeting tonight at the Presidency of the Council, when in fact we shall initial the agreement.

I should have said that yesterday Head and I, accompanied by John Hamilton, made a tour of the muski and bought various things for our families. I got slippers for Julian and Catherine, some Egyptian silk for N. and a small ivory model of a felucca for Robin. This afternoon I went for a sail on the Nile with John Hamilton[1] for about an hour. Glorious heat and interesting talk with him about Egypt and the Sudan. He is entirely with us over this agreement and bitter about the attitude of Killearn and Hankey. He also agrees that we are right to bring the British officials out of the Sudan as soon as possible so that the Sudanese realize their independence rests with themselves. He said one of the tragedies of the

1 John Hamilton, Oriental Secretary at the Embassy.

Sudan had been that the British Administration there had got completely out of touch with Egypt. This had been partly due to the advent of flying. In the old days the Sudan Government officials from the Governor-General down always passed through Cairo on their way to and from home leave. They met their opposite numbers, discussed their projects with them and thus kept the Condominium a reality. Since they had all begun to fly home they had forgotten the existence of the other co-dominors and had proceeded to govern the Sudan, so to speak, in a vacuum. Few of them had a broad political view of world affairs. I found John sensible and wise on all these matters, and was much encouraged to find that he approves so strongly what we are doing. We drove round old Robert Greg's house, which was recently sold with all its contents after his death, and gave a lift to Cairo to one of his former servants. In the upper room where Lady Greg used to live with such solemn refinement I saw five or six black women peering out of the window.

Back to dine with Mrs Murray, Countess Neipperg and Anthony Williams,[1] whom they had invited at my request. He seems to be settling happily down in Cairo with 'a nice flat and a good gramophone'. He says he can get the Third Programme on his radio, which seems an odd thing to do on the banks of the Nile. After dinner we formed up again at the Embassy and off to the Presidency of the Council for the initialling ceremony. Rather crowded and not very agreeable, but the Egyptian Government conducted themselves most seemly and properly towards us. After it was over they kissed one another and were embraced by many supporters, but there was no crowd at all or public enthusiasm to be seen. I got Nasser's autograph on a visiting card of Fawzi's, but unaccountably mislaid it on the journey home. Straight from the ceremony to the aeroplane where we were seen off by the Ambassador, Benson and Murray. Three suffragis carried on a large tray of beer and sandwiches, so that we did not suffer in the same way as on the journey out. Smooth flight home and good sleep.

28 July

We escaped the press at London Airport and there was a message waiting for us to see the Secretary of State as soon as we got to London. Though we were absolutely sure we had done a good job we were a little apprehensive about our reception, but A.E. was enthusiastic and in no way critical of the terms we had got. We helped him prepare his statement for the House this afternoon. There is to be a debate tomorrow at which the strength of

1 Anthony Williams had been with us at the Embassy in Prague after the war; later Ambassador to Argentina.

the rebels will be tested.

I learned on return to FO that the Moscow visit is off after a terrific struggle in Cabinet. Situation was saved by the opportune arrival of a most uncompromising Soviet note to the three powers which enabled the would-be traveller to say 'I have been intending to give you a formal proposal for the visit but I see from your note that you have nothing new to say, and there is therefore no point in meeting you.' (My own words.) To be saved from our own embarrassments by a clumsy action on the part of the Soviets is quite like old Stalin times. I do not understand why Malenkov and Molotov have let us off so lightly.

The statement went quite well in the House and the Opposition line is going to be 'why did you not do it before?' and I am told that the rebels' ranks are thinning. Fitzroy Maclean in particular is alleged to have left them. Took the evening train home and found both children back from school.

29 July

Spent all morning preparing for the debate in the afternoon. Head required no brief or notes and made the opening speech entirely without notes. A.E., on the other hand, was in rather a stew and we were briefing him up till the moment he rose, i.e. 9.30 p.m. The debate went well, and the rebels (Waterhouse and Amery) whom I heard were quite dignified and rather pathetic. A.E.'s wind-up was one of his best and it is clear that his stature in the House stands high at the moment. Waited to see the Division and only twenty-six voted against; the Opposition for the most part abstained, which I think was rather despicable of them considering they certainly support the agreement. I walked back to the Albany from the House, feeling altogether rather pleased with myself, as I do think that I played some part in pushing this agreement through. Certainly, from the moment when I first took over Middle East work, I consciously set out to do it and it has been on the whole well received in the House of Commons and in the press.

30 July

In the meantime we have signed an arbitration agreement with Saudi Arabia, and are getting near the final stages of our negotiation with the Persians. This has been very active in my absence, and is going well. Ian Samuel[1] and Robert Belgrave[2] (mainly the latter) have been handling it.

1 Ian Samuel, First Secretary in the Foreign Office; later Principal Private Secretary; resigned 1965.
2 Robert Belgrave, Second Secretary in Baghdad 1950–53; now serving in the Foreign Office.

The Persians have said they will make a nett payment of twenty-five million pounds to AIOC in final settlement of all claims and counter-claims. We are still trying to get them up to thirty million pounds.

19 August

Roger Makins, on leave from Washington, came to see me. He is pleased with our three Middle East agreements and applauds my proposed visit to the Middle East. He thinks I should go to Washington after that, to meet my opposite number, whoever it is that succeeds Byroade. Byroade is now definitely going to be Ambassador in Cairo.

Lunched with the FBI directors to meet Troutbeck[1] in connection with the Baghdad fair. Stafford Hotel in St James's Place. Sir Norman Kipping[2] (preoccupied with the contractors' problems in Suez) and Lady Kipping, and about eight others. A meeting in the afternoon in which after some rather unpleasant exchanges I seem to have persuaded the Colonial Office (Bill Gorell Barnes and Sir Bernard Reilly) that it would be a good thing to have talks with the Yemenis about the Aden Protectorate. They want me to go out and do it, but unfortunately it can hardly wait until November. Perhaps Selwyn Lloyd should go.

An interview also, much against my will, with Ben Welles. I have a nasty feeling he trapped me into confirming that Byroade is going to Cairo. But perhaps he knew it already.

Acted as host at a Government reception for five Iraqi journalists, but met no one of any interest except an old socialist MP who railed against the Israelis and begged me not to give them any more help.

Supped with Martyn Beckett at Bentley's and he decided to re-learn the clarinet so that we can all make music together, with Pinkie at the piano.

Received a very disturbing and alarmist letter from Glubb Pasha[3] about the proposed Israeli manœuvres this autumn. He says they amount to total mobilization and are intended to provoke Jordan. He suggests that the Great Powers should call them to order. (Later) I took this rather seriously, especially as it was backed up by Duke[4] in Amman, and submitted telegrams to Washington and Paris asking whether the US and France would join us in a 'friendly enquiry' as to the motives of the mobilization. Neither were at all keen, and it emerged then that Glubb had greatly exaggerated the scale and duration of the manœuvres. The Secretary of State was very down on us for this, though in fact the manœuvres coincided

---

1 Sir John Troutbeck, Ambassador to Iraq 1951–55.
2 Sir Norman Kipping, Head of the Federation of British Industries.
3 Sir John Glubb, Commander of the Arab Legion (see footnote on page 292).
4 Sir Charles Duke, Ambassador to Jordan 1954–56.

with a new series of Israeli 'reprisal' attacks on Jordan. No one ever wants to condemn the Jews. Long talk with Kirkpatrick about them. He thinks they are doomed to failure in the long run, because they cannot learn to live alongside their neighbours. US money and support will not always be forthcoming, and the Mediterranean will not necessarily always be open. Then they will be rats in a trap.

27 September

Back to work. Whole day on Egypt, preparing Tony Nutting for his journey tomorrow to Cairo to conduct the final stages of the negotiation. I had been warned of the decision to send him, and Tom Bromley came over (with wife and six-year-old son) to lunch on Sunday to give me the background. This is a second eye-wiping for Ralph Stevenson and I was unhappy about it. But he seems again to have forfeited the confidence of people in London. Found that the Secretary of State and Kirk were expecting me to go with Tony, but we talked them out of this and Tom Bromley is going instead. Long meeting in the Treasury under the Financial Secretary (Brookes), at which they took a very stiff line about any more concessions to Egypt. It is all very well, but this is the *end* of the negotiation, not the start of a haggle. However, Tony Nutting thinks he collected enough to make a bargain, and is off first thing in the morning.

Lunched with the Secretary of State at Carlton Gardens for Nuri Pasha. Nuri looking much better, and very pleased with his election results. All sorts of plans for defence arrangements with Turkey, Pakistan, Arab League, etc. But he is clearly after some permanent link of Syria with Iraq – he spoke of having a Governor-General of Syria, similar to British Commonwealth Governors-General.

In the evening I played the violin with Captain Adams in Albany. This woke me up rather to the inadequacy of my playing.

4 October

Last ten days rather exhausting as N. still in bed (broncho-pneumonia) and I have been driving the car to and from home every other day. Tony Nutting seems to be getting on quite well in Cairo without sending us too many telegrams, and has not asked for any new concessions yet. Douglas Busk[1] and the Governor of Somaliland are at daggers drawn over their negotiation with Ethiopia (The Haud) and consequently of course making no progress. Had long talks with Nuri and the Israeli Ambassador, but no

1 Douglas Busk, Ambassador to Ethiopia 1952–56.

prospect of a detente between them for the time being. Possibly after our Treaty is signed we might persuade Egypt to make some gesture; not before.

A.E. is having new triumphs with the London Conference, but I never see him. Nor do I ever see any other Ministers, who were my constant companions a year ago. Thank God. (With a few exceptions. I miss Salisbury and Monckton.) Lunched with Lord and Lady Salter, to talk about Iraq development, but it is too boring a subject for my diary. Salter wants to build houses and clear slums, rather than concentrate entirely on long-term irrigation projects. He is very doubtful about Nuri's prospects, and thinks him most unwise to have 'driven the respectable opposition underground'. Troutbeck seems to share these doubts, but nobody thinks we can do other than support Nuri, and get the best terms out of him we can for the replacement of the Anglo-Iraqi Treaty. The question is, when he dies or disappears, will any agreement made with him 'stick'?

11 October

A newspaper strike, which conveniently dampened speculation on Tony's return from Egypt. Lunched with him at Chester Square (also his daughter Zara and nannie) and heard the story. Quite clear we must accept alternative accommodation, and that we shall have to get A.E. in person to swing this with the contractors. After lunch we repaired to Carlton Gardens where A.E. received us, Douglas Dodds-Parker, Tom Bromley and Guy Millard in his bedroom. He is not ill; just resting. Now that I am less used to them, I find these bedside sessions almost humiliating to the Foreign Secretary. We spread an enormous blue map of Moascar across his bed. He seemed to accept our line, and said he would talk to the Chancellor tomorrow morning, and the contractors (or rather, FBI) in the afternoon. Then he quizzed me at some length about what we are doing to settle the Israel–Arab dispute. Why are we not getting on; why haven't we a policy? I welcomed this opportunity to express my belief that *for the moment* the most we can do is to keep things quiet, prevent incidents if we can, get small improvements on the frontier; and that no real progress is possible until *after* the Anglo-Egyptian agreement, Jordan elections, etc. He seemed to accept this. Then he agreed to see the Israeli Ambassador and give him some encouraging statement (I had said I was worried by Israeli neurosis, their sense of isolation and frustration, and had been disappointed that A.E. cut out a warm passage about them from his Blackpool speech).

18 October

Lunch with Smart[1] at St James's. He thinks well of King Saud – easily the best of Ibn Saud's sons, but not a natural leader like his father. He says one can always speak frankly to the Beduin Arabs, as opposed to the townsmen and sophisticated Palestinians. He deeply distrusts the Jordan Arabs west of the Jordan. Quite agrees with me that it is no good rushing matters, either in defence or in Arab-Israel.

22 October

Nutting back – and had account from him of his talks with Nasser. He was very outspoken with them and they seem to have been impressed. He thinks they would like eventually to have a treaty with us, but not for some years. Cairo have coined the word 'NECMU' for 'New Era of Co-operation and Mutual Understanding' which is now the slogan.

Lunched at the Ritz alone with Soheily, the Persian Ambassador. He started by handing me a note asking for two Persian Gulf islands, but after that became very interesting on the Persian character, the differences between the Shi-ite Muslim religion and that of the Arab states, the greed and materialism of the Arabian Sheiks, Persia's need for British investment and British goods.

26 October

Walking to the FO in the sunshine – very nippy though – I met the President of the Board of Trade leading a minute brown poodle on a long red lead. Bought two nylon shirts. Faint signs that the dock strike, now in its fourth paralysing week, may be breaking. Anthony triumphant over his Paris agreements, and the settlement of the Saar, but some fear Adenauer may have difficulty in getting it through his Parliament. John Hope thinks the French were secretly hoping for complete breakdown, so that they can make an alliance with Russia! Kirkpatrick thinks this overestimates them; thinks they do not know what they want, like a child that won't eat. Only Mendès France [the French Prime Minister] knows what he wants, and therefore gets a good deal of it, unlike former French politicians who always said, '*Que voulez vous que je vous dise?*', shrugging their shoulders, if you asked them a question. Had a quietish day at the office, collecting my briefs and pacifying Peter Hayman[2] who is distressed about the Haud

1 Walter Smart, formerly Oriental Counsellor at the Embassy in Cairo; a great expert on the Middle East.
2 Peter Hayman, First Secretary in the Foreign Office dealing with North African affairs; later High Commissioner in Canada.

negotiation having run into eleventh-hour difficulties. I assure him it will be all right.

Went over to No. 1 for a drink with the Edens, but owing to rain and no taxis arrived after A.E. had gone up to change. Clarissa with Ronnie Tree, very friendly. Dashed back to Albany to put on white tie and decorations and back to No. 1 for A.E.'s dinner for the Emperor of Ethiopia. Sat next Kirk, who told fascinating stories about post-war Germany, notably about a poor FO librarian, a Mr Thompson, who was in charge of the German archives in some schloss, and who one day had delivered to him by some GIs in a lorry four parcels, for which he signed. When opened they were found to contain the bodies of Hindenburg and Mrs H., Frederick the Great and Kaiser Wilhelm I. After dinner, interesting talk with Salisbury and Kirkpatrick about the H-bomb. Question whether the Russians realize the full horrors of it. Kirk thinks they do, and are acting accordingly. Doubt whether the Chinese do – that might be a grave risk.

Selwyn Lloyd was at the party, and genuinely distressed at having left the FO. He is now Minister of Supply. Alexander telling him it is quite simple, if you can only get the Service Departments to say what they really need, consistent with what they can afford. One can never tell whether Alex's remarks are profound or completely naïve.

Took Jo Grimond and Tom Bromley back to Albany for a drink and stayed up late packing.

27 October

Interview with the Secretary of State. He authorized me to give personal messages to various Middle East personalities at my discretion; also to try out on the Arabs the Israeli offer of a free port at Haifa. He seemed quite keen on my tour and gave me good wishes.

Then I gave lunch to John Hamilton at the Turf. He was most interesting about the Sudan and the Middle East. Thinks the eventual solution must be Jordan–Syria merger and Lebanon–Israel (Israelis becoming more and more 'levantine' as the Western European Jews fade away). He sees a natural affinity between the Israelis and the Lebanese, both being forced to a Mediterranean character. Suggested I should examine the old Roman frontiers in the Levant; these are the true boundaries.

In the Sudan he fears gradual loss of authority by the central Government in the southern Provinces, and reversion to pre-Omdurman condition. We ruled by right of conquest – this was clear to the tribes and they accepted it. But black men sent down from Khartoum, or local headmen from the towns, command no such respect. He does not think the Egyptians will penetrate much – they hate going to the Sudan, and never filled the posts they were allowed under the 1936 Treaty. John expressed unbounded admiration and liking for Smart, whom he regards as far the wisest adviser on Middle East questions living. Hope I may see him again in Cairo.

Handed over to Jack Ward and took the train home with luggage and portable dictaphone, ready to pack for tomorrow.

Chapter Nine

In Search of a Palestine Settlement,
1954–55

*In the autumn of 1954 I made a six-weeks tour of the Middle East (accompanied
by my wife) in order to acquaint myself with the problems of the area, with
particular instructions from Eden to look out for any possibilities of an Arab–
Israeli settlement. I had interviews with the leading figures, including the Shah
of Iran, Nuri Pasha the Prime Minister of Iraq, King Saud, King Hussein,
Moshe Sharett the Prime Minister of Israel and Gamal Abdel Nasser of
Egypt. At the conclusion of the tour I chaired a conference of British Middle
East representatives in Beirut at which British policy in the area was reviewed.
My diary of the tour is not reproduced here.*

*On the subject of Palestine Eden and Dulles at this time saw eye to eye. On
other aspects of Middle East policy, however, British and American views were
beginning to diverge. Dulles was increasingly dubious about British attempts
to organize the 'northern tier' of States (Turkey, Iraq, Iran, Pakistan) into
a defence pact against Russia, and steadfastly resisted British pressure for the
US to join the Baghdad Pact. The conflict of British and American oil interests
was also affecting the situation.*

*As this chapter opens, I was off to Paris to report on the conclusions of my
tour at a meeting between Eden and Dulles.*

16 December

To Paris with A.E. and Harold Macmillan.[1] Long delay from weather at
London Airport, which I made use of to sell my ideas to Harold. Found
him very keen to do things in the Middle East.

My moment came at dinner in the Embassy – Dulles, Eden, Livvy
Merchant, Douglas MacArthur, Ambassador Dillon, Gladwyn, Harold Caccia and Tony Rumbold. Already at the soup stage Dulles said, 'Couldn't
Mr Shuckburgh tell us his ideas?' and as A.E. concurred, I launched forth,
with some hesitation, but satisfactorily I think. Found them amenable to
the idea of trying to get concessions out of Israel. Also Dulles won't have

1 Now Minister of Defence.

the French in at any price. 'They are already over-stretched in the Far East and in Africa. It makes no sense to invite them to play a part in the Middle East.' Full agreement that we should have secret Anglo–US talks, probably in London, in mid-January. Roger Makins to work out 'cover story' with State Department. Felt pleased about all this, for it is the climax of my tour and it went well. Gave them copies of my report to A.E. on Arab/Israel. Dulles, however, gave us an enlightening account of the power and influence of the Jews in America. Subscriptions to Israel, alone of all non-local charities, are (quite illegally) exempt from tax. But he said we have just about twelve months to do something in, before another election looms up and makes all action impossible. A.E. for his part admitted the influence of the Jewish lobby in the House of Commons.

After this I sat and listened to their talks on atomic-bomb control and on Far East. Old Dulles in his best form, and I still like him. He said that USA would be perfectly happy to let India take the lead in establishing relations and influence with Laos and Cambodia – the Americans would gladly stand back, for he realized how much less good at this sort of thing they were. I thought this characteristic of Dulles. Acheson would never have said it.

17 December

A day in Paris. Worked until 9.30 in bed in the Bristol Hotel then called with Pat Reilly[1] on Roland de Margerie and talked to him for an hour and a half about my tour. This was a great success. The French had been suspicious and were said to be annoyed by my refusal to have talks 'at Under-Secretary level' about Middle East problems; and I was expecting to be pressed on this and on our policy over defence, etc. But I talked so much and so gaily around the topic that de M. never asked for anything more and seemed delighted, though I told him nothing really. Pat thinks it did a lot of good.

Lunched with John Beith[2] and his wife in the Counsellor's house over the Gate. Tony Rumbold was there too, and the two little thin, pale Beith children played around after. Tony and I did a little window shopping, and he told me that the PM is now much nearer resigning than I thought. Apparently he has become convinced that the Russians do not particularly love him after all, and that he has not got a great role to play with Malenkov.

---

1 Patrick Reilly, Assistant Under-Secretary at the Foreign Office 1950–53; Minister at the Paris Embassy 1953–56; later Ambassador to the USSR and France.
2 John Beith, Counsellor and Head of Chancery at the Paris Embassy 1954–59; later Ambassador to Israel and Belgium.

Also, Ike has told him plainly that there is no foreseeable chance of a four-power top-level meeting.

1955

Started the year recovering from flu which I caught on Christmas Day. N. and the children off to Gstaad with the Becketts, and had eight wonderful days of sun and good snow, and two of rain.

Many people wanting to see me as result of my M.E. trip, including Dr Edith Summerskill[1] who was thoroughly rude from the outset; Crossman in his urbane, Wykehamical mood (both of these off to Israel with ambitions of solving everything); Elizabeth Monroe[2] who gave me lunch at her club and was highly intelligent; the Israeli Ambassador fishing for information about our intentions, the Greeks, the Italians and the French wanting to know what Nuri is up to, and whether we are pressing him to join a Defence Pact. When he did so, suddenly and without warning during Menderes'[3] visit to Baghdad, I found myself a little off balance for I had been telling everyone that I thought he would be very careful and that we did not want to press him. Great pressure by Harold Caccia to make a separate and independent post of Kuwait and to get a high-powered outsider to occupy it. I am not really at all certain that this is justified – unless it is really impossible to ask a member of the Foreign Service to spend more than two or three years in such a post. There is a lot of 'Whitehall politics' in this; Treasury, Ministry of Fuel and Power and Bank of England tend to accept the suggestion of the disgruntled contractors that all their troubles stem from the inadequacy of our representatives to the Ruler. John Maud says that none of the Gulf counts compared with Kuwait; I doubt very much whether this is true. If IPC [Iraq Petroleum Company] get oil in Muscat – as they expect – in large quantities, it will be 'outside the narrows' of the Persian Gulf and might become at least as important to us as K. My feeling is that we can only preserve our position in any of these Gulf States if we preserve it in *all*, and that consequently the great thing is to maintain the prestige of the Political Resident, keep up naval visits, and 'acts of presence' of all kinds, and introduce as many long-service Arabists into the area as we can. Also I am keen to get our relations with the Yemen right, because fundamentally they are in the same position in regard to Saudi ambition as our own Gulf States.

Spent this fortnight completing my report on my tour, and am not very pleased with it. Difficult not to be platitudinous.

1 Dr Edith Summerskill, Chairman of the Labour Party 1954-55.
2 Elizabeth Monroe, historian and journalist specializing in the Middle East.
3 A. Menderes, the Turkish Prime Minister.

19 January

Off to America, with Geoffrey Arthur[1] in attendance, for the first round of my attempt to work out an Anglo-US solution of the Israel-Arab dispute. This is the first time I have been charged with a mission of my own, and I am feeling rather overwhelmed. Arthur has done a lot of work in the last three weeks, writing briefs for me which expand and explain the policy I set out in my original paper, written in Cyprus. Am glad to find that most of my ideas are accepted by the FO experts. Comfortable flight (with an hour's delay at Shannon) but not much sleep. I won a bottle of champagne in a lottery on the time of arrival.

20 January

Landed at Idlewild and caught another aircraft almost at once for Washington, where we were met by Harold Beeley.[2] Quiet lunch with the Makins and Edmund Hall-Patch[3] who gave us a very gloomy account of affairs in the Far East.

In the afternoon Alice Makins took me for a walk and we called on Mrs Wood Bliss at Dumbarton Oaks. Large dinner party at Embassy in my honour, to which Eric Johnston and George Allen [of the State Department] came forty-five minutes early, for talk with me. I told Eric Johnston we could support his coming efforts to get agreement on a Jordan waters plan, and he seemed very pleased with this. He told me that our former Ambassador in Amman more or less sabotaged his earlier efforts, despite A.E.'s assurances to him that we would back it. It is clear that my unequivocal support has started my talks off in a good atmosphere.

21 January

First meeting with State Department in the morning. General survey. Broad agreement about the problem, need to solve it, method of approach. But a tendency of the Americans (especially Francis Russell) to doubt whether we can expect Israel to make sacrifices.

Before I left London, Kirkpatrick told me that Rob Scott,[4] Pat Dean and I are the three candidates he has put up to the Secretary of State for succession to Ralph Stevenson in Cairo. Roger knows about Rob Scott being a possibility and says he will resist it, because Rob is such an outstanding success here and so essential to him, besides being an orientalist

---

1 Geoffrey Arthur, spent most of his diplomatic career in Turkey and the Middle East; Master of Pembroke College, Oxford, 1975–84.
2 Now Counsellor in Washington.
3 Sir Edmund Hall-Patch, British Director of International Monetary Fund 1952–54.
4 Robert Scott, Minister in the Washington Embassy; later Permanent Secretary to the Ministry of Defence.

who should be reserved for the Far East. And nobody thinks it right to move Pat Dean from the FO — so it rather looks as if I may find myself Ambassador in Cairo before the year is out.

22 January

Roger and Alice left at crack of dawn for a tour of Southern states. My morning meeting with Russell dealt with the question how to guarantee any settlement we might reach. It was a great success, the Americans declaring that Mr Dulles is willing to advocate treaties binding the United States to ensure the permanence of the frontiers. This is half the battle. I said that HMG would do whatever US does. We also discussed whether and if so when to bring in the French and the Turks, and were in entire agreement. Very strong anti-French feeling in the State Department delegation, and I had to counter-balance this a bit by pointing out how much damage the French could do to our exercise if we allowed them to get really huffy.

At this stage I was optimistic about the way forward, as this letter to Sir Ivone Kirkpatrick shows:

> British Embassy
> Washington
> 22 Jan. 1955

My dear Kirk,
As there is a bag this evening I take the opportunity to let you know that my talks with the State Department have begun very well. There is little or no difference between us about the necessity of working towards a settlement, or about the broad methods of approach. They have, to all intents and purposes, accepted the papers I wrote. What is more, Dulles has said that he is prepared to recommend to Congress (if we get to the stage of a settlement) that the US should guarantee it by means of treaties with the two parties This is a substantial thing. I have told them that the Secretary of State authorized me to go as far as they in any guarantee.
> *I suspect there is going to be a slight difference of emphasis between us as to how much sacrifice Israel can be expected to make. Francis Russell does after all come straight from Tel Aviv and although there is certainly no sign that he (or any of the other Americans) is pro-Israeli ... he does see their point of view very clearly, and I think that is rather a good thing, since we are rather short on Israeli expertise.*
> *The result of the progress we have made is that we are already getting*

down to much more detail than I thought would be achieved in this round. For example, we are drafting sample treaties, and next week I suspect we shall be drawing up various territorial proposals. . . .

> Yours ever,
> *Evelyn Shuckburgh*

24 January

Meetings morning and afternoon. A lunch in my honour, given by Hoover at Blair House, and dined with Freddie and Frances Leishman.

27 January

This was the climax of my week. In the morning a meeting with Byroade, George Allen and a lot of others at which I expounded our ideas on Middle East strategy and the need for British bases, etc. After lunch Rob Scott took me to call on Hoover, Assistant Secretary of the State Department, and finally on John Foster Dulles himself who listened at great length to our story and made some damaging comment. His first point was that the Arabs should be told that unless they make peace with Israel now they will miss their best opportunity, because American efforts to 'deflate the Jews' over the last two years will not be sustainable much longer, when elections draw near. The second was that the promised US guarantee, which is so essential to our plan, will not be easy unless the Arabs really make 'peace' (which I said I don't think they will). I fear that we are going to be forced to put forward a solution much too favourable to the Jews.

28 January

Lunched today with Allen Dulles[1] at the CIA. Kim Roosevelt[2] was there, and the talk was about Communism in the ME – especially Iran. Allen Dulles is a friendly and gentle soul, and I should think sensible. He told me that he read my Arab–Israel paper in bed last night, in the interval between telephone calls about an atomic bomb scare. It seems someone rang the police with an anonymous warning that some atomic bombs had been planted in New York, and the Civil Defense Organizations were alerted. But we are still alive. There is a great sense of crisis over Formosa.

In the evening after a very long day I had to face a cry of suspicion and alarm from Laboulaye, the French Counsellor, about France's role in the

1 Allen Dulles, head of CIA; brother of John Foster Dulles.
2 Kermit Roosevelt, Middle East expert of CIA.

ME. Why are they left out of everything, what am I doing here, why cannot we have tripartite talks on ME defence, what are the Americans and British up to? It was rather charmingly done, as a matter of fact, and I was disarmed.

1 February

A busy last day in Washington. Byroade attended our morning meeting, when we discussed the tactics for the approach to Egypt, which A.E. is to start off and B. will follow up. Then I lunched at the Metropolitan Club with Seager (Harold's brother) and Norman Paul, Middle East directors of the FOA, who control all the US aid to development projects in Iran, Iraq, Egypt, etc.

Then I walked to the State Department for a meeting with Hoover, at which he expounded in grave terms the consequences of British Petroleum (Willy Fraser again) selling Kuwait oil at 40 cents below Gulf prices to American importers. Thinks this may undermine the whole policy of trade delegations on which the President has been working, and affect the convertibility of sterling.

After our final meeting in the afternoon (at which we congratulated ourselves on being so united – if a little pessimistic – on our whole operation), I went for a drink with the Ray Hares and had a very gay time with them, the Russells, the Jernegans, the Baileys[1] and Harold Beeley, reeling back to a quiet evening by the fire with Rob and Rosamund Scott. During the party (and after consulting Harold) I told Ronald Bailey of his promotion to be Head of Chancery. He and his wife were quite over-whelmed with pride and delight.

2 February

Snow – and my plane to New York cancelled, so I went by train. An hour in New York, during which time I saw Bob Dixon again and Tony Rundall the Consul-General and Reggie Secondé who is off to Lisbon. Our Stratocruiser would not leave the tarmac because its brakes were frozen, but when this had been corrected we had an uneventful flight home. One Stephens, of Shell, talked a lot to me.

3 February

N. was at the airport to meet me and I went home for the night. Lovely warm, wet England. Robin in bed with chicken pox. Played flutes with N. and early to bed.

1 Ronald and Joan Bailey. He was later Counsellor at the British Embassy, and Ambassador to Bolivia and Morocco.

4 February

Perturbation in the Office because the Chinese Communists have refused the UN invitation.[1] Kirkpatrick barely had patience to listen to my story, but S/S has had my telegrams circulated to Cabinet and Tony Nutting is showing an interest. Monsieur de Beaumarchais of the French Embassy came round and formally requested Anglo-French talks 'at the Under-Secretary level'. I have been expecting this and cannot escape it any longer. The Egyptian Ambassador, Hakki, also called and tried to induce me to persuade the Turks and Iraqis to put off signing this pact. I said he could be quite sure we should do no such thing. He thinks the pact is a Turkish–Iraqi plot for the eventual dismemberment of Syria.

10 February

We lunched with the Egyptian Ambassador (Hakki) for Sir A. and Lady Eden. The Egyptians are in a state of fury about Nuri's determination to sign a pact with Turkey, and will not be comforted. I had no idea they were quite so jealous of Iraq; or that they would put themselves quite so foolishly far out on a limb despite every possible good advice – for they cannot stop it, and may be forced to carry out their threat and leave the Arab League. I am counting on A.E.'s visit to Cairo to put some sense back into Nasser.[2] At the lunch I talked mainly to John and Liza Hope, and to Lady Helm (off to Khartoum to be Governor-General's wife).

11 February

We lunched at the House of Lords with Pat and Ann Rathcreedan to meet the Dukes (Ambassador in Amman). Tony Nutting tells me in great secrecy that the PM now really *is* going to resign, immediately after A.E. gets back from Bangkok (i.e. about mid-March). As I have observed before on similar occasions, I shall believe this when I see it. Ribald Foreign Office proposals (originating from Kirkpatrick) are for a 'top-level' meeting between Truman, Mendès France (who resigned a week ago), Malenkov (resigned five days ago) and W.S.C. This would be quite safe, and would be enjoyable for all four.

1 On 31 January the UN invited the Chinese Communists to attend the next meeting of the Security Council. This offer was rejected by Peking on 3 February.
2 In the event, Eden's meeting with Nasser in Cairo was not the success we hoped for, though there were friendly moments (see photograph).

16 February

I went to Whites for lunch with Hugh Fraser, MP, who wanted to talk about Middle East. He was mainly interested in Gulf oil problems, about which I am not very knowledgeable. There I met Antony Head, and the place seemed to be dominated by the loud voice of Christopher Soames ragging everybody round the bar. Thank God I don't belong. I walked back with Jock Colville who told me he is leaving the public service when he leaves Winston. He has been offered a job in the City. In the evening I went with Tony Nutting to Waterloo, where with the Duke of Gloucester we received the Shah-in-Shah and Queen Soraya in our top hats, and back to the Persian Embassy where we drank a glass of the Soheilys' champagne and chatted with their Imperial Majesties. She is lifeless – glamorous and seems in great despair. The rumour from Tehran is that the American doctors say she is sterile, so presumably she will be replaced in due course, poor girl. She was friendly enough, however, and so was he, but he talked solid shop to Tony in a morose kind of way and Tony says there was not a word he had not read in my account of my talk with him in Tehran. Afterwards I gave the Nuttings and Noreen Parkes dinner at Wheelers, costing £7.

17 February

Long meeting on Middle East defence with the Chiefs of Staff. Dined at Carlton Gardens to meet the Shah and Soraya. Nancy looking wonderful in her new diamond–emerald and pearl necklace. Attlees, Morrisons, all the Chiefs of Staff and their wives, Thorneycroft, Geoffrey Lloyd, Alexanders, etc. Good party but the Shah stayed rather late, and we took the Rumbolds back for a drink in Albany. Tony is resigning from the Service. He says it is now definitely fixed that W.S.C. will retire in April. Macmillan to be Foreign Secretary. Attlee talked to me after dinner about his coming visit to Holland, where he is to talk to 'our people' (the Dutch socialists). He has a profoundly British point of view about foreigners – likes the Dutch – 'good people' – and thinks the French perfectly frightful. He is bitter against them for failing to approve the German military contributions, because this is causing him acute troubles in his own party. He also told a number of quite funny stories. Kirk asked N. at dinner how she felt about going to Cairo. N. much embarrassed because at heart she hates the idea. So, in some ways, do I.

18 February

We went to lunch with the Queen and Duke of Edinburgh, in honour of the Shah and his Queen. Queen Elizabeth, the Churchills, Edens, Tommy

Lascelles, Nuttings, Harold Nicolsons, Peter Flemings, Salisbury-Jones and some Household. Really excellent lunch, far beyond the cooking of Government hospitality. After lunch the children and the two corgis came in and played around. They were quite unspoilt and natural, yet very well behaved, and their grandmother took them round to talk to people. The little princess was fascinated by Winston, who sat slumped in his chair, looking just like the Sutherland portrait. I was drawn into some talk with him, and he said the FO was 'riddled with Bevinism' on Middle East questions, i.e. anti-Jewish. He had heard (from James de Rothschild) that the Israelis would like to join the British Commonwealth. 'Do not put that out of your mind. It would be a wonderful thing. So many people want to leave us; it might be the turning of the tide.' I congratulated him on the success of the Commonwealth Prime Ministers Conference. He said, 'I have worked very hard with Nehru. I told him he should be the light of Asia, to show all those millions how they can shine out, instead of accepting the darkness of Communism.' 'But you ought to let the Jews have Jerusalem; it is they who made it famous.' He also said that large numbers of the refugees ought to be settled in the Negev. I'm not sure whether he was aware that this is something the Israelis are resisting. I was surprised that the guests of honour were not given an opportunity to talk to any of the 'Persian experts' (Harold Nicolson, etc.) whom we had so carefully collected for them. They talked to the Queen and Duke exclusively before, during and after lunch.

21 February

We went to the Savoy Hotel for a dinner and reception given in honour of the Shah by the Soheilys. Hundreds of friends there, and afterwards we brought the John Mauds and the Jo Grimonds back to Albany for a gossip until 1.30 a.m. Jo said that he drove recently into Nazareth and saw a large slogan chalked up on a wall, in English and Arabic, saying 'Shuckburgh, go home!'

26 February

I have been thinking seriously about Cairo and have come to the conclusion that it would be (a) a mistake by the FO to send me there (b) thoroughly inconvenient personally, since N. hates the idea, Julian would be left alone, Catherine would miss 'coming out' and (c) I should be promoted too high too soon. Went to see Roddie Barclay and told him of these thoughts. He thinks there are other 'possibles' – notably Kit Steel and Humphrey Trevelyan. I shall write a note to Kirkpatrick.

28 February

Sent my minute to Kirk, and heard from him later in the day that A.E. is beginning to think I cannot be spared from my present job. This is only common sense – after I have spent six months 'preparing' myself to do it. Began second round on Palestine with Francis Russell.

7 March

During last week Russell and I completed our scheme for a settlement of the Palestine question. It is a full blueprint for a settlement, including territorial adjustments, compensation and resettlement of the refugees, raising of the 'secondary blockade' and guarantees for both sides by the US and UK. We both saw A.E., to whom I outlined the scheme and who, as I expected, was keen to put it to an early test despite the unfavourable conditions created by (a) Nasser's fury over the Iraq–Turkey pact and (b) the Israeli raid on Gaza last week in which thirty-eight Egyptian soldiers were killed. He suggests that we should get Byroade and Stevenson in Cairo to give us a joint opinion as to whether there is any prospect of launching it with Nasser in the near future. If Dulles agrees, we will do this, and I fully expect their answer to be 'no'.

14 March

Last week we started work on a treaty with Iraq, to replace the 1930 Treaty and to be dependent from our accession to the Turkey–Iraqi Pact. Nuri wants to do it in a hurry and seems ready to give us the things we want. The idea of 'joint training', which I think I cottoned on to during my Middle East trip, is to be the basis of it. I had a rather wearing lunch with Hakki, the Egyptian Ambassador, where I was confronted with bitter complaints by the Egyptian QMG about his inability to get any delivery dates for arms which we have (politically) released.

16 March

N. and I lunched with Marshall-Cornwalls,[1] drank with Drew Middleton (where we met Attlee and Gaitskell fresh from their decision to sack Bevan) and dined with Betty Montagu.[2] I saw the Israeli Ambassador looking disconsolate (we have reacted very sharply to the Gaza attack) and asked

---

1 General Sir James Marshall-Cornwall had commanded the British forces in Egypt when we were in Cairo before the war.
2 Lady Elizabeth Montagu, novelist.

him to call next week for a talk. The Israelis are beginning to feel the air, and the more they do that, the more reckless and foolish they become. Jack Nicholls[1] says they have to be treated with the same patience and understanding as juvenile delinquents.

Harding, the CIGS, has agreed to lecture on ME defence at the FO Summer Course at Cambridge, at which I am to take the chair in June. I like him very much and feel that we are both pulling the same way on ME questions. We catch one another's eye at meetings of the Chiefs of Staff and support one another.

23 March

Oliver Esher's birthday – a dinner party at their Mayfair flat, to which Lionel came with a volume on tombs, being about to design one for Oliver. After the others had left, Antoinette presented N. with an emerald bracelet and a beautiful diamond tiara! I took them back to the Albany and hid them in a cupboard, and we all went out for a glass of beer at the White Bear whence we were soon ejected owing to closing time.

27 March

Andrew Cohen[2] and his wife are staying at Watlington, and we dined there to meet them. The Iraq negotiations are going well and we hope to initial in a few days. We went to Oxford last week and ordered a virginals to be made for us by a Mr Goble. The PM is still trying to hedge on his retirement, though all the newspapers now declare the date to be 4 April and I know this is the date fixed.

30 March

Worked with Michael Rose[3] and Powell-Jones[4] till 11.0 p.m. on Monday getting the Iraqi agreement in order, and a statement for A.E. prepared. All went well, and today it was initialled in Baghdad. The House of Commons took it well.

1 April

A.E. sent for me last week to ask whether I thought Donald McLachlan would be a suitable person to be his publicity agent between the moment

1 Sir John Nicholls, Ambassador to Israel 1954–57.
2 Governor of Uganda.
3 Now Head of Eastern and Levant Department of the Foreign Office.
4 John Powell-Jones, then a Secretary in Eastern and Levant Department of the Foreign Office.

when he becomes PM and the elections, presumably in the summer. The job would probably lead to his being PRO at No. 10 and Treasury when the present man goes. I said I thought him too senior and respectable for what A.E. really wants – which is a knock-about publicity man to go round with him to meetings. A.E. seems relaxed and confident, all being set for the hand-over by Winston on about 5 April. There have, however, been a number of last-minute efforts by the Old Man to escape the inevitable. He misread a lot of telegrams from William Hayter about meetings with the Russians, thinking they related to 'top-level' meetings, and sniffed the air for a whole day, A.E. says.

5 April

The Jews are beginning a great pressure campaign, to get us to give them a treaty similar to those we are negotiating with Iraq, etc. We have seen the instruction to their press attaché, and immediately after came the articles in *Manchester Guardian, New Statesman*, etc., speeches by their supporters in the House (especially Crossman who made an outrageous appeal to the use of force and blackmail on their behalf) and even a visitation to A.E. by Messrs Morrison, Dalton and Shinwell,[1] at which I was asked to be present. Letters and telegrams and resolutions have begun to pour in too. (Evan Wilson tells me that he was given the Palestine Desk in the State Department largely because he is 6 ft 2 ins; the former occupant having been a small man had been physically submerged by Zionist telegrams at moments of stress.) A.E. has turned the pressure aside by promising that *if there were a settlement* we would consider a new treaty to guarantee it.

Meanwhile Byroade has launched 'Alpha' on to Fawzi and Nasser, with quite promising results. If the Jews will just keep quiet for another four or five weeks we might get some sort of negotiation going, but I don't suppose they will.

Winston handed in his resignation today. It was a fine day, and the buds are coming out on the trees in St James's Park. I saw the Duke of Edinburgh land again in his helicopter in the garden of Buckingham Palace. A.E. will be sent for tomorrow.

6 April

When I got to London I rang up Clarissa to congratulate her on this day (A.E. had just left for the Palace). She said, 'Yes, after all you and I have

---

1 Emanuel Shinwell CH, (Lord Shinwell), distinguished Labour statesman; Secretary of State for War 1947–50 and Minister of Defence 1950–51; Chairman of the Parliamentary Labour Party 1964–67.

been through.' It is indeed a thought. I said that I felt as if I was being sent for myself, which is just how I do feel. It was not a Greek tragedy after all. I sat in the box this afternoon after Questions, and saw A.E. get his ovation as he entered the House for the first time as PM. Good speeches by Attlee and Walter Elliot about Winston, and a good one by A.E. too. He is filling out with security and confidence. I think he has the general respect and affection of the House, despite being of so much lesser stature than Winston. It is a relief that one can now revert to admiring W. for what he has done and been, and not worry about what he is doing or will do. I began to feel, as I listened to those speeches about 'the greatest Englishman of our time', that my diary contains a great deal of unworthy and even scurrilous criticism, and ought perhaps to be suppressed. 'The myth' will now take over, and none will want to listen to the carping voice or the awkward derogatory fact. But it doesn't matter, of course. The great thing is that he has gone from the active scene and can be a great man again without damage.

7–11 April

Easter weekend at High Wood. Nice weather for most of it, but things are very backward and the daffodils not yet out.

Very bad situation on the Gaza border, and threat of serious trouble during the weekend. Macmillan is Foreign Secretary.

13 April

I had a tiresomely bad-tempered interview with Elath, the Israeli. He took a really intolerable line about everything being our fault. He not only belittled the value of our reaffirmation of the Tripartite Declaration but picked holes in practically every sentence Eden used in the debate and had the impertinence to suggest that we had weakened the force of the Declaration. I got cross, and was glad I had Michael there to record the conversation. Meanwhile the Jews are organizing every sort of pressure and propaganda to get a treaty guarantee of their present conquests, so that they shall not have to make any concessions. The Labour Party are taking it up as an election stunt, so we may have trouble.

14 April

My first meeting with Macmillan – about Alpha. He was very polite about the paper I had written for him, and discussed the whole problem helpfully.

1 Walter Elliot, Conservative MP.

We are going to try and get Francis Russell over again. M. compared these troubles with those on the Irish border where he says IRA forays are a daily occurrence. He told an amusing story about IRA men being smuggled across the frontier in a horse-box – most of the guards being at the races. 'Sure, it's the Colonel's horse.' Today I also attended a meeting (with Nutting) at the Colonial Office, where we successfully diverted them from some bellicose plans in the Gulf. Henry Hopkinson[1] much less complacent than his officials.

16 April

I drove up to London for the morning and back again for lunch. Things look better on the Gaza front and I think the immediate danger is over. Dulles has quietened the Israelis by giving them a very clear hint that 'Alpha' is in the wind. Only Glubb is still wildly excited, and asking us to adopt a strictly anti-Israeli policy which we cannot do.

17 April

Tennis with the children, tea with Lionel and Christian in a new corner of the kitchen garden where they are making a terrace, and 'mixed instruments' at the house of some people called Clerke Brown, at Kingston Blount, where the RAF are ruining the woods with a radio station.

18 April

Russell has agreed to come over again for more talks on 'Alpha'. It is clear that Nasser will not play unless we can give him something more of a land link with Jordan than is provided by the 'two triangles' in our plan. I had an idea today of using the 1947 frontier line south of Gaza and building a triangle on that, pointing eastwards to the Negev Road. This would mean Israel giving up a substantial slice of the Negev, but I think all of it desert country and they would still have their port of Elath. They will not like it. We might in return save the demilitarized zone east of Tiberias for them. Put this to Washington.

19 April

Glorious spring weather still and London looking wonderful: daffodils everywhere. Walked through the parks to Piccadilly, where I got Catherine's

---

1 Henry L. d'A. Hopkinson (Baron Colyton), Minister of State at the Colonial Office.

sleeper to Paris for next week. I concocted a further message to Sharett from Macmillan, to balance Dulles's revelations.

Aldrich[1] told me he has never liked or trusted Byroade, and that if he was Mr Dulles he would not have him around. He is also highly indignant with the French, as everyone is. Dulles and Macmillan have refused to go to Paris until the French have deposited their ratification of the Bonn treaties. A. asked me to go round and talk to him about Middle East.

21 April

I caught an early train and drove straight to Stonor, where I had a bath and changed into a dinner-jacket for their 'children's dance'. It turned out that there was, besides the young people's party upstairs, a sit-down dinner for about fifty grown-ups, with champagne and all. Sat between Patricia Hambleden[2] and Mrs Duncan Sandys.[3] The latter seemed excitable and even neurotic, and told me numerous anecdotes about her father. She had an argument with John Piper, the other side of her, about the Sutherland portrait. She had, however, never heard of John Piper, and I thought this typical of the Churchill entourage, who really confine themselves entirely to political gossip and racing, though managing to convey the impression that all English life is embraced by their gaze. She also told me that she had recently heard a very amusing story about me, in which I had 'scored someone off' – but then she refused to tell it. This upset me – one is always shocked and surprised to hear that other people have been talking about one, however friendly the things they are alleged to have said.

25 April

Francis Russell is here for the third round on 'Alpha'. I had an uphill job convincing him of the merits of my new idea for the Negev. This is, to take the frontier of the Gaza strip from north to south, then follow the line of the 1947 UN Resolution southwards and construct upon that a triangle of territory based on Jordan. This gives both parties a free and sovereign way through. He thinks it will not be much better for Nasser than the original, small triangles of the 'Alpha' plan, and will be much more painful for Israel.

1 US Ambassador in London.
2 Lady Hambleden, wife of third Viscount.
3 Diana Spencer Churchill, eldest child of Winston and Clementine Churchill; married the Conservative MP Duncan Sandys in 1935.

27 April

N. and I to lunch with the Kirkpatricks, where we met the US Ambassador and Mrs Aldrich and Sir John Wheeler-Bennett[1] and his American wife. Wheeler-Bennett is writing the life of George VI. Kirkpatrick told us amusingly about his identification of Hess during the war.

28 April

I lunched at No. 10 for the first time today. The PM (A.E.), Macmillan, Morrison, Hartley Shawcross,[2] Selwyn Lloyd, Turton[3] and Guy Millard on the British side, Nuri and his Ambassador on the other. Morrison got into rather an embarrassing discussion with Nuri about Palestine, during which he said in a patronizing way, 'I should not pay too much attention to the 1947 Resolutions if I were you.' He is sold on the Israeli thesis, I fear, and does not realize that he is taking their side when he blandly demands of the Arabs that they 'sit down at a table with the Jews, without any prior conditions on either side'. After lunch I walked over to the FO with Harold Macmillan and had half an hour on Palestine with him in his office. I said I was worried by the importance Nuri seems to attach to the internationalization of Jerusalem, since I do not believe it is possible. He seemed to think we might devise some method of leaving the two halves to Jordan and Israel respectively, but superimposing some common authority to look after particular aspects of the city's life – e.g. the hospitals, municipal services, etc. He did not like the idea of UN doing this (because he thought that would mean a committee of Central Americans) but agreed that someone sensible like Burns[4] would be all right, under UN auspices.

Russell and I have been hard at it for three days and are getting our ideas sorted out. We both feel that we cannot let the approach to Israel be left entirely to our Ambassadors in Tel Aviv, and are thinking of going out ourselves for a secret meeting with the Israelis in Malta or Cyprus. We might also meet Nasser secretly in the Canal Zone if necessary!

1 May

N. and I went to Locks and bought me the first bowler hat of my life. I hope to look less like a seedy Home Office official in this hat. Called on

---

1 Sir John Wheeler-Bennett, historian; adviser to Foreign Office on publication of German Archives; author of inter alia *King George VI*.

2 Sir Hartley Shawcross had been Attorney General and President of the Board of Trade in Attlee's Government; created a life peer 1959.

3 Robin Turton, Conservative MP and member of the Government.

4 Lieutenant-General E.L.M. Burns, Canadian; Chief of Staff of the UN Truce Supervision Organization in Palestine 1954–56; later commanded the UN Emergency Force in Palestine 1956–59.

Hugh McClure Smith, formerly Australian Ambassador in Cairo, now going to The Hague, and had a gossip with him about the Egyptians. He thinks Nasser insecure.

Throughout May we were quiet in the Office, our Ministers being all away in their constituencies, electioneering. The only trouble in my part of the world was the growing tension on the Gaza front, with shootings and reprisals almost every day. The Israeli Ambassador has begun to build up a case against any 'interference' between Israel and the Arabs by the Western Powers. Our role, in their eyes, is quite simple; we are to compel and cajole the Arabs into sitting round a table with them, without conditions. They are afraid (rightly) that if we have a hand in it we shall suggest concessions by Israel. He and his Washington and Paris colleagues were summoned home for consultation towards the end of the month, which caused our eyebrows to be raised a little, and the Americans took fright at once thinking the Israelis were going to come out with a rival 'Alpha'. Actually, they came out with a plain negative – 'no concessions of any sort by Israel. Keep off the grass.'

23 May

I lectured to the Imperial Defence College this morning on the Palestine question. Had written it all very carefully this time and it went quite well. I found that it cleared my own ideas on the subject, and am left with the strong conviction that the Jews are doomed if they don't change their ways. But they show no signs of recognizing that.

24 May

My birthday, and I went home early to vote for the Tory candidate – an act of supererogation, since his majority is secure beyond any doubting. N. and Robin give me their presents – gold cuff-links and brushes from N., a shoe horn from R., which he bought himself.

9 June

I saw Sir Walter Monckton in the Private Secretary's room this morning, and he seemed to be very lively despite his strikes, but not optimistic. N. and I gave a glass of champagne in Albany to the three Heads of my Departments, Michael Rose, Bunny Fry and Tom Bromley in honour of the CMG which all three of them were awarded in today's birthday list. Then we went on to the Festival Hall for a Gala performance by the Israel Philharmonic Orchestra (Brahms No. 4 and Honneger No. 2) and afterwards to the Israeli Embassy where far too many people had been invited. But we were early and got some food, and away. Met Anne and George Barnes,[1] and Theresa Clay who wrote the book about fleas.[2] Kenneth Younger told me he has despaired of Aneurin Bevan, whom he used to admire so much; says he has none of the qualities of a leader, cannot be loyal to his supporters, cannot play the game as a member of a team. I told Kenneth I had voted Tory, but hoped that the Labour Party would make it possible for one to vote for them in four years' time. He agreed with this point of view – just as, he said, he thought it would be too early for the US to change back to the Democrats next year, much as he disliked the Republicans. Lord and Lady Moran were rather sweet and cosy to us, and we saw Isaiah Berlin trying vainly to be heard in the howling bedlam.

10 June

Thought for a moment today that I might have to go to New York next week with Macmillan. Dulles has had 'new thoughts' about 'Alpha'; wants to announce it publicly now. But we decided M. should say he cannot possibly agree to such a thing without consent of his colleagues – and invite D. to send Russell over again. Had a long session with William Clark, about ME problems. He seems to be angling for the job of press agent to the PM.

11 and 12 June

Tom Bromley and his wife gave me a lift to the Christmas Common turning on A40 (there being still no trains) where N. and Robin were waiting for me in Greeners. We played tennis with the Dixons, had drinks with the Eshers and went down to Watlington to sing madrigals. Many new ones which I was reading, and I was the only tenor. On Sunday I learned how to turn wood on Mr Dixon's lathe, and began the centre column for my music stand. Horrible weather – a continuous wind which ruined the garden and frayed our nerves.

13 June

Called on General Templer at the WO to hear about his recent trip to Jordan, Iraq, Libya, etc. He has strong views about people; Nuri the only

---

1 My cousin Anne and her husband Sir George Barnes, formerly of the BBC.
2 *Fleas, Flukes and Cuckoos* by Miriam Rothschild and Theresa Clay (Collins, 1952).

'man' in the area. Great admiration for General Glubb though he admits he is excitable. He, Keightley, Duke and Glubb drove together round the country, visiting Arab Legion posts, and Templer says that after an hour or so they realized that all the applause, the interest, the panache, was for Glubb alone. His Beduin bodyguard swarm around every time he gets out of a car, constantly alert for his assassination. It is said they have let it be known that they fully expect him to be murdered, but that whoever does it will be guaranteed two or three hours of the utmost torture before he dies. Templer agrees fully with my theory that British troops in Arab countries must find some means of living closer to the local communities, and making their presence seem advantageous to the population. More mixing, more joint training, more spreading of the economic benefits by letting out contracts to local men, etc. etc., just as the oil companies have learned to do.

15 June

Half an hour with Macmillan at No. 1 Carlton Gardens – very different from the Eden days. Instead of my trailing up to the bedroom, Macmillan himself opened the front door to me and we had a cosy chat in the small study. It was all about defence, 'Alpha' and the Gaza trouble. After lunch I went to the offices of the COI and lectured, entirely extempore and without notes, for one and a half hours about the ME to a group of about twenty of their directors. Dined with M.

16 June

Drove out with Michael Rose and John Summerhayes [of the Foreign Office] to Northolt aerodrome, where I tagged behind the Duke of Gloucester, Selwyn Lloyd and Tony Nutting in receiving King Hussein of Jordan and his new wife Dina. Gloucester arrived in a helicopter, Hussein in an Arab Legion Dakota. The assembled cameramen were only interested in Queen Dina, who looked very nice but rather podgy in her 'Dior' coat and skirt. Her King very young and solemn, taking the salute of the RAF guard and shaking hands without a smile with the assembled Arab diplomats.

17 June

Nutting and I called on King Hussein at the Dorchester. To our surprise he did not have his 'wicked uncle', Nasser, with him, but two Court officials and his Ambassador. I got rather cross with the Egyptian Ambassador, Hakki, and the QMG, General Riszk, when they called and asked for more arms. I made a kind of outburst and told them they ought to pay more attention to preventing incidents on the Gaza front than to getting a lot of arms. They said they must deal with Israel 'from a position of strength'.[1]

19 June

Spent the morning with the Morans, he reminiscing about Winston, and very sharp and critical of many of the others, especially Montgomery whom he considers to be a phoney. He doesn't seem to think much of A.E., though admitting that he has good judgement of men and politics.

22 June

Reception at Claridge's for King Hussein, and afterwards to dine with him and his attractive Queen at the Jordan Embassy. R.A. Butler and his young son, the Mountbattens, the Turtons and ourselves the only English present. Rab next to Nancy talked very peculiarly, about himself mostly, but touching upon the Edens, the state of national taxation, the undesirable boom on the stock exchange and how he wishes we could pay more to the engine drivers. Mountbatten talked a lot about his deep-sea diving in the Mediterranean. Not much opportunity to talk to the King, as Rab left early and the party broke up by 11.

23 June

To Cambridge by train with Roddie, John Henniker,[2] and Norman Bentwich[3] who is to lecture to our weekend course tomorrow. Arrived to find I have rooms in Trinity Great Court. Lovely evening, walked into the Fellows Garden and along the Backs. Denis Robertson[4] made his number with us at dinner in Hall.

First talk by Dr Hourani, on the Arabs. A sympathetic account of the philosophy of Islam, rather idealistic I should think; and a gloomy picture of the corruption and decay in Arabia. He thinks the Sudanese likely to become one of the great nations – their character, intelligence, untouched by any but the best influence of the West. But he is convinced the Arabs will never make peace with Israel, and have no interest in doing so.

1 This was subsequently described by Nasser as 'pressure' and used to justify his arms deal with Czechoslovakia.
2 John Henniker-Major (later eighth Baron Henniker), Head of Personnel Department at the Foreign Office; later Ambassador to Jordan and Denmark, and Director-General of the British Council.
3 Norman Bentwich, Professor of International Relations, Hebrew University, Jerusalem, 1935–51.
4 Denis Robertson, economist, Fellow of Trinity College.

24 June

Lovely sunny morning, and I walked out of Trinity into King's after breakfast, and met Adcock[1] who gave me free run of the Combination Room. Also Patrick Wilkinson who showed me round the new rooms they are building at the end of Bodleys. Everything looking beautiful, well kept, prosperous.

Morning lecture by Professor Norman Bentwich on Israel – optimistic but not very convincing. I had rather to protect him against critical questions. After lunch I walked about again, and took a bus to Lensfield Road to visit the site of our old home, Stokeslea. Not only the house, but the entire landscape has disappeared and an enormous engineering school or something, half built, has arisen in its place. An extraordinary sensation. The whole ground on which our garden stood has been dug away, and basements and concrete foundations take its place. Only the old gate into Stokeslea, vestigial and one or two trees round the edge, remain there, derelict traces of the old scene.

At 3.45 we all collected on the Backs behind Trinity to watch the CIGS land in his helicopter. Lady Auriel, wife of the Master, and Denis Robertson with whom CIGS is staying. Then I had tea with them in Denis's room. The Bursar of Trinity told us about the difficulties of running a college of 750 undergraduates and seventy dons. No landlady class nowadays, and those there are prefer American airmen.

CIGS's lecture at 6.0, a little disappointing, but the discussion after dinner was better. Then I went to drink beer in Bene't Street with Robin Hooper,[2] John Henniker and Alan Dudley, and we gossiped in the Great Court until bedtime.

25 June

After breakfast we gathered on the Backs to see the CIGS off in his helicopter. Quite a crowd of spectators, children, and great excitement amongst the birds, who flew chattering in to the air space above the field after the helicopter had risen out of it.

Brilliant lecture on oil by Brigadier Longrigg; much the best we've had.

After lunch I began to think over my speech for tomorrow, which is now worrying me. At 3.30 the Cromptons picked me up outside the gates of Trinity and drove me out to Newton, to their modern-American-colonial farm house, Thriplow Farm, for tea. Scorching hot day. Cows, foals,

---

1 Professor Adcock, Fellow of King's.
2 Robin Hooper, Counsellor in Baghdad 1953–56; later Ambassador to Greece.

flowers. On the way back we looked in at Newton Hall, which is an oversized structure amongst glorious trees. Very luxurious inside, with unattractive modern paintings by people like Stanley Spencer. Walstons[1] not there. Back at 6.15 for Jack Troutbeck's lecture on social and economic conditions in the Arab world, a very good but pessimistic, not to say lugubrious picture. As the sun was still shining hot outside our discussion was not very lively.

After dinner Jack, Robin Hooper, David Scott Fox[2] and I went walking on the Backs and soon found ourselves locked in – or out – being unable either to get back into college or out into Queen Road. After much running about we stole a punt and escaped. All this time a white swan was chivvying a small white duck on the smooth, darkening surface of the river. Back in college, we found the younger members of our party organizing a race round Great Court while the clock struck 11. They said this was a practice run for a midnight attempt – for it is said to be just possible to run round while the clock is striking 12. I went to bed.

26 June

After walking up and down in Great Court for an hour in the sun, getting my ideas in order, I gave my lecture on British policy in the Middle East. Spoke without notes, and despite one dry-up in the middle it went quite well. Good discussion followed it.

This course has brought out still more clearly our dependence on good relations with the Arab world, and the impossibility of doing anything for Israel if she will not herself 'buy' a settlement with substantial concessions. It has also confirmed my feeling that the State of Israel was founded, both from the Jewish and from the Western point of view, on a false premise and in unnatural, impermanent conditions. The Jews were under the impact of the Hitler persecutions, desperate, on the run. This, despite ghettos and frequent persecution, is not their natural condition. It was also a moment of unnatural and emotional aberration on our part. We had a bad conscience about the Jews. In so far as we were not bullied by the Americans, we gave way to the passionate panic of Zionism out of weakness of will, war-weariness and confusion. Above all, we had not become aware of the extent to which we were becoming dependent on the Arab world for oil and for area defence against Communism. By 1943 we ought to have seen it, but we evidently did not.

After my lecture was over and last lunch in the Hall of Trinity (gradually filling up with scaffolding for the cleaning of the panelling) I went to the

---

1 Harry (now Lord Walston) and his wife Catherine; agriculturalist, politician and author.
2 David Scott Fox, Minister to the UK delegation to the UN; later Ambassador to Chile and Finland.

Backs and lay in the sun watching the punts and canoes go by. Wonderfully quiet and happy – no gramophones, no discordancy, even American GIs with shop girls seemed to behave discreetly and quietly, as though the ancient university had taken hold of them.

29 June

I lunched today with Bill Elliot, who told me a fascinating story about our lecturer of last week, Norman Bentwich. B. was his secretary during the war, and was foolish enough to take home to Hampstead one day, and to drop in the street while getting on to a bus, a copy of a minute by the PM which gave away the impending African landings and discussed the next moves thereafter. A real red-hot one. B. was arrested and Winston took the line, 'Here am I, with all my supreme responsibilities, and you let a man do this to me.' He wanted to have him shot.

4 July

Long session with the Vice Chiefs of Staff attempting to persuade them that a policy of trying to put a ban on arms for Israel is self-defeating. They are going to fight to the death against our releasing the six Centurion tanks, which we promised six months ago and held up on account of the Gaza raid. Ivelaw Chapman, in the Chair, saw my points clearly, but the VCIGS was adamant. I am not much helped in all this by Kirkpatrick, whose sharp logic is a little too thin and brittle to cover this emotional problem.

6 July

Called on the Sultan of Muscat in the morning at the Dorchester, accompanied by Bernard Burrows. Spent an hour with him, he told me of his confident expectation of being able to 'clean up' the Imam of Oman by a brief show of force as soon as his forces are ready. He is a charming, friendly little man with apparently complete confidence in us and in himself, and a contempt for the Saudis and their bribery which was very encouraging.

In the afternoon I had the Israeli Ambassador and Mr Peres (Secretary-General of their Ministry of Defence) for one and a half hours asking for arms, and I took the occasion to deliver to them most of my innermost thoughts on Israel and her prospects. Perhaps this was rash: I hope it does no harm. In particular I tried to show why the US and UK must necessarily nurse their relations with the Arab world and cannot, even if they should be inclined to do so, sacrifice their major interests there for Israel. But Peres was quite unmoved and uncomprehending. His philosophy is that the West have one job: to show the Arabs unequivocally that Israel – *in toto* – is there to stay because they will see to it that she does stay. Very exhausted by this performance, but recovered over a drink at Albany with the Burrows who then took us out to dinner at Quo Vadis in Soho.

7 July

Today N. and I had lunch with the Queen again – this time a much smaller party (for Sultan of Muscat) in a smaller room – a nice gay one with orange and gold pillars, to the right of the circular reception room on the ground floor. This I think is the room in which I once interpreted for King George VI and the Argentine Foreign Minister. Only ten guests – Sultan, Edens, Burrows, ourselves, Lord Chamberlain and Lady Scarbrough, Duchess of Devonshire and Adeane. After lunch I had what seemed like twenty minutes' conversation with the Queen. I was a little handicapped by having a cigarette in my hand, which steadily burned to my fingertips behind my back. A.E. was looking wonderfully fit and relaxed, and was very friendly to both of us. So was Clarissa.

In the afternoon I had a session with Francis Russell, who had arrived about two hours earlier from Washington, about our old topic, 'Alpha'. He told me why Mr Dulles wants to make a public statement of the 'Alpha' plan, instead of waiting for the secret negotiations which we have always contemplated but for which the Egyptian Prime Minister never seems ready. His account was reassuring. It is not, as I feared, that D. is weakening on the 'Alpha' demand for sacrifices from Israel, or is contemplating any abandonment of the position that Israel can only have a US guarantee after a settlement. His point is that only by getting the US Government publicly committed to this policy now can he insure himself against being compelled later on, in the atmosphere of US elections, to make a much more pro-Israeli stand. He thinks that if he (and Macmillan) make the statement now, he will get a lot of support in US, even from Democratic leaders such as Stevenson; whereas if he does nothing, and the Administration appears to have no policy, other Democratic leaders like Harriman are bound to take a position favourable to the Jews, from which they will not be able to withdraw and which will compel him to compete with them. There is a lot of force in this. We realize of course the risks – the outburst of protest there will be from both sides, and the bad times we may have to go through, rioting no doubt and the breaking of windows in US and British Embassies. We also realize the great danger that the Jews might 'accept' our plan, and then try to argue that since the Arabs reject it we must give Israel the guarantees without the settlement. Discussed all this with Nutting and I think we shall come to accept Dulles's broad proposals, though having some comments on the text he has prepared.

8 July

A desperately busy day, with 'Alpha' talks as well as trouble in Muscat, arguments about whether we need defence facilities in Lebanon, attempts to work out a policy on arms for ME (to replace the idiotic concept of a 'balance' between Israel and the Arab world as a whole), quarrels with the Egyptians about the composition of the 'Neutral Commission' to supervise the Sudan self-determination process, disputes with the French about the Fezzan (they want us in effect to divest ourselves – so far as Fezzan is concerned – of our responsibility for defence of Libya and give it to them without consulting the Libyans; this I really cannot accept, despite pressure from Sir G. Jebb). The day ended with my acting as host to a party of Lebanese journalists at a cocktail party in the Ambassador's Waiting Room from 6 to 7 and then going on to a garden party in Walt Butterworth's house, where I talked to Averell Harriman, Governor of New York, who is shortly going to Israel. He is of course going simply in order to make sure of the New York Jewish votes, and in order to make it quite plain that he is doing politics, he is also visiting Dublin and Rome. He asked me, 'What shall I say to the Israelis?', so I improved the shining hour. It was a beautiful sunny evening, and after going back to FO to clear up some papers I caught the 9.25 home.

9 July

A Saturday off, for the first time for many weeks. Did a lot of gardening – my new roses are in full bloom and looking wonderful. Took Robin swimming at Watlington Park; he now swims to the centre of the pool with a rubber ring, having been unwilling to do that last week. A sociable evening, for the Frank Wilsons came round to fetch their child from a party (he's just been accepted, at last, as a Queen's Messenger), and had drinks with me in the rose garden, and Christian came later to meet Francis Russell who came for the night. N. and C. were at Oxford for a performance of the *Messiah* by the combined village choirs of Oxon but returned about 9.30 and I made them omelettes.

Chapter Ten

Rough Going, 1955

From July 1955 to the end of the year the situation in the Middle East became increasingly confused. 'Alpha' was still under discussion and the diaries continue to show some optimism over it. But its prospects were fading. Opposition to the Baghdad Pact began to place a heavy strain on Britain's friends in the area (and notably on Jordan) and the Americans continued to refuse to join it. The conclusion by Egypt in September of an arms deal with the Soviet satellite Czechoslovakia revealed the Russian intention to play an increasingly active role in the Middle East. Difficulties with the World Bank over the financing of the High Dam at Aswan were to result eventually in a deal with the Soviets. All this led to recrimination between the United States and the United Kingdom Governments and to growing British impatience with Dulles. The descent to Suez was gathering pace.

14 July

Up early, fetched at Albany by Francis Russell and driven out to Northolt, to fly to Paris in Aldrich's Convair. Very luxurious. On the way out, Francis talked about the qualities of Eisenhower. His picture is that E., never a good strategist or commander in the field, had a genius for making people work together, relax and unite on sensible progress. This was his triumph as Supreme Commander. When he became President, people thought he had not the quality for it, and for a year it seemed as if he was not handling it. Yet imperceptibly it became evident that with his old skill he had calmed the inter-party bitterness, eliminated the recriminations of treason, etc., between Truman and the Republicans, 'cut McCarthy down to life size' and generally got the Americans working together again. Next, he had performed the same feat of quiet healing in the relations of USA with her allies of the Free World, and restored the confidence of the European and other free peoples in American policies and intentions. Now – who knows? – he might be embarking on the final stage of this progression, in reducing tension and suspicions between East and West. He goes to Geneva for the 'Summit' talks on Sunday. It is a pretty picture.

On arrival I called at the Embassy and had lunch in the garden with Gladwyn and Cynthia Jebb. They have vastly improved the garden by pulling out certain large trees, and have planted flowering shrubs and posted a large urn in a suitable position. I have told G. the main bones of our 'Alpha' story and naturally he thinks we should give the French longer notice. Sat in the Private Secretary's room all the afternoon, reading despatches about Egyptian intrigue in Libya and the deteriorating state of affairs in Iran, and writing up my diary. A great thunderstorm burst over Paris, and I stood watching it from the drawing-room window with a gin and tonic and the butler (full of stories of his days with Sir A. Cadogan in New York and Lord Derby in Paris), wondering whether the Secretary of State's party would land safely despite it. Half an hour with Macmillan after his safe arrival, when he showed a complete grasp of the 'Alpha' problems, outlining what he would say to Dulles tonight. The PM and Cabinet were evidently fed up this morning at being presented so suddenly with the change of plan. It was 'very hot', they had other difficult topics, such as Cyprus. They were not willing to commit themselves. I supped with Francis Russell off a chicken sandwich and some raspberries, and then we went off at 9.30 to Ambassador Dillon's house where the great were assembled at dinner. As soon as they were finished, Dulles and M. came out to us in a separate room, and gave us about forty-five minutes on 'Alpha' while the 'Summit' experts waited impatiently. All my old friends were there – Livvy Merchant, Doug MacArthur, and that old scoundrel of a 'press adviser', William McCardle. Doug said, 'When you were Private Secretary you never let people like you get in like that.' R. and I dictated our record to an American girl, and went off to bed, leaving the conference to begin. Paris, having been empty all day, was beginning to fill up with returning holiday makers. I don't suppose one can get to sleep with so much traffic in the streets.

15 July

Francis and I worked all morning in the Hôtel Talleyrand, which seems to be not an hotel at all, but given over entirely to American officers. We agreed a joint minute to our masters – 'Alpha' to be postponed until 7 or 8 September; British Cabinet to decide after H.M. gets back from the 'Summit' whether they will be co-sponsors of the proposals or merely applaud and support a Dulles initiative; in the meantime, US Government to tell us whether they will promise to join Iraq–Turkish pact in event of a settlement of Palestine, and (more important: I am making a great 'condition' of it) whether they will decide to equip Iraq Army with Centurions by off-shore purchase. These two things, we are saying, will make all the difference to Nuri and will help to reduce the risks of 'Alpha'.

Lunched with Tony Nutting at La Truite. We sat outside and ate *truite aux amandes* with a bottle of Chablis. Tony tells me that A.E. and H.M. are 'watching each other' a little cautiously. It must be difficult for H.M. having the past master sitting there behind him, and now coming forward to take the lead at Geneva. It seems that there have been some slight fireworks already about something. Tony told me Selwyn Lloyd is getting on well now with A.E., and is thought to be doing fine as Minister of Defence. Selwyn said the other day to him, 'I bet the best-organized part of the FO is the Middle East, under Evelyn.' It looks as if Turton is going to be moved elsewhere when the Cabinet re-shuffle (or shake-up) takes place. Monckton is to get Lord Chief Justice, though nobody has yet explained how they are going to get rid of Goddard, who is determined 'not to make way for a divorced party'.

After lunch I got half an hour with H.M., and sold him the results of our morning's work. He himself dictated there and then a paper for Cabinet, most cogent and correct. Russell came round and said Dulles has accepted our recommendations, too; so we've completed our task here. Dulles has also let it be known to us that the Pentagon are the niggers in the woodpile about supplying British equipment (tanks) to Iraq, but that the President is in favour. Therefore I've drafted a minute from H.M. to A.E., urging the latter to have a word with Eisenhower at Geneva. That done, I was foot and fancy free, and went off drinking with Eddie Tomkins,[1] Tony and Barbadee Meyer,[2] Johnstone the Private Secretary. Gramophone records, supper, walk along the quais, Ste Chapelle flood-lit, hot night. Another sleepless night owing to the traffic.

16 July

Stayed late in bed and caught the mid-day 'silver wing' to London after buying a French novel (*Les Aristocrates* by Michel de Saint Pierre), a bottle of brandy and some sweets for the children. N. met me in the new Heathrow airport – not finished yet, but in full use and looking rather promising. Back to High Wood where it was so hot that we sat in the wood playing flutes, and then to Watlington Park to bathe.

As we were sitting having supper on the lawn, a perfectly hot and still night, a large beech tree broke in half 100 yards down the hill, and fell across the lane into our field. Beech disease.

---

1 Edward Tomkins, later Ambassador to The Netherlands and to France.
2 Sir Anthony and Lady Meyer. He was a member of the Foreign Service in Paris and Moscow until 1964 when he became an MP.

17 July

Sunday. Lunched with the John Hopes, and in the afternoon I played cricket for his team against the village of Grey's. Blazing hot, and we fielded till teatime. After that I went in 10th, and was bowled first ball. We only made 80 to their 168, despite all our I Zingari and Harlequin caps. John's uncle, Lord Charles Hope, a picturesque figure in a straw boater; Lord Linlithgow his brother, George Thorne the hero of our side, Dick Troughton and a bevy of wives. A most enjoyable day, and afterwards I went with Robin to bathe in the pool.

19 July

Messrs Herridge and Dawson of the IPC [Iraq Petroleum Company] came to tell me of a new oil trouble looming ahead. Quite a serious one. The Syrians are trying to insist upon being paid half the difference between the price of Iraq oil at the Iraqi border and its price at the Mediterranean port – i.e. half the increased value resulting from its passage through Syria by pipeline. The IPC are prepared to pay them more money than they are getting, but not on this principle. We must support them, for once you admit the right of a transit country to a share in the increased value of the property after transit, where are you? Suez Canal would be the next case. IPC want to base their payments on a percentage of their invested capital in Syria, but this unfortunately would not give the Syrians enough money unless the percentage were higher than 'normal American practice', and in that case they would again be setting a precedent. All this against a background of Syrian political weakness, greed and xenophobia.

20 July

Knox Helm[1] came to see Nutting, and we discussed whether to stand firm with the Egyptians over the composition of the Sudan electoral commission, even at the expense of a real row. He is for it. He thinks we will have to have a show-down with Salah Salem over Sudan sooner or later (because S.S. is determined to get unity with Egypt by fair means or foul), and that we will never get a better issue to stand upon than this, with the Sudan Government and people entirely behind us. It is a question of having an entirely neutral commission, without Egyptian or British or Sudanese members.

In the course of this I asked Helm whether he confirms the opinion

1 Sir Knox Helm, Governor of the Sudan.

expressed at our Cambridge course – that the Sudanese have it in them to become a really independent and stable nation. He thinks they have. He definitely does *not* think we are wasting our time in trying to get them over the 'hump' of self-determination. He agrees that they are unspoiled, uncorrupted and that they have absorbed enough administrative competence from the British to run themselves easily, anyhow for the experimental years. Only Egyptian bribery in the South is a danger.

Lunched alone with the Jordanian Ambassador at the Dorchester; he told me nothing new, but his distrust of Fawzi el Mulki and the King's advisers is deep and personal. He said what a mistake it is that the Prime Ministers are always men from east of the Jordan – never Palestinians. He is a Palestinian himself, one must remember. He has read that the King is going in for motor racing and wants someone to stop it.

I hear from Geneva that A.E. has tackled Eisenhower to some effect over 'Alpha' and the tanks for Iraq. This may be a great triumph – if we can get a decision in principle that US will supply British equipment by off-shore purchase. Ike wants us to start with a gesture – some free tanks – and I think with A.E.'s support we may get Chancellor to agree.

25 July

Terrible day, with too much talk and too much food. Shell gave a lunch at Claridge's for Humphrey Trevelyan. I sat between Loudon, the host (the Dutch Production Manager of Shell), and Stephens who I think is their advertising man. Very interesting discussion about the dependence of the West, including USA, on Middle East oil in coming years. The Western Hemisphere oil, Venezuela etc., will be increasingly absorbed by American consumption, especially S. America, and USA will become a large importer of ME oil. So they, like the rest of us, will become dependent upon the Arab world for this commodity. Stephens said that although they are looking to atomic power to 'help out' over the next twenty years, there is no prospect whatever that it will replace oil except for *static* power production (i.e. electricity plants, etc.). There is no means of splitting the atom without producing beta and gamma rays, and these have to be carefully contained in protective covering which (in case of a car) would be ten times the weight of the car. Even if this ratio were reduced, it would still be much too dangerous to put an atomic device into a mobile thing like a motor car, since 'if you ran into a tree you might kill five million people'. Not quite sure how this fits in with the atomic submarine already launched in USA. Stephens implied that this was in fact an extremely dangerous object, and that if it hit another ship, or an iceberg, and were split in two, it would become the equivalent of an atom bomb. Robert Belgrave thinks all this is 'oil propaganda' by Shell.

27 July

Lunch at the Hyde Park Hotel for Sultan of Muscat – given by the IPC. Sir John Cunningham, the host, talked to me at length about the feebleness of the FO. 'You have an American Section, a European Section, a Latin American Section, a Chinese Section. What you need is a British Section.' He seemed pretty foolish, but they are backing the Sultan of Muscat up to the hilt, which is enlightened of them. Their technical man, Mr G.W. Bunkley, told me it is 50–50 whether they find a tremendous oil field in Muscat, or a lot of salt water. The structure is a perfect textbook example; but the oil might be absent. They hope to begin drilling this year. They want some very big aircraft to fly in their drilling gear (minimum weight twelve tons) and I may be able to help them with the Ministry of Supply. In fact, I obtained support of ME Oil Committee this afternoon in doing so.

28 July

Lunched at Lancaster House in honour of Hakki, the retiring Egyptian. I had Colonel Banks, MP, on my left, a bumptious charlatan if ever there was one, who fancies himself as a potent intermediary in Middle East affairs, devoted primarily to the interests of the Arab refugees but doing oddments on the side to bring in a little business 'for the British people'. He told me Nasser had assured him that he would take one Palestine refugee family for every five Egyptians to work on the Aswan Dam. I told him I did not believe it. Every time you mention an important person to Colonel Banks he says that of course he has had 'a very long talk' on several occasions with that person, and is in a position to assure you that he holds Colonel Banks in high esteem.

On my other side, Lord Henderson,[1] quiet, cockney and seriously worried by the turn of elections in Israel. He thinks Ben-Gurion[2] very dangerous, and fears that a recent speech by him may be taken as an

---

1 W. W. Henderson, Labour MP 1923–24, 1929–31; Parliamentary Under-Secretary at Foreign Office 1948–51; first Baron, 1945.
2 David Ben-Gurion, Israeli statesman, Prime Minister and Minister of Defence 1948–49, 1949–53, 1955–63.

incitement to murder Nasser. He shows great courage in standing out against the views of his party when he thinks them wrong, as he often does.

29 July

Meeting with two rather indecisive representatives of the IPC (Herridge and Lawson) about the iniquities of the Syrians; then forty-five minutes with the Secretary of State on 'Alpha' (about which the Cabinet took reasonable decisions yesterday) at the end of which I ground my axes on Iran, Syria, Aden and Muscat and got his support on all four; then a futile interview with the little Yemeni Chargé d'Affaires to whom I could only say that if his country would just talk to us we would talk to them; then the intellectual and moral effort of a 'round up' with Evan Wilson; and finally Catherine turned up, to be taken out to lunch with Christopher Ironside who is to paint her portrait. Discussed dress, position, form, etc., with him and went to Harrods with C. to find a high-necked shirt.

On return to my office, found Roger Stevens awaiting me and had to go through the whole problem of what to do about the Shah (and, incidentally, how sorry he is that we don't like his reporting or the sharpness of his style). Then a summons to No. 10, where the PM (A.E.!) wanted to ask me whether I thought William Clark would make a good publicity agent for him. On the whole I gave W. a favourable chit, and I hope he will get the job and won't disgrace me. I said he would be devoted, intelligent and imaginative and not an intriguer; but that there were elements of vanity and sycophancy (the latter, on the whole, quite a useful quality for the job). He would 'take his colour from his surroundings' – this pleased A.E.

Then A.E. (sitting and walking about the Cabinet Room) kept me talking quite a time. He described his and Clarissa's plans for redecorating the Cabinet Room. She has been studying the history of it, and is going to put silk again in the wall panels, and replace the (hideous) Ministry of Works ceiling lights and wartime blackout curtains. Then I asked him about Geneva. He said Bulganin had a sly look, 'like a Chekhov clerk or school-master', and that 'the other' (Khrushchev) was just like any other totalitarian police chief. He said that his own private view was that the Russians were looking ahead, and saw in ten or twenty years a very strong China to the east of them and a perhaps very strong Germany to the west, and were looking out for someone to hold their hands a little. They could not expect anything from America, and they saw that the French were no use, so they were looking to us. I said this was a gratifying thought – just the sort of role we would like to play – to which he replied that perhaps it was only wishful thinking. He agreed emphatically when I said that their change of front seemed due mostly to the H-bomb and their economic difficulties, but reverted to their fear of Germany. I wonder whether this means that he is moving away from German reunification. He cannot, I am sure, be moving away from German participation in defence and NATO.

David Pitblado I found to my amusement speaking in awed terms of A.E.'s 'flair' for politics, and impressed by the way he has handled the first, very difficult months of his premiership. He spoke well of Clarissa too.

After this I had to go through the whole of our Egyptian policy with Humphrey Trevelyan and send off a lot of telegrams about 'Alpha', and I retired to Albany to cook myself eggs and bacon, and to read papers, quite exhausted. But it is my last day before my holiday and nothing matters.

29 August

Returned to work after four weeks' holiday at High Wood, during which the sun shone almost continuously. Highlights of the holiday were arrival of our spinet from Mr Goble, a two-day visit to Hayling Island, where Robin learned to swim; several pleasant interludes with the Troughtons; my music stand nearly completed; arrival of Mr Gwyn Hughes [a holiday tutor] to take Julian off to Holland, and his great initial success with Julian (and with the rest of us) which we hardly dared to hope. Tonight I gave them both dinner at Bucks Club and saw them off at the Waterloo Air Terminus for Amsterdam. I stopped smoking a fortnight ago.

30 August

The Middle East looks if anything worse than when I left it. Mr Dulles has made his statement on Palestine and it has been unexpectedly calmly received; but apart from that things are very bad. Open fighting on the Gaza border; strikes in Bahrain; rapid internal deterioration in Iran; mutiny in South Sudan; mass outbreaks of murder and pillage in Morocco and the sacking of General Grandval; Soviet activity in Syria. 'Alpha' seems like a beautiful dream.

Supped with George and Joanna, and saw their two little girls (very bouncy and free) and their new baby. George said it is merely a matter of chemistry to find an antidote to radiation, and he feels sure that it will be found in the long run, so that the devastation of the H-bomb would be confined to its heat and blast effect and thus much circumscribed.

31 August

I walked to Bucks Club for lunch and found myself lunching there with Harold Macmillan. He was excellent company. He said that this morning's speech – at the conference on Cyprus – by Stephanopoulos[1] was very

---

1 Stephanos Stephanopoulos, Foreign Minister of Greece; later Prime Minister.

moderate and set forward a programme not very far removed from what we are trying to get ourselves. He hopes the conference will end with two conclusions – *first*, that all three parties will work for the establishment of self-government as a first step – consulting together on such matters as minority rights, etc; and *second,* that the question of self-determination (which for the Greeks means Enosis) be tacitly regarded as something for further study and discussion. He thinks this can be done by extending the conference (at working level) more or less indefinitely. But there is likely to be trouble because the Turks are being extremely tough and will not hear of self-determination for Cyprus at any price. They say that it is Turkish territory once the British, to whom they ceded it, cease to possess it.

H.M. also spoke strongly against abolition of the H-bomb. He thought any such thing would lead directly to war. For of course, he said, if there were an agreement to abolish it, along would come General Brownjohn and Pat Dean and would say to the Government 'of course, we must keep just a few', and the same would happen in the other countries, and you would then have produced the one sure condition for war, viz. misleading one another as to your powers and intentions. He thinks the only hope for the world is for the bomb-possessing powers to band together to prevent any other people having it, and to keep the others in order in their use of conventional weapons. It is worrying, otherwise, to see how the main danger of war today lies in places like Palestine and South-East Asia, where tanks and machine-guns and jet aircraft are still the decisive weapons because the Great Powers are not directly involved.

I had an argument with Kirkpatrick this morning about the Sudan. I have a feeling that we cannot entirely wash our hands of the Southerners and leave them to be massacred, partly because of the responsibility we have acquired for them during the last sixty years and partly because of the effect this will have on our own (related) tribes in Kenya and Uganda. But K. takes the logical, ruthless view that we have decided, and are committed, to get out of the Sudan, and that the quicker we do so the better, regardless of the consequences. He has a contempt for indecision and 'hovering between one policy and another'. I expect he is right really, but I said that Palestine was not a very good advertisement for the policy of 'getting out' from a difficult responsibility. There is a row between Knox Helm, Governor-General of the Sudan, and Andrew Cohen, Governor of Uganda, because the latter (instigated no doubt by former Sudan officials now on his staff) has urged us to send British or even Belgian troops into South Sudan to restore order and to protect the Southerners against Northern reprisals. Helm calls this 'Bog-baron' policy. I am instructed to go and see the Minister of State for Colonial Affairs (Henry Hopkinson) and tell him to tell Andrew Cohen to keep his nose out of Sudanese affairs, and to curb his ex-Sudan officials.

Macmillan is suffering from prime ministerial interference by A.E.! He said, 'He has got the habit of writing minutes on telegrams. It is a nuisance, especially as he is not even in London – or even at Chequers, but at Broadchalke where he has no room for a Private Secretary. But I am biding my time. I ignore most of them.' This afternoon we had a scene exactly identical (though more restrained and discreet) to hundreds I have witnessed with A.E. in the different role. My draft telegram to Dulles about next steps in 'Alpha' had to go to A.E. in the country, and he suggested all sorts of changes. We met most of these, but when M. was told that A.E. wanted the text cleared again with him, he threw the papers on the desk and murmured, 'I might as well give up and let him run the shop.' At lunch M. told me that when he went to see Winston after fixing up with the Americans and Russians the top-level meeting at Geneva last June, W.S.C. looked at him with a sly smile and said, 'It is wonderful what a difference it makes to your views about a top-level meeting when you get to the top.' This was his only comment.

1 September

I had to go over to Colonial Office and see Hopkinson at the behest of the Secretary of State, to warn him of the interference of ex-Sudan officials (now employed in Uganda) in the affairs of the South Sudan. Rather embarrassing and it meant a criticism of Andrew Cohen, Governor of Uganda. But he took it well. He looked utterly exhausted, but I don't know why.

7 September

M. has handed over to me all the letters I have ever written home, beginning with letters from The Wick, Hove (about 1919). I am going to sort them out and have the most interesting ones bound together. Am struck by my unjustifiable optimism and self-confidence as a boy; also my constant concern, when at school, with the progress of certain blades of grass in our 'back garden' at home. I seem to have got very much above myself when up at King's.

13 September

Bill Montagu-Pollock, now Ambassador in Lima, took me to lunch at the International Music Club, a rather smart place in Mayfair where I once had a drink with the Schumans. His main object was to tell me that he feels neglected and even slighted by the FO, because he is not in the 'political swim', and this despite the fact that he's had two nice Embassies and likes being in Lima. Some of the Ambassadors feel very far away, and they *are* very far away, and their reputation with the FO often depends on chance reports from businessmen or foreigners; whereas people like me who are at the centre can always get a hearing.

21 September

Outcry against the FO on account of Burgess and Maclean. All the vultures are after us – Crossman in the van. At luncheon today for the King of Iraq I told Duncan Sandys that I was shocked to see that Herbert Morrison had made statements hostile to the FO officials; this had not been at all his line when he was our Chief, and when he took farewell from me in 1951 he had expressed his admiration for us. D.S. went straight across the room to Morrison and told him, 'Your former Private Secretary is disappointed in you.' So Morrison came over to me and said, 'One is so often misquoted; the only point I was trying to make was that some enquiry should be made into FO to see whether the Foreign Secretary's burdens can be lightened.' John Hope has come out good and strong in our defence, saying that decisions about B. and M. were Ministers' decisions, not ours, and he is now being torn to shreds by the Beaverbrook press. He says that this does him a great deal of good. What I shall be keen to observe is whether the PM will stand up and take his personal responsibilities.

After this lunch I spoke to the Crown Prince of Iraq about the troubles of King Hussein of Jordan. He was quite understanding but will do nothing, I'm sure. He deplores the driving of fast cars by his own nephew, King Faisal, who has just bought a 120 mph Mercedes. But at least F. does not want to fly all the time, like Hussein.

We have had a crisis over Buraimi, Sir Reader Bullard having resigned from the Arbitral Tribunal on account of Saudi corruption and bribery. I am beginning to think we should denounce the Arbitration Agreement and resort to methods of straight force. They are crooks of the deepest dye.

22 September

Francis Russell is here, and our calm deliberations about the next step in 'Alpha' have been broken in upon by the news that Nasser is going to buy arms from Russia. Spent all day frantically discussing this, and concluding (with Harold Macmillan in the evening) that we cannot allow it. But how to stop it? The folly and fragility of our Palestine policy is beginning to come home to roost at last. As long as the Russians played no role in the ME we were just able to run with the hare and hunt with the hounds. But now they are obviously beginning to make a bid for Arab support.

23 September

Secretary of State wants me to go to New York, so as to be present when he discusses the Egypt business with Dulles. More confirmation this morning that Nasser really has committed himself to the Russians. But the Israeli Ambassador, who called on me this afternoon, swears that his Government have had an assurance from the Russians that it is not so. The poor Egyptian Ambassador, Abdel Fattouh, who was paying his first courtesy calls at FO today, got it straight between the eyes from Harold Caccia, Secretary of State and me. Francis Russell and I prepared instructions together for our Ambassadors in Cairo – very high-powered affairs in which we assure Nasser, in the name of President Eisenhower and the Prime Minister, that he *cannot do this*.

Life goes on underneath all this. I lunched at Hyde Park Hotel to meet a three-man mission of Egyptian water experts, over here in connection with the High Aswan Dam, Toby Low[1] being the host.

I was in a great state this afternoon, because of Egypt. I am indignant that the department think we must sit down under the Egyptian blockade of the Gulf of Aqaba, without even protesting, because protest will be vain and our shipowners are ready to 'live with' the regulations. At the same time I have to issue a strong warning to the Israeli Ambassador against taking the law into their own hands (as we have good reason to think they may) and bombing the Egyptian batteries. Elath's reply is, 'I agree; but it would be much easier for us to restrain ourselves if you will tell us what you are going to do about it.' Answer: nothing. The process of betraying Israel is going to be both dangerous and painful.

24 September

Very worried about Egypt, and in particular over having so openly exposed my lack of confidence in Israel to the Secretary of State. William Clark drove me down to Watlington, via his cottage at Lewknor, and discussed his first week with the PM. He said the most difficult change, after being a journalist, is to remember that bad news is bad, not good; also to

---

1 Toby Low (now Lord Aldington), Parliamentary Secretary at the Ministry of Supply 1951–55; later Minister of State at the Board of Trade.

remember that Sunday is not the day of the week up to which all politics lead.

Walked from Watlington Park to High Wood after looking at the state of the former's building, and met Christian, Lionel and Christopher out shooting. Talked with them rather gloomily in the autumn sun (they had one pigeon) about the three topics that depress me – Egypt, the Burgess/Maclean scandal which has just broken out again (White Paper in my pocket) and my having to fly tomorrow to America. N. fell from her horse this morning, out riding with Robin, and seems pretty bruised. Dined with the Eshers, where we met the Austrian Ambassador Prince Schwarzenberg (which saved me from being quizzed about Burgess and Maclean) and Lady Phipps.

25 September

A most beautiful sunny autumn day, High Wood views being quite marvellous, and the grass bright green after a summer of burned grey. Played much spinet, with N. and C. on recorders, and went through Robin's 5- and 6-times tables over and over again with him. Over to the Williamsons to get sleeping pills for my journey and we had a drink with them before lunch.

I left the house about 6.30 in an FO car for London Airport, thinking to get there by 7.15. But traffic blocks in Henley, Maidenhead, Slough and even on A4 near the airport were such that it was 7.40 before we arrived. I was greeted with the news that my booking had been cancelled and given to another! Utter consternation; but not for long. They were most obliging and forgiving, and got me aboard in record time, in fact not a whit later than Malcolm Campbell the racing motorist, who was a fellow passenger. But I was shaken by all this and repaired at once to the bar for gins and tonic before dinner. We landed at Keflavik, in Iceland, where I washed, cleaned my teeth and swallowed two of the blue capsules which Robin Williamson had given me in the morning. Result – six hours' solid sleep despite no sleeping berth.

26 September

New York at 8.30 a.m. (their time) after seventeen and a half hours altogether. Feeling quite fresh, and it is another lovely day, the same autumn sun sparkling over the city. Found Harold Macmillan very serious about the Egyptian arms deal with Russia. But I could not think how to handle it, being I suppose still a little fuzzy with flying and not knowing what news Francis Russell would bring from Washington. H.M. seems keen on taking it up with Molotov.

Roger Makins gave me lunch at an excellent small Italian restaurant the other side of Park Avenue, and I had little to do in the afternoon until Russell arrived about 7.0 p.m. But I wrote a paper setting out the various alternatives before us, and concluding that we must first try to frighten Nasser, then to bribe him, and if neither works, get rid of him. I dined with John Russell[1] and Henry Hopkinson at the Racquets Club, and found John uncertain whether he ought to be offended at having been posted to Tehran. Back in time for first meeting with Dulles and H.M. about Egypt. Livvy Merchant and Doug McArthur were there, silent spectators. Dulles and H.M. got more and more worked up against the prospects of a Soviet arms deal with Egypt as they warmed to the subject. The thought of Soviet technicians sitting on the airfields which *we* built, and to which we have to return in case of an emergency under the Treaty, was too much for H.M., and Dulles could not bear the Egyptian ingratitude for all the money US has spent on her. So they decided to go for Molotov, and Messrs. [Francis] Russell and Shuckburgh were instructed to draw up instructions for the Ambassadors in Cairo, designed to bring home to Nasser the enormity of his actions. But we left this until the morning.

27 September

Spent the morning on instructions for Cairo and lunched at a Swiss restaurant with Moore Crosthwaite.[2] He brought with him an ingenious idea for taking the question of ME arms before the Security Council as a threat to the peace, and urging a ban on all arms to the signatories of the Palestine armistices. We must study this if Molotov is quite intractable tonight.

Francis and I got our drafts examined at the tail end of a tripartite meeting (Pinay,[3] Dulles and H.M.). Dulles is puzzled and worried by the reactions of the US press, who are taking the line despite State Department denials that US is offering large amounts of arms to Egypt in order to offset the Soviet offer. He wonders if this is being worked by the Jews as cover for some impending outburst, or even war against Egypt. He is more than ever worried by the prospects, and suggested that if our efforts to dissuade Nasser fail we may have to 'start getting tough around there'. Pinay claims to have information that Nasser's deal with USSR is even

---

1 John Russell, Director-General of British Information Services in New York; later Ambassador to Ethiopia, Brazil and Spain.

2 Moore Crosthwaite, Deputy UK Representative to the UN in New York; later Ambassador in Beirut.

3 Antoine Pinay, French Foreign Minister.

more far-reaching than we thought, and includes an undertaking by USSR to support the Arabs against Israel and by Egypt to hot things up for the French in North Africa. This sounds to me like a too clever French supposition. H.M. has a poor opinion of Pinay, whose words for his own Prime Minister, M. Faure, are too strong for quotation.

Getting back about midnight I found H.M., Roger Makins, Geoffrey Harrison and Pat Hancock[1] mulling over the evening's dinner with Molotov. It went quite well. No disagreement about procedures for Geneva; some bickering about new admissions to UN and finally the assault upon Molotov about Egypt. He took it calmly; said he was not fully briefed but that when he left Moscow nothing had been sold to Egypt. We are wondering whether Nasser has been bluffing us. Harold Macmillan rather likes Molotov. He thinks that the Soviet leaders have a great desire to be considered respectable, like other people, reliable. The only thing is, they have a very hard core in their character which prevents relaxation. Macmillan very pleased that poor Armitage[2] has been removed from Cyprus. He thinks it most self-sacrificing and patriotic of Harding to take on the job – 'a thankless job, just as he was looking forward to his farm in Cornwall. But of course they all hate their farms in Cornwall after six months, so perhaps it is just as well.'

28 September

I had been worrying a little as to whether London would think we have made a mistake in approaching Molotov about Egypt (tho' actually Dulles did it first, on his own, and there was really no option for us) when a telegram arrived from the PM urging us on in the most explicit terms – in fact even suggesting that we should agree to four-power consultation on Middle East matters, and that he (A.E.) should if necessary telegraph to Bulganin. Shades of W.S.C! H.M. was very much surprised at this, and said it was 'the same illusion that Winston had, that there is a sort of club of men at the Summit. There is no such thing as Bulganin in that sense.' He can also see that A.E. is anxious to make peace all over the place, without much regard for the consequences. We are worried about letting the Russians too much into our ME counsels, and I suggested that the best way out is to steer the business towards the UN, which is already in charge of Palestine, and thus to try to limit it to the Palestine problem. H.M. and Roger Makins agreed with this, and I am to go to Washington

---

1 Pat Hancock, Principal Private Secretary to the Foreign Secretary (Harold Macmillan); later Ambassador to Italy.
2 Robert Armitage, Governor and C.-in-C. Cyprus 1954–55.

tomorrow to sound out the Americans – and Dulles himself if I can get hold of him, for he is busy with constitutional problems resulting from Ike's illness.

29 September

Up early, lovely morning sunshine over Manhattan, packed and made arrangements with Andrew Stark for a possible change of all our plans. I am to ask Dulles if it would suit him for H.M. to come to Washington on Saturday and stay until Monday evening for further talks about ME. If so, I shall stay over too. Early out to La Guardia, but the aircraft was delayed. 'The equipment skeduled for this flight is no good. Another equipment is coming in.' I am now sitting in the spare equipment hoping it has been well oiled.

The question is, how far ought we to bring Molotov in on this business of arms for ME? It would have been much better if we could have stopped the Egyptian arms deal at the Egyptian end, and I think we might perhaps have done that if it had not been for the wrong handling of Nasser by Byroade. It is clear that they are hopelessly embroiled, and Dulles has sent George Allen out to try and put it right. But it is probably too late. Pity that Trevelyan has not had more time at the job.

Since we almost certainly can't stop it in Cairo, there is no alternative to trying Molotov. The hope would be that he could be persuaded that this was an exercise in Great-Power policy, designed to prevent the outbreak of a local war which might set off a greater one. But if we are not extremely careful we shall (a) give him an excuse to claim a say in ME policies generally, to demand the abandonment of the Defence Pact and so on and (b) give the impression to our Middle East clients that there is no further need for them to suppress Communism, hold off the Russians, join together for defence. They might easily all run for cover.

Therefore I think the only safe way is to treat this as a *Palestine* question and handle it through the Security Council. Then we should have a frame within which to contain the contacts with Russia; and should not really be doing anything new. I hear that there is a letter on its way to me from Harold Caccia on this subject and I am sure it must be his cry of alarm at the PM's concept of four-power talks on Middle East, messages to Bulganin, etc. He would not like to telegraph. His letter will be opened in my absence and shown to Secretary of State. (This 'equipment' takes an awful long time winding up.)

(Announcement it is no use either!)

(11.30. Now sitting in a third equipment, having rung up Andrew Stark to fix me an appointment with Russell in Washington the moment I arrive.)

On arrival Washington went straight to State Department to see Francis Russell and Ray Hare (acting for George Allen) and ask whether Dulles would find it convenient for H.M. to come here for the weekend. Then to lunch with Leishmans, with whom I am staying.

In the afternoon telegram arrived for me from Secretary of State, forwarding a message from the PM which repeats in more urgent terms his desire to send a message to Bulganin about the Egyptian arms deal. I am really astonished that A.E. should act so exactly in the manner of W.S.C., considering how he hated it when he was Foreign Secretary. And there is less excuse, for the idea of sending messages to Bulganin over the head of Molotov is even more ridiculous than that of approaching Eisenhower over Dulles, or Stalin over Molotov. I think that A.E. really models himself on W.S.C. in a sort of perverted way. For instance, all that bedroom work is an imitation. H.M. would never dream of being so indelicate as to have the FO staff in his bedroom.

H.M. wants me, without mentioning the PM's desire, to sow the seeds of doubt, which I will do.

30 September

Long discussion with Russell, Hare and Fraser Wilkins of State Department which I have reported fully to H.M. It is clear that Dulles would be strongly opposed to any further approach to the Russians – especially a British 'top-level' approach.

1 October

Spent the morning at the Embassy and State Department but nothing very new to say. It becomes more and more doubtful whether George Allen and Trevelyan will succeed in preventing Nasser doing this deal. I had lunch at a restaurant called La Place Vendôme with Laboulaye, who as usual lectured me about the inadequate attention we pay to the French on ME matters. We kept being interrupted by TV raptures about the world series, in which the Brooklyn Dodgers today drew level with the New York Yankees. I had the greatest difficulty in refraining from saying that all this trouble has been caused by the French smuggling arms to Israel and selling them Mystères. Laboulaye shrewdly suspects that a merger of Iraq and Syria may become a possibility as a result of all these troubles, and solemnly warned me that such a thing must be done, if at all, in full consultation with France.

Then to the airport to meet Harold Macmillan who arrived in Roger Makins' nice four-engined Heron. I drove back to Washington with them, and found that H.M. is worried about the PM's insistence on sending a message to Bulganin. Bob Dixon has advised against the idea of a friendly discussion in the Security Council of the question of arms for Palestine – thinks it could only be done as a challenge to the Russians, and the danger of that is that we might not be able to avoid their posing as the friends of the Arabs. Foster Dulles has changed the character of tonight's dinner party, and I am not to be asked to it. Vice-President Nixon[1] is to be there, and Alan Dulles.

Back to the Embassy early and went to bed; but I was woken up at 11.45 and brought down in my dressing-gown to hear H.M.'s account of his dinner. Nixon was quite taken with the idea of a message to Bulganin from A.E. and Eisenhower, and suggests it might be the latter's first move on his return to active work next week. We are still not keen on this idea, but we may be able to work it into something fairly harmless.

2 October

To church with H.M., Roger and Pat, at the new Washington Cathedral. Very fine choir singing; full congregation and impressive service, marred by the reading of a long Pastoral Letter by the Bishops of the Episcopalian Church recently assembled in Hawaii. Actually it was quite a good message, urging a modest understanding of the peoples of Asia. But there were certain cracks about colonialism in it, including the inference that America's unpopularity with Asiatics is an 'inheritance' from more wicked Western empires. As H.M. said, 'We got the stick, as usual.'

A.E., to our surprise, is not content to wait until next week for his message to Bulganin. He seems to have got the Winston bug in a big way.

R.M. [Roger Makins] asked me to go out to lunch, so I went with Pat to lunch with the Ropers out in Virginia, in a house deep in the woods overlooking the Potomac. We had a very gay lunch, and the sun was shining, trees turning, berries red on the dogwoods. At 4.0 I had another session with the State Department, at which we exchanged the reports of our Ambassadors' interviews with Nasser yesterday. They do not give us much encouragement. Trevelyan got quite a lot out of Nasser, but the nett effect is that he cannot possibly go back on his contract with Czechoslovakia. Maybe he can be induced to limit it and make it politically innocuous by other gestures.

At 6.0 I was driven off for an hour's painful and vigorous arguments with the Israeli Minister Sheloah and the Head of the Arab desk in the Israeli Foreign Ministry, one Rafael whom I met in Tel Aviv. They

---

1 Richard Milhous Nixon, later President of the United States 1968–74.

(especially Rafael) are quite frantic about the Egyptian arms deal, and breathing fire and slaughter. They told me solemnly that Israel will not sit by and see the balance of strength turned against them by Soviet arming of Egypt. The West must denounce Egypt, arm Israel and give a guarantee of security without conditions. At the height of this I got annoyed and told them that I thought it was all their fault for pursuing a policy of reprisals against Nasser, putting his army in a humiliating position with their boastings, and in fact doing exactly what I had urged them *not* to do when I was in Israel last year. They were much astonished by this – though Rafael admitted that it was consistent with what I had said to Sharett in December last. They said Nasser was a crook, and that any policy of compounding with or appeasing him would be 'dealing with evil'. They mocked openly at the idea that Nasser, if given a chance, would work towards a decent settlement with Israel; this was a naïve illusion which 'certain people' both in London and Washington were nurturing to their own confusion. He had now shown his true colours, etc., etc. Here I said that Sheloah seemed to be making fun of me; which distressed him as it was meant to, and he was full of apologies until I left. Sheloah is very intelligent, and turns every argument to account. The line is to make the utmost use of this golden opportunity to show that the interests of the West coincide with those of Israel and demand the suppression of the Egyptians. It is an extraordinary thing that these sort of arguments appear irrefutable but wholly unconvincing. I left in Sheloah's car with Rafael, sadly contemplating this tragedy in which the Israelis are embroiled surely to their eventual perdition.

Alice Makins arrived during the afternoon from England and we dined quietly with them. After she had gone to bed H.M., Roger, Pat and I sat a long time drafting a telegram to A.E. trying to stop him inviting Bulganin to a round-table conference about all this. The telegram added, 'I must ask you to hold up your message until we can discuss the matter on Tuesday.' Rather weary – but sober – to bed.

3 October

A very long day indeed. Up early to prepare some notes for H.M.'s meeting with Dulles at 10 a.m. To our amazement A.E. has rejected last night's plea, and says he *is sending* off his message this evening. But he has removed the bit we most objected to – namely the proposal for a meeting. At our meeting with Dulles we went over the whole ground and decided that we must 'live with' the Czech contract, tho' we will try to get Nasser to limit it and offset it with political concessions – e.g. support of the Johnston Plan. Dulles treated us to a very interesting philosophical statement about methods of handling the Soviet 'new policy'. He said that if we consider ourselves entitled to go visiting Moscow, talking to the Russians, dealing between East and West, how can we complain about small countries like Egypt doing the same? Maybe we will have to ride through a certain amount of Soviet penetration in such countries, until such time as the Soviets come up against the difficulties and heavy burdens of sustaining a position. In any case, he said, we have little choice, since US aid for foreign countries is spread so thin, and has become so burdensome, that they cannot expect to compete with a Soviet effort concentrated at a particular point such as Egypt. Wait until the Soviets find that a 'one shot' aid to such a country has little value unless it is followed up by more and more expensive and continuous support.

All this confirms the general trend of our thought. At one moment Dulles suggested that I should stay behind to work out detailed policy, but Macmillan fortunately demurred. I may have to go back – but first I must get back in touch with FO and see what the PM is up to. Anyway, I suggested that we should let Nasser wait a little before we make our next move.

Back to Embassy for a quick lunch (Jim Thomas there) and then said goodbye to Alice and flew in Roger's Heron to New York, where we changed into the BOAC plane after a cup of tea with Bob Dixon. Cynthia Makins and John Russell were there to greet us. Hardly out to sea when we learned that the aircraft had a defect, and we landed at Gander to change aircraft. Sat there about two hours, during which H.M. was fascinating on the subject of the UK economy, the need to restrict public and private investment, instead of letting it flow and then taxing it ('turning off the tap instead of mopping the floor'), the uselessness of fighter aircraft, minesweepers, etc., in the H-bomb war.

4 October

Took a strong pill and awoke feeling very stuffy when breakfast came. Good landing at London Airport, where a helicopter was awaiting us. We walked straight into it, and in fifteen minutes were descending gently upon the South Bank, and getting into the car. Straight to Downing Street, where H.M. dived into Cabinet before an admiring crowd.

Plunged straight into very hard work. Not only consequential action from the Washington visit, briefs for H.M. to see the PM this afternoon and correcting the Bulganin message, but all the work of my three departments dumped unceremoniously on my desk by Ivor Pink.[1] Spent all the lunch hour eating sandwiches in H.M.'s office with him and Harold Caccia; then out for a shave. I find Harold Caccia has rather been taking the PM's side over the Bulganin message, but he seems to have seen our point on the whole, and at least there is now no suggestion in it of a meeting.

5 October

Desperately busy, and ended up the day with a bag full of work undone. During a meeting of Ministers today H.M. succeeded in getting agreement (a) to offering Persia the inducement she needs to join the Baghdad Pact (i.e. a statement by HMG of our vital concern for Persian independence) (b) to offer the Sudanese immediate independence (this will show Nasser we don't like his ways) (c) not to take the question of Egyptian arms before the UN. This was A.E.'s idea – and mine at an early stage – but I'm now convinced it is too dangerous.

Lunched at 10 Downing Street for the King and Crown Prince Abdulilla of Iraq. I sat between Harold Caccia and Robin Turton – the former preoccupied in lecturing Selwyn Lloyd on the other side of him about the importance of the ME and the latter talking complete rubbish to me about his recent visit to Israel and Jordan.

Later I sat in a circle where A.E. was being highly indiscreet to the Iraqis about 'Alpha'. He said that for over a year we (and notably Mr Shuckburgh) had been working out with the Americans a full and detailed plan for a settlement; but that greatly to his annoyance Mr Dulles had insisted on making a public statement (for internal political reasons): naturally this statement had contained none of the detailed proposals of the plan so laboriously worked out, but these remain in existence. Mr Shuckburgh has them, etc, etc. I only hope his guests did not understand what he was saying. Mr Morrison, who was also in the circle, kept muttering about the need to do something to help Israel, and this too I hope was not heard by the Iraqis; but I fear it all was, for they seemed bright and lively. At least A.E. has ordered the Minister of Defence to see what he can find for Iraq in the way of arms.

The Israeli Ambassador called upon me to find out my impressions of Washington and what we are going to do about the Egyptian arms deal. He was very quiet and reasonable, but feared we were about to appease Nasser. I told him there were no grounds for this fear. He asked of course

---

1 Ivor Pink, Assistant Under-Secretary of State; later Ambassador in Santiago.

for arms. What are we to do about that? After supper I went round to No. 1 Carlton Gardens with some telegrams to show H.M., and stayed with him until nearly 1 o'clock talking. He is a most entertaining companion. He told me all about his experiences with Eisenhower at Casablanca during the war; how E. had at first resented his appointment (not having been warned of it) but that at the Casablanca Conference some six weeks later when he was ushered in to the presence of the great, Roosevelt sitting in his chair, Winston deferential colleague at his side, Eisenhower at attention, Roosevelt spread wide his arms and shouted 'Harold, how are you? I haven't seen you in years'; and Eisenhower was amazed that H.M. had never mentioned that he was a friend of the President. 'You English, I don't understand.' Typical. He also told me a story – which he has put in his diary – which Bedell Smith told him after lunch last Sunday in Washington. It was to the effect that Eisenhower told Bedell Smith that he had been invited to run for President by both the Democrats and the Republicans and asked B.S. which he thought he should choose. B.S. asked whether he was a Republican or a Democrat. E. said his father was a Republican but his politics are democratic. But he decided to stand as a Republican because the system would only work if both parties had a turn. The country needed a change of party.

We also talked over all our ME problems, and evolved a Machiavellian scheme which I must carefully think over. We might even get USA into the Baghdad Pact in these conditions and really build up a serious Northern Tier.

7 October

Bernard Burrows is keen on our denouncing the Saudi arbitration, but he cannot think of any way in which we can scupper the fifteen Saudi policemen in Buraimi without seeming to be very dirty dogs indeed. They are there, after all, in full agreement with us under an international agreement, and sitting amicably alongside our own fifteen. If there were to be resistance and some of them got shot it would not look good. Yet we must get control of Buraimi. The Saudi Ambassador called more in sorrow than in anger to complain of our public accusations of Saudi bribery. He said our statement was more like an Egyptian broadcast than a British Government statement. I said the distinction was that every word we said was true. His line was that no Saudi, not even the King, knows what a million is, so that if they said to someone we will give you £30 million, it meant merely 'we'll give you thirty big piles of money'.

Gardener[1] called: he says he can bring about the merger of Syria with

1 Sir John Gardener, Ambassador to Syria.

Iraq any time we like if given enough money. Also Rob Scott, on the way to the Far East to be Malcolm MacDonald's[1] successor [as Commissioner-General for the UK in South-East Asia].

8 October

Long talk with Claude Lebel [of the Quai d'Orsay], in which he revealed the basic French opposition to our way of handling Middle East questions. They think all the ills come from the 'Northern Tier', which split the Arabs and forced those who were left behind to be even more violent about Israel than before and more hostile to co-operation with the West. Actually I think this is quite untrue. And if the French believe it one would have expected them to be particularly careful in their policies towards Israel not to give the 'remaining Arabs' – e.g. Syria and Egypt – grounds for being more scared of Israel than they need be. Yet it was talk of French Mystère aircraft for Israel, and the French ban on arms to Egypt, which set Nasser off on buying from the Iron Curtain. I invited M. Roux to come over next week for some more talks. We really must try to get the French to stop messing everything up.

17 October

This weekend I succeeded in calming myself down to some extent after a week of worrying about the state of the Middle East. I was helped in this by Ralph Stevenson, who came in from his retirement idyll to tell me not to worry about the Egyptians taking arms from the Iron Curtain, saying that it means nothing, they will be compelled by facts to remain allied to the West. Only don't imagine that they like us – they hate us, just as we hate and despise them. *The Economist*, too, is taking it philosophically.

I had a desperately busy week, during which I had to explain our thoughts to every sort of diplomat, including a whole day of M. Roux. My main objective now is to prevent Egypt taking economic aid from USSR – e.g. for the High Aswan Dam. But the World Bank are being very difficult about financing the dam, and insisting on public tender which is contrary to our interests since the Anglo-German Consortium is well ahead of the field.

Kim Roosevelt called, on his way back from Cairo, and gave me a fascinating account of Nasser's attitude which I recorded in a minute for Secretary of State. He sent it over to the PM. Main point was that the

---

1 Son of the first Labour Prime Minister, Ramsay MacDonald; later British High Commissioner in India 1955-60.

Soviet Ambassador in Cairo at once told Nasser all about the three Foreign Secretaries' approach to Molotov in New York, and urged him to stand firm. So they are obviously quite conscious in their drive upon our Middle East position.

We prepared a paper for Cabinet urging immediate abandonment of the Buraimi arbitration and seizure of the oasis and disputed areas of Abu Dhabi. H.M. accepts it, but I have fears of the Prime Minister. We have another paper, drafted by Robert Belgrave, urging an additional £1 million of Government expenditure in the Middle East.

18 October

The Cabinet accepted our Buraimi policy today, and tomorrow the Defence Committee is to discuss the means of carrying it out. They also agreed to our expenditure paper, and a working party is to be set up to produce concrete projects.

Meanwhile I had written a policy paper over the weekend, and H.M. sent it over to the PM who has instructed that it be circulated to the Defence Committee for discussion tomorrow. I showed it to Ralph Stevenson, who thought it a good paper. He thinks there is little danger of Communism in Egypt, even if they do accept Russian arms, because Nasser and the CRC [Cairo Revolutionary Committee] are so fanatically anti-Communist and have suppressed them so fiercely. He said, 'Egypt is fully committed to the West, but hates the idea of acknowledging it.'

22 October

Yesterday among other things I called on King Hussein at the Dorchester and had a nice chat with him. This morning came the Jordan Ambassador to say the King is upset about [Colonel] Dalgleish being taken away. So I cancelled my passage to Paris on Monday morning, and will spend Monday talking to the King. We cannot have Jordan going sour on us at this moment.

I summoned Elath to tell him H.M. will see Sharett – but preferably in Geneva – and he launched into a passionate plea – a demand, rather, for arms and guarantees. He tells me it is our *duty*, and I fail to see what duty we have towards Israel. But I did not argue.

24 October

Even in the Bristol it took us nearly two hours to get to town. The traffic in and around London gets worse every week. I spent most of today on

Hussein of Jordan, first preparing the ground with the Under-Secretary for Air, George Ward, and the Vice-Chief of the Air Staff, Air Chief Marshal Ivelaw-Chapman, as to what sort of air force we could supply to Jordan; then calling on the King after lunch. After the others had dealt with the air force question I stayed behind for a private talk with the King about: (a) the return to the RAF of Colonel Dalgleish, his pilot and head of the Arab Legion Air Force, which the King laments, and (b) his relations with Glubb.[1] It seemed to go quite well, and he asked me to come to Amman whenever I could. After this I worked until 8, got in an office car, drove to London Airport and caught the 9.0 p.m. Elizabethan BEA aircraft for Paris. Straight to bed in the Bristol Hotel.

25 October

A completely useless and frustrating day in which I achieved nothing. Could not get any attention from the S/S for my Middle East affairs, because the poor man had to sit all day in NATO listening to the smaller allies talk about the Geneva Conference and how they must not be left out of account. Yet he kept making me show up at different places, in order to have five minutes' talk with me in the car, or on a sofa in the Palais Chaillot, or on the steps of the Quai d'Orsay. So I could do nothing else. I got one hour in the morning, however, with Francis Russell, Hank Byroade and Ambassador Lawson from Tel Aviv, and found them in a state of great disarray and gloom. Could not contribute much enlightenment. Ended the day nicely by dining with John and Diana Beith and going to hear the Hallé Orchestra play Vaughan Williams and Brahms under Sir John Barbirolli at the Th. des Champs Eliseés.

26 October

Early this morning we reoccupied the Buraimi oasis and the main part of the disputed Abu Dhabi territory. It seems to have gone off all right,

---

1 It is a pity that the diary does not describe this conversation, since it has been suggested that the King warned me on this occasion of his wish for a change in the command of the Arab Legion. My own recollection, which may well be mistaken, is that I was on the look-out for a chance to sound the King out on this question, being well aware that he could not be expected to continue forever with a British general in command of his army; but that he did not give me an opening and that I did not have the courage to make one. Perhaps the official records will show.

I have always regretted that we did not deal with this matter amicably and in good time; we might have avoided the explosion which took place when the King dismissed Glubb four months later. But anything of that sort would, of course, have been described as another case of 'scuttle'.

according to telephone messages from the Resident Clerk. At 8.30 I was briefing Gerry Young[1] about it; and 9.00 dictating a note for the Secretary of State to use in telling Dulles, and by 10.0 a.m. (at last) we got Macmillan and Dulles together for a two-hour talk about ME. Dulles had all his experts – Doug MacArthur, Russell, Lawson, Dillon, Aldrich; but there was little unanimity and few ideas of what to do. Dulles explained how terribly hard to handle the US would be if the pro-Jewish lobby were to join with the extreme anti-Communist lobby in urging support for Israel against the 'Communist-aided' Egyptians and Arabs. I said, would it not be a good long time before our public opinions regarded the Arabs as Communists? And he replied rather sharply, 'Not in the United States.' This all seemed very depressing. D. did not like the news that we had occupied Buraimi; he thought it would react against the interests of Aramco. But he was not unpleasant about it. There was absolutely no discussion about what line should be taken with Molotov in Geneva, and we broke up (Sharett having arrived to see the S/S) without any sort of policy or plan.

Then Sharett for an hour, making a brilliant plea for arms and guarantees, taking us to task for our past policies and telling us how our duty and interest combine to impose upon us the necessity of supporting Israel more fully in future. He gave us the impression that his chances of avoiding a preventive war by Israel are very slender unless we grant him his demands. H.M. was quite firm, promised him nothing and told him he should consider making concessions for the sake of a settlement.

From there I rushed off, half an hour late, for a lunch I was giving (with John Beith, at Government expense) for Messrs Roux and Maillard in a private room at the Restaurant Carton Lukas, 9 Avenue de la Madeleine. Talked without stopping for an hour, this being the only meeting with the French which I was able to fit in during my visit. I took them frankly to task for the way the French talk in the ME of 'Anglo-Americans' as having a completely different set of interests and policies from the French, different Arab clients, historical rivalries. I said it also seemed to me out of date and meaningless. Their general line of defence was to attack me for the Baghdad Pact, which they said was responsible for splitting the Arab world, annoying Nasser and the Russians and *hinc illae lacrimae*.

27 October

Today was a low point – I hope the lowest – in my morale. I could not see any sense or prospect of sense in our Middle East policies, and there was none who would discuss it with me. Kirkpatrick too busy getting ready

1 Sir George Young, baronet, Head of the Foreign Office News Department from May 1955.

for Geneva; Nutting just back with a heavy cold. The Syrians are evidently about to break with the IPC and shut the pipeline; the Israelis about to attack someone or other; the Saudi Ambassador about to call on me, doubtless with the intention of breaking off relations or declaring war; Nasser riding high and 'eliminating the last vestiges of Western influence in the Arab world'.

In the end poor Hafez Wahba had nothing to say and was quite friendly though sad, and at one point came out sharply, in reply to an intervention by Mr Riches,[1] with the remark that 'the Statement of the Prime Minister [in the House yesterday] is not the word of God'. He said he lamented that his country was getting so close to Egypt, but blamed us for it and said our action in Buraimi would push it further still. Then I was summoned over to see Kirkpatrick in his house, and gave voice to my gloomy prognostications, to which he gave little quarter and equally little relief. I could see that he was very tired and unwilling to hear about the complexities of the situation, and he took refuge in those verbal gymnastics with which he so easily confuses almost anyone. He said it was no use 'being like Sir Victor Wellesley, moaning about the deterioration of events but producing no advice which Ministers can be expected to take'. He has written, at the Prime Minister's request, a message to Nasser which in my humble opinion is worse than useless, couched in sharp and inquisitorial terms and demanding that he 'declare unequivocally whether he wishes to be our friend or not' – because if not, we shall draw the requisite conclusions, etc.

28 October

Better today. Had a visit from Walter Lippmann,[2] to whom I gave a lively and perhaps not very discreet account of our dilemma in the ME and the danger of a wedge being driven between US and UK by the Palestine problem and the influences of the Jews. The Saudis have protested rather politely about Buraimi, but are clearly up to some mischief, perhaps involving the expulsion of British subjects from Saudi Arabia. I have drafted a different message for Nasser, and a line of talk for the politicians in the House about why we won't sell lots of arms to Israel; and I feel better. Drinks with Pinkie and Martyn, and dinner alone at Veeraswamy.

30 October

I don't see how we are going to compete with the Russians in the Middle East. Not only are they dishing out masses of more or less free arms, but

---

1 Derek Riches, Head of Eastern and Arabian Departments at the Foreign Office; later Ambassador to the Congo.
2 Walter Lippmann, leading American political commentator and journalist.

they are openly espousing the Arab cause against the Jews, and are even reported to be starting anti-Semitic policies in Russia itself. This forces us irresistibly to the other side, where we *must* not find ourselves. Syrians are about to break with IPC – so Iraq may want to march in there. Russians are opening diplomatic posts in Libya, Yemen; Egypt signing agreements with Syria, Saudi Arabia – perhaps Lebanon next. What do we do in face of all this? Kirkpatrick's method seems to me quite useless, and I have written an alternative outline approach to Nasser – in the form of a consultation, rather than an appeal or a lecture. I am still sure that the key lies in Egypt, and that we must make sense of Nasser by some means or other.

But the weekend was really soothing and comforting. Lovely autumn colours, to begin with, and we dined on Saturday night with the Ronald-shays, and met Lord and Lady Carrington. Nice dinner, very warm and squire-like atmosphere, good port and some excellent coloured slides taken by Pen.

On Sunday Alfred and I laid the foundations for a new garage for Catherine's car, in the woods; then we went to have drinks with Celia and Peter Fleming and met almost all our local friends and enjoyed ourselves greatly, driving home at a great pace in time to receive the Watlington Orchestral group with whom we played Handel, Bach, etc., all evening. Nothing like this to drive away one's anxieties. Robin has been moved up to the next form at half-term, and is now to be taught by 'Sister Bridget, who is very strict'. I said I hoped he would not get into trouble. 'Don't worry, Father.'

31 October

Meetings all day, and not much comfort, but I have purged myself to some extent of the excessive sense of personal responsibility and despair which weighed on me last week. Dulles and Macmillan got nowhere with Molotov over the weekend in Geneva; in fact they found themselves confronted with an almost frank insolence. 'I don't quite understand what it is you are proposing. Do you suggest that we should consult together about the level of arms supplies to ME countries?' At which, of course, they took fright and dare not speak to him again. Much better not, I think.

I went over to the Secretary of State's room in the House this afternoon to see Tony Nutting prior to a meeting on arms with the Minister of Defence. Found Tony looking very haggard and unhappy and he told me suddenly that he and Jill are separating. I was entirely surprised and distressed.

2 November

Anglo-Israeli Association dinner, and a set of the most lengthy, dreary speeches by the Ambassador, Edmund de Rothschild, Sir Andrew McFadyean (a sad bore) and Clement Davies. All the Jews telling us it is our duty, political, moral and historical, to stand by them in their hour of need. Rothschild wants us to invite Israel into the Commonwealth and assures us that that will make everything in the ME calm and stable. It crossed my mind that we might offer Commonwealth membership to Israel *less the Negev*; but that won't do either, I suppose. Clement Davies said we ought not to be guided by selfish British interests, but by the higher duty, etc. Of course they all say that it is only because of our sordid, materialist interest in oil that we fail to follow the course of higher righteousness in supporting this democratic, forward-looking, peace-loving and pro-Western state against the rotten Arabs who misused the land for so many centuries. But it is terribly tragic, however angry it makes one. They are all at their wits' end.

4 November

This was an almost intolerable day, during which I was continually being summoned by Nutting, Caccia, etc., to stand over them while they mulled over papers submitted by me, or (in the case of N.) thrashed about for action of some kind. There is real fighting in the El Auja section, and large claims of killings on both sides. I don't believe the Egyptians can do very much about it, and the Israelis are evidently not yet starting a preventive war; but the situation deteriorates rapidly. Hundreds of Parliamentary Questions to make our life miserable, and a series of Arabs (Bustani, Saeb Salam) came to warn me of the vast, unmanageable unpopularity of the West amongst the Arabs. These 'friends' of ours tell us that everything we do to stand up for ourselves is a fatal mistake. The reoccupation of Buraimi is a folly; we ought rather to do whatever King Saud says, because he is so rich.

In the afternoon General Burns came, looking much aged and very grim, and we discussed how to stop the fighting without much confidence. It is now a case of ordering the Israelis out of the El Auja demilitarized zone, and nobody thinks the three Great Powers have the will or determination to do it. But we are afraid of the Security Council, because of the Russians posing as friends of the Arabs. Every day the weight of Israel round our necks draws us further down into the mud.

The PM has expressed an urge to take a hand. It has occurred to him that with Eisenhower sick, Adenauer sick, Macmillan and Dulles engaged with Molotov in Geneva, there is only one great man left in the world capable of giving a lead and that is himself. So he would have liked to go to Cyprus in a broad and generous gesture of Peace, and summon the Egyptians and Israelis to his side. Unfortunately Cyprus is not in a proper condition for such a scene; and so he is driven back to the idea of making a stirring declaration at the Mansion House dinner next Wednesday. The only question is, what shall it be? Harold Caccia and I went over to No. 10 to talk about this. Naturally I pointed out that the Egyptians are not going to pay any attention to just one more appeal from the West to make peace with Israel, and that any initiative, if it is to be realistic and to avoid damaging even more seriously our position in the Arab world, will have to be something which the Israelis will detest. This very considerably reduces the attractions of the project; but the idea of doing something deliciously bold and dramatic while the others are not looking prevails, and I am to draft a passage for the speech, bringing in some mention of the 1947 Resolutions as a factor to be taken account of in any settlement. At one point in the discussion A.E. said: 'You are much more pro-Arab than you used to be' – as if it was a matter of one's preferences. This is really incorrigible.

After all this, and clearing up the accumulated paper work until about 9.0, I was completely sick with weariness and went to Bentley's for some lobster and early to bed but could not get to sleep for a long time.

5 November

Secretary of State, back from Geneva for the Burgess/Maclean debate, tells me I am to go there next week for two days for another round of talk with Dulles. He says that Dulles has confidence in me, and that whereas when he or Kirkpatrick suggest some Middle East action Dulles thinks they are grinding some political axe, when Russell and I recommend it he thinks it must be right!

8 November

Off to Geneva early by air, with H.M., Gerry Young and Pat Hancock. Lunched at the villa where H.M. is staying, with him, Kirkpatrick, Pat and John Wyndham.[1] H.M. is very pleased with the way the Maclean/Burgess debate went off, and indeed he seems to have had a triumph. When it came down to it, the House did not want to increase the rights of the state over the individual. Kirk told me that he had asked Molotov to tell him where

---

1 John Wyndham (first Baron Egremont), Private Secretary to Macmillan during the war, joined the Private Office at No. 10 when Macmillan became Prime Minister in 1956.

M. and B. are and what they are doing, since this would have given the Secretary of State's speech a special importance. M. hedged, saying why should he help Mr Macmillan with his speeches when he had such brilliant assistants as Kirkpatrick. They are amused at Molotov using the phrase 'Moscow was not built in a day', and think of telling him 'We have a saying – when in Moscow do as the Muscovites.' Then I spent the afternoon with Francis Russell and got his comments on Kirkpatrick's policy paper. It is quite clear that the Americans will not join the Baghdad Pact – for two very serious reasons. First, they think the accession of Iran has made the Russians very sensitive to the Pact, and very much afraid that Western air bases may be set up in this limitrophe country. Second, they set store on not driving Nasser more deeply into Soviet arms. I made a note of all this and sent it up to the Secretary of State's villa with the kind assistance of Alan Hare.

9 November

This morning was to have been devoted entirely to a Middle East discussion between Dulles and Macmillan, followed by a tripartite talk with Pinay. That is what I came over for. But as usual it was quite otherwise. Owing to Molotov's uncompromising speech on Germany yesterday the Conference is on the point of dissolution and we were forced to be content with forty-five minutes of the inattentive time of the two Ministers. Nothing was decided – but D. did approve of the passage about Palestine in the PM's speech tonight at the Mansion House. He told us of his plan to get Eisenhower to issue a statement tomorrow forestalling Sharett, who arrives in US on a propaganda visit that day, asking for arms. Lunched with Francis Russell in the cafeteria of the Hôtel du Rhône, and was attacked without provocation by McCardle, Dulles's press secretary, about some alleged leakage to the press on the part of Gerry Young. It was to cover a leakage of his own. In the afternoon we worked out a joint paper, recording the unanimity not reached by our Ministers in the morning. I had a steak alone in a nice popular bar, and then visited the Secretary of State's villa at 10.0 p.m., where I reported my day's work to the Secretary of State and Kirkpatrick. Found them very cosy with Hancock and Wyndham, reading their books and looking at telegrams about Cyprus. They had a copy of the *Evening Standard* with a large piece about me. At last I was able to talk to the S/S, and cleared a number of things with him. He and Kirkpatrick half hoped that the secret reports I was bringing them were true, and that the Israelis would attack Egypt, and have a good fight before going under for good and all. H.M. thought we ought to take the Jews away and settle them in Madagascar.

10 November

Went round early to see Russell at the Hôtel du Rhône and put finishing touches to our paper. Then we went in to see Dulles, who was sitting behind a small desk in a converted hotel bedroom with the inevitable stars and stripes standing beside him. Outside the window workmen were building a huge new block. He read our paper with great attention and made a few changes. Then he repeated his fear that if we build up the Northern Tier too ostentatiously it will seriously upset the Russians. He thought that their activity in Afghanistan and threats to Pakistan are at least partly caused by the accession of Iran to our Pact. I told him that our prime motive in asking for arms for Iraq was to show that good Arabs do as well as bad ones, or better, and that we were not advocating a great military build-up on the edge of Russia. He used the phrase 'it might be better to keep it a paper pact'. I told him of our Israeli reports, and he had not heard the same from his people. He hardly thought they would attack while Sharett was in the US.

Back to the Delegation office, where I worked until 1.15, then had some cold ham and beer with Ivor Pink at the Beau Rivage and was reminded by him that I owed him 6/-. Caught the 2.30 Viscount for London and was in my office by 4.30 (London time), having read a bit of *The Great Gatsby*, which I bought at Geneva airport together with a lot of Toblerone for N. and the children. Caught the usual train home. A very windy night at High Wood, but warm.

Just before I left Geneva, Pat Hancock told me he was worried about the possibility of our losing H.M. It seems that Rab is 'no good any more'; he must have had some sort of a breakdown since his wife died, and there is the chance that H.M. may have to be made Chancellor of the Exchequer. In that case it is hard to see who we should get – perhaps Selwyn Lloyd.

11 November

Harold Caccia and I were summoned early to No. 10, where we found A.E. with his press adviser (William Clark) worrying about the press reactions to his speech. Nobody seems yet to have suggested that it was asking too much of Israel to mention the 1947 UN Resolutions, but he has been criticized for being too weak in his references to a possible aggression by one side or the other. He has now forgotten that he originally thought of this as a move in which he would 'take the lead' in the absence of Ike, etc., and is anxious that the Americans should at once back him up. I told him that if he wants Ike to back his speech, he must back Ike's; for both of them tend in the same direction – to show that there is no future for Israel except in a settlement.

I had a visit from Dr Kaissouni, the Egyptian Minister of Finance, a young, tall serious soldier with whom I felt ill at ease. The new Ambassador was with him – looks somehow like a German, with Himmler spectacles: but he seems quite a sensible man. Kaissouni was only interested in the High Aswan Dam and did not fail to make the point that if we Westerners do not put up the money there is another source. When I gave him a homily about the evil intentions of the Russians he said I was preaching to the converted; but I wonder!

14 November

Ended the day with the PM again, at No. 10, getting him to agree instructions to Trevelyan for an 'Alpha' talk with Nasser on Wednesday. He is still standing firm in his intention to press for Israeli concessions, despite the criticisms of the Jews and the *Manchester Guardian* which, according to William Clark, he did not realize was a Jewish paper. From this I went on to give Tony Nutting dinner at the Turf Club. He said very little about his family troubles.

We talked a good deal about A.E., and Tony is greatly disillusioned with him. He has in fact not seen him at all, any more than I have, since he became PM, and feels that there is nothing left of the human relationship. We agreed that A.E. has no heart. Anyway we always knew that.

15 November

I had a very heavy day, with too much talking. In the morning I was engaged in trying to get the Americans to back up A.E.'s statement about Palestine, and in the process went over to No. 10 where I was received by the PM. 'My ex-Private Secretaries have the right to come in here.' He was somewhat preoccupied by certain Bishops' attack upon him on account of his divorce, and the proposal to disestablish the Church of England which is to be advocated in the House this afternoon. But he is sticking to his guns on Palestine despite the Jewish clamour. In the afternoon I had to talk to the Chiefs of Staff about reinforcing Jordan in case of an Israeli attack on Egypt (I am for it), then to lecture for half an hour (in the presence of Jack Ward and Frank Roberts) to the Yugoslav Secretary-General about Egypt, so that Tito can do good work on Nasser when he visits Cairo (I had difficulty here, as I kept finding myself saying, 'Of course Nasser does not want Communism: he is anti-Communist', as if all present would agree that was a good thing); then an interview with a man from *Newsweek* who is doing an article on Tony Nutting; and finally a set-to with the Israeli Ambassador in which we both got rather heated and I said, 'After all, we did not ask you to go there: we have no obligation to keep you there,' and he said, 'We absolve you from any obligation: you are pro-Arab; we have some friends, thank God; we lost four and a half million in the ghettos, perhaps we shall now lose another million. God help us, but we will fight for our lives and we will not give up a single inch.' I said, 'You are committing suicide for your people: you will have a heavy responsibility to them.' It was terrible. By the time N. came to collect me and drive me home I was more or less gibbering. Quiet supper at home, and we played recorder and spinet.

16 November

I am feeling better about Palestine, and see glimmerings of hope. Nasser and Nuri have taken A.E.'s statement very well and both talk of a settlement. Jack Nicholls thinks even the Israelis would like to be forced into a compromise despite Ben-Gurion's flat and absolute rejection.

18 November

Nancy drove up and we went with Askari (the Iraqi Chargé: a Kingsman) and his wife to hear Rubinstein at the Festival Hall and to the Colony in Berkeley Square for dinner after. Nasser and Fawzi are nibbling strongly at 'Alpha', and we now want to make a move with the Israelis. It is even quite exciting, though I suppose it is doomed to failure.

19 November

Saturday. Glubb is pouring out desperate telegrams of doom, which Michael Hadow[1] takes delight in thrusting under my nose. Glubb thinks we shall have to spend another £10 million a year on Jordan if we are to keep her in the fold – by adding a division to the Arab Legion. Even the CIGS rang me up to ask what we should do. I do not trust Glubb's panics. I am sure the Egyptians and Saudis are doing all they can to undermine our position in Jordan, but we have good cards left in our hands, and I don't see why we should fall at once for blackmail.

Finished my work at 2.30, had a quick lunch in St Stephens Dive, and got in an FO car for London Airport again, picking up Pat Hancock on the way. He lives in Pelham Crescent, next to the Humphrey Brookes.[2] We

1 Michael Hadow, later Head of Levant Department and News Department at the Foreign Office, and Ambassador in Tel Aviv.
2 Humphrey Brooke, Secretary, Royal Academy, 1952–68.

are off, I should explain, to Baghdad, for the first meeting of the Baghdad Pact Council. This at least is something to do, something stable, gathering together our friends. A Constellation, crowded, cold, no sleepers, constant interruptions. H.M., CIGS (Templer) and a few Staff officers.

At Rome (11.0 p.m.) we were met by Ashley Clarke,[1] looking very fit and filled-out, and had an hour's talk with him in the airport. He was mainly worried about PQs next week on the subject of Italy's sales to ME countries of British aircraft manufactured under licence in Italy. I asked him whether he thought Italy could help us at all in the ME and he said they were most anxious to, and might have some influence in Egypt (hardly elsewhere except of course Libya, where they are at present having a small row over UN Commission). I think at least we should tell them what we are doing about arms for ME countries.

Took two strong capsules and slept solidly through the miserable four and a half hours between Rome and Beirut.

20 November

At Beirut we were met by Ian Scott,[2] who handed us a Lebanese paper with the welcome headline that Lebanon accepts the Eden plan for a Palestine settlement, and says the Arab states are unanimous in doing so. (I fear they are misrepresenting the PM as having said that the settlement should be *based* on the 1947 Resolutions). The only critical voice today is our old friend Victor Khoury, formerly Syrian Ambassador in London, who takes the extreme line that there can be no discussing the *existence* of Israel. We had coffee and dry chicken sandwiches, but we did get a shave and began to wake up. It was cool, and raining, and the airport full of movement. Arrived Baghdad about 10.30, to be met by Nuri, Michael Wright, Robin Hooper, Kellas,[3] etc., a lovely sunny day, not hot. I was to stay with Robin so I drove straight to his house with him in his chauffeur-driven Jaguar and there found Con and (surprisingly) Barley Alison.[4] No time for a bath, as I had to get to Embassy for meeting with S/S about plans for the day. Was rather gratified to find myself in a large Arab city where there seemed to be no hostility towards us, and even the most slovenly looking 'intellectuals' paid no attention to our Union Jack. Lunch at the Embassy, much smartened up since the Wrights took over from the Troutbecks. The garden wall along the house has been painted pink (doesn't go very well with evening light, the main point of that view) and

1 Ashley Clarke, Ambassador to Italy 1953–62.
2 Ian Scott, First Secretary at Beirut Embassy; later Ambassador to the Congo, Finland and Norway.
3 Arthur Kellas, First Secretary in the British Embassy; later Consul-General in Tel Aviv, and Ambassador in Nepal and the Yemen.
4 Later a publisher and director of The Alison Press.

the furniture within somehow less drab, though probably little changed really. Nuri was at lunch, and very deaf, and I thought Esther [Lady Wright] coped extremely well. Had a bath after lunch in Pat Hancock's little bathroom near the roof, and then went along to a dreary 'meeting of experts', at which the Turks were most tiresome, trying to make points of substance while we were only talking mechanics. In the meantime I had dictated H.M.'s main statement for tomorrow – on our association with the Baghdad Pact countries, trying to make some logical link between us and this odd collection of ME states. Dinner at the Embassy and talked a lot to Gallman (the US Ambassador) and Admiral Cassidy (CINCNELM) who explained that the L stands for 'Atlantic' and the Iraq Foreign Minister, Boshayan, a big bull of Bashan sort of man, dark and thick-lipped whom I liked. But I don't remember much of the evening because after dinner we worked till late on the speech with H.M. and I drank a lot of whisky while being very lucid, and had to be given two Alka Seltzers by Robin when I got home.

21 November

A long morning session in which old Nuri, in the Chair, succeeded more or less in getting through the business by dint of having had every intervention typed out for him beforehand by his (British) Secretariat. The Persian, Ala, who had a patch of sticking-plaster on the back of his head, where he had been banged by a terrorist who had missed him with the bullet, was interested solely in getting himself named next year's chairman, and wanted it to begin on 1 January 1956. The Turks questioned every single point. At 1.15 H.M., the Ambassador and I set off for lunch with the Pakistani Ambassador to meet Mohammed Ali their Prime Minister, but we were kept waiting over an hour for lunch by the CIGS and his Pakistan colleague who had been in a meeting. During this hour we had one small glass of orange juice, and I actually went to sleep while talking to the Pakistani Ambassador, sitting on the sofa. I woke with a start, talking about Bahrain, but I don't know if it was relevant.

Ghastly session all afternoon. Once H.M.'s speech was over my eyes drooped again, and I had to leave the room once to wake myself up.

We all went to a sheep-bash with Nuri – several hundred of us, and I tore some tender lumps off a whole lamb, some rice and pickles. Very good. But I avoided speaking to many people, being at my last gasp with sleep.

Got a night's sleep despite the howling of dogs.

22 November

A much better day, though a long one. After completing our business in the morning we went into secret session – the five Ministers and US observers plus one each. Very interesting discussion. The main point which emerged was that everyone thinks Saudi bribery and corruption (allied with the Communists) is ruining the Middle East and distorting political life in all the countries of the Levant. There was a strong appeal by Nuri to Mr Gallman, the American observer, to find means of preventing Saudi Arabia from earning so much money. He naturally explained the difficulty for the US Government in interfering in the affairs of private oil companies like Aramco. The fact is that the American oil men have gone into Saudi Arabia with this vast enterprise which utterly submerged the old economy of the country, without assuming any responsibility for the political effects. It is as if the East India Company had regarded themselves as 'just neutrals'.

In the afternoon we finished our business, set up our Pact machinery and agreed upon the communiqué. Then we went to dinner with the King, where I was most friendly received both by him and by the Crown Prince. They both said, 'We thought you had not come,' because I was not with Macmillan when he called yesterday. Abdulilla took me aside for a talk about Jordan; he thinks Glubb is being too rigid. I like him. The King also talked to me for a long time – mostly jokes about Harrow and Winchester. Nuri was there, too, very deaf, but full of enthusiasm and vigour. He seized my arm and poured out his views on the iniquities of the Saudis and the danger of Communism in Syria. The oil companies should get together and save themselves before it is too late. The King and Crown Prince signed my menu for Julian.

After dinner we went back to the Embassy for a further talk with Charles Duke, our Ambassador in Amman, who had flown over to tell us of the parlous state of that country, torn between joining the Baghdad Pact and linking up with Egypt. Needless to say the remedy is said to lie in our doubling the subsidy of £10 million by giving them an extra division if they will join the Pact. Secretary of State, CIGS and I are all determined not to do this; but I suggested a 'package' offer, including revision of the treaty, some guns, Comet tanks and oddments, a reaffirmation of our guarantee and more British aeroplanes.

Michael Wright took no part in all this, having apparently retired to bed. When I got home I went out on the balcony outside my bedroom and listened to the dogs howling. A crescent moon faintly illuminating a desolate grove of palm trees, under which a lot of mud houses had long since crumbled to decay.

23 November

First the Crown Prince and then Nuri called upon H.M. at the Embassy, and we sat out on the terrace beside the river. Nuri said that he was perfectly willing to support Nasser if the latter made a move towards a Palestine settlement; he only hoped that Nasser would not change his mind under Saudi pressure. He evidently thinks Nasser unreliable and not strong. After this the entire staff were paraded past the Secretary of State, who made a very nice speech to them, and I was amused at Esther solemnly calling Michael 'H.E.' to me and the Secretary of State. I talked to the British Council man, who said there is a huge demand for teachers in Iraq which we cannot meet simply because no one will agree to go abroad. Then a press conference, then a very quick lunch with Robin and Con Hooper and Barley Alison and a dash to the airport. H.M., Pat, the detective and I went ahead in an RAF Hastings to Beirut, so as to have an hour or so to talk to the Lebanese. Very bad weather and apparently we had some difficulty in getting over the mountains; but I had taken a Dramamine and slept through it.

Called on the PM whose name I forget [Rashid Karameh], who lectured us for twenty minutes, very slowly, in Arabic, about the iniquities of Zionism. We lectured him back about the wider picture. Then to the Palace, where President Chamoun looked more worried and older than last year, and spoke to us bitterly about Saudi/Communist intrigue. He says all decent people are helpless in the face of massive Saudi corruption, and that it is all being done in co-operation with the Communists. We dined with the Ian Scotts and caught our BOAC for Rome. London after dinner.

28 November

It is difficult to write one's diary in these circumstances. So much work that one is worn out mentally and physically by the end of the day. I tried, on return last week, to get Ivor Pink to continue looking after my departments at least for a few days, while I handled the consequences of Baghdad; but he was most indignant and more or less refused to do it. So I am already submerged in paper, and on top of this there is a terrific scare that the Egyptians are going to give the Aswan Dam project to the Russians. It begins to look as if Nasser is even more unreliable than he seemed, and may even be consciously handing over his country to Communism. But I do not quite believe that. I think he thinks himself supremely clever, and is playing East off against West to the last moment.

On Saturday, N. and Robin and I went down by train to Winchester to attend Julian's confirmation. Over ninety boys confirmed by 'History Bill' (Dr Williams, Bishop of Winchester). We sat in the front row of the choir, exactly where I used to sit as a treble in the school choir. Tea afterwards with the Hamptons, where we met the old Bobber now looking very decrepit but full of reminiscence.[1]

Dinner on Saturday night for the Eshers (her birthday) and Bretts, plus Catherine and Christopher. Oliver attacked me violently about Cyprus, but Lionel took it on for me.

29 November

When I got to London this (Monday) morning I found there had been a tremendous hullaballoo over Saturday night about the Egyptians: PM and Foreign Secretary had come up to London; Kirkpatrick had been unable to get anyone from African Department; telegrams had gone to Washington, special message to Eisenhower and Nasser; and indeed, the evidence that Nasser is playing closely with the Russians is very disquieting – unless it has been planted on us, which I think is very possible. The PM is taking a strong lead in the direction of getting the World Bank and the US Government to put up quickly whatever is needed for the Aswan Dam, so that Kaissouni goes back satisfied from Washington. We shall be obliged to contribute too, I'm sure, tho' we claim righteously to have done our bit already by releasing the sterling balances.

30 November

Nancy came to town to keep me company, as I was in the slough of despond and not feeling very well. We went to a movie with Martyn and Pinkie after dining at the Carlton Grill. Today I have begun to console myself for the general *dégringolade* of Middle East affairs by getting on with certain matters; first, the means to get Jordan into the Baghdad Pact (at a meeting with Selwyn Lloyd I think we got substantial increases for the Arab Legion, and the S/S has blessed my idea of sending the CIGS [Templer] out to 'sell the package' to the Jordanians); secondly, an arrangement with Iraq whereby we let them off payments for the installations at Habbaniya, etc., in return for their buying arms from us; thirdly, my plan to get Peter Fleming into Muscat for the closing drama of the Imam of Oman next month; fourth, putting some content into the economic side of the Baghdad pact: I've got Denis Wright[2] to work on this with Treasury and Board of Trade. William Armstrong, the best Treasury man I know, is keen on this. Finally, IPC have reached agreement with the Syrians, which is a very good and unexpected piece of news. So we are beginning to recover our spirits.

---

1 Marcus Hampton was Julian's housemaster; the Bobber (Malcolm Robertson) had been mine in the same house.

2 Denis Wright, Assistant Under-Secretary at the Foreign Office; later Ambassador to Ethiopia and Iran.

I am indignant, however, at the treatment meted out by Kirkpatrick and the PM to Peter Matthews [of the News Department] for saying at a press conference that Krushchev was 'hypocritical'. It is the plain truth, and he ought never to have been disgraced for saying it.

1 December

N. and I did some Christmas shopping at lunchtime and bought a ukelele for Julian in the Charing Cross Road. Long session with Secretary of State. Very satisfactory.

2 December

Kirk tells me I'm likely to have another year plus a month or two before going abroad. That is, spring of 1957, when he himself, so he says, retires, and I suppose there will be a great shake-up. They think Bernard Burrows might succeed me – quite a good idea. I shall be nearly forty-eight by then, and a hardened old Whitehall figure.

Defence Committee today approved the 'package' for Jordan, and Templer is to go out, accompanied by Michael Rose. We all had an hour with H.M. about it this afternoon. It is a great gamble, for the Egyptians are thick as flies in Amman, trying to stop the King from joining the Pact, and we have got to overcome them now or never. I rather wish I was going – but I'm also relieved I'm not.

Had supper with William Clark and one David Panter-Downes in Albany. William tells me the PM is furious with the Israeli Ambassador for a letter he wrote in *The Times* this week and thought seriously of asking for his recall. Instead, Kirkpatrick is to be invited to dress him down. That is regarded as the equivalent of six of the best.

Subsequently some friends of the Arabs, including General Spears,[1] tried to get *The Times* to publish a rejoinder, but were refused so they got the Jordanian Ambassador to sign it and it duly appeared. Quite a good letter. Low, the cartoonist, has set the Jewish readers of the *Manchester Guardian* about the ears by publishing a letter in which he correctly defines the dilemma in which Israel now finds herself and urges an effort to reach a settlement with the Arabs.

3 December

This was a nice peaceful Saturday (from 2.30 onwards) and Sunday, during which I completed the garage and put in the windows, and N. burned leaves outside the kitchen door. A dark red sunset, and all nature very

1 General Sir Edward Spears, First Minister to the Republics of Syria and the Lebanon 1942–44.

relaxed and autumnal. Two messages from the PM over the weekend, both about Israel, but no change of policy.

5 December

Spent the morning and early afternoon getting Templer and Michael Rose off to Amman with their instructions all in order and their 'package' offer all tied up. In intervals I had a visit from the new Australian Minister in Cairo, a large unwieldy man looking rather like a police constable, who held the conventional views on Nasser. Kirkpatrick advised Templer to tell the Jordanians that bilateral pacts are no longer *à la mode*, and that the smart thing is to wear the new kind of hat. Can't see this going down very well with the Arabs.

6 December

Dulles has replied, after a fortnight, to the message H.M. sent him on return from Baghdad, saying that he thinks we should 'wait a little' before getting Jordan or Lebanon into the Baghdad Pact. It is of course too late. D.'s message is also very unsatisfactory on the subject of Buraimi (he wants us to return to arbitration) and of Saudi corruption (he does not think US Government can limit or control the use of Saudi earnings).

In the later afternoon I had a quiet forty-five minutes with the Secretary of State, and went over our many problems with him. He thought our Middle East position 'rather exciting' – so many issues on a knife-edge: will the Dam come to us? will there be a Palestine settlement? will Jordan come into the Pact? what will King Saud do? etc. He has dictated his own speech for next week's Middle East debate, and it is very good. He is reasonably hopeful about Cyprus even, though he deplores the weakness of the Greeks and fears that their lack of courage may undo them. The Greek Government is at least trying to reach a settlement with us.

7 December

Bernard Burrows is now expressing doubts whether Peter Fleming will be allowed into Muscat by the Sultan. We told him to damn well get permission. Rest of the day spent in vain competition with the CRO over the drafting of a reply to Nehru's complaint to the PM about the Baghdad Pact. The trouble was started by the PM asking both FO and CRO to do a draft and then telling his own Private Secretary to do one too.

We both lunched with the new Lebanese Ambassador and Madame Ahdab, the Chapman-Andrews being the only other guests. Ahdab told me the French, even more than the Saudis, are responsible for the anti-British and anti-Baghdad Pact attitudes of Lebanon and Syria. While the Saudis influence the Muslim minority in Lebanon against us, the French do the same for the Christians. Dined at Albany with Harry Walston, Hugh Dalton and Jack Ward. Unexpectedly enjoyable evening. Dalton said there is a story about me which he has been spreading around – that when A.E. succeeded Morrison as Foreign Secretary I said, 'With Morrison one could have helped' – which I daresay I did say; in fact I know I said it. I went over our whole Palestine philosophy with Dalton and he seemed quite impressed though he kept saying he would not commit himself not to attack us in next week's debate. He said something which confirmed my belief that I am regarded by the Jews and their friends as an evil counsellor to the Foreign Secretary. Attlee resigned today from leadership of the Labour Party and Dalton says it is certain Gaitskell will succeed. He says Morrison's friends have all been trying to persuade him not to run, since he is likely to be bottom of the poll and it will be a humiliating end; but he is not listening to them. Harry Walston is cock-a-hoop because he has got his visa for USSR.

8 December

Telegram from Washington saying that Sharett has pretty well flatly rejected Dulles's suggestion that they make sacrifices in the Negev, but that there are slight chinks in their armour and D. wants to know, by this afternoon, whether we see any objection to Francis Russell telling them of the 'Alpha' plan. Can't object, but sent some warnings back and asked that Russell should not indicate that his suggestions result from talks with us.

Good news from Muscat, where the followers of the Imam (cut off from their Saudi paymasters by our occupation of Buraimi) are beginning to come over to the Sultan. We may be able to get rid of the Imam without a fight.

9 December

Pat Hancock is depressed about how things are going in the Government. He says the PM is trying hard to make H.M. Chancellor of the Exchequer, and that we shall be landed with 'that bloody Selwyn Lloyd'. H.M. doesn't want to leave the FO and doesn't want to be pushed around and seems to be in a bad mood. Meanwhile Tony Nutting is getting into bad trouble (as expected) in New York and the PM wants to order him home. It could be said that A.E. is not doing very well.

10 December

There is another reference to me in this week's *Jewish Observer*.

On Sunday morning I began veneering the second frame of my music stand, but the FO were ringing up all day long and eventually I had to come up to London in the evening by train. Visited the Secretary of State at No. 1 Carlton Gardens with Kirkpatrick and Hadow, and we discussed the next move in Amman. I think Templer will get some sort of an assurance, or letter of intent, out of them. He wants authority to use certain threats if they don't. Kirkpatrick said, 'I don't trust these Arabs,' to which H.M. replied, 'But you say that about every foreigner that is mentioned.' They were talking of the breakdown of talks on Cyprus, and the need to 'bring it to a head' this week by the arrest of the Bishops and a real suppression of the terrorists (if it can be done!). K. said he would take away all wireless sets, bicycles and cars; and make them carry identity cards and stay in their own villages. It is a grim prospect.

12 December

Today was day of Middle East debate in the House. H.M. had written his own speech, to which we had made a number of amendments designed primarily to prevent him being too explicit on Palestine. I had a talk with him during which he said that Nehru (who had expressed such strong objections to the Baghdad Pact) is really doing his best to hold the balance between Right and Left in India, and that after his death there seems a very fair prospect of India going Communist. 'But there are some very tough people on the Right, too, who might be able to prevent it.' There is a rumour today of more trouble in the Kremlin, and one has a glimpse of the nice prospect of Khrushchev and Bulganin coming back from their elephantine tour of India and Burma to find themselves under arrest! Clark,[1] of the CRO, tells me that Nehru has given us explicit assurances of his continued independence of policy, refusal to buy arms from Russia, etc., but in the lucid watches of the night I could not avoid the conclusion that all Asia is moving steadily out of our ambit and that our Western civilization will be seen strangled and subjected, with its bombs unusable in its pocket. Fortunately in the daylight such gloomy prognostications are overlaid by veneers of busy confidence.

I had an hour also at No. 10, sitting at the Cabinet table with Kirkpatrick, Buchan-Hepburn, Guy Millard, Robert Carr and Clark while A.E. went through the draft of his speech for the debate. He is mainly concerned to

1 Sir William Clark, Deputy High Commissioner in Delhi.

defend his Mansion House statement on Palestine. He is quite firm about it, and not wanting to make any concessions to the Jewish lobby: but at the same time hoping that by some trick of words or charm he can please them. He kept turning to Robert Carr saying, 'Is that all right for the Jewish lobby?'

14 December

The days go too quickly for recording. Last night I did get home for the night, but as soon as I arrived the telephone started ringing and it went on until just before midnight, with news first good, then bad, from Templer. Finally came the report that the Jordan Government had resigned and that a new man, Hazza Majjali, who is in favour of joining the Pact, is being asked to form a Government. This sounds just all right. T. is coming home.

Today we were thrown into a rage with the Americans upon receiving two notes or messages – one telling us that we had better go back to arbitration on Buraimi because otherwise the Saudis will be very annoyed and may take us to the Security Council; and the other practically ordering us to call off the Sultan of Muscat's impending clear-up of the rebellious Imam of Oman, again because the Saudis won't like it. Kirkpatrick is breathing fire and has sent for the US Minister, poor man, a Mr Barbour, who is new.

After an interview with the Egyptian Ambassador and a nice dinner at the club, I caught the night ferry for Paris, took two strong pills and was asleep within ten minutes of reaching the sea.

How the Arabs hate us really. I was talking to Haikal, the Jordanian, a friendly one. They will never forgive us Israel.

15 December

Met at the Gare du Nord by a London taxi belonging to the Embassy. Raining. After clearing my yard-arm with the Secretary of State I went to see Francis Russell at the Hôtel Talleyrand, and spoke at great length and suitable vigour about the Dulles messages. He said that there were differences of opinion in the State Department about all this; that some were doubtful about the policy of giving way to the Saudis, but that all had the feeling that we tend to act without due consideration for American interests. He said he thought someone ought to go to Washington to explain our policy, and that it ought if possible to be me.

Lunch at the house of the American Ambassador, Dillon. I sat between him and Francis Russell, opposite H.M. who was on Dulles's right. Dillon seems to think (and Gladwyn Jebb confirms) that it is only the Quai d'Orsay and a few newspapers like *Le Monde* who care so much about France's alleged position in Syria and Lebanon. They neither of them think that the French people would be much concerned if Syria were merged with Iraq. After lunch we retired to the room where I have now attended so many meetings, including the terrible one with General Radford a few days before the fall of Dien Bien Phu, and had a session on the ME. There was only a limited time and I was rather horrified when H.M. began with 'clearing out of the way a few small points', and got the meeting launched on to German support costs, Chinese membership of UN, etc. The usual story; we lost half our time, and never really got down to the Middle East. But H.M. did make a statement, based on my brief, about the need to retain our positions in the area, including especially the Persian Gulf, and I think we may now regard ourselves as having 'side-stepped' the Dulles messages, especially in view of the sharp attacks which both Kirkpatrick and I delivered respectively in London and Paris this morning. I got a telegram from K. saying, 'I made a fairly savage attack on the American Minister this morning emphasizing that Americans were playing the Russian game and violating justice'! Better still, news came that Nizwa has fallen without any resistance, and the Imam fled to some mountain village.

It was agreed that I shall go to Washington in January to prepare for the Eden–Eisenhower meeting on Middle East. When this was being mooted I said that Francis Russell and I had the impression that the only aspects of ME policy on which there was not Anglo-American identity of view were those on which he and I had not yet worked. I thought for a moment that this was not going to be thought funny, but Dulles eventually laughed and applauded us for being willing to take on another difficult topic.

I think H.M. told Dulles this afternoon that he will no longer be Foreign Secretary by next week. It is a real blow to the FO. Rab is to be Leader of the House, H.M. to be Chancellor of the Exchequer and Selwyn Lloyd Foreign Secretary. Somehow I don't see how A.E. and Selwyn are going to get on with one another with Selwyn at FO. He will resent A.E.'s interferences so bitterly. I hope I shall succeed in retaining the moderately successful relationship I have with S.L. The great thing is to stand up to him, for he is a bit of a bully. I can't imagine what will happen if the Democrats win the US election and Acheson comes back. He once called S.L. a 'crooked Welsh lawyer' – as appears somewhere in this diary.

My last appointment of the day was a meeting at the Quai d'Orsay, where the three Foreign Ministers met, mainly for French appearances, to talk about the Middle East. Pinay had a whole list of tiresome little points, many of them irrelevant or out of date, and his four or five advisers kept shouting things in his ear all the time the others were talking. So it was with utmost difficulty that H.M. and Dulles extracted from him an assurance that he would not despatch twelve Mystère aircraft to Israel at the present juncture. He speaks and understands no English, so that very little of what is said penetrates beyond Massigli, de Margerie, etc. Old Dulles made quite extensive use of his very slow and inadequate French, steeped in American accent.

16 December

Home in time for supper with George and Joanna; Catherine also there with two other young people. C. is up having her last sittings for the portrait.

17 December

A little worried by reports of demonstrations in Jordan against the Baghdad Pact, though the Government and King seem to be quite firm. Home with C. and I worked on the veneering.

18 December

Today (Sunday) was the occasion of a kind of Royal Visit to Watlington Park by the Eshers; their first sight of the house since the alterations began.[1] They seemed on the whole quite favourably impressed, and it was fortunately a sunny day. The Hutchinsons (Peggy Ashcroft) were also there for lunch, and I explained Buraimi to them all with a map. (What a bore I am becoming.)

19 December

Serious rioting in Jordan, and for some reason a very bad day for me which left me utterly depressed about our affairs. I feel we may have 'torn Jordan in pieces' as I feared we might. Nasser is jumping the gun on us over the Sudan, not that that matters, and we have made a good offer to him on the Dam. But if Saudi/Egyptian/Communist intrigue can prevent Jordan joining the Pact despite our offers and despite the King and Government

---

1 On inheriting Watlington Park, Lionel Brett had decided to reduce the house to its original Georgian form, pulling down various accretions including an extension which had been added by his own father.

wishing to do so, how far the rot has spread! I'm also depressed by A.E.'s reported intention to remove H.M. from the FO and give us Selwyn Lloyd. I dined with Tony Nutting at Boodle's, where we met Guy Millard. When I told Guy that the FO was astonished and depressed at losing H.M. he seemed quite surprised, and asked whether we didn't think he might do better in the Treasury. I suddenly realized that this change is *not* being made because A.E. is desperate for a good man to succeed Rab; but rather because he is critical of H.M. as Foreign Secretary. I could see it all in a flash; he is *never* able to be loyal to anyone, and he does not like H.M. having a policy of his own. Tony Nutting thinks Selwyn will be a pure mouthpiece of A.E. But Tony has his own reasons for being discontented. I'm sure he realizes he's being removed from the FO; he spoke of having been sounded out as to whether he'd take the War Office – and having refused. I doubt it.

Everything is in a mess – the economic prospects very bad, relations with the Arabs, Asiatics, Chinese, Russians very bad, no longer any lead in the atomic field. I am tired and depressed, and all the nonsense in the newspapers makes me angry. Today I had lunch with the Jordanian financial delegation at the Dorchester, sat next to Sir Edward Boyle, the Financial Secretary to the Treasury, who could not think of a word to say to his Jordanian host, and seemed utterly emptied of content by political showing-off. One never seems to meet a Tory MP nowadays who does not talk as if he was a member of a TV quiz team. I also had wearing interviews with the CIGS, Dick Crossman (who told me that we ought to be advocating neutralism for the Arab world, with a vast US/UK base in Israel); the Lebanese Ambassador; also the Secretary of State (perhaps for the last time); Nutting; and Turton. Tonight I feel that the whole ME situation turns on whether Glubb can keep order in Jordan.

21 December

Found out this morning that after his talk with me on Monday Crossman went straight off and rang up the Israeli Embassy and told them all about it. He said I was a nice chap, but very anti-Israeli, completely bankrupt of policy, conventional in outlook and no good. What with this and the lies which the Egyptian press are spreading about our policy in Jordan, I became almost as depressed during the day as I have recently been at night. Lunched with the Eshers, where I had a good talk with Freya Stark about the Middle East. She thinks we are losing the Arab world because we have de-personalized our relations with them. Instead of sending men out who will spend their lives there and get to love and be loved by the Arabs, we deal them institutions, pacts, etc. Short-term officials, who change every

two or three years and have no spirit in it, are a poor substitute for
Cornwallis, Kirkbride, Glubb.

This afternoon I went to say goodbye to Harold Macmillan. He is deeply
distressed at leaving the FO. He was enjoying the Middle East problems
'so much happening, so many projects that can go right or wrong'. He
thinks we shall have more troubles before we succeed in stabilizing the
situation, and he is certainly right. He agreed with Freya Stark's complaint,
and suggested that we might send out distinguished figureheads to the ME
countries, to act as Ambassadors for considerable periods with someone
else to do the work. He spoke of Cromer's influence in Egypt, based entirely
on personality and not on force or rank. Thinks we could manage it again
if we really tried.

22 December

Got away this evening for ten days' rest, feeling that I could not have
borne another hour of it. All three children at home, and a wonderful
Christmas and New Year. Eshers gave C. a Morris Minor convertible for
Christmas – great emotion. I finished the music stand, planted a fifty-yard
hedge of holly, beach, yew and box, and played a certain amount with N.
on the Dolmetsch treble recorder, with ivory mouthpiece, which she gave
me for Christmas. Robin and Julian both got ukeleles, and both started
quickly to learn them. We gave a New Year's Eve party at which Peter
Fleming was very severe to William Clark (who had been running down
A.E. in an all too familiar boasting way). It seems, however, that A.E. has
been behaving very badly, and rang up poor Selwyn thirty times over the
Christmas weekend from Chequers. He *cannot* leave people alone to do
their job.

Thinking about Crossman, etc., I think they are mad not to see that
unless they can reach some accommodation with their neighbours and learn
to live with them, they have no hope of a stable and peaceful homeland for
which they have yearned since the diaspora. But if you say this to them,
they say you are anti-Jewish. They seem to have a sort of ghetto instinct.
I had an argument about this with Arthur Koestler at Pinkie's house. He
saw the point, of course, but did not accept it.

Chapter Eleven
Downhill, 1956

In this last chapter the diaries record the deteriorating position in the Middle East during the first six months of 1956 and my increasing despondency. Harold Macmillan, to his own regret (and mine), had been removed from the Foreign Office at the beginning of the year and replaced as Secretary of State by Selwyn Lloyd. By the end of March I was asking to be released from the Middle East work and I left the Foreign Office on secondment to the Imperial Defence College (IDC) on 20 June, five weeks before the nationalization of the Suez Canal. The diaries throw light on the process by which Anglo-American co-operation in the Middle East became eroded and finally broke down over Suez.

2 January

Badly received by the new Secretary of State, Selwyn Lloyd, who was (perhaps naturally) upset that both Kirkpatrick and I were away for his first week. Preparations for a complete review of our Middle East policies, first at a conference of ME Ambassadors to be held this week and then in my talks next week in Washington where I am to prepare for the visit of the Prime Minister and Secretary of State to Ike and Dulles. I shall have to cross the Atlantic four times in a single month!

Dined at the Turf Club with the Wyndhams and Lionel Brett, and later we came up to K.3.[1] for a gossip. John is leaving us shortly, following Harold Macmillan to the Treasury.

4 January

Conference all day with the Middle East Ambassadors; Selwyn Lloyd in the Chair during the morning, Reading in the afternoon. Good statements by all the Ambassadors, especially Michael Wright and Humphrey Trevelyan. I went to lunch at Claridge's with Persian Chargé d'Affaires for Dr Amini, to whom I sat next and found very entertaining. His brother,

---

1 Staircase K.3. in Albany, Piccadilly, where I rented a room from Harry Walston.

Military Attaché in Paris, was there too. After the Conference we had drinks in the Ambassador's Waiting Room with Selwyn Lloyd and I then went over the points covered during the day with him. Found him in more mellow mood and very quick to deal with. Took John Hope to dinner at Turf Club, where we joined Selwyn and Oliver Poole (Chairman of the Conservative Party) who were dining together there. Amusing evening. Poole thinks the present criticisms of the PM amongst the public – and especially party workers – stems from his delay in making changes in the Government. They are all obviously worried by the press campaign against the PM, which includes Conservative press as well as Labour. But Selwyn is loyal and spoke of his great qualities, tho' suffering so severely from his less great qualities.

5 January

Second day of Conference. Selwyn conducted it well, though called out three times by the PM on account of some muddle over the Brazilian President's visit. Tony Nutting surprised us all by advocating quite impractical moves like announcing that we will back a claim by the Arabs to part of the Negev, or telling Nuri he can march on Arabia, overthrow Saud and put Abdulilla in his place. I prepared a summary of the conclusions of the Conference but was not able to get Selwyn to approve it. He is very coy about agreeing to anything. Dined at Veeraswamy with N., who was fogbound in London after taking Robin to the circus.

6 January

Preparing for Washington and trying to get the recent Conference in perspective. I have written to Kirkpatrick urging that the authors of the proposed Eisenhower–Eden declaration should pay some attention to the uncommitted millions of Asia, and not confine themselves exclusively to stale clichés from the European cold war.

The Jews are after me again; they say I am to get the sack because of the failure of 'my' policy. They took a long movie picture of me yesterday, coming out of the Conference.

Spent an hour with Selwyn Lloyd, talking to him about how to stand up to the PM and how to evolve a policy for the Middle East. I told him how Anthony used to say, when pressed by No. 10, 'They can get another Foreign Secretary' – 'They' being a sort of mixture including the Queen, Winston, the Tory backbenchers and Christopher Soames. I told him that he should bide his time, and then one day when A.E. is being tiresome on the telephone he should bite back sharply and say why can't you leave me alone to do my job? Then A.E. will be very upset, for he hates the thought of someone not in the immediate neighbourhood who is annoyed with him, and he will be 'sweet' to Selwyn for at least a week.

Meanwhile the Tory attacks on A.E. gather in strength. I dined tonight with Tony Nutting who says all A.E.'s friends have more or less been driven from his side, and there is none now to defend him. But Tony thinks Beaverbrook, with his flair for controversy, is about to come out on A.E.'s side. That will be a fine reversal – and probably a kiss of death. We ate caviar and grilled sole at Wilton's.

7 January

Saturday. Very worried about events in Jordan, where Glubb seems to be near panic. We were always told that the Arab Legion was absolutely certain of being able to handle any internal trouble; but now Glubb says that if the wives of the British officers get frightened to the extent of wanting to be concentrated in the cantonment at Zerka, the morale of the Legion will collapse. Only King Hussein seems to be keeping his head.

8 January

Michael Rose rang to say there is very serious trouble in Jordan. Also, Selwyn Lloyd has spent the whole weekend meditating upon, and correcting in detail, the action telegrams we submitted to him on Saturday. The Government is still in a state of jitters at all points. Peter Fleming, as Stryx, has written an article based on his row with William Clark at our house on New Year's Eve. Very bad manners in my opinion.

9 January

Real worry about Jordan all day. The King wants an Iraqi Division to march in to his aid, and we are thinking of sending British forces (a) from Habbaniya (RAF regiment) (b) up to Amman from Aqaba (Armoured regiment) (c) to Cyprus from UK (Parachute Brigade). Meeting with the PM in Cabinet Room at 7.0 p.m. at which we discussed these plans, and Selwyn succeeded with some difficulty in getting past A.E. an instruction to Humphrey Trevelyan to see Nasser and reason with him about his anti-British actions in Jordan. A.E. was in the mood that Nasser is a cad and why should we have anything to do with him. But Selwyn stuck to his guns and with Harold Macmillan's support got his way. Then we went off for supper, I with Chilver, of the Cabinet Secretariat, to the St Stephens Dive, where he told me A.E. is 'rattled', not only by the criticism but by a series of leaks which have been taking place of Cabinet documents, so that he feels he is dealing with his colleagues *in foro publico*. We met again in the Cabinet room at 10.30 and got our telegrams cleared.

10 January

Visited by George Brown, MP, the only member of the Labour Party who is not besotted with Israeli propaganda (with the exception, he says, of Aneurin Bevan); the French and Italian Counsellors, the Jordan and Israeli Ambassadors. Besides I forgot to say that yesterday I went over to the Ministry of Defence to give Walter Monckton a lecture on the Middle East.

This was one of those days that never ended. I tried to get someone to give me comfort and guidance for my visit to US but Selwyn Lloyd was not available, Kirkpatrick was in a particularly sharp dialectic mood and only poor Nutting, who is at the moment rather blown upon and out of touch, was helpful. I have a feeling that the Washington visit of the PM and Secretary of State is being prepared somewhere else, by someone else, and that although ostensibly I am going out to prepare it (on the Middle East side) I have not been told all. However, perhaps I can prepare it my own way and override the anonymous others. At 6.30 Ian Samuel, Geoffrey Arthur, Myra Sully [my secretary] and I set off for London Airport for the USA. But we had not been there long when delays were announced, and we were given drinks and dinner by BOAC and sat awaiting news until after midnight in the company of a troop of motor car manufacturers (technicians) from Manchester and Birmingham who were on their way to Australia. The Governor-elect of British Honduras, Townley, and a man called Salisbury, General Manager of East African Airlines, were also in the party and I had some talk with them. By 1.0 a.m. we were embarked in a bus for Sanderstead, Surrey, where we spent the night at a vast bogus mansion called the Selsdon Hotel, and away back in the morning to London Airport. This time lucky. All day in the aeroplane – Gander. I read my briefs.

11 January

We got off about 11.30 and spent the whole day in the aeroplane, stopping at Gander and arriving at New York about 10.30 at night, local time. We were put up in the New Weston Hotel, where I went off into a deep sleep as soon as I laid my head on the pillow.

12 January

Bob Dixon rang me up in the morning, and told me he was quite looking forward to handling the Buraimi dispute in the Security Council. I find that I am quite a feature of this morning's news – my arrival reported in all the papers and my name mentioned in the first leader of the *New York Times*! We all got on to an aeroplane at La Guardia and flew to Washington in the morning. I lunched with the Makins family, saw Francis Russell and had a nice cold, windy, sunny walk with Alice and her son Christopher and youngest daughter, Virginia, along the Potomac river. V. and I went up the Washington Memorial and walked down the 900-odd steps. She is a silent and shy child, but very gentle in character like her mother. Francis Russell tells me that there is a negotiation about to start with the Egyptians and Israelis.

Dinner with Ronald and Joan Bailey; a delightful party including the Roosevelts, Russells, Coulsons[1] and Rountrees (Rountree is now Deputy Assistant Secretary for Middle East in State Department). Everybody is talking about Dulles having dropped a brick by saying (in remarks quoted in an article in *Life* magazine) that the art of diplomacy is to bring nations to the brink of war. Of course he did not mean that, and it is clear from the words he used that he did not mean it. But there is a great row none the less. Election year.

13 January

First meetings at State Department, morning and afternoon. We ran over the ground – Baghdad Pact, Israel, Jordan, etc., and I gave an account of the conclusions of our Ambassadors' Conference. I also spoke very frankly about the Jordan incident, and said we did not regret the action we had taken, since it had revealed facts about Communist penetration which we might not otherwise have uncovered. This went quite well; but George Allen seems worried about our position in Jordan and to think we ought perhaps to give it away. He is very discursive and makes wild suggestions for which there is no official backing. One cannot tell what to take seriously and what to ignore. Mr Bowie [of the State Department] attended in the afternoon and asked various searching questions about the value of the Baghdad Pact which subsequently got around to the newspaper. None of it meant anything – I mean they are all 'talking out of the top of their heads'.

1 John Coulson, Minister at the British Embassy; later Ambassador to Sweden and Secretary-General of EFTA.

14 January (Saturday)

Very satisfactory talks with Francis Russell about policy towards Israel. In the afternoon I moved over to the Coulsons' house (same house, same room as [their predecessors] the Scotts last year).

15 January

Ian Samuel and I are preparing my statement for tomorrow about Buraimi. We are making it strong. I can see that this is to be my most formidable task.

16 January

I spoke for one and a half hours on Buraimi this morning. Cannot tell yet what impression it made, but have the feeling that it opened their eyes to a lot of things. George Allen had not even realized that the Geneva case was not the arbitration itself. In the afternoon I was questioned at length about my Buraimi statement, and emerged very exhausted in time for cocktails with Willie Morris[1] and dinner with the Leishmans, where a woman called Sophie Prentice, with a cosy manner and a strong Southern accent, sang songs to the guitar all evening.

17 January

More talks all day. Lunch at State Department, at which Allen Dulles talked most interestingly about his experiences at the end of the war, when he extracted the Ciano diaries from Edda Ciano in Switzerland after she had smuggled them out of Italy on her person, pretending she was with child. It seems that he did her some disservice, for the money she earned from her book, based on the diaries, was eventually blocked by the American Custodian of Enemy Property and she still has nothing of it (according to a strange elderly female I met, called Mme Brambilla, who knows her).

This evening I called with Ian Samuel and the Petroleum Adviser upon Mr Terry Luce, the Aramco adviser to King Saud. Apart from being allowed to sit upon a pair of nail scissors, inserted upright between the cushions of the sofa, I was not actually assaulted. But he was very cagey and so was I. He told me the figures of Aramco payments to Saudi Arabia during 1955, and of the bank loans she had received against the backing of Aramco tax vouchers. I don't quite see why.

1 Later Sir Willie Morris, Ambassador in Cairo.

18 January

More and more disturbed about Buraimi. The Americans seem unwilling to look at the merits of the matter, and take 'a neutral position between their two friends' – by which they mean advocating a renewal of arbitration or some other form of mediation. They are convinced, they say, that we shall find it impossible to sustain a completely negative attitude in the Security Council, if it comes to that; and that they could not support us in such an attitude. The more we protest the strength of our case and of our evidence, the more they say 'Then why can't you face a really impartial arbitration?'

19 January

My last day. As I expected the American position on Buraimi is very unsatisfactory. They treated me to a long account of the hopeless position we should be in in the Security Council; we would never get the item off the agenda; it would be a sword of Damocles hanging over us; and it will gravely embarrass the US in their relations with Saudi Arabia and help the Russians to make all sorts of trouble. Therefore – what? I said, therefore you had better stop the Saudis taking it there. They doubted if they could, unless I would 'come up with some alternative'. I outlined the limits of the alternative – direct talks with Saudi Arabia on 'all topics of common interest', but without conditions and on the understanding that only minor modifications of the frontier are discussable.

I lunched alone with Roger and Alice and told my griefs to Roger. I feel depressed about it, and wonder whether I have left any stones unturned. Pity I haven't seen Dulles.

At 6.30 p.m. Roger took me to call on Herbert Hoover. Very unsatisfactory interview: no discussion to speak of, though I did question his assertion that but for Buraimi (and Palestine) the Saudis would be much easier to handle. They had not been all that easy while the arbitration was going well. Hoover handed me a most depressing note and I handed him one back, giving an account of my arguments. After sending off telegrams recording this failure of my mission I got back to supper at 8.0 and a quiet evening with the Coulsons.

20 January

John woke up with bad lumbago. We went early to the Embassy, where I talked for over an hour to the Commonwealth Ministers or Counsellors, giving them a full account of my meetings and showing them maps of

Buraimi, etc. I then received a telephone call from Francis Russell and gladly went down at once to see him in the State Department. His object was twofold, and both parts most helpful and encouraging – I needed it! First, he said he had some advice to give me about Buraimi. Dulles was much more ready than Hoover to take account of our views. He had not yet made up his mind, and a message from Selwyn Lloyd might be very effective. Let me not quote Francis, but Hoover looked at these matters rather from the point of view of Aramco and American oil interests; Dulles had had to point out to him 'rather sharply' only last week that Britain, too, was an American interest. This cheered me up. Second, Francis said that the first talks with Nasser have been on the whole not discouraging. He is ready to see an agreement reached, but not published for about six months because 'public opinion must be prepared'. This is, I am afraid, a common cry of Arab politicians when you want them to do something sensible. Unfortunately they never undertake the task of preparing public opinion. But I suppose Nasser might. Next thing is, what are his terms and what will the Israelis offer?

Anyway I set off for New York (after bidding farewell to the lumbago-bound John and his friendly hospitable Mavis) a good deal more reassured than before, and on the Eastern Airlines aircraft I drafted a telegram to FO recording this conversation.

At 4.0 Bob Dixon and Moore Crosthwaite arrived and we had forty-five minutes' talk in the BOAC office there. Bob was less optimistic about Security Council action than I had expected from his telegrams; but he does agree we must face it out and thinks that with minimum American support (i.e. abstention and some good advice to Cuba and Peru) we can defeat any hostile resolution. But he, too, obviously thinks we ought to have an alternative up our sleeves.

21 January

Met at London Airport, 1.30 p.m., with a message that the Secretary of State wants to see me tomorrow, Sunday, at noon in London. Quite reasonable really, though it annoyed me at the time. I made a discreet statement to the press and was driven to High Wood in an office car. N. and Robin to greet me. We went for a walk through the woods to Elisabeth's[1] house and back. Lovely to be home. C. is away staying with Asquith friends but will be back tomorrow. Very sleepy and went early to bed.

1 Elisabeth Beazley, architect and author.

22 January

N. and I and Robin drove up to London and they dropped me at Chester Street, where Selwyn Lloyd lives, deserted by his wife, with his little three-year-old daughter and a nurse. Tony Nutting, Harold Caccia and Pat Hancock were there. Selwyn listened to my story and seemed more or less calm; he said that he had had twenty-four hours' 'respite' between the PM's speech at Bradford and his TV appearance last night; but even as he spoke the PM rang up about something. I hear we now consult No. 10 about the appointment of Embassy guards in Amman. Tony Nutting talked to me afterwards, pacing up and down Chester Street while we waited for Nancy and Robin to return, and seemed despairing. He thinks Selwyn likes acting as an office boy.

We lunched at the de Vere Hotel (Robin very impressed) and drove home quickly amongst busloads of Welshmen returning from their victorious rugger match. William Clark came round for a drink and we commiserated with him on the behaviour of Peter Fleming, whose article is still causing trouble. Randolph Churchill, out to make trouble for anyone he can, has guessed that the article is about William and he is trying to find out more about it. He rang Pinkie yesterday but she kept her mouth shut. Meanwhile Peter and William have exchanged apologetic letters. William looks even more thin and drawn, and is obviously having a terrible time with the PM. But he says he enjoys it. Clarissa is ill, having spilled boiling water over herself; and she is in trouble with the gutter press on account of having asked a cottager to remove some unsightly washing. One has the impression that England is being run by a pack of quarrelling yapping dogs.

23 January

Dentist; talks with M. Roux; collection and preparation of briefs; drafted a message from Selwyn to Dulles about Buraimi which I succeeded in getting S. to submit to the PM and approve. He was extraordinary about it; pretended that he thought it awful and concealed from me the fact that he had already cleared it with PM and colleagues – until he had been right through it with me, making verbal changes.

24 January

Got away early with Pat Hancock; and we caught the 4.45 boat train to Southampton and went aboard the *Queen Elizabeth*. Dined on board with the Menuhins[1] after writing to N. and sending Robin a postcard. Then a talk with Harold Caccia and saw a documentary film about New Zealand with him. We are both concerned about the the poor FO with a Foreign Secretary who wants to be a cypher. I must not let this fall into the hands of Randolph Churchill, who is on board this ship for the express purpose of exposing the Prime Minister and all his works.

25 January

Breakfast with Leslie Rowan, who spoke with very great respect of Harold Macmillan's first weeks at the Treasury. He said H.M. has first-class, tough plans for dealing with the inflation, and that since he has been put there specially to do this and is committed wholly to achieve it he will have to insist on acceptance of his proposals in the main. But A.E. will oppose them because they will hurt.

I worked all morning on my briefs and came in to lunch at 1.15 when I found S.L., Rowan, Harold [Caccia] and Pat Hancock at my table. S.L. greeted me with the accusation that I had 'abandoned him' last night for the Foreign Affairs debate, that he had had no advisers, no advice and had been compelled to improvise, etc. I pointed out to him that he had himself personally told me not to concern myself with the debate, and to leave it in the hands of Denis Wright and Michael Rose, but he went on in an aggressive way accusing me of having let him down. I said that I would offer him a humble apology but that I refused to be put out of countenance by this attack. Then he started saying that Harold, too, had let him down over something. An extraordinary way to gain the co-operation of your advisers; especially as I don't think he has it in for me in any way really, or dislikes me. It is his idea of humour I think. Later in the afternoon he was rude to me in a slightly more clearly humorous way, and I could see that this was meant to be amends. But what a bore it is, and how one regrets Macmillan. *having left FO.*

26 January

Most of our masters' energies today were taken up with deciding how to avoid Randolph Churchill; and A.E., who was longing to have Liza [Hope], Mrs J. J. Astor and Lady Ednam (the Carcano girls) to dinner, was too frightened to do so in case the press should hear of it, so Selwyn did it instead and upset Anthony truly. Randolph got his own back by telling the press that A.E. is ill in bed, which is half true. I lunched with S.L.,

1 Yehudi and Diana Menuhin.

Rowan and Caccia, and S.L. was quite polite. I think I can get out of going to Cairo, Tehran and Baghdad with him next month.

I had a Turkish bath, and a walk round the deck in exiguous sunshine. Then an hour and a half session with the PM and S/S, during which we went through the agenda. PM seems satisfied with the line in my paper, but he is very suspicious of American intentions and absolutely distrusts Nasser. He seemed thin, nervy and in a curious way frivolous. I don't think he is at all well or at all happy.

27 January

A strong S.W. wind got up in the night, and the boat started pitching violently. It kept me awake most of the night but I did not feel ill until I got up (without breakfast) for our 10 o'clock meeting. After that I had to retire to bed with a half Dramamine which just saved me, and slept until 2.30. Had my Turkish bath at 3.15 after dictating a Middle East section for the communiqué. Dinner with Harold and Guy Millard,[1] when we discussed A.E. and S.L. on the usual lines and wondered whether H.M. will have the courage to insist on carrying through the economic reforms which he knows are necessary to save us, but which A.E. will oppose as too drastic. Guy loathes his job, and has tried to get out of it.

At 10.30, when we were still talking about all this, along came A.E. into the office, having restlessly got rid of his dinner party for the Menuhins on account of having work to do, asking. 'Is there nothing in? Is there no work? What are you doing there so busily?' He had wanted to take them to the cinema, but did not dare 'because there are so many press about'. He asked us in for a drink, and we went through my communiqué. Restless, impersonal, unsteady. I am very depressed again – perhaps my Dramamine is working off, for the boat is pitching badly again. Guy and I wandered around until we found Liza, and I told her how gloomy I am. Gloomy for her.

28 January

Much calmer. A good morning's work, and then lunch with Leslie, Harold, etc. Before my Turkish bath I had a walk on the boat deck in a hailstorm with Allan, the PPS, who expressed enthusiastic admiration for A.E.'s integrity, goodness, ideas. He hopes to make his speeches interesting – just as I used to hope.

Meeting at 5.0 with A.E. and S.L. and we finally cleared our ME

1 Now the Prime Minister's Private Secretary.

communiqué and the bit of 'what we want out of the conference' which we then telegraphed to Roger Makins. After the meeting S.L. kept me back with a whisky and soda, and told me how furious A.E. had been with him for agreeing to have lunch with Randolph Churchill. He had cancelled it, and had offered C. a drink instead. He thought he had made an impression on C. and that this would be helpful to A.E. I doubt it. S.L. said it was absurd of A.E. to think he could be disloyal. 'I am a contented animal; I know I have been over-promoted; there can be no question of my disloyalty.' PM gave a cocktail party and afterwards I dined with Aldrich's party and finished up in the Verandah Grill with Guy, Chicita Astor and Liza. A scene with Randolph over Florence Desmond, who declined to perform to us all but apparently did a turn twenty minutes after we had left.

29 January

Last day on board. All the staff with their hands out, palm upwards. I did not go to church, but read my book and walked on the boat deck in the wind. Very smooth, and several ships passed us by. Lunch with the Menuhins and Liza. Diana Menuhin was very amusing indeed about their tours through South America, when locusts infested the concert hall and one sat on the bridge of Y's violin while he was playing. On one side of us was a solemn lunch party for A.E., given by the US Ambassador, and on the other Randolph Churchill holding forth in a loud voice to a group of tycoons and their wives.

Had a swim but no Turkish bath, and a meeting with A.E. and S.L. at 5.30. A.E. threw a tantrum because according to the programme just received from Washington he is not going to see Ike as much as he would like. 'I am not going to be treated like this. I will take the next boat home. We shall achieve nothing. It is no use talking to Dulles and the State Department, though you will do it very well, Selwyn dear; they cannot treat the British Prime Minister like this. Remember Yalta,' etc., etc. Great indignation against poor Roger Makins about it. But after this had blown over, an interesting meeting in which he disagreed with me over Egypt, and wanted to place all the emphasis on the Baghdad Pact. He compared Nasser with Mussolini and said his object was to be a Caesar from the Gulf to the Atlantic, and to kick us out of it all. He all but called me an appeaser. I said I mostly feared our using instruments which would break in our hands – e.g. Jordan, and the negligible influence of Iraq in Syria. He wants us to prepare the Fertile Crescent, and to build up a defence against Egyptian broadcasting, etc. This is quite right, I think, but there is the $64 question of Nasser – do we write him off or try to work with him?

After a drink with Drew Middleton and Guy I dined with Selwyn, Harold, Pat, John Graham[1] and Guy in the main dining-room. (Should have said I also had a drink in Selwyn's cabin with Harold and Chicita Astor.) We had a very good dinner, and a good Burgundy with it, and it must have been as a result of this that I made a remark which astonishes me now. I was telling Selwyn about Buraimi, over the coffee and brandy, when he said jokingly: 'What is the use of telling me this without a map?' So I said, 'Do you want to see the map? I'll go and get it straight away. Only you must bloody well stay there until I come back.' Then I dashed off, and returned with the map, wondering what reception I should get. It was a great success. Selwyn pretended to rise from his seat at my approach but he had left £2 under my plate (his contribution to the common tip which he had previously refused to cough up) and it was clear that he was amused and rather pleased. However, this is not really the way for a Foreign Service officer to address the Secretary of State. I played Housie Housie this evening with a stockbroker called Pott and his wife, but won nothing. Early to bed.

30 January

One of those long days. At 3.0 a.m. we ran into fog and the ship's fog-horn kept us lugubriously awake. Up at 6.30, breakfast with Leslie and Harold (who ate onion soup out of bravado); then Roger Makins and Bob Dixon came on board and we had a short conference with Selwyn. Tremendous scrimmage on the boat. Randolph Churchill got in amongst the pressmen before the PM appeared and performed on his own in front of the tele-cameras, etc. Couldn't bear to hear A.E.'s speech: full of 'the work we are doing together for peace' – it gets more insincere-sounding every day. Drove off to La Guardia in the rain. President's special aircraft awaiting us, but we were early so we had to spend an extra half-hour in the sky, in order not to arrive ahead of schedule. A.E. got cross in the aircraft because Senator George said yesterday that his visit was necessary in order to bolster up his position at home! So tonight in his speech he made a point of saying that the visit had been arranged last November before the attacks upon him by the Tory Party began.

A.E. and Selwyn went off to Bliss House with PPS and Private Secretaries, but the rest of us lunched with Roger and Alice and then off to the White House. First hour with Dulles, when we discussed mainly the measures to be taken if Israel attacks Egypt. Dulles ready to recommend military discussions, but wants some UN advance cover for action by the

---

1 John Graham, Assistant Private Secretary to the Foreign Secretary; later Ambassador to Iraq and Iran.

US/UK. We touched on Buraimi but Dulles said he would reserve that until the President came.

When he did come, Eisenhower was in extraordinarily good form and health. He had an obvious grasp of the subjects – better than our man, and he joked away in the most cheerful manner. He had re-written our 'declaration' and greatly improved it. Dulles said 'The President does not like the word communiqué,' to which Ike replied, 'because I don't understand French'. He at once authorized military talks with us, and sent orders to Admiral Radford to meet our General Whiteley tomorrow. He is thinking of various moves by the US air forces and navy in the Mediterranean, as a deterrent to Israeli aggression. He seemed to enjoy this. On Buraimi it soon became apparent that the President and Dulles were much nearer to us than Mr Hoover is. They pretty well accepted that we cannot go back to arbitration, and pressed us to agree to some sort of negotiation 'to save King Saud's face'. We stood on the offer to discuss 'minor modifications' of the frontier, but Ike wanted us to put a little more jam in this for the Saudis. We might be able to – but not of course in Buraimi. We thought all this not at all bad.

The Prime Minister and Eisenhower discussed Nasser, and this is clearly the unanswered question. The President said, 'What kind of a fellow is Nasser?' Selwyn answered, he is ambitious, dreams of an Arab empire from Atlantic to Persian Gulf under his leadership. President: 'Does that go well with the other Arabs?' The crucial question, he said, is whether Nasser is with the Soviets. If he proves to be, we shall have to back either Israel or the Arabs who don't like Egypt. PM mentioned Nasser's very bad speech of yesterday and said it was difficult to go along with such a man. Ike: 'Maybe he doesn't have good staff to go over his speeches.' Pause – then Dulles, sweetly, 'I wonder what you mean by that?' (Reference to the trouble D. has been in recently over his speech about bringing USA three times 'to the brink of war'. The current joke about Dulles is – 'three brinks and he's brunk'.) After the meeting Ike gave A.E. a penknife with his initials on the blade, and I had to cough up a shilling as 'payment'. Then he retired to his study and as we went out through the garden we saw him through the garden windows sitting at his desk.

Back to the Embassy with Selwyn Lloyd for discussion, telegrams, etc., and then a desperate rush to change into a white tie at the Baileys' house, where my luggage was still unpacked and everything in a buffle. A huge dinner at the Pan American Union. I sat between a Miss Thomas, cousin of Dulles, very attractive and intelligent, and the Californian wife of the President of the Ford Foundation, an institution which has $600 million to give away. She says it is very hard work. A charming and most friendly speech by Dulles, followed by a much less good one by A.E. in which he

omitted to propose the toast of the President. I think he is greatly deterio-
rated: seems to be thinking only of himself. I envy the Americans having
Ike and Dulles to deal with over their foreign affairs. It seems to me that
these two have continuity of policy, serious ideas and courage, and that
our team by comparison is frivolous.

31 January

A long and exhausting day, during which we lunched with the President
at the White House and dined with Foster Dulles at his house in George-
town. After dinner we worked on the communiqué until after midnight.
At lunch the chief excitement was a strong statement by the President
about the admission of China to the UN. He said that if this were to
happen, not only would the US be driven out but he doubted whether the
HQ of the UN could remain in the USA. He said that he, personally,
though a moderate, agreed with public opinion in this, for so long as
Communist China remained a declared aggressor, retained American prisoners and conducted herself as a pirate, he did not see how she could
rightly be included in the company of peace-loving nations. Someone
pointed out that UN is supposed to be universal and that USSR is in it,
but it made no difference. It looked as if some of the Americans present
(except of course Walter Robertson) disapproved of this extremely rigid
line of the President's. He was in wonderful form, wearing a NATO tie
and eating a large lunch after a whisky and soda. He ate nuts throughout
lunch.

After Foster Dulles's dinner we all sat down to go over the draft
communiqué. A.E., with unusual restraint, detached himself from the
discussion and picked up a book (one of Winston's). Foster Dulles and
S.L., surrounded by advisers, went straight on with the job and after a
while A.E. began to look rather isolated and uncomfortable. So I went up
and had a talk with him. This is the only occasion on the trip (or since I
left him nearly two years ago) on which he has talked to me with any
intimacy, and it was a curious occasion, standing in front of the fire in a
room full of people sitting around the two Foreign Secretaries. He has in
my opinion greatly changed in the last two years. He is far away, thinking
largely about the effect he is making, not in any way strengthened in
character, as I hoped, by the attainment of his ambition. Our conversation
was mostly about him, and his position; how Winston had been 'sweet' to
come and see him last month, at the height of the press attacks against
him, and had patted him on the back and growled, 'Pay no attention to
the filthy press'; how at a party when Randolph Churchill had been slanging
him, Winston had silenced his son by saying, 'He is my best friend.' (I

had heard this story from Liza on the boat, and it was through her that A.E. heard it. But at that earlier stage in its career it had simply run 'He is my friend.' Rather a characteristic Eden amendment; less effective, too.) After twenty minutes of this saddening conversation I suggested to A.E. that he should go to bed, which he did with alacrity, bidding farewell to Foster Dulles and the rest of us in what seemed to me an affected way. I am wondering whether my extremely critical feelings about him are due to changes in him or in me. Anyhow I can see that there is no prospect of my ever being intimate with him again, and I don't think his present Private Secretaries like him enough to want to be.

1 February

It is clear by now that the President and Dulles take a much more realistic view of Saudi Arabia than their advisers, and that they are not going to try to pressurize us into arbitration. All talk has ceased about the dangers of the Security Council and the imminence of Saudi appeal to it. Moreover we have now had a private approach from King Saud through his Private Secretary in Jedda. I am sure the Saudis are very reluctant to appeal to the Security Council and that our firmness is paying dividends.

Today was spent almost entirely on the draft Declaration and communiqué. We met all morning at State Department under Dulles, and ate sandwiches there for lunch; and in the afternoon we met again at the White House with the President. I took a hand in securing an amendment to the first paragraph of the Declaration, which seemed to suggest that the Western camp believes in God while the enemies believe 'Man is designed solely to serve the state machine'. Even if we all believed in God it would not be true to say that the Communists believe that about Man. They 'believe' (i.e. their bible says) exactly the contrary, i.e. that the state will wither away. So we got it changed to a statement that they *treat man as if* he were designed merely to serve the state machine. Personally I thought the reference to God quite unsuitable, and so did Bowie and Allen on their side and Selwyn Lloyd on ours. But Leslie Rowan and Harold Caccia (largely, I suspect, because they did not want changes at this late hour) were for leaving it.

The President was extraordinarily quick and resourceful during all this, and every time there was a drafting difficulty he came up with a solution. He cuts through differences with wonderful precision. Some argument about what to say to the press about atomic tests. Eisenhower: 'You have the choice sometimes between keeping your mouth shut and being thought dumb or opening it and removing all doubt.' There was a curious moment of difference between him and his advisers about the bomb. He maintained that future US tests would be concerned with small bombs, for precision use, whereas his advisers thought there were going to be big explosions. He took a very sturdy line about the absence of danger from bomb tests so long as the bombs are exploded well up in the air; only ground explosions, which throw up tons of earth, create the fall-out problem on a significant scale. A.E. seems to have been talked out of his plan for reduction of tests. He was not in any case in a very strong position as we are about to make tests ourselves.

2 February

This morning we all trooped off to Congress to hear A.E. address the two Houses. I personally thought very little of the performance, but it seems to have been a great success. Randolph Churchill was in the Press Gallery looking scornful and subsequently wrote a nasty piece about it. I was sitting with Rowan for the House of Representatives speech and we both thought it very poor, and the emphasis all wrong. But we were wrong. The Coulsons, Harold and I then had a snack lunch at the National Gallery and spent two hours looking at the pictures. Also some rather ugly Steuben glass with modern oriental designs. Meeting at S.D. with Douglas McArthur to go over the points arising from the Conference, after which Geoffrey, Ian Samuel and I dined quietly with the Baileys and watched A.E.'s television performance which I must say was not bad. During the late evening I was summoned to the Embassy by S.L. to go over with him the draft letter to Dulles about Buraimi which I had drafted. He finally approved it, but this did not prevent it being torn up by the PM in the night, on return from his TV act. I would not be Foreign Secretary in such conditions for anything in the world.

3 February

Selwyn Lloyd left early this morning for Chicago and I spent the morning re-doing the Buraimi action. No letter to Dulles, but a telegram to Phillips[1] in Jeddah telling him to follow up an approach which he has had from the King. Cleared these with the PM in his sitting-room before lunch and then went off for a snack at the Shoreham Hotel.

I should have been at lunch with the Commonwealth Ambassadors at the Embassy, but never received my card. Joined them afterwards while A.E. was telling about the Conference. Then to the airport to see PM and party off to Canada.

---

1 Horace Phillips, Chargé d' Affaires in Jeddah.

7 February

Drove in to New York with Bob [Dixon] in the morning and drew some money and spent a couple of hours shopping. Bought Catherine a white nylon net evening dress, ballet length, and Robin Williamson [our local doctor] six bottles of immune globulin. Lunched in a low joint with Moore Crosthwaite and Peter Ramsbotham[1] to the sound of a juke box and frequent interruptions from drunks. In the afternoon I had meetings with Bob and his staff, and with Ormerod[2] of the BIS [British Information Services]. Then after taking a telephone call from Roger in Washington and dictating a telegram to Baghdad I drove home to Wave Hill and showed the dress to Ismene Dixon and her young daughter. They seemed to think it a good buy.

After a brief visit to Ottawa, Eden and his party returned home on 9 February.

11 February

Weekend at High Wood. Dined with Bretts and William Clark, and heard more about A.E.'s troubles. William stood up for him rather well: I am going through a phase of strong disapproval of A.E., his lack of stability, sensitivity to criticism and vanity. William says it is a superficial frivolity, and that really he is still rather a big man. Cocktails on Saturday with the Osbert Lancasters. O. has done a pocket cartoon on our aircraft landing at Gander and I have asked him for it. Very cold, everything covered with snow. Did not go out at all, but played the spinet with N. and C. On Sunday morning Robin was suddenly taken with a pain in his back and started screaming. Most alarming. Doctor says it is kidney trouble, I hope not bad. Turned out to be a stone.

12 February

The Russians have put out a statement about the Middle East, accusing us of interference in the sovereign affairs of ME states, slanging the Baghdad Pact, the Tripartite Declaration and the Washington Communiqué. They take the very words out of the Egyptians' mouths – 'Baghdad Pact is a British prison for the Arabs', etc. They are getting very skilful at this – bidding for a power position in the area. I was asked at short notice to give Gerry Young a piece to put out this morning to the press, in refutation of this. I said we should not put anything out 'on the record' until we had

---

1 Hon. Peter Ramsbotham, UK delegation to the UN; later Ambassador in Washington and Governor of Bermuda.
2 Berkeley Ormerod, Director, PR, BIS, New York, 1945–62.

thought a bit and obtained approval of Secretary of State and Prime Minister, but I dictated a piece for background guidance. Nutting, without consulting me, authorized it to be issued, and then of course it turned out to be highly controversial. My piece suggested that we will act under the Tripartite Declaration only if asked to do so by the victim of aggression; journalists say the Declaration itself does not mean that, and accuse us of 'watering down' the Declaration. I worked all through lunchtime on this, and in the end (when I was sitting, lunch-less, with the Chiefs of Staff), was called to the telephone to advise the PM what he should say in the House about it. I suggested he should refuse to 'gloss' the Tripartite Declaration, and this he did. We shall have to clear the point up with the Americans and French.

13 February

Very cold. A good day's work with no interviews or meetings. Cleared my tray and paid my income tax. The calm and arrogant assurance of the Russians is very disquieting. Speeches by Bulganin and Khrushchev at Party Rally. 'Half the population of the world is already on our side.' And then one thinks of the neurosis of the Americans, and our economic difficulties. Oh, dear.

17 February

The last three days have been more or less bearable in the Office, because Ministers have been concerned solely with the financial situation ($5\frac{1}{2}$ per cent bank rate, £18 million cut on food subsidies, etc.) and the debate at which the House voted to abolish hanging. At one moment I had five urgent telegrams and a submission which got 'lost' at ministerial level, and I eventually put ferrets in, to find that they were all at No. 10, waiting for the PM's approval. I suggested to the Private Secretary that we might just as well abolish the system of using personal minutes from Foreign Secretary to PM, and simply send our Office submissions over for him to see. It would be interesting to know the number of minutes S.L. has sent over since he became Foreign Secretary, and compare it with others.

20 February

Missed the train at Henley for (I think) the first time. Went on to Reading and arrived FO at 10.30 just in time for a meeting with S.L. about arms. He is understandably confused by the tergiversations of the Americans who in the course of the weekend released eighteen tanks to Saudi Arabia, banned all shipments of arms to the ME, and lifted the said ban. But his concern seems as usual to have been prompted by the PM. Today he let us down twice as a Department, allowing the Colonial Secretary to impose upon us Lord Lloyd [his Parliamentary Under-Secretary] as a member of a negotiating team for Addis Ababa (FO no longer allowed to conduct negotiations with foreign Governments): and not allowing us to discuss with the Arab Legion what is to happen if we suddenly have to fly troops in to Jordan. (This is the PM again.) Kirkpatrick renewed his scathing comment. 'Selwyn's only ambition is not to get in trouble.' He has let me off going to Cairo with him. (At least, I would say he has given way to some pressure by H. Caccia to this end.) I am delighted.

We had a large meeting in Tony Nutting's room today, to discuss the conduct of the cold war, and I made myself unpopular by asking why, if 'there ain't gonna be no war' (Macmillan's phrase), it is necessary for us to devote ourselves to pacts, armed forces and hydrogen bombs, when we could make so much better use of the money bribing uncommitted countries. The reply as regards the H-bomb was that it is terribly cheap, really.

21 February

Lunched with Neville Berry and his wife and seven or eight other well-selected persons of moderate importance, to meet Mr Hughes, the *Sunday Times* correspondent who recently saw Maclean and Burgess in Moscow. Hughes gave a confident account of Soviet intentions, and expressed himself as 'frightened' by their assurance, efficiency and progress. But he told us little about Donald and Guy, except that they seemed well dressed and prosperous and gave the impression of 'two English gentlemen'. He got the feeling that they lived in Moscow, but he was so busy being furious with the Reuter man for being there too, and so much concerned over getting his 'scoop' that he forgot to ask any questions or make any close observations. He seemed full of pompous theory about why Malenkov is not dead and how he and Khrushchev share a suburban house with a common bullet-proof grille.

22 February

Lunched with Paul Grey[1] at Brooks's at his request, thinking he would have lots of ideas about winning the cold war in the Middle East. But he had none. Oliver Esher came up to our table and talked to us. 'What a Government!' he said. 'There is even a Liberal revival.' I re-wrote the piece for Selwyn Lloyd to say to Nasser. Dined in decorations at the top table, facing 1250

---

1 Paul Grey, Assistant Under-Secretary at the Foreign Office; later Ambassador to Czechoslovakia and Switzerland.

other diners, at Grosvenor House in aid of the Institute of Petroleum. Two unspeakably boring and pointless speeches by the Minister of Fuel and Power (Aubrey Jones, a Welsh mining engineer's son) and the President, Colonel Auld, respectively, followed by a well-turned and witty speech by the American Naval Attaché, Rear Admiral Lyman. He sat down with the remark, 'The human body is the only instrument yet invented that makes more noise when it is well oiled.' I sat next to a nice Professor of Chemical Engineering at Birmingham University, Professor F.H. Garner, and an old bore called Sims who makes petroleum equipment. Left after the speeches.

Met David Stephens[1] on Horseguards Parade. He is now with the PM, appointing bishops, and says trade is humming. He told me that A.E.'s morale is very high at the moment; I can't imagine why.

24 February

Not feeling at all well this morning, and N. persuaded me to stay in bed until 10.0. Caught a train at 11.02, just in time to get to lunch at the Egyptian Embassy (in honour of S.L.) where I had a lot of conversation with the Yugoslav Ambassador, the Swiss Minister's wife, the First Secretary in the Egyptian Embassy and Mr Krishna Menon. Velebit, the Yugoslav, told me that the recent changes of tone and tactic in the USSR are in his view to be taken seriously, since they represent the first signs of revolt by the newly matured technical classes against the rigid dogmatics of Stalinism. But he does not think we can regard the battle as finished; there might easily be great upheavals, and in particular there might be a military coup, for the army is increasingly powerful. In the long run, however, the trend will be towards greater freedom of expression, a greater insistence on consumer goods and an insistence by the 'privileged classes' on stability and peace. This came well, I thought, from a Communist.

Krishna Menon was much less realistic and gave me the whole Indian case on the wickedness of pacts, especially the Baghdad Pact, and the follies of our Middle East policy. When he said we ought to back democratic regimes rather than old-fashioned autocracies, meaning Egypt rather than Iraq, I asked how he could possibly describe the military junta in Cairo as 'democratic'. He insisted that they were, because they were giving land to the peasants – or were going to do so – and that they were 'in harmony with the trends of the future' in some way which Nuri is not. That is typical Indian thought – just because they happen to agree with Nasser, he must be a democrat. Menon (who invited me to drive back with him in his large car) said many things against NATO as well as the Baghdad Pact, and when I said NATO had saved us he replied, 'Perhaps it only

1 David Stephens, Secretary for Appointments 1955–61.

postponed you being saved.' I said, 'This means you think we might be saved by becoming Communist; but we do not want to be Communists' (Velebit said – 'Why should you?'). Menon then said, 'Perhaps you would change Communism by diluting it.' That is, I am sure, the Indian pacifist hope in a nutshell.

A very great mass of papers – on Buraimi, Jisr Banat Yakub and the Johnstone Plan, Morocco, briefs for the Secretary of State's tour, etc. Then I dined with the Guy Millards. They had a successful Jewish publisher called Weidenfeld, who has just published Tom Driberg's critical life of Beaverbrook, and who I am told is being cited as a co-respondent by Cyril Connolly; also a rather intelligent woman called Rosa Something who was at school with N. Weidenfeld told us how Driberg quarrelled with Beaverbrook over this Life and how he was treated like a footman. We talked politics of course, and Weidenfeld and Guy think both parties are completely without philosophy or ideals; just two rival groups of not very competent administrators.

25 February

The Jordan Government asked us urgently ten days ago, what we should do if they became involved in war with Israel as a result of an Israeli attack, not on them but on another Arab state. We have been working out our reply, cleared it with the Chiefs of Staff, and had it ready today for Ministers. But as it will take them a day or two to consider it, I put up an interim reply too, saying we will answer soon and that meanwhile if Jordan herself is attacked of course will come to her aid under the Treaty. S.L. would not even send off the interim reply without the PM's approval. It all had to be typed out again and sent down to Chequers, and it won't go off until Monday. It becomes daily more apparent that we have no Secretary of State. We have a rather nervous official who has not the inclination or the courage to take decisions of any kind. This afternoon (Saturday) the PM rang him up to complain that Lord Mountbatten, who is passing through Cairo on his way to S.E. Asia, should be seeing Nasser. So the 'Sec. of State' rang me up in the country to ask whether we had ever given Mountbatten permission to see Nasser. You would think the PM might employ his time better than getting into a jealous temper over one of his own Chiefs of Staff paying a courtesy call on a foreign ruler with whom he is friendly; and you would think the Foreign Secretary might deal with such a situation off his own bat, and not reply, as he tells me he did, 'I know nothing about it: I will find out who authorized it.'

The new French Minister called on me this morning. I found him quite robust, for a Frenchman, and I told him the line S.L. is going to take with

Nasser. There is one chance in 100 that we shall get Nasser to move helpfully to check the landslide of Arabs towards Russia and Communism. An intermediary is off again at the end of the month, and could succeed in bringing Nasser and Ben-Gurion together.

Home for lunch, glorious sunny day, and the snow still thick on the hills. Did some tobogganing with R. Tonight it got very cold again and N. and I drove down in C.'s little car to dine with William Clark in his remote, cosy little cottage at Lewknor. Full moon on the crisp, crackling snow and ice. We heard Harold Macmillan make a very good party broadcast on the war against inflation, and both spoke to him on the telephone when it was over. He said he would like me to lunch with him alone when he gets back from OEEC in Paris next week. Very gloomy talk about the state of the Government and A.E.'s failings as PM. The latest muddle (apart from the fact that it took seven Cabinet meetings and a threat of resignation by H.M. to get the one-third cuts in the bread and milk subsidies and the increased bank rate) is over the abolition of hanging. The Government evidently did not expect to be defeated (on a free vote) and had made no preparations against that event. The fact that it now proposes to rely on a Private Member's Bill (in the name of Mr Silverman, of all people) instead of producing one of its own is thought to be dishonest and – more serious – ludicrous.

27 February

Foreign Affairs Debate today, with all ministerial business at a standstill. Session with S.L. in the morning about his speech, and with the PM in the evening about his. But I could not bring myself to care what either of them say; there is no sense in the debate, nothing to debate, nothing new to say. These debates, and the endless PQs, are marvellously calculated to distract Ministers from their duty, rattle them, take their eye off realities.

28 February

I had a real set-to with S.L. today in an endeavour to get some of my telegrams off. Saw him before and after Cabinet, but had very little success. He seems absolutely determined not to take decisions of his own, even on the simplest matters. He came back from Cabinet saying they 'would not hear of' his inviting Nasser to the UK. Why should we do this honour to him when he is attacking us? But I asked why in that case do we invite Bulganin and Khrushchev. The object of inviting Nasser is not to honour or give pleasure to him, but to widen his horizons, influence him in our direction. It makes me furious the way Ministers – especially A.E. of course – take emotional attitudes on questions like this. We have no diplomacy at all, no flexibility. Selwyn was rather taken aback at my expostulation, but of course will do nothing. He cleared thro' Cabinet my draft reply to the Saudis re-proposing talks, but wanted some extra 'sugar' put on the end. When I produced the sugar he said he thought it fine, but insisted that the telegram go back again to the PM for approval. At that he left the UK for his Karachi trip, and within two minutes of his departure the PM was ringing up Kirkpatrick.

29 February

The party left this morning and we had a quiet day. I took a Turkish bath in Jermyn Street and, coming out, met William Clark in St James's Square, writhing under abuse from A.E. because 'the American press' – it turned out to be the Paris edition of the *New York Tribune* – had not given enough attention to his speech in the House yesterday.

Had a gossip with Tony Nutting, who shares my despondency about the Middle East, the FO, the Government and the future. But in his case there is also personal cause for gloom – he has now asked Jill to divorce him.

1 March

There was very little work today, and after a lunch with Sir H. Pilkington at the top of Selwyn House (looking over the Green Park), where Sir Norman Kipping, Head of the FBI, Loombe of the Bank of England and a number of others discussed how to sell more goods in the ME, I was preparing to go off early in order to see Robin in Reading Hospital and to visit Dr Williamson about my knee. Five minutes before I was due to leave Michael came in with a telegram saying that King Hussein has sacked General Glubb. I took my car to Paddington, found N. sitting in the carriage waiting for me, told her the sad news and returned to FO. Went over with Tony Nutting to No. 10 and cleared two telegrams with the PM. Then after making arrangements to cover any publicity for the night I caught the 7.0 p.m. train to Henley and got a lift home from the Charles Steels. Supper with N. and C., and early to bed. At midnight I was woken by the PM on the telephone, with a really nasty tone. 'Where are you? Are you in the country? I thought you were supposed to be looking after your business. Nutting is here with me. I thought you knew things were wrong . . . etc.' I mumbled a few inconsequential excuses, asked what I could do to help and was told 'No, there is nothing, as you are not here.' So I leaped into my clothes and dashed up to London at 80 mph in Greeners, arriving

FO at 1.15 to find Tony and Michael with the Resident Clerk. The King has done it, and Glubb leaves in the morning for Cyprus. It is a monstrous piece of ingratitude and the Jordan Prime Minister, Samir Rifai, is obviously embarrassed or at least makes a very good show of being. But I don't think it means Hussein is sold to the Egyptians or Saudis. For A.E. it is a serious blow, and he will be jeered at in the House, which is his main concern. He wants to strike some blow, somewhere, to counterbalance. Hussein has blandly ignored his message, and tells Duke that he is convinced he has 'acted for the best'.

2 March

The Glubb crisis occupied everybody's time all day. I had to go nevertheless to the Chiefs of Staff, to talk about Israel, the impossibility of going to war with the Arabs if they aggress, and the question of re-disposing our forces so as to get round what they call the 'air barrier' – the line of countries from Syria down to Egypt which we can no longer fly over without permission. Mountbatten and the new CAS pressed me to produce a statement showing 'our policy in the ME' which they both professed to think must be stateable. Templer and Dixon were more realistic. I promised to write a paper on the problems of the ME. When I told Kirkpatrick this he gave me a quotation from Palmerston to use next time this happens: 'When people ask one what is one's policy, the only answer is that we mean to do what may seem to be best upon each occasion as it arises, making the interests of one's country one's guiding principle.'

The Chiefs are not a very effective body at present. Dixon has an ulcer and talks too much, Mountbatten is full of undigested bright ideas and is really a simpleton though very nice. They all argue with one another.

Very gloomy this evening, especially as I still have a bad knee, and a cold on top of it, and have a compact with N. not to drink gin. Turkish bath at lunch, and supped with the Becketts.

3 March (Saturday)

Chaos in the FO – every time I tried to talk to Kirkpatrick or Nutting their telephone rang and the PM came on the line, dictating messages, asking questions, complaining about life in general. He is mainly perturbed this morning by a terrible speech of Pineau, the French Foreign Minister, criticizing US and UK policy over the last few years. But Glubb too, and also the final break-down with Makarios over Cyprus. A.E. says M. has now shown that his sole aim is 'to become King of Cyprus'. We are to publish the documents, and A.E. says this will 'look well – we shall have no trouble in the House'; and this seems to satisfy him. After that, I suppose, we suppress the rebellion by force and deport Makarios.

At 11.45 I set off in Greeners for Chequers to lunch with the PM and Lady Eden to meet Mr Jack McCloy, formerly US High Commissioner in Germany, now head of the Chase Bank. The Aldriches also there. Very speedy journey in the rain. A.E. talked loud and excitedly throughout lunch and after, with many histrionic remarks such as 'I never move a step without our American friends'. McCloy gave a factual account of his talks with Nasser and King Saud, which A.E. interrupted with (I thought) rather light and ill-tempered comment, as if M. was supporting the views expressed. He is now violently anti-Nasser, whom he compares with Mussolini, and he spoke darkly (to the Americans) of having a good mind to revise the evacuation of Suez. He talked twice on the telephone to Gladwyn Jebb in Paris, and invited the French PM to stay at Chequers next weekend. This seemed to excite him very much, and a lot of trouble was taken over the communiqué; also to ensure that the press know Aldrich was here to lunch.

After the Americans had gone, A.E. took me aside and said I was seriously to consider reoccupation of Suez as a move to counteract the blow to our prestige which Glubb's dismissal means. (News came in while we were drinking coffee that Selwyn was stoned in Bahrain!)

A.E., Aldrich and McCloy were all agreed that the Foreign Secretaries ought not to travel about so much. A. said that there was no co-ordination of policy in the State Department when Dulles is away, and McCloy thought there should be a special Ambassador to cover the whole ME. The spectacle of Dulles, Selwyn Lloyd and Pineau going off to Karachi at this moment (when the pot was boiling over in the ME) seemed absurd. A.E. summed up the whole business by saying, 'We are in a mess', which is an understatement. He added, 'We are at our best in a mess', and a sort of 1940 look came into his eye. McCloy appeared to have swallowed the Saudi line over Buraimi, and I arranged to see him on Monday.

Got away at 5.0 p.m. and drove straight home along B4009, at the foot of the Chilterns, arriving just in time to go with N. and C. to see Robin in Reading hospital, where he is having X-rays and observation. Played snakes and ladders with him for half an hour and home for supper. Deeply worried by everything in the Middle East – Cyprus, Algeria, Jordan. Everything in a mess, and the Arabs hating us more and more. So far from reoccupying Suez, my inclination is to get out of some of these untenable positions. I am thinking of a combination of steps to put ourselves right – withdraw from the Tripartite Declaration, from Jordan, from Cyprus, and Libya bases (which we don't really need); declare a solution of Palestine on basis of Negev going back to Egypt; give the Jordan subsidy for buying support for the Fertile Crescent and encourage Iraq to join Syria and Jordan.

Great wind all night, with rain beating on the windows, and I could not sleep.

4 March (Sunday!)

Left High Wood in Greeners at 9.0 a.m. for London, this being the first really lovely day of the year, with sun shining on the snowdrops and the grass beginning to get green. Meeting at 10.30 with Tony Nutting and at 11.0 with poor Glubb. He made a most noble impression – no harsh words against the King of Jordan, and a real understanding of the boy's desire to get rid of him, Glubb, who was always preventing him from doing foolish things. He said, 'It would not be right to come down on Jordan like a ton of bricks. Take what they say at its face value; they want to remain friends. Do not pull out, do not cut the subsidy (you cannot reduce it). Stop sending telegrams and let the dust settle down'! He thinks the Legion will break up, however, with the British officers gone, and the question is, how can we go on paying £9 million for a useless Legion?

When he had gone (and I had been called to the telephone once, and Tony twice, while the meeting was on, by PM ringing from Chequers to ask why we were wasting our time gossiping with Glubb, instead of answering Duke's telegrams) we drafted a statement for the PM to make tomorrow, had a quick lunch at Boodle's and set off by car for Chequers again. Tony and Kirkpatrick went in an official car with a very speedy and adventurous woman driver, and I chased them in Greeners. Glorious drive, but too worrying for enjoyment. We met in the fifteenth-century 'Long Gallery' round a fine log fire, from 5.0 until 8.0. PM, Salisbury, Monckton, CIGS (Templer), CAS (Boyle), Nutting, Kirkpatrick and me. Kirk was for a drastic statement, looking towards a withdrawal of the subsidy and denunciation of the Treaty. They all rather wanted to be tough, and to withdraw the remaining British officers without any 'by your leave' to the Jordan Government who employ them. I tried to reduce the sharpness of this, fearing that it would lead to cries of treachery and fresh outbursts against our people, who with their families are quite unprotected and whom we could not save. I was not altogether successful, but we did get it agreed that Duke should be sent the text for comment and I felt confident he would ask for amendments on certain points, which is exactly what he did. A.E. asked me to stay on to supper, so that we could look at some more telegrams after. So we all had a cold meal there – with Clarissa and Lady Monckton too. After dinner we sat in the main hall, talking gloomily about Middle East problems, while Kirk wrote out a message for PM to the

President asking him once again (a) to join the Baghdad Pact, and (b) to give Nuri some more Centurion tanks. This has become our double theme song. Finally I got away around 11.0 and drove home through the starry night. Yesterday afternoon a Meteor training aircraft from Benson fell amongst the Big Beeches in Watlington Park and the two occupants were killed. Catherine saw it all, with the firemen and Alfred.

5 March

Duke having asked for just the changes I wanted in our statement, it was duly made today and went well. We have simply asked the Jordan Government to relieve British officers of executive commands. This can hardly trigger off a riot, and it leaves the door open for a reconciliation between us after the dust has settled. Very busy day. Chiefs of Staff in the afternoon, some trouble in Bahrain, two Israeli patrol boats captured by the Syrians on Tiberias, etc. But I am beginning to see a glimmer of hope that the King and Government of Jordan may want to mend their fences with us, if we could find a way of letting them back through the Iraqis. Why not induce Iraq to supply officers in the place of ours? If the net result of Glubb's dismissal were to enable the King to bring Jordan in the Baghdad Pact it would indeed be turning the tables on Egypt. Tony N. and I worked out a paper on these lines for the PM, having been summoned for 9.30 tonight to discuss future policy. Quite a big gathering round the Cabinet table. PM, Salisbury, Chancellor of Exchequer (H.M.), Rab, Lennox-Boyd,[1] the Chief Whip, Norman Brook, Templer, Boyle, Kirk, Nutting and me. We got them to accept the policy in our paper with great assistance from H.M. (sitting next to me) who disagreed with Salisbury and Butler. S. wants to scrap the subsidy and the Treaty, but quite agrees that we must give the Iraqis a chance to see what they can do first. Rab wants to get rid of the Treaty obligation to defend Jordan which he dislikes largely, I suspect, for pro-Israeli reasons. But H.M. wants to save what we can in Jordan. At the end he wrote on an envelope for me: 'I have gained you a day or two to rescue the work of forty years. Do try to work out a plan on which we might stay in Jordan.' Afterwards he asked me in to No. 11 for a drink and talked a lot more to the same effect. I like him very much and think him wise.

The meeting also talked about Cyprus, and the plans to deport Archbishop Makarios and the other bad Bishop. Lennox-Boyd confident and keen but rather repetitive. All are agreed on the deportation from Cyprus, but the question is, where to? Greece, England, Mombasa, the Seychelles?

1 Alan Lennox-Boyd (later Lord Boyd of Merton), Secretary of State for the Colonies.

After a long pause, Salisbury came out boldly, 'I'm for the Seychelles', and made everybody laugh. There is a very nice house there, they say – called Sans Souci! – and S. wanted a good photograph of it for the press, so that people cannot say we put them in irons. I was only half listening to this, while I re-wrote a telegram on Bahrain. The Ministers – led by the PM – were mad keen to land British troops somewhere, to show that we are still alive and kicking; and they thought Bahrain a good place because of the recent stoning of Selwyn Lloyd.

6 March

I started today in a terrible muddle; had prepared myself for writing the telegram to Baghdad as a result of last night's meeting, but the PM called for it by 10.30. I did not know this, Nutting and Kirkpatrick did it without my knowledge and I was furious. Told K. I would like to be relieved of this job; made a bit of a scene. He told me to take a deep breath and sit down. I am at the end of my patience and also very depressed. Everything goes wrong. N. came up and we met for lunch at the Austrian Embassy, but I had to leave before the others so I never spoke to her. A bloody afternoon, not seeing how I shall ever escape from this foul Middle East job. Walking back to Albany I met Harold Nicolson, who said he was sorry for me. Malenkov is coming to London next week, the evening papers say. At lunch I sat next to Lady Alexander, who said it was a tragedy of her husband's life that he ended up with 'a failure' (as Minister of Defence), when he never should have been asked to take on so unsuitable a job. He is now President of the MCC and spent his morning telephoning to Pakistan to apologize for the conduct of the MCC team, who ragged an umpire or something. The poor British, they appear to have entirely lost their touch.

7 March

The whole of today was devoted to preparing Nutting's and A.E.'s speeches for the Middle East debate this afternoon – the third in two months. How can democracies conduct foreign affairs if they have to do it in the open like this? Yesterday the PM, in order to placate the party, told the Foreign Affairs Committee of his plans (a) to get the US Government to join the Baghdad Pact (which they won't, despite his message to Ike) and (b) to get the King of Iraq to persuade the King of Jordan to come back into the fold. All this appeared in the newspapers this morning – A.E. was furious, I'm told, and said he would withdraw the whip from them all. But what does he expect; why can't he keep his mouth shut?

The debate was a calamity. The PM was shouted down, the Speaker had to call for order. Gaitskell spoke excellently – entirely pro-Zionist and quite wrong-headed but very impressive. The PM lost his temper with Robens (who sounds like a real shocker) and made an ass of himself. I went back after with William Clark to Albany. He is deeply depressed and thinks the 'Eden must go' movement will be redoubled. I really can't wish that it should not. He seems to be completely disintegrated – petulant, irrelevant, provocative at the same time as being weak. Poor England, we are in total disarray.

8 March

Bought all the newspapers from the pavement vendor in Piccadilly and found universal jeering at the PM. And yet the main thing he did in this debate – refuse to commit himself to a policy on Jordan – was absolutely right and courageous.

Kirkbride arrived from Amman with placatory messages from King Hussein. Spent all morning talking to him and gradually formulating a policy. Sandwich lunch, after which we went with him to a ministerial meeting in the PM's room at the House of Commons, and I circulated a set of headings for agreement which were more or less accepted. Harold Macmillan very helpful. Kirkbride told us of the remarkable reception he himself had had, both in the bazaar and on the steps of the Palace, at the height of the demonstrations.

Today both we and the Americans really gave up hope of Nasser and began to look around for means of destroying him. Kirkpatrick thinks that the PM's description of him as a second Mussolini shows that feminine flair for which he is so famous.

It is lovely spring weather, but I see nothing of it – out for twenty minutes only at lunchtime, and sick with work by the end of the day. We thought by 7.0 p.m. that we were emerging from the Jordan crisis, and Kirkpatrick told Michael Rose and me to get some rest tomorrow. But immediately after that the PM began ringing up from Leamington or somewhere, demanding weekend meetings at Chequers about Bahrain (quite unnecessary) and defence in the Persian Gulf. Having survived this, I was just leaving for supper with M. when Nutting's private secretaries caught me and told me to stay. I went down, found him talking endlessly on the telephone to his wife, lost my temper with the unfortunate Starkey and stalked out of the building. We are getting near the end of our patience.

10–11 March

Another spoiled weekend. I got away by the 2.25 on Saturday, quite exhausted, but had to go back at 5.0 p.m. on Sunday. This did not give me long enough to stop worrying about the Middle East, though it was wonderful spring weather and I had a nice walk down the long field and through Howe Wood where they've been thinning the trees. Burned off some of last year's grass from the field and played with Robin, who chucks a ball extremely hard and accurately. Betty Montagu was with us for the weekend and drove me to town on Sunday, her chow, Ming, breathing down my neck. Read the current telegrams with Tony Nutting and dined with him at Boodle's. He told me his separation is now complete. Tomorrow I am to drive down to Chequers with the CIGS for a meeting with Kirkbride.

12 March

Owing to more trouble in Bahrain the PM came up this morning and the meeting was held at No. 10 instead of Chequers. He began by cursing us for not telling him about the Bahrain telegrams last night (Sunday), and proceeded to be pretty bloody to everyone present. But by the end of the meeting he had calmed down and was quite polite to me – pleased with my scheme for detaching King Saud from Nasser. He was quite emphatic that Nasser must be got rid of. 'It is either him or us, don't forget that.'

13 March

A slight reduction of tempo today. The King of Jordan is to meet the King of Iraq at H.4;[1] and he has refused to go and see Nasser in Cairo. But we are working ourselves up against Nasser and deciding that the time has come to overthrow him (if we can) or isolate him. Unfortunately the PM has refused with violence and indignation to look at the paper which Nutting sent him last night, outlining a long-term policy for dealing with the Tripartite Declaration, Palestine, Baghdad Pact, etc., and weaning Saud from Nasser. He cannot bear long-term thoughts, and wants only to discuss how to answer this morning's telegrams. I was summoned by Norman Brook, Secretary to the Cabinet, this evening and asked if I could produce reassurance for the PM about coming events in Bahrain and Kuwait. Nutting, Kirkpatrick and I feel that we, alternately, are rejected by the PM as no good, not on the job, unhelpful; and the Chiefs of Staff, our Ambassadors abroad and other Ministers undergo similar periodical eclipses. No one is trusted to the extent that his advice is regarded when unwelcome.

    N. and I dined with Neville Berry and his wife Christobel. The Aldriches,

1 A pumping station on the oil pipeline.

the Portuguese Ambassador (so dark under the eyes that we thought he would die), Lord Linlithgow (John Hope's brother; rather a prim and dry figure in pince-nez), Lady Willoughby de Broke who thought most Foreign Service officers queer and when asked whom she had in mind said Burgess and Maclean, after all these years! She said, 'I put you top of a very short list', and at that I managed to turn to my other neighbour, a hard-voiced woman from Sunningdale whom I found quite entertaining called Waddington or something. Jim Thomas was there, bemoaning the state of the Government and the jumpiness of the PM.

14 March

Much controversy at long range with the CIGS about the extent to which British officers can remain in the Arab Legion. He sent General Poett[1] over to see me about it, and with him came an excellent Brigadier Frank Brooke, who set up the Military Mission in Burma and knows how to do it. I thought him very sensible and strong. He is going out to Amman to help Duke. He was quite keen to be as flexible as possible, which was what I wanted – I think that if we are not too inflexible we may find ourselves running the Legion once again after all.

A Turkish bath at mid-day and the masseur said no wonder I had taken off half a stone through stopping gin; it has got something called fusel oil in it, which is a marvellous creator of adipose tissue.

Dined at the club and read depressing FO papers about the advance of Communism. Was disturbed around midnight over Bahrain, where Bernard Burrows is unable to make up his mind whether he wants 100 Iraqi policemen or not. Rioting, strikes, stone-throwing.

15 March

The PM has seen the Bahrain telegrams and is in a state of excitement, which he has communicated to Nutting. He seems to want to march troops in and arrest the 'Higher Executive Committee' with which Bernard [Burrows] is now negotiating. Great agony in Tony's office from 10.0 to 11.0 because he insisted on drafting a telegram to show to the PM *before* Cabinet, without having decided what the policy was to be. Kirk's protests and mine were unavailing. We have now got to a state where each telegram that comes in causes Ministers to meet, telephone one another, draft replies and curse everybody. Not only does each of our telegrams contradict the one before, but each paragraph in each telegram contradicts the paragraph before.

George Allen called in the midst of all this and I was unable to see him.

1 Major-General Nigel Poett, Director of Military Operations, War Office, 1954–56.

But I heard Kirkpatrick giving him a sharp homily on Cyprus, proving that the US, where her direct interests were concerned, has always cheerfully ignored the principle of self-determination. Then I lunched with the US Minister, Mr Barber. Aldrich was there, and Allen and Jack Ward. There was no serious talk, except that George Allen seems to think the Israelis will attack and defeat the Egyptians in the near future, and that seems to give him comfort. It *would* be nice if they could do it, and do it quick before any of us (including the Russians) had time to save Nasser: then we could fall upon them as aggressors. Lunch was taken up with anecdotes about Arab rioting, narrow escapes of British and American diplomats (including some tragedies) at Arab funerals, and crowds stampeding. I had a feeling of appalling weariness at the thought of the Arabs, and the diplomats too, and I wonder why ever I go on with this career.

By evening, after spending hours in Nutting's room, an hour in the PM's room, two interviews with oil men and a conference with Gorell Barnes of the CO about the Horn of Africa I was again utterly drained. Went to a gala showing of a Rank film about Libya with Michael Rose and a girlfriend of his.

16 March

Selwyn Lloyd back from his tour. Meetings with him morning and afternoon. Masses of work and no quiet. But for some reason I am feeling cheerful. Malenkov called on S.L., who thought him 'the nicest Russian I have met; he has a good, appraising look in his eye, unlike the usual wooden blocks.' I supped with Martyn and Pinkie, and Myra came round after supper so that I could dictate to her a Cabinet paper on future Middle East policy (how to do down Nasser). Back to the office at 11.0 p.m. to collect it, with Michael Rose, and while we were there the Resident Clerk brought in a telegram, just drafted by the PM and Secretary of State over the telephone, about Bahrain. Fuss, fuss; no confidence in anyone; teaching Bernard Burrows his business. The PM has never understood that it is far more courageous to accept a humiliation than to do a damn silly 'bold' act. The object of his telegram is to make quite sure that B.B. does not negotiate the withdrawal of Belgrave[1] (which he never intended to do); though everybody knows that Belgrave ought to go, and soon.

21 March

I lunched with the Swiss Minister and had a long argument afterwards with Gaitskell about the Middle East and Israel. I was amazed at the vehemence of his pro-Israel sentiments. I told him that I did not see how

1 Sir Charles Belgrave, Adviser to the Ruler of Bahrein 1926–57.

he could logically distinguish between British 'positions' in the area, which he describes as 'colonial' or 'semi-colonial' and the position of Israel, which to the Arabs is the most colonial position of all. This made him quite indignant. He simply denies that arming Israel would drive the Arabs into the arms of Communism, and then, if pressed, he says, 'What if they do go Communist, they will still want to sell their oil to us.' He gave me a lift to the FO and continued the discussion in the car. He said our Middle East policy was 'hypocritical' and did not welcome my suggestion that there should be more discussion between Government and Opposition on it. He said that we 'always got bad advice from our people in the Arab States'.

In Haymarket we saw a small man in a bowler hat holding on a short lead a goat, which was quietly making water in the midst of the stationary traffic.

22 March

I lunched at the Garrick Club with Drew Middleton, who is even gloomier that I am about the Middle East, and also about the ability of this country to survive its economic problems. He has been visiting some new working-class estate, where he found them 'more reactionary, self-satisfied and idle than any body of London club-men'.

23 March

Lunched today with Roddie Barclay and told him I really must be released from the Middle East work. He was sympathetic, but does not see what he can do for me, short of sending me to Rio which I do not care for. Managed to get away this evening (with great difficulty and some public obloquy) from a meeting of the Middle East Official Committee, in order to catch a train to Dorchester with N. to stay with the Stones. We had dinner on the way down. Met by Reynolds Stone. He and Janet have a lovely old vicarage in a hilly village called Litton Cheney, with rooks in the elms and cascades of spring water running through their garden. Two glorious days there, in which N. threw off to some extent her flu and I my worries. But it made me sick with envy to see Reynolds at his lithography and woodcuts, working in his own time, in his own house, creating beautiful objects in a beautiful countryside. Selwyn Lloyd rang me up on Sunday morning to say that he and the PM had been looking at the Sunday papers and didn't like the interview Nasser had given yesterday to the *Observer* and *Sunday Times* correspondents; consequently they had decided to issue a counter-statement. They had debated whether to wait until Monday and do it in the House, or issue it through the FO spokesman this afternoon, and had decided on the latter (presumably because it is quicker and gives them the feeling of prompt action). S.L. read me the text, which is harmless and says nothing new at all – but really! We have come a long way down when the British Foreign Secretary has to spend Sunday morning answering a press statement by the Egyptians.

29 March

This week has been a misery of depression and weariness. I see myself caught in another twelve months of perpetual crisis. I have written Roddie a letter saying I *must* be relieved. His idea is to bring in Harold Beeley to take over one of my three departments and act as my 'alternate' – thus enabling me to get an occasional weekend off. This might help considerably; but I find it does not much console me for the fact that I have got to *think* about the Middle East for another year. I can hardly bear to think of it, and lie awake at night worrying about the headlong descent of our fortunes. I started writing a minute this week to the effect that if things go on as they are we shall within six months be getting our oil, if at all, by courtesy of Communist Powers.

Tonight I looked in at the Soviet Embassy and shook the hand of Malenkov. Then I talked for ten minutes with Norman Robertson [Canadian Ambassador] and the Italian Ambassador and we slipped out. Norman gave me a lift to Paddington. He disapproves of the line Tony Nutting is taking over the latest Soviet disarmament proposals; he thinks 'very big changes' are taking place in Russia, and we ought not to miss opportunities to help along the favourable tendencies. Then he said, 'But I'm afraid that your Minister of State and I hardly ever agree about anything.'

30 March

Good Friday, but I had to come up to London for a day's work. Drove C. and J. up too, and they went to hear the St Matthew Passion at the Festival Hall. This was C.'s second hearing of it within a week, and she is deeply moved by it. So is Julian. They are certainly remarkable children and in no way affected. C. is reading Tolstoy as hard as she can.

2 April

Three days' complete rest over Easter and I feel better. Spent most of the time gardening and playing quartets with the family. Half an hour's tennis on Sunday was about all we could manage. We had a small cocktail party for the John Hopes and Tony Nutting and we dined with the Troughtons.

Dick is optimistic about the effect of the Chancellor's 'squeeze' on our economic life. He seems to think it is beginning to work – but he admits he is only generalizing from the effect upon W.H. Smith & Sons, who are spending £800,000 less on development this year than they had intended.

3 April

A colourless, dreary day in the office, during which I was quite unhelpful to all and saw how easily one could drift into becoming a fifth wheel. Long meeting with Selwyn Lloyd at which Harold Caccia (*vice* Kirk who is on leave) made all the running and my three Heads of Department took all the catches. Had a fried sole at Scott's and finished reading *Elephant Bill*.

6 April

More bad news from the Middle East. Fighting on the Gaza frontier.

After dinner I went round (with Selwyn Lloyd's permission) to see Kenneth Younger and talked with him for three hours about the Middle East. He thinks we ought to clear out of many positions, including Cyprus and Jordan. But not, of course, Israel. I spoke to him of the illogic of that, and he understands it perfectly well. But he takes the party line. I begin to see what Kirkpatrick means when he says that Kenneth Younger has charm and great intelligence, but no courage whatever. It is clear that he is no longer a runner for Foreign Secretary in Gaitskell's Shadow Cabinet: Robens has that now.

9 April

The question is, can we somehow move away from the concept of tripartite action on Palestine and put the responsibility where it should be – in UN? The Tripartite Declaration of 1950, which we continuously harp on, is quite out of date, first because the French cannot play any part whatever, second because the Americans won't put their backs into it and third because it is becoming unacceptable to the states in the area that the three Western Powers should arrogate to themselves special responsibility for keeping the peace. The trouble is, we have made so much of the declaration during the last year, by statements in Parliament, etc., that it is almost impossible to get out of it without the Government being accused of betraying Israel. (The Opposition forget that the Tripartite Declaration was originally designed, and has for six years served, as a defence of Arab states against an *Israeli* attack.)

N. and I took Christian to a wonderful French film called *Race for Life* about twelve Breton fishermen suffering from botulism on a trawler in the middle of the North Sea. Then we went on to a party at the Savoy given by William Douglas-Home and Celia Johnson. Every actor and actress in London was there, and lots of others. Great fun, but by 2.0 a.m. N. and I were exhausted.

10 April

Eisenhower has issued a statement which does precisely what I would like us to do – emphasize the UN (as opposed to the Tripartite) responsibility for peace in the Middle East. Fortunately S.L. is ready to 'welcome' this. I lunched with Norman Robertson alone at his house in Upper Brook Street, and he spoke strongly in the same sense. He thinks we ought to bring the Russians in, too, and face them squarely with responsibility for their actions.

I applied last week to Roddie Barclay for the job of Civilian Instructor to the IDC, and he told me today that Kirkpatrick is putting this to the S/S.

11 April

I have got the job with IDC! Kirk told me this evening that the PM has agreed to it, and Roddie suggests I should start in June. I am tremendously relieved, and feel sure that it is the right thing. It means at least two more years in England, and a very civilized existence too, I think, without the agonies and pressures and limelight of the last five years. I had lunch in the House of Commons with Robert Carr, who now has a ministerial job (Ministry of Labour) and seems much happier than he used to be. I took Janey and Christopher Ironside to the *Threepenny Opera* and thought it quite awful – noisy, squalid and unfunny. Nice dinner afterwards in their house, with smoked cheese.

13 April

These days are deep in concern about the future of the Middle East. Endless meetings, on oil, on the Suez Canal, on the Palestine question (open fighting goes on despite Hammarskjöld's efforts), and they all show up the same grim truth – that Western Europe is *dependent* on the oil, and that Nasser can stop it coming if he wants to, by closing the Canal or the pipelines.

Dined with the Aldriches to meet the Lord Mayor of London and a lot of his city dignitaries with their wives – they are just off on a visit to

New York. Old Aldrich was mysteriously enthusiastic about 'what we are planning to do in the Middle East'. Can't imagine what he means.

15 April

A delightful weekend with the Nichols[1] family at Lawford. Tennis, music, conversation. C. and J. were with us, and the four Nichols children and three extra young men, mostly Wykehamists.

16 April

Nothing terrible happened in the Middle East over the weekend. The fighting has simmered down a bit and Nasser hasn't done anything particularly beastly to us. Hussein seems to have done rather well in Damascus, and to have impressed the Syrian soldiers whom he met. No link with Egypt.

19 April

Khrushchev and Bulganin have arrived, and the public reception has been cool. William Clark thinks that from their point of view the 'preview' of Malenkov was a mistake, as it has taken off the freshness and enabled our press and people to look at these two more soberly. I saw Bill Barker,[2] who has been acting as interpreter, this afternoon. He says that they are 'very tough', and are putting on a tremendous act about how humanity is lost unless Russia and Britain get together and agree upon world problems. The general objective seems to be to make the Americans stick out as the tiresome ones. He, of course, has never seen these two or any other Communist leaders doing the 'expansive' act; in his time they wouldn't speak to anyone. He thinks it very formidable, and seems afraid that the PM and Secretary of State were falling for it, especially at lunch today. I told him that A.E. always looks as if he was falling for that kind of thing; but that in reality he has a very shrewd idea of what he is up against. However there is no doubt that the Russians are absolutely brimming over with confidence, and that they won't refrain from pressing their advantages.

But they have made a very peculiar statement on the Middle East, which seems to put them back into a neutral position between Jews and Arabs. Great dismay amongst the Arabs, of whom I met a lot at the Syrian and

---

1 Sir Philip and Lady Nichols. He had been my Ambassador in Prague.
2 William Barker, linguist and expert on Soviet affairs, who had served with me in Prague; later Ambassador to Czechoslovakia; Professor of Russian, University of Liverpool.

Lebanese national day parties yesterday and the day before. The Lebanese Ambassador insists that we must exploit this to the uttermost; and we are doing so to the best of our ability.

My appointment to IDC is confirmed and I start in on 25 June.

20 April

A message from Dulles came in from Aldrich this morning, suggesting that we might sound out B. and K. on the possibility of sponsoring a UK Resolution giving the Secretary-General a mandate to mediate between Israel and the Arabs. Michael Rose and I thought it a very important suggestion and one which HMG could not have made unless it had been suggested by the Americans. So I wrote a minute urging that it be done – subject of course to consultation with Hammarskjöld himself, who is still out in the Middle East trying to enlarge his success in arranging a cease-fire yesterday. When I wrote this I was under the impression that the Middle East was to be discussed with B. and K. this afternoon; but when I took it to Kirkpatrick at lunchtime I found that they had already had two hours on the Middle East in the morning, and that it had been 'very sour'. The Russians rejected as an 'insult' our suggestion that we might all forgo using the veto against a resolution defining the aggressor; yet this is the only logical way of making UN action speedy and certain enough, and if they would agree to it we might dispense with the Tripartite Declaration. They also took umbrage at the PM's statement that we would fight if anyone interfered with our oil. Kirkpatrick thinks this shows how important it was to say it, but he says the PM began to wish he hadn't when the reaction was so sour! Anyway we handed them the bit of paper which I had written, and this will make good publicity even if they reject it. Roger Makins was delighted to hear that the morning's talks went so badly – because he is concerned lest we become carried away by smooth talk. This afternoon's session was equally grim, I'm told. They let out some of their bile about America. Kirk says they are both thoroughly unpleasant characters, and B. even worse than K. He finds them primitive and brutish. They are getting a curiously cold reception from the London crowd. I saw them going into No. 10.

21/22 April

Glorious spring weekend, with all our daffodils in their prime and the beechwoods starting to bloom copper-coloured with fattened buds. Our local orchestra came to High Wood, and we were still playing when Kirkpatrick arrived from Chequers at about 11.30, having been there all

afternoon and evening with Khrushchev and Bulganin, to stay the night
with us. He says they are extremely realistic men and refuse to take refuge
in expressions of false agreement when there is no real agreement. He
compares them favourably, in this, to our side. Here there is a great deal
of 'I am sure my Soviet friends will allow me to say. . . . ' It seems that they
were much ragged at Oxford this morning, and a portrait of Stalin had
been inserted in one of the frames of the ancient colleges: also a flash bomb
let off. They took it quite well. They are going to go on ragging us in the
Middle East, Kirk said, because they see quite well that we are going on
with the Baghdad Pact.

23 April

Because the Saudis have signed an agreement with Egypt and Yemen, the
PM wants *again* to hold up the Dodds-Parker mission to Riyadh. Only
last week we wanted to hold it up because of something they had done,
consulted the Americans, were advised by them to go ahead regardless,
and decided firmly to do so. Every wind that blows diverts us from our
course.

30 April

Spent an hour talking to Queen Zein at Claridge's, where I met her little
son, Hassan, very bright and keen, speaking good English and understanding French. Then to the Esher's cocktail party for C. at the House
of Lords.

3 May

To Paris early in the morning with Selwyn Lloyd. Lunch at the Embassy
with Dulles, Livvy Merchant, Rountree, etc., where we talked Middle East
but nobody had many ideas. I outlined a suggestion for an 'agreement to
exercise restraint' in supplying arms to Israel and her neighbours, but
nobody seemed much interested in it.

4 May

Lunched alone with Rountree and Bill Burdett, and did not enjoy it at all.
They do not see our point of view about Saudi Arabia and I beat my head
against a wall. I am hating foreign affairs these days and longing to give it
a rest.

   Called on Diana and John Beith for a drink; she has just had a daughter and is in bed in the living room, looking out on to the front of the Ambassador's house. Spent the evening with Julien Françon and family [with whom I lived twenty-five years ago when learning French] and had *a porto* with them at the Dôme.

5 May

It is glorious spring, almost summer weather and the chestnuts are at their finest. Nothing much for me to do, so I went for a walk along the quais below Chaillot, ending up in a small garden under the Eiffel Tower. Lunch for the Turk (Koprulu) at Kit Steel's flat, where Selwyn Lloyd and Harold Caccia were both taking pills and saying that they felt like death. In the afternoon I sat in the Embassy's garden in a deck chair under an enormous chestnut tree, while the little Beith girl and a friend played together on the lawn.

20 June

Today I left the FO for (I hope) at least a year and a half, and perhaps I shall never work in it again. Archie Ross, who takes over African and Levant Departments from me, came in on Monday and I have spent two days sitting in his (my) room talking to him about the job. I am thankful to be quit of it. Not to have to think about Nasser, Saud, Hussein is in itself a relief from anxiety and strain. It is true that during the last six weeks the Middle East has been more or less quiet, but the general trend is still against us and the bad feeling worked up by Egyptian propaganda is deeper and deeper. I find it intolerable to have to work in this hopeless hatred, and exasperating that we should be too inflexible to make any counter moves. It looks as if Nasser were now completely under Communist influence, and he is playing a role amongst the Great Powers for which there is no justification in the strength of his country. The writing on the wall is there all right, but he may destroy a lot of things before he is brought down. We have decided (with the help of the Americans) that we are *not* going to build the Aswan Dam. Probably Shepilov will promise Russian money for it when he is in Cairo this week. *Tant pis.* The Arab states will have to see the Russians actually carrying out some project before they will believe that Communists are not selfless paragons of brotherly love.

The Egyptian national day, Monday 18 June, was to celebrate the evacuation of Suez. It was built up into a frenzy of anti-British feeling, despite all Fawzi's promises and the invitation to General Robertson to attend it. Obviously my policy and efforts to save relations with Egypt have been all wrong. I was in favour of Robertson accepting, and I pressed the Secretary of State to write a friendly message to the Egyptian press (through Mr Zaghloul, the London correspondent of *El Akbar*): but the response from Nasser was negligible. Meanwhile I wonder whether my other ideas are wrong too. I have been saying that we must try and build on these 'new' types of Arab leader – Abu Nuwar in Jordan and Ben Halim in Libya – because being young and ambitious they have an interest in preserving the independence of their countries against Egyptian or Communist control. Abu Nuwar is now in Baghdad, which is a good sign, and he may evolve in our direction. But Ben Halim, who is in London, is openly demanding more money, an army, navy and air force, as a price for remaining loyal to us. At a lunch for him at No. 10 Downing Street on Tuesday A.E. tried to persuade him that armies, navies and air forces are out of date and nobody ought to want them – but that is not much good to an Arab leader who has no atomic weapons and who anyhow needs armed forces for internal prestige and public order. A.E. was particularly maddening at this lunch; when Ben Halim asked Selwyn Lloyd what the FO thought of Eisenhower's chances of running again for President A.E. interrupted, before Selwyn Lloyd could answer, by saying he had had a personal message from Ike yesterday – 'I don't think I told you about it, Selwyn' – but it emerged that the message threw no light whatever on the answer to Ben Halim's question. Selwyn, sitting next to me, said that he congratulated me on getting a rest from the FO. He said he thinks being made Foreign Secretary is a death sentence – two or conceivably three years and you are dead. I took this occasion to tell Selwyn, as my last piece of advice before leaving the FO, that I think he ought to exploit the ferment of opinion in the satellite states, especially Poland. I suggested that he should invite himself to Warsaw for a start. The Polish Government would be embarrassed, and would probably ask the Russians. If the latter advised a refusal we should say, 'What? Do the Russians think it safe for themselves to have Eden in Moscow and unsafe for you to have Lloyd in Warsaw?' But if they accepted, then I thought Selwyn Lloyd could have the same sort of popular success as B. and K. had in India. Once there he could ask to broadcast, to see the university, etc. Why should we allow the Russians to go trumpeting around the capitals of *our* clients, and do nothing to increase their difficulties in holding down theirs? S.L. said he thought I was quite right. But (a) the FO advice was against it and (b) the PM would never allow it. But the idea may sink in and I am sure it is right. The only real weapons we have against Communism are the reality of our freedom and the higher standard of living of our people. The more we can make the Soviets' subjects resent the restrictions and sacrifices which are forced upon them, the more capable we shall be of competing economically with them. We ought to be flooding the satellite countries with visitors, missions, exhibitions, etc., to increase their restiveness. I don't think it is much good trying to affect the Soviet people themselves; they have gained too much and have too much yet to gain from their system.

The only things of interest that I seem to have done in the last six weeks were to lunch with Isaiah Berlin to talk about Palestine (he thinks Israel no longer represents an ideal for Jews, and that it will become more and more another Levantine state) and to attend a lot of meals for Persian Gulf Sheiks.

We spent Whitsun at Petworth with John and Pamela Wyndham. The Hambledens were there, and Peter Quennell[1] with a girl he was about to marry. Tennis and sunshine, and some gentle ragging of Maria Carmela [Hambleden] about her Italian accent, which she took very well. Pamela took me for a walk up Chanctonbury Ring, and we visited Uppark, where the process of stitching and hemming old seventeenth-century curtains back to life goes on and on, to the despair of the old Admiral Meade-Fetherstonhaugh, the owner.

23 June

We drove yesterday to Aldeburgh to stay with Humphrey and Natalie Brooke in the house of her father, Count Benckendorf, for the last weekend of the Aldeburgh Festival. Stephen Runciman[2] the only other guest until another pair called Pilkington arrived, he a director of Sotheby's. Concerts in Aldeburgh Church (sonnets of John Donne by Benjamin Britten, beautifully sung by Peter Pears) and the Jubilee Hall (Poulenc playing a thing of his own with orchestra) and a lovely afternoon on the lake at Thorpeness listening to madrigals and recorder playing.

I was now Chief Civilian Instructor at the Imperial Defence College (later re-named the College of Defence Studies).

20 July

It seems to be more difficult to write a diary now that I am less busy. There is less to say and I doubt the interest of what I might say. My first month at the IDC has demanded of me a complete change in my outlook towards political and economic problems. The purpose is no longer to get a decision and apply it in action, but simply to discuss and to stimulate

1 Peter Quennell, author and literary critic.
2 Stephen Runciman, historian and author.

thought. On all matters of administration and organization the military show a care and attention to detail which is entirely alien to the FO. I find myself solemnly discussing arrangements for the reception of some Home Office officials in the hall downstairs three weeks hence, of deciding in which order two officers shall speak at an inter-syndicate discussion next term.

24 July

Expedition to Marham (RAF) Bomber Station. We (the staff) flew in a Valletta from Northolt, the rest of the IDC in two Hastings. Saw the inside of an atomic bomb and lifted a heavy object like an enormous thermos flask containing one million pounds' worth of plutonium. It was warm on the outside. Interesting talk at lunch with a man called Llewellyn, technical adviser on radar to C.-in-C. Bomber Command. He agrees with me that the H-bomb has made any sort of war between the Great Powers impossible.

General Thompson gave me a lift from Northolt as far as the Lambert Arms, and I spent the evening playing the spinet. Wonderful sunset, strawberries, roses, music, and I feel that the vile bomb I saw this afternoon is going after all to preserve these things.

26 July

Another lecture on the consequences of nuclear warfare, which now appear to me to have become so universal as to be on a par with death itself and consequently hardly noticeable. It is an illusion to suppose that when the people learn all about it they will become ridden with fear or panic. People cannot remain afraid for lengths of time. Even those who know they are going to die soon (the old and the sick) do not spend all their time thinking about it and being frightened. I am therefore strongly opposed to the Home Office politician line of not letting the people know the full horrors in case they start demanding shelters and evacuation plans which the nation cannot afford. The mass of the people will decide these things better than the officials.

Tonight, while Nasser was nationalizing the Suez Canal, I went to have a drink with Brian and Alfreda Urquhart,[2] met Richard Wollheim[3] who doesn't agree with me that city life has been made intolerable by traffic,

1 Brian Urquhart was active in the organization of the UN Emergency Force in the Middle East 1956. Later he became Under-Secretary-General UN and the leading expert on UN peace-keeping operations.
2 Professor Richard Wollheim, philosopher and writer.

subtopia and noise, drank nearly half a bottle of champagne, dined with my mother and went round later (at the Urquharts' suggestion) for coffee with the Tines, with whom they were dining. Brian went off to the country in a defrocked taxi which he has bought. If I had not escaped a month ago I should be in the midst of this major Suez crisis. As it is, I need have no more anxiety than any other British subject – though in fact I do.

30 July

We gave another cocktail party in Albany. Robin was there and came on to supper with us afterwards. This he did not enjoy and says he will not go out to dinner again until he is at least nine!

Michael Rose tells us that the Government are taking the Suez business very seriously, and he hints that military measures against Egypt are being prepared. If so, it is good news. The time has come when we must show strength, and Nasser should be overthrown. I only hope we can do it. Michael says the other Arabs (Iraqis and even King Saud) are not backing Nasser. But they will if he gets away with it.

24 September

Drove up to London today after seven weeks' holiday, feeling altogether more robust. Nothing much doing at the IDC (term really starts tomorrow) but I found that all the summer tours (except the American) were cancelled on account of the Suez crisis and that all the RAF officers (including Air Vice-Marshal Hudleston) have been withdrawn from the course. Enrolled myself as a temporary member of the London Library in order to be able to consult Spanish dictionaries. (Reynolds Stone has asked me to translate a book on calligraphy by the Spanish writer Yciar, published in Saragossa 1550.)

I called on Pat Dean by appointment at 4.0 p.m., but as he was not ready I looked in on Kirkpatrick. Never have I heard such black pessimism. Set off by some mild criticism I made of the PM's handling of the Suez crisis, he said the PM was the only man in England who wanted the nation to survive; that all the rest of us have lost the will to live; that in two years' time Nasser will have deprived us of our oil, the sterling area fallen apart, no European defence possible, unemployment and unrest in the UK and our standard of living reduced to that of the Yugoslavs or Egyptians. He said that all the newspapers except *The Times* are concerned only to criticize the Government for 'making trouble' over Suez, while exonerating the brigand Nasser from any blame for his felony, while the press correspondents' main pleasure is to come to the FO and put awkward questions to the News Department, designed to weaken the British hand in the dispute. I was embarrassed by all this, and went to Pat Dean for comfort, which to a certain extent I received. He does not think that all is lost; nor does John Maud whom I met later at Harold Caccia's farewell party. There are pressures still to be brought and tricks to be won and forces are beginning to make themselves felt in the Arab world against too intransigent an attitude by Nasser. It is not good, but there is something to play with.

After this I went to the Royal College of Music and did a voice test before Dr Jacques, and was admitted to the Bach Choir.

4 October

Called at the Foreign Office today and found them all more cheerful. Michael Hadow tells me that the Iraqis are about to send a force into Jordan (at Jordan request) to help them against Israel, and that the Americans have told the Israelis they are not to take it amiss. This will upset Nasser and reduce his prestige. Meanwhile Harold Macmillan is pushing hard for a European Common Market and there is serious study of our joining some sort of European confederation system. The Tories are beginning to think that something of this sort is essential for their own electoral prospects, which are at present very dim. Kirkpatrick has the idea that we might get Western Union into the Sterling Area (we would describe it as creating a common currency) thus getting the vast German capital reserves pooled with our own.

I am on the track of a Spanish priest, Father de Zulueta, to help me with my book.

Nasser had nationalized the Suez Canal Company on 26 July 1956, precipitating a major international crisis which lasted for the next three months and ended with the Suez operation of October/November. In the hectic negotiations which followed nationalization Eden's objective was to establish some form of international regime for the canal which would prevent canal traffic falling under exclusive Egyptian control. The 'Canal Users' Association', representing the major maritime powers, was set up for this purpose.

On 29 October, while these negotiations were still in being, but making little progress, Israeli troops invaded the Sinai peninsula and on the following day an Anglo-French ultimatum was delivered to Israel and Egypt demanding an end to the fighting and the withdrawal of both parties ten miles from the canal. The Israelis accepted, the Egyptians refused and on 31 October British and French forces began bombing Egyptian airfields. An invasion force was landed several days later. By 3 November, however, under extreme international pressure, the British and French Governments accepted a cease-fire subject to

*certain conditions, including the establishment of a United Nations force to
keep the peace. On 6 November Eden announced a cease-fire from midnight
and the two Governments began the withdrawal of their forces from Egypt.
The Egyptians then sank ships in the canal which remained blocked for many
months.*

1 November

In the month that has passed great events have taken place in Poland and
Hungary and we were all thinking that for the moment the tide had turned
in our favour when suddenly the Middle East flared up again. The first overt
sign was Israeli half-mobilization last week, and the alarmed warnings to
American residents in Egypt and Jordan to leave for home. This was
immediately after the Jordan elections, which had gone in favour of the
left and the Egyptian party and had been followed by the creation of a
joint Egyptian–Syrian–Jordan command. But it was only gradually that
we in the IDC began to get the smell of something fishy in the air. There
were visits by M. Mollet[1] to London and by Eden and Lloyd to Paris;
rumours of French fighters on Israeli airfields; and hints dropped by Ivone
Kirkpatrick, in a lecture to us, that 'if you want to play a trick in the
diplomatic game you don't want always to have to tell the press in advance'.
I heard from Michael Rose that he, too, thought something was going on
which the FO did not know much about, but we were not prepared for
what occurred.

On Monday the Israelis launched an attack into Sinai. Good, we thought;
now let them chew up Nasser's army a bit and then the Security Council,
after 'working to rule' for a little perhaps, might order them back. Eisenhower condemned them, and I took it for granted that we would seize the
opportunity to show that we, too, were ready to honour our Tripartite
Declaration and take action against the aggressor. Not a bit of it. On
Tuesday night, on getting home for a quiet evening by the fire, we turned
on the news to hear how the fighting was going, and heard that the Prime
Minister had announced that afternoon an Anglo-French ultimatum, with
a twelve-hour time limit, to Egypt and Israel to 'withdraw' ten miles from
the Canal so that we might move in. Staggered by this. It seems to have
every fault. It is clearly not genuinely impartial, since the Israelis are
nowhere near the Canal; it puts us on the side of the Israelis; the Americans
were not consulted; the UN is flouted; we are about to be at war without
the nation or Parliament having been given a hint of it. We think A.E. has
gone off his head. What can be done? Sleepless night, thinking of all that
I have done to get us *out* of Suez; now we are going back. Next day, a very

---

1 Guy Mollet, French Prime Minister.

gloomy one at the IDC. The Commandant, Geoffrey Thompson,[1] Bill Crawford[2] and I tried to persuade the students that there must be better reasons behind it than we know, but the general feeling is one of amazement and horror. Lunched with Harold Beeley who told me that the FO, with one exception (Kirkpatrick) are equally depressed and astonished. I met poor Charles Mott-Radclyffe[3] on the steps of the Reform Club and told him that I thought it a disastrous decision. He seemed quite taken aback.

Next morning we learn that the UK and France have vetoed a UN Resolution put forward by the US! A picture in *The Times* of poor Bob Dixon sitting between Cabot Lodge and Shepilov who are both voting against us. It looks more and more as if there has been collusion with the Israelis, for we have not said anything about the need for them to return behind their frontiers. I wrote Kirkpatrick a note yesterday afternoon suggesting that we ought to do this, if only to put ourselves aright with the other Arabs, and to give some verisimilitude to our story that we have gone in to 'separate the contestants and safeguard the Canal'.[4] But it begins to look as if we have moved over to a policy of using Israel. Mountbatten (First Sea Lord) came to lecture this morning, and could not conceal from us the fact that he, too, profoundly disapproves of the policy. He said he had spoken against it up to the limit of what is possible, and was surprised that he was still in his job. This added greatly to our gloom, and the poor Commandant, Admiral Russell, who had been hoping for some comfort and robustness, looked suddenly about ten years older. I myself had not had any comfort to give. I had rung up Tony Nutting in the morning to find out if he would abstain in the vote, and found that he had already resigned from the Government. But I felt the IDC needed a little encouraging so I went to the FO to find out what there was to be said on the other side. Saw the Private Secretary and Pat Dean, and built up quite a fair picture. First, Nasser was winning too fast. He had got his command over Syrian and Jordan armies; he had a plot far advanced for a coup in Libya; another in Iraq; a third in Saudi Arabia. He was a stooge for the Russians, and was being sent really large supplies of arms including submarines, for use against us all, etc. Second, the French could not wait. Their troubles in North Africa, largely fomented by Nasser, were having a dangerous effect and it was a question of keeping France in NATO.

1 Major-General Geoffrey Thompson, Senior Army Instructor, IDC, 1955–57.

2 Rear-Admiral William Crawford, Senior Naval Instructor, IDC, 1956–58.

3 Charles Mott-Radclyffe MP, Chairman of Conservative Party Foreign Affairs Committee 1951–59.

4 31 October 1956; Forgive me for interfering, but is it not necessary to adjust the impression which our 'ultimatum' has given that the Israelis are to be allowed to remain on Egyptian territory? Should we not at once make it clear that we insist upon their withdrawal? Only thus, it seems to me, can we prove that the action we have taken really is on behalf of our own Suez Canal interests, and not on behalf of Israeli expansion. We may save some credit with the other Arabs in this way.

Third, the Israelis would not wait. There was evidence that they meant to have a go. So, HMG were confronted with the situation that the slow methods of 'reducing Nasser to size' which the Americans were willing to sanction (problematical in any case and taking a year or more) would almost certainly be no good and too late. They felt they must grasp the nettle. Along came the Israeli attack, and this was the opportunity they could not let pass. (I did not press anyone on the subject of collusion, but I feel sure there was some, probably on the part of the French.) Anyway, the Israelis are doing the major fighting. They are now chewing up Nasser's forces in Sinai, about one-third of his army, while we are destroying the Russian aircraft on the Egyptian airfields, and our amphibious force is on its way. The world at large is screaming blue murder but (a) Eisenhower's statement was reasonably mild and (b) Australia and New Zealand support us. Dean says the great hope is that Nasser will collapse before we land, or at least not oppose our landing.

This story comforted Russell quite a bit.

Dined with Tony Nutting. He told me the whole story from the beginning, and he is in a state of profound indignation with Eden and Lloyd. We went through the speech he is to make in the House, announcing his resignation, and I got him to tone it down a bit, because I thought that too bitter an attack on what the Government had done might injure the nation in a very difficult time. There was the fullest collusion with the Israelis. Selwyn Lloyd actually went to Paris incognito to meet Ben-Gurion with the French. It is true that he did not actually urge Ben-Gurion to make an attack, but he gave him to understand that we would not take a serious view. Later they even knew the date on which it was to take place. They deliberately deceived the Americans and everyone else.

The scheme was devised by the French. The broad idea was that there would be an Israeli attack and we should send forces to separate the contestants. There would be parachute landings and the parachutists as they fell from the sky would say '*Tiens! Voilà le canal.*'

Tonight the Government got a majority of sixty-nine against the vote of censure, and I have a feeling that public opinion is going to veer round to a little greater comprehension of the Government's action. Certainly if it is successful, the damage to our prestige and reputation and to our relations with Asia and the other Arabs, though serious, may not be so terrible. If it fails to get a result in two or three days, or if there is bad fighting when we land, God help us. It is horrible to be bombing and sinking ships.

Mountbatten told us that our Canberras were intercepted at 47,000 feet by Egyptian fighters, greatly to their surprise. Perhaps Russian or Czech pilots; but they did no damage. He also said that French ships are actively co-operating with the Israelis in the Sinai battle, while we are trying to pretend we've nothing to do with them.

3 December

It is a great pity that I have not written my diary daily during the past
month, because it would have shown how terribly uncertain and changeable
one's opinions are in a crisis. After my initial shock, and the appalling
experience of a week of bombing Egyptian airfields and radio stations by
the RAF, I began to think for God's sake get the landing over and complete
the job. It took nearly six days for the force to arrive from Malta, and
according to William Clark it was delayed twenty-four hours by the
American 6th Fleet getting in its way. William resigned his job in a frenzy,
and I met him in the Albany Rope Walk one night saying that the PM
was mad and that we could never work with the Americans again until he
had been removed. Then at last we landed, and it went well, but the
decision to call it off before we had got the whole Canal seemed like another
act of absolute folly. The pressures from USA and the threats from Russia
must have been very great indeed; but having gone in, surely we should
have done the job. As soon as we stopped, the Egyptians sank dozens of
ships in the Canal and we had lost the capacity to clear it. The American
attitude continued to be unbelievably hostile. I think this must have been
the main miscalculation of the Government. I do not think anyone imagined
that Eisenhower would actually drive the UN to take positive action at
unheard-of speed against us; but this is what he did. Cabot Lodge would
not give Dixon an hour's respite; Dulles cut him in public, and for
the next fortnight (until we declared our readiness to withdraw) neither
Eisenhower nor Dulles would speak to us. E. went off to play golf and D.
was in hospital. Meanwhile A.E. had broken down and gone off to Jamaica.
This is the most extraordinary feature of the whole thing. Is he on his way
out, has he had a nervous breakdown, is he mad? The captain leaves the
sinking ship which he has steered personally on to the rocks. That is how
it is looked at by the Commandant and officers at the IDC. They think it
is inconceivable that he can come back and remain in office; but I am not
at all so sure.

In all this one has been trying (vainly for the most part) to fight off the
feeling that we are doomed, heading for mass unemployment or even world
war. The breach with USA is the most dangerous thing, with the Russians
maddened by the Hungarian revolution. Next comes the hostility of Canada
and the apparently irremediable breach with India, Ceylon and Pakistan.
But here I feel less fatalistic. In the end the Indians will be glad to make
use of us when they need us, and that goes for everyone else.

We've had the house painted, the chimneys repaired, a new fireplace
put in the sitting-room. About fifty new roses have arrived from Burrell's
and are safely planted. Also I have completed the first draft of my translation

of Yciar and have begun to learn the guitar. These things console one for –
or divert one from – the horrible world scene.

5 December

Norman Brook came to lecture this morning and showed us afterwards (in
private) that he too thought the Suez expedition a folly. He thinks however
that the PM will return and assume charge again as if nothing had
happened, because the Tory Party would split, without him, into Macmillan
v. Butler groups, with the Suez diehards as a third.

   Now that our withdrawal 'without delay' from Suez has been announced
by Selwyn Lloyd everyone at the IDC has become suddenly very gloomy
and all the Services feel they have been betrayed, and that we will never
be able to show any independence as a nation again. A long letter from
Admiral 'Lofty' Power, who has been on the operation, and who describes
it as 'conceived in deceit and arrested in pusillanimity'. Petrol is up by one
and sixpence.

Postscript

Having recovered my spirits after a two-year academic interlude at the IDC, I was seconded from the British Foreign Service for two years as Political Assistant to M. Paul-Henri Spaak, the Secretary-General of NATO in Paris. I returned to the Foreign Office in 1960 as the Deputy Under-Secretary responsible for relations with the USSR in Europe and was deeply involved in the Berlin crisis of 1961–62. I then served for four years as British Permanent Representative on the NATO Council. I ended my diplomatic career in 1969 as Ambassador to Italy.

After my retirement from the Foreign Service I was for ten years Chairman of the British Red Cross Society and was elected Chairman of the Standing Commission of the International Red Cross. I was a Director of the Commercial Union from 1971 to 1980 and a Regional Chairman of the National Trust.

The corner cupboard, whose laborious construction the reader will have followed with anxiety through the diary entries of 1952–53, still hangs in the corner at High Wood where it was placed in 1953. In the following years, I continued to do cabinet work in my spare time. In 1973 I was taught how to build clavichords by the late Thomas Goff, and have so far made twelve of these instruments. Nancy and I have three children, nine grandchildren and one great-granddaughter.

List of Family Members

M.: my mother
N.: Nancy, my wife
Catherine ⎫
Julian ⎬ our children
Robin ⎭
Diana and Harold Seager: my sister and her husband
John and Paddy: my brother and his wife
Joanna and George Simon: my sister and her husband
Oliver: third Viscount Esher, Nancy's father (married Antoinette Heckscher of Philadelphia)
Lionel (now the fourth Viscount Esher) and Christian Brett: Nancy's brother and sister-in-law
Pinkie: Nancy's sister, married to Sir Martyn Beckett (half-brother of Eden's first wife, Beatrice)
Aunt Louise (Mrs John Thatcher) ⎫
Augie and Claude Heckscher ⎬ Nancy's American relations
Bunny and Philip Hofer ⎪
Catherine and Ted Leach ⎭

Index

QUEEN ELIZABETH
  p. 78.

sardonic comments